Deposit Insurance

AF740204

Deposit Insurance

Edited by

Andrew Campbell
Director of the Centre for Business Law and Practice, University of Leeds, UK

John Raymond LaBrosse
Secretary General, International Association of Deposit Insurers, Switzerland

David G. Mayes
Adviser to the Board, Bank of Finland

Dalvinder Singh
Senior Lecturer in Law, Oxford Brookes University, UK

City University
Library Information Services
Cass Learning Resource Centre

palgrave
macmillan

Editorial matter and selection © Andrew Campbell,
John Raymond LaBrosse, David G. Mayes and Dalvinder Singh 2007
Individual chapters © contributors 2007

All rights reserved. No reproduction, copy or transmission of this publication may be made without written permission.

No paragraph of this publication may be reproduced, copied or transmitted save with written permission or in accordance with the provisions of the Copyright, Designs and Patents Act 1988, or under the terms of any licence permitting limited copying issued by the Copyright Licensing Agency, 90 Tottenham Court Road, London W1T 4LP.

Any person who does any unauthorized act in relation to this publication may be liable to criminal prosecution and civil claims for damages.

The authors have asserted their rights to be identified as the authors of this work in accordance with the Copyright, Designs and Patents Act 1988.

First published 2007 by
PALGRAVE MACMILLAN
Houndmills, Basingstoke, Hampshire RG21 6XS and
175 Fifth Avenue, New York, N.Y. 10010
Companies and representatives throughout the world

PALGRAVE MACMILLAN is the global academic imprint of the Palgrave Macmillan division of St. Martin's Press, LLC and of Palgrave Macmillan Ltd. Macmillan® is a registered trademark in the United States, United Kingdom and other countries. Palgrave is a registered trademark in the European Union and other countries.

ISBN-13: 978–0–230–00699–7
ISBN-10: 0–230–00699–X

This book is printed on paper suitable for recycling and made from fully managed and sustained forest sources. Logging, pulping and manufacturing processes are expected to conform to the environmental regulations of the country of origin.

A catalogue record for this book is available from the British Library.

Library of Congress Cataloging-in-Publication Data
Deposit insurance / edited by Andrew Campbell . . . [et al.].
p. cm.
Includes bibliographical references and index.
ISBN-10: 0–230–00699–X (cloth)
ISBN-13: 978–0–230–00699–7 (cloth)
1. Deposit insurance. I. Campbell, Andrew (Andrew B.)
HG1662.A3D47 2007
368.8′54—dc22 2006052727

10 9 8 7 6 5 4 3 2
16 15 14 13 12 11 10 09 08

Printed and bound in Great Britain by
Antony Rowe Ltd, Chippenham and Eastbourne

Contents

List of Tables

List of Figures

List of Boxes

Preface

The subject of deposit insurance has become increasingly important in recent years with the result that there are now almost one hundred deposit insurance systems in operation around the globe. A significant feature of the last century was the series of banking crises which many countries experienced. Countless numbers of bank depositors in many countries have seen their savings wiped out and in many instances governments have had to absorb substantial losses due to banking failures. One reason for the development of explicit depositor protection arrangements is that they contribute to financial stability by protecting depositors and they avoid bank runs by providing safeguards to unsophisticated depositors. A second reason, and in the view of many the most important, is that explicit limited deposit insurance limits the exposure of governments to banking problems. While the use of explicit limited deposit insurance in the promotion of financial stability is becoming the norm rather than the exception internationally, the debate about many aspects of its use needs to be developed further. At the time of writing many countries are in the process of introducing deposit insurance systems for the first time, while a number of countries, which already have systems are considering making changes to make them more effective.

The idea for this book developed from the papers presented at the Fourth Annual Conference of the International Association of Deposit Insurers which was held at The Grand Hotel in Taipei, Taiwan, in September 2005. It is thanks to the very existence of the International Association of Deposit Insurers that it has been possible to gather such expertise in one place and to assist in promoting a significant amount of vigorous debate. The papers have been updated and expanded upon where appropriate and two introductory chapters, written by the Editors, have been added. We are fortunate to be able to present such a wide ranging collection of papers which deal with many aspects of the subject and which have been written by people who have real expertise in the area.

The book deals with a wide variety of relevant issues and these include such matters as the rationale and purpose of providing protection to bank depositors and the legal position of bank depositors as unsecured creditors. Readers will find that there are many different approaches to such matters as: the level of protection to be provided; how systems are to be funded; what the role of the deposit insurance agency is to be – should it be narrow and act simply as a 'pay box' or should it have a wider function and be involved in the regulatory and insolvency aspects? The book is deliberately forward-looking, considering the way the role of the deposit insurer is likely to develop, particularly in a world where national institutions have to cope with increasingly international banks.

In particular the book deals with the problems of the internationalization of banking and how deposit insurance provided by national organizations can handle the fact that the depositors and the banks' assets are spread over many countries.

We intend this book to be a major reference point for all those with an interest in the provision of deposit insurance. This includes deposit insurance agency officials, government officials, policy makers, central bankers, commercial bankers, economists, lawyers and academics. We hope it will be of interest and use to all of these and will also have a major role to play in stimulating further debate on the subject at all levels.

ANDREW CAMPBELL
JOHN RAYMOND LABROSSE
DAVID G. MAYES
DALVINDER SINGH

Notes on the Contributors and Editors

The editors

Andrew Campbell is the Director of the Centre for Business Law and Practice at the University of Leeds in the United Kingdom and a Solicitor of the Supreme Court in England and Wales. He regularly acts as Consulting Counsel to the International Monetary Fund, Washington, DC, USA. He is co-author, with Peter Cartwright, of *Banks in Crisis: The Legal Response* (2002) and a co-author of *Butterworths Annotated Guide to the Financial Services and Markets Act* (2nd edn, 2005).

John Raymond LaBrosse has been the Secretary General of the International Association of Deposit Insurers (IADI) since it was founded in May 2002. The objects of IADI are to contribute to the stability of financial systems by promoting international cooperation and to encourage wide international contact among deposit insurers and other interested parties. After starting his career at the Bank of Canada, he served in many senior positions at the Department of Finance and was a key adviser on financial sector policy issues for the Government of Canada from 1976 to 1999. Prior to his appointment as Secretary General he was Director, International, Canada Deposit Insurance Corporation (CDIC); he was also the Executive Director of the Financial Stability Forum's Study and Working Groups on Deposit Insurance which finalized its report in September 2001.

David G. Mayes is Adviser to the Board at the Bank of Finland and Professor of Economics at London South Bank University. He is currently Visiting Professor at the University of Auckland. He has published widely on problems of financial and monetary integration in Europe, including *'Who Pays for Bank Insolvency?'*, (2003).

Dalvinder Singh is Senior Lecturer in Law at Oxford Brookes University in the United Kingdom and Managing Editor of the *Journal of Banking Regulation*. He is an Associate Research Fellow at the Institute of Advanced Legal Studies, University of London. He has also acted as a consultant to the International Monetary Fund.

The contributors

Gulen Atay is Principal Counsel in the Office of the General Counsel of the Asian Development Bank (ADB) where she is involved in processing and administration of development loans made to the member countries. ADB is a regional multilateral development finance institution owned by 64 member countries, 46 from Asia and the Pacific and 18 from other parts of the globe. ADB helps its developing member countries through policy advice, loans, technical assistance, grants, guarantees and equity investments. She previously worked as a lawyer in Istanbul, Turkey, advising major international banks in their local and cross-border operations, and other project finance matters. Prior to that, she worked as a bank inspector, reviewing compliance of a major local bank with the banking rules and regulations, and reporting thereon.

Christine E. Blair is Senior Financial Economist in the Division of Insurance and Research at the Federal Deposit Insurance Corporation. She has been active in the FDIC's international programmes, including the development of the FDIC's 1998 International Conference on Deposit Insurance and the 2000 Symposium on Establishing a Deposit Insurance System jointly sponsored by the Financial Stability Institute (FSI) and the FDIC. As a member of the Research Committee of the FSI's Working Group on Deposit Insurance, Ms. Blair was a major contributor to Guidance for Developing Effective Deposit Insurance Systems. She holds a PhD in Economics from Fordham University.

Frederick Carns is Director, Office of International Affairs, Federal Deposit Insurance Corporation, and Chair, Research and Guidance Subcommittee, on the Evaluation of the Effectiveness of Deposit Insurance Systems, International Association of Deposit Insurers.

Winston Keith Carr was formerly Deputy Governor of the Bank of Jamaica (the Central Bank), which he served in many capacities for 36 years. During his tenure at the bank, he was a member of Jamaica's negotiating team with the IMF, The World Bank and the IDB. He was instrumental in the establishment of the Cambio system in Jamaica in 1994. He was Chairman of the Task Force set up by Government of Jamaica in 1995 to identify the necessary requirement for introducing an explicit deposit insurance scheme in Jamaica. When the Jamaica Deposit Insurance Corporation (JDIC) was legally established in August 1998, he was seconded from the Bank of Jamaica to the JDIC as the first Chief Executive Officer and an ex officio member of the Board of Directors, a position he currently occupies. He was a member of the Working Group on Deposit Insurance which made its final report to the Financial Stability Forum in September 2001. He is a member of the Executive Council of the International Association of Deposit Insurers (IADI), established in May 2002 in Basel, Switzerland. He is a member of many of the Association's Standing Committees and is Chairman of the Training and Conference Committee and the Caribbean Regional Committee. He is a director of the National Export Import Bank of Jamaica. He was awarded the national honour of the Order of Distinction, Commander Class, for outstanding service to Banking, effective 6 August, 2003.

Pilsin Choi is Assistant Professor of Economics at Konkuk University in Korea having previously been Team Head at the Financial Supervisory Service and a Senior Economist at the Korea Deposit Insurance Corporation. In 2002–3 he was a Visiting Lecturer at the University of Texas at Austin in the United States.

Marc-Andre Flageole holds a Master in Finance from HEC Montréal. He is currently employed at the real estate group of Caisse de dépôt et placement du Québec as an International Equity Analyst. He was also Lecturer in Portfolio Management at HEC Montréal.

George G. Kaufman is the John Smith Professor of Finance and Economics in the School of Business Administration at Loyola University, Chicago. He previously taught at the University of Oregon and as visiting professor at the University of California, Berkeley, Stanford University and the University of Southern California. Prior to his academic career he was a Senior Economist at the Federal Reserve Bank of Chicago and has served as a consultant to the Bank since his return to Chicago. He has published widely in major professional journals and books, is currently co-editor of the Journal of Financial Stability, a founding editor of the Journal of Financial Services Research, and a member of numerous editorial boards. He has served as president of the Western Finance Association, the Midwest Finance Association, and the North American Economic and Finance Associations. He currently serves as co-chair of the Shadow Financial Regulatory Committee and as Executive Director of the Financial Economists Roundtable.

Dong-Il Kim is an Executive Director of the Korean Deposit Insurance Corporation. He has formerly been Director of the Asset Management Department and President of the Resolution and Finance Corporation. He has been an Adviser to the Federal Deposit Insurance Corporation in Washington, DC, USA.

Lawrence Kryzanowski is currently a Full Professor and Concordia University Research Chair in Finance. He is an active educator, mentor, consultant and expert witness in financial economics, including investment management, risk pricing and management, and regulation and operations of global financial markets, institutions and participants. He is author or co-author of over 95 refereed journal articles, seven books or monographs, and over 150 papers presented at learned conferences. His various research awards include the OSFI Award (with Dr. Roberts) for excellence in research on regulation of financial institutions. He is currently an advisory Editor (*European Journal of Finance*), editor (*Multinational Finance Journal*), Associate Editor (*International Review of Financial Analysis*) and editorial board member (*Canadian Investment Review; Finance India*). He has appeared as an expert witness in regulatory board hearings dealing with rate of return and capital structure applications by Canadian utilities and stock market insider trading court proceedings. He represents retail investors on the regulation advisory committee of Market Regulation Services Inc.

Rose M. Kushmeider is Senior Financial Economist in the Division of Insurance and Research at the Federal Deposit Insurance Corporation. She has been active in the FDIC's international programmes, including the development of the FDIC's 1998 International Conference on Deposit Insurance and the 2000 Symposium on Establishing a Deposit Insurance System jointly sponsored by the Financial Stability Institute and the FDIC. As a member of the Research Committee of the Financial Stability Forum's Working Group on Deposit Insurance, Ms Kushmeider was a major contributor to Guidance for Developing Effective Deposit Insurance Systems. She holds a graduate degree in Economics from the University of Maryland.

Ganiyu A. Ogunleye is Managing Director and Chief Executive Officer of the Nigerian Deposit Insurance Corporation and Chairman of the Africa Regional Committee of the International Association of Deposit Insurers.

Jean Roy holds a PhD in finance from the Wharton School of the University of Pennsylvania. His major field of interest is the management and regulation of financial institutions. Since 1990, he has been Professor of Finance at HEC-Montreal. He is a regular consultant to government and industry.

William Su is the Director of Risk Management Department, Central Deposit Insurance Corporation (Taiwan). He is the project coordinator of the Sub-committee on Resolution of Bank Failures, Research and Guidance Committee, International Association of Deposit Insurers (IADI). He is experienced in dealing with failing/failed bank resolutions, including being appointed as Deputy Supervisor of Conservator Team of Chung Shing Commercial Bank, Taiwan, during 2000–2 (the largest bank failure in Taiwan banking industry).

David K. Walker is Director of Policy and International Affairs for the Canada Deposit Insurance Corporation. He is responsible for developing advice on policies affecting CDIC; conducting research on emerging financial sector issues; and coordinating CDIC's international activities. Prior to joining CDIC, he was Senior Economist with the Royal Bank of Canada.

Acknowledgements

The editors would like to thank the Central Deposit Insurance Corporation of Taiwan for hosting the Fourth Annual Conference of the International Association of Deposit Insurers which provided a venue for the presentation of most of the papers contained in this book.

Andy Campbell would like to thank his daughter Marianne and his colleague Lindsey Brooke for their invaluable help with the preparation of the manuscript. He would also like to thank his wife Shirley and his daughter Elise for their continuous support throughout the project.

Ray LaBrosse would like to thank his wife Gail for her continued encouragement and Jean Pierre Sabourin, Chair of the Executive Council, for his role in founding the International Association of Deposit Insurers and through that organisation there continues to be wide, international discussion of ways to improve the functioning of deposit insurance systems.

Chapter 1 was written while David Mayes was visiting the University of Auckland and he is grateful for the facilities provided.

Dalvinder Singh would like to thank his wife Sarbjit and his daughter Amaryn and son, Arvind for their love and support.

All the editors would like to express their appreciation to Lauren Anderson for her assistance at the final proof stage. Andy and Dalvinder would like to thank Ross Cranston for his much appreciated comments on Chapter 2.

ANDREW CAMPBELL
JOHN RAYMOND LABROSSE
DAVID G. MAYES
DALVINDER SINGH

1

Promoting Financial Stability through Effective Depositor Protection: The Case for Explicit Limited Deposit Insurance

John Raymond LaBrosse and David G. Mayes

At the beginning of the twentieth century there were only a handful of explicit deposit protection arrangements in existence. By the end of those hundred years, however, the number of systems in operation had grown to close to one hundred explicit or implicit arrangements with many of the explicit systems being created in the 1990s.[1] Why has there been so much interest in having such systems? After all in the nineteenth century there had been a string of financial crises.

In the early part of the twentieth century one could look to the fallout from the bank[2] runs that precipitated the Great Depression as a cause.[3] However, the period following the Second World War was characterized by greater stability partly in response to the extensive controls and limits on risk taking. More recently with liberalization and extended international lending there have been new problems, with the Tequila Crisis in Mexico, the Nordic crises, the Asian financial crises, the Russian and Argentinean defaults, to name only some of the 117 crises since 1980 that Caprio and Klingebiel (2003) identify. This has led to a reaction in regulation with Basel I and more recently Basel II and to a rethinking of foreign lending and the risks involved. The introduction of explicit deposit insurance systems is clearly part of the reaction to the losses and, more particularly, a part of the drive for financial stability both nationally and internationally that has arisen during the last decade (Schinasi, 2005; Allen and Wood, 2006).

The concern is two-fold. In the first place, as laid out in Diamond and Dybvig (1986), simply by providing confidence, deposit insurance helps ensure that problems with a bank in difficulty do not spread over to a general loss in confidence and run on the banks as a whole. This, supported by the role of the central bank as lender of last resort in providing emergency liquidity against collateral for banks that are solvent but subject to pressure, is intended to limit the contagion from the shocks that inevitably hit the economic and financial system. It is the knowledge of the existence of these two facilities that provides the confidence so that a shock is much less likely to result in a crisis. A loss of confidence causes people to alter their rate of time preference and to rush for more secure assets, thereby causing a rapid decline in asset prices and the circle of debt deflation (King, 1994).

The other part of this two-fold concern is that it is thought unlikely that ordinary individuals are capable of monitoring the risks that their banks take and acting appropriately to manage such risks. Indeed, many people view banks as places that look after their savings, much in the way that Gringotts Bank in the Harry Potter books keeps each depositor's money in a numbered vault. They are not properly aware that their money has been used to finance other activities, each of which has a risk attached. Since deposit insurance provides a comfort in this respect it can also be seen as reinforcing a moral hazard. As banks are aware that the authorities will step in in the event of difficulty they may be tempted to take greater risks in the pursuit of profitable activities than they would if they faced a greater risk that investors, creditors and depositors would withdraw. It could therefore be argued that depositors should be encouraged to pay greater attention to the risks. Then in turn the banks would have a greater incentive to make sure that they lent prudently and profitably to give the necessary confidence to their depositors.

There is considerable debate in the literature about the extent of moral hazard in practice and the contribution of deposit insurance to it. Wheelock (1992) finds evidence in favour of increased risk-taking in the USA and Demirguç-Kunt and Detriache (2000) find evidence that deposit insurance is associated with an increased risk of banking crisis in a substantial cross-country study. Others fail to find evidence one way or the other. However, Gropp and Vesala (2001) not only provide strong evidence that the introduction of deposit insurance has tended to be associated with a *reduction* in bank risk-taking in the EU but they do so in an encompassing framework that explains why other studies have found the opposite in specific cases. In particular, they show that moral hazard tends to be greatest when the banks are weak, hence introducing deposit insurance in that framework may indeed encourage risk taking.[4] Similarly, if banks are in some sense 'too big to fail' they find, not surprisingly, that the introduction of deposit insurance appears to have no impact on risk taking. Most promisingly they find that deposit insurance interacts positively with the holding of subordinated debt, or at least non-bank subordinated debt holders. Those particular subordinated debt holders are not only among the groups that are likely to be able to offer the most effective market discipline on the bank but they are typically not also insured depositors (or at least their exposure as insured depositors is trivial compared to their exposure through subordinated debt). The logic is simple, depositors will tend to be treated more favourably than other unsecured creditors and therefore the extent of any recovery by subordinated debt holders will be reduced – thereby heightening their incentive to monitor the bank to protect themselves. This, therefore, seems to provide the compatible incentives that designers of the safety net are so keen to achieve, that the safety encourages others to improve prudence and hence stability.

It is essential to consider the structure of each deposit insurance system in judging its impact in retrospect or prospect. Similar to Gropp and Vesala (2001), Bartholdy, Boyle and Stover (2004) in looking at the case of Denmark, find that large banks reacted favourably to the introduction of deposit insurance while small and risky banks tended to increase risk taking. However, they regard two features as being crucial in determining this response, namely the use of market value accounting and the existence of a strict closure policy in the event of difficulty. These two features tackle two of the trickier parts of credible deposit insurance. If the risks are to be well managed and market discipline (and regulatory discipline) to be placed on the bank it must be possible to obtain useful valuations of the assets and liabilities of the enterprise. Historical cost measures are not helpful, especially when the market starts to crumble. What is needed is valuation in the market. (Other countries have been slow to follow the Danish lead. One problem specifically relates to the role of the deposit insurer. Opponents of marking to market argue that in the case of banking many banks intend to hold assets to maturity, so short run variations in them are unimportant. However, the key issue is the stance of the deposit insurer when the firm reaches insolvency.[5] If the deposit insurer is going to act on a mark-to-market basis then this is the appropriate accounting framework. However, if the deposit insurer is inclined to take the longer term view then a more qualified valuation may make sense.)

As we develop in more detail later, having an effective strategy for exiting banks irrelevant of size, is crucial to the success of the system. In a small country like Denmark (Mølgaard, 2003) the supervisor (in this case on behalf of the deposit insurer) can develop a close relationship with the banks and demonstrate clearly by its actions, discussions and preparations that it can intervene rapidly and effectively when the time comes.

There is thus some scope for debate about how the insurance of deposits should best contribute to maintaining stability. Clearly a blanket government guarantee would offer the greatest potential protection to depositors but it would limit the incentive to banks to manage their risks prudently which could expose Treasuries to potentially enormous costs. At the other end of the spectrum, the absence of any insurance at all, whether implicit or explicit might lead people to avoid the banks and hence reduce the contribution that the financial sector makes to wealth creation and economic growth. Indeed, it is unclear whether a lack of implicit insurance is believable in any circumstances. Governments have tended to take action in times of crises because of their fears of the impact on society as a whole if they did not, even where they have made strong prior statements about not bailing out banks. One of the strongest arguments for explicit but limited deposit insurance is that all parties have a better chance of knowing where they are likely to stand in the event of difficulty. Only some deposits will be protected, shareholders may have limited protection and hence those creditors and others with something at risk will still have a strong incentive to monitor and discipline the banks.

It is sometimes argued that an element of ambiguity is advantageous as people will want to protect themselves from loss if they are not certain whether the state will step in (Talley, 1994). However, the argument can easily be turned on its head so that such ambiguity is no longer constructive. People may believe that more insurance will be provided than the authorities intend and hence take greater risks, exposing the moral hazard. While this may appear advantageous when all is going well it both increases the chance of a crisis or failure and the depth of the consequences that will follow. People who are unprepared for problems will have to take far more costly steps than those who are well prepared.

In this framework deposit insurance forms just one component of the system that will come into play in the event of a problem and, therefore, cannot be evaluated on its own but in concert with insolvency legislation, the nature of the lender of last resort and other aspects of the safety net. Similarly its existence forms one component of the system for encouraging prudential management and the avoidance of problems, along with supervision of individual financial institutions and macro-prudential analysis of the threats to the system as a whole. Costs are reduced when the components are mutually reinforcing rather than contradictory (Beck, 2003).

In this book we explore several of the major facets that are required to make a system of explicit depositor protection convincing and hence encourage financial intermediation and its contribution to the faster growth of the economy without simultaneously encouraging imprudence and the financial instability that could more than offset the faster growth. It is worth recalling that the crises of recent years (Hoggarth and Saporta, 2001) have on average led to a loss equivalent to 30 per cent of gross domestic product. It would take very substantial growth rates to offset such a loss even within the course of a generation. In the case of the Finnish crisis on the early 1990s the cumulative loss has been estimated to lie between 20 per cent and 50 per cent of GDP. Indeed if unemployment is used as a measure of loss the cost is still continuing to mount 15 years later.

In what follows, therefore, we begin examining some alternatives to deposit insurance and then set out the framework on which explicit limited deposit insurance exists and its appropriate structuring before going on to discuss two major issues that have to be resolved if crises are to be handled effectively for deposit insurance:

- prompt payment to depositors;
- cross-border banks.

1.1 Alternatives to deposit insurance arrangements

As financial systems are liberalized and rely more and more on market forces, they also become more vulnerable and subject to greater instability (Caprio and Honohan, 1999). Depositor protection has become an important feature of most banking systems to reduce the instability and minimize the probability of a crisis (Talley, 1994; Barajas and Steiner, 2000). There has been a strong argument in favour of establishing a deposit insurance system in order to prevent the disruptive and costly effects of the types of depositors' runs (Diamond and Dybvig, 1986; Barajas and Steiner, 2000). The cost of such systems it is argued is moral hazard, as insured depositors no longer have a strong incentive to monitor the behaviour of banks where they hold their deposits, and thus banks may also have an incentive to assume greater risks. Therefore, when designing a deposit insurance system, policymakers often face a tradeoff between the reduction of risk coming from bank runs and the additional risk induced by moral hazard (Barajas and Steiner, 2000).

However, deposit insurance is not the only way to protect depositors. Another option is so-called implicit deposit protection, which usually means taxpayers rescue banks that would otherwise fail, although it could be customary for other banks to acquire those that are in difficulty or actually failing. Governments also have the option of providing no protection – but this is a rare policy choice in practice, even if it is the stated policy stance. In the course of deciding which option to choose, policymakers have to consider some wider public policy objectives, including the prevention of contagious bank runs, and promoting market discipline through minimizing moral hazard (Talley, 1994). Deposit insurance systems have several advantages over implicit protection. Deposit insurance gives the banking system more protection against bank runs, provides more protection for small depositors, and provides a faster, smoother administrative process to undertake payouts when a bank fails. On the other hand, deposit insurance probably creates more moral hazard for depositors, thereby contributing to the erosion of market discipline and increased bank risk-taking. Deposit insurance can tend to be a more expensive mechanism for protecting depositors because it offers less freedom of action to policymakers than an implicit scheme (Talley and Mas, 1990; Talley, 1994).

Policymakers often look to a variety of alternatives to deposit insurance before introducing such systems. They do so by examining practice and the literature and seeking advice from academics and others (Garcia, 1996 and Financial Stability Forum, 2001a). It is helpful, therefore, to examine the usefulness of the alternatives. Some countries have implicit protection that arises when the public, including depositors and other creditors, expect some form of protection when a bank fails (Tally, 1994). This expectation usually arises because of the governments' past behaviour or statements made by officials. Implicit protection is, by definition, never formally specified. There are no statutory rules regarding the eligibility of bank liabilities, the level of protection promised or the form in which reimbursement of funds after a failure will take. By its nature, implicit protection creates uncertainty about how depositors, creditors and others will be treated when a bank failure occurs.

Funding under those kinds of arrangements is discretionary and often depends on the government's ability to access public funds. Although it can be argued that a degree of uncertainty can lead depositors to exert greater effort in monitoring banks, the Financial Stability Forum's Study Group on Deposit Insurance (2000) found that in reality most depositors are not capable of doing so, or have little incentive given the diversity of interests.

Since decisions to reimburse depositors are discretionary and based on the willingness and capability to reimburse depositors, depositors in failed banks are often treated differently. This creates inequities and does not promote stability. As the number of claimants mounts, for example, the generosity of the pay out may fall. Conversely, a deepening crisis may encourage a government to issue a blanket guarantee, which may not compensate those with the foresight to protect themselves earlier in the process. Finally, there are cases where countries have had to fund failures through government appropriations which have forced them to reduce spending on needed social programmes and infrastructure programmes for several years.

Some countries have had to introduce explicit blanket guarantees during a financial crisis to protect all bank depositors and creditors fully. The provision of such guarantees may be unavoidable in periods of extreme financial distress to maintain domestic and international confidence in a country's banking system. However, such blanket guarantees are the extreme in moral hazard and it can have a number of adverse effects. We can identify many countries that have had to resort to blanket guarantees – Sweden, Mexico, Japan, Malaysia, and Thailand. Blanket guarantees are easily announced but difficult to eliminate or reduce, Japan being an example.

At its extreme, blanket guarantees could encompass unregulated or 'free' banking where entry and exit are uncontrolled, supervision is nonexistent or minimal, competition is intense and there are no implicit or explicit guarantees. It is argued that given market discipline and full disclosure, depositors would have the incentives and capabilities to look after their own interests. Losses to depositors and creditors would occur, but it is argued that such a system would see fewer problems to begin with and losses would be minimal. The model is very conceptual and no country follows it exclusively. Although, some would argue that New Zealand, which we will discuss in more detail later, is close to this model – it should be noted, however, that they do not have any significant domestically owned banks.

Depositor preference is discussed by Garcia (1996) and articulated in the Consultation Paper that was issued by the Hong Kong Monetary Authority in 2001. Countries without deposit insurance, it is advanced, can provide their depositors with some protection from loss by giving them priority over the assets that are recovered from a failed bank. Essentially, this means that while secured creditors have first priority, followed by liquidation/receivership expenses, depositors are ranked immediately afterward with all other unsecured creditors (such as, employees, unsecured central bank claims, taxes) and subordinated claims and shareholders following them.

Depositor preference is, in fact, found in a number of countries. In the USA it is used in conjunction with deposit insurance for domestic depositors. Germany provides depositors priority over secured as well as unsecured creditors. In Australia, depositors receive priority over all other unsecured creditors and it is used in a financial system without explicit deposit insurance (although some observers argue that an implicit deposit protection regime exists in Australia). Canada has a limited form of preference for depositors (such as, deposits held 'in trust') and this has been a factor contributing to lower resolution costs, in some cases, for trust companies[6] compared to banks.

The advantages of depositor preference are that it can encourage more market discipline (by increasing the loss exposure of general creditors) and substantially limit depositor losses in a failure. Disadvantages are that since non-deposit creditors could suffer substantially higher losses than depositors, they could react by shortening maturities and in some cases withdrawing all or part of their funds thus making it more difficult for banks to offer longer-term funding. But, implementing depositor preference can be a formidable challenge for government authorities given the interests of other creditors in the system (for example, central banks or commercial banks). Moreover, depositor priority in itself does not provide a mechanism to reimburse depositors quickly. Hong Kong is implementing a deposit insurance system at this very time for that reason. It has depositor preference but the payment of claims by liquidators may take years. In such cases, the potential for bank runs are still very much a part of their system.

A key element in promoting market discipline is to ensure that there are strong governance incentives for owners, directors and managers of institutions. It has been the experience in Canada in dealing with failures that deficiencies in corporate governance are among the most important causes of problems.

We know that there are a variety of mechanisms that exist for enhancing corporate governance. Although shareholders are exposed to the potential for investment losses in most market systems, 'double liability' proposals have been made whereby investors could be subject in a failure to covering shortfalls and losses to creditors. It has even been proposed (by Kane and Wilson, 1997, Beck, 2003, and Saunders and Wilson, 1995) that 'double liability' could be used as an alternative to deposit insurance. Double liability was in place in Scotland in the nineteenth century and in many states prior to the 1930s where it appeared to play a positive role in limiting bank failures. It was a feature of the Canadian system until 1954. However, the problems with implementing such schemes in practice are numerous and include creating incentives for investors to participate, knowing their further potential liability, and in creating the legal structure necessary to enforce the contracts.

Taking legal action against directors, managers and auditors of problem financial institutions is also helpful in creating strong incentives against moral hazard. During the 1990s, Canada Deposit Insurance Corporation recovered close to C$175 million through litigation involving directors, managers and auditors of failed CDIC-member institutions.

A third incentive comes through subordinated debt proposals (Garcia, 1999, Calomiris 1999, and others) usually require institutions to issue – on a continuing basis – debt which would be subordinate to all other debts, ranking only ahead of shareholder equity. The proposals usually involve ensuring that banks maintain minimum ratios of subordinated debt relative to deposits. It is suggested that the debt be held by parties unrelated to the bank or bank holding company. Necessary conditions for the scheme to work include a liquid market for the debt and a belief by debenture holders that institutions will be closed before or when they become insolvent. If not, high rates of interest are likely to be demanded by debt holders and/or liquidity problems could result.

The main advantage of subordinated debt is that it provides for additional market discipline as those debt holders should have strong incentives to monitor and use information about each institution. Supervisors and the markets could benefit from the market's rating of the subordinated debt as additional signals. However, the major disadvantage of the scheme is that not all institutions would be in a position to issue such debt because of their corporate structure. Therefore, there may not be sufficient market liquidity (or even sophisticated investors) in many countries. Questions also arise as to how the authorities (and depositors) would treat institutions with low ratings. In the absence of rules-based closure regimes, this is likely to be a serious concern. Such regimes force closure or require a minimum level of subordinated debt that, if not met, would trigger requirements for the bank to buy back its debt. A variation on this concern is too-big-to-fail considerations. If certain institutions are deemed too-big-too-far, this would reduce the incentives of the subordinated-debt holders to exert market discipline.

As articulated by the Financial Stability Forum's Working Group on Deposit Insurance (2000) an explicit deposit insurance system is preferable to any other type of deposit protection. It is preferable because it clarifies the authorities' obligations to depositors and limits the scope of discretionary decisions that may result in arbitrary actions. To be credible and to avoid distortions that may result in moral hazard, such a system needs to be properly designed, well implemented and understood by the public. However, an explicit system needs to be part of a well designed financial safety net, supported by strong prudential regulation and supervision, effective laws that are enforced, sound corporate governance and risk management in banks and sound accounting standards and disclosure regimes.

To be credible, statutes or other legal instruments need to stipulate explicit deposit insurance systems. Typically, rules governing insurance coverage limits, the type of instruments covered, depositor ranking of claims, the process and method of reimbursing depositors claims, the manner and method of funding, need to be described in law. An explicit system can also provide an orderly process for dealing with bank failures, mechanisms for resolutions, reimbursing of depositors claims and the monitoring of the liquidation of an estate's assets.

An explicit system protects insured depositors against the consequences associated with bank failures but it is not designed to protect banks from failing. An effective system limits government fiscal exposure, assume banks pay the cost of the system, and it also reduces the political risks of allowing banks to fail. It can also contribute to the maintenance of confidence and reduce the likelihood of bank runs. To be effective, an explicit system needs a clear mandate to reinforce the stability of the financial system and to contribute to its own sound governance and greater accountability. An explicit system also requires the powers to fulfill the mandate. All deposit insurers require the ability to enter into contracts, set appropriate requirements, and have access to timely and accurate information to ensure that they can meet their obligations to depositors promptly. Interrelationships between safety net players need to be well defined to ensure close coordination of activities. There are a number of design features that need to be decided upon to ensure that an explicit deposit insurance system is effective. These are: which institutions should be eligible for membership (commercial banks, foreign banks, state banks and non-financial institutions), the need for compulsory membership to avoid adverse selection, what considerations are necessary for granting membership (when the deposit insurer is established and after new banks are chartered), coverage and limits (scope and level, co-insurance, adjusting coverage limits, foreign currency deposits), funding (levies, *ex ante* or *ex post* premium assessments, flat rate or differential premiums) level and size of a fund (target ratio or range), public awareness, bank resolutions, reimbursement of depositors claims, claims and recoveries, among other things.

In short, the establishment of an effective explicit deposit insurance system is rather complex but the benefits far outweigh the complexity of establishing one. There are always criticisms of explicit systems. But if one considers the options, effective explicit deposit insurance systems do promote and contribute to the stability of the financial system. We need, nonetheless, to add one word of caution. Effective explicit systems can deal with a bank failure or a wave of failures but cannot by themselves deal with a financial system crisis. That is the role of the government. Finally, the complexities of explicit systems require appropriate skills and resources to be effective. Such skills are in short supply, more so expert practitioners.

1.2 The importance of deposit insurance in the evolution of the financial system – the Canadian case

In 1964, a Royal Commission (the 'Porter Commission') reviewed the question whether Canada should adopt an explicit system of deposit insurance. The Commission concluded that such a system was not needed, based on the argument that sufficient protection to depositors was provided through the concentrated nature of the financial system, good supervision of that system, and a collaborative approach by government and industry to addressing the rare problems that arose (Canada Deposit Insurance Corporation (CDIC), 2003). In hindsight, it was rather odd for a group of prominent economists to conclude that more concentration, resulting in less competition, was such a good thing. However, failures of a number of financial institutions later in that same decade and an apparent unwillingness of the large banks to collude in dealing with them in a way that was expected caused the government to rethink the advice that it was given. In 1967, a bill was introduced into the House of Commons to establish the Canada Deposit Insurance Corporation. The legislation argued that deposit insurance would make a substantial contribution to the government's goal of achieving greater competition and flexibility in Canada's financial system. By levelling the playing field, depositors should have greater choice among equally secure institutions, both new and established. Was the policy successful?

There is no doubt that the existence of deposit insurance provided a solid basis for a more competitive Canadian financial services sector. From 1970 to 1979, CDIC's membership grew from 73 to 115 institutions and insured deposits grew from C$25 billion to C$83 billion (an increase of 232 per cent). New members included both federal and provincially regulated financial institutions (6 banks, 49 federal and 54 provincial loan and trust companies). It is interesting to note that the federal government's comfort level with the banks' collusion did not start to diminish until the passage of the Bank Act in 1980 when the banks were finally brought under the Competition Act, for the first time. However, even with that smallish step the Minister of Finance retained the ability to permit banks to enter into certain agreements if the Minister felt that such agreements met a public interest test. Determining just what is in the public's interest is an interesting point. More competition in the financial sector should have been high on the list but recent history indicates that such a policy is not always the case as political interests can rise above that.

In furthering the argument that deposit insurance promotes competition one could draw an analogy with another industry. In North America, at least, Home Depot is one of the firms taking over the consumer hardware and building supply distribution system. They are doing so by wiping out small firms. Indeed, it would be difficult to imagine a small hardware store opening up next to a Home Depot even if it promised a high level of 'service'.

Is the same thing happening in the financial services sector? The answer is no. In Canada, small or internet banks can compete right along side the 'big 6' banks because they can offer the same government guarantee – protection to C$100,000. If that were not the case, small institutions would not exist for very long as they would have to pay higher rates of interest and take on much riskier assets otherwise depositors would only deal with large institutions under the guise that they will not be allowed to fail.

Another aspect of the benefits of explicit deposit insurance is the time that it gives the prudential regulatory authorities to deal with a problem financial institution. To illustrate this point one only needs to look at the way some of the banking failures were handled in Canada. In the early 1990s, the regulatory authorities in the Province of Ontario forced one of its regulated trust companies (Shoppers Trust) to issue a News Release stating that the company could only accept insured deposits. In that way the public received protection of their deposits in that institution while solutions to the problem could be found (eventually the company was closed).

Further evidence of the use of deposit insurance in limiting the government's guarantee (that is, moral hazard) can be drawn by looking at the experience in the handling of the failures of Canadian Commercial Bank and the Northland Bank. In those cases, the banks failed but the Minister of the day decided that all depositors – insured and uninsured – should be compensated because of statements made by the authorities as to the condition of those banks (CDIC, 1985 and 1986). The cost of reimbursement to the federal government was over C$750 million. CDIC now maintains an active public awareness at a cost well under the losses incurred during those two failures.

Before closing this section it is interesting to speculate on what might have happened in Canada in the absence of deposit insurance. There is little doubt that small deposit accepting institutions would not have been able to survive for very long (the 'Home Depot' effect) and markets would have suffered from less competition and innovation. Second, there have been 43 member failures in the time since the establishment of CDIC. It could be argued that they might not have started in the first place. But if anyone or some of them had, would that have opened up the federal or other governments to lawsuits from depositors? There would have been a move, at a minimum, for governments driven by politics to compensate depositors in any of the failures, especially if they occurred around the time of an election. If governments chose not to compensate depositors, then the prudential regulatory authorities would, at the very least, have wanted to see ratings available for the organizations they regulate.

1.3 The nature of deposit insurance

Deposit insurance *per se* is not a route to greater financial stability nor is it the 'mother of all evils'.[7] But carefully designed, tailored to the environment in which it operates and supported by a strong business environment it can offer an important supporting role. 'An effective deposit insurance system needs to be properly designed, well implemented and understood by the public in order to be credible. It also needs to be supported by strong prudential regulation and supervision, sound accounting and disclosure regimes, and the enforcement of effective laws' (Financial Stability Forum, 2001a). A closer look at deposit insurance systems around the world reveals that there is no single approach that has been universally applied. Recent work by the International Association of Deposit Insurers finds that the types of deposit insurers range from simple 'payboxes' to 'risk minimizers', who have an active duty to manage the system according to specific criteria, and everything in between (INSOL INTERNATIONAL, 2005).

In a paybox system the deposit insurer is a small organization responsible for administering the insurance system. If the system is contributory it will ensure that the contributions are made. If it is funded then it may manage the funds. And in the event of a successful claim it will pay out as instructed. All of the aspects of deciding what form of system works well, acting before any bank reaches the point that the insurer may have to pay out or adjudicating whether a pay out is needed will occur elsewhere. Such an organisation can then be very small – the Finnish deposit insurer is staffed part time by a member of the staff of the Banker's Association (www.talletussuojarahasto.fi).

At the other end of the spectrum the deposit insurer itself handles the whole process and is able to structure the system to achieve a particular objective, such as minimizing its losses. This then involves a much more substantial organization with research, legal, executive and other divisions in addition to asset management, perhaps even having the power to adjudicate. It is likely to be able to participate in banking supervision.

The differences are rather marked, in fact, with mandates, business powers, structures, and characteristics of systems being quite diverse. Decisions have to be made over what sort of deposits to insure; whether there should be cutoffs, both for very small and large deposits; whether depositors should share in the risk; whether the taxpayer or the banks themselves provide the finance; whether there should be a fund to cushion against the initial impact of shocks (and add credibility)[8] and so on.

As a starting point for the proposition that explicit limited deposit insurance can make a substantial contribution to financial stability, it is important to distinguish between 'explicit' and 'implicit' systems. Every country, today, has some form of depositor protection, whether they acknowledge it or not, because the public wants to have and governments want to promote, confidence in the banking system (Sabourin, 2000). This is due to the fact that intermediation by banks in transforming depositor funds into loans provides important economic activity and growth.

From a global perspective, we could look at the different forms and alternatives to deposit insurance and from that analysis focus on some key aspects of explicit systems in order to examine the contribution that they can make to financial stability. The evidence is that banks will fail, in one form or another, in all jurisdictions around the world. The risks are no longer such that bank failure can be treated as being sufficiently unlikely that no provision is made for it and each case treated at the time on its merits without some particular regulatory foundation for the way to proceed.

Explicit deposit insurance systems have a clear benefit over other forms of protection in that they clarify the obligations of government and limit the scope for discretionary decisions that may result in arbitrary actions.[9] When properly designed, well implemented, understood by the public, and with appropriate prudential regulation and supervision and laws supporting them, adverse consequences such as moral hazard can be mitigated, and an effective deposit insurer can contribute substantially to a country's financial sector stability and depositor confidence.

Those general observations are reflected in the Financial Stability Forum's (2001a) Working Group Report, which cites four reasons in support of deposit insurance. The first relates to uncertainty regarding the cost of bank failures. The second and third relate to shortcomings in implicit insurance – namely uncertainty and inequity. Alternatively, these can be expressed as positives, namely that *explicit* deposit insurance clarifies the obligations of the insurer and limits the scope for discretionary decisions that may result in arbitrary actions. The fourth reason is that an explicit system provides a basis for a pre-determined contingency plan that more clearly defines the role and extent of government support in the resolution of bank failures. The achievement of this last objective does not in itself require the creation of a deposit insurance system; but the creation of one does render clarity of role and extent of government support an essential prerequisite.

Bank regulation in most countries encompasses a lender of last resort, deposit insurance and supervision. These functions are interrelated and therefore require coordination among the authorities responsible for them and each, in their own way, contributes to moral hazard that is associated with the financial safety net. In support of strong prudential regulation and supervision there needs to be a clear and transparent closure regime. Some countries, notably Canada, have done this by publishing a 'Guide to Intervention'[10] which outlines in important detail the steps that the supervisor and the deposit insurer will take through the 'life cycle' of a regulated financial institution. The 'Guide', supported by a clear mandate for the supervisor that makes it explicit that one of functions of the supervisor is to close 'troubled' financial institutions, is a key factor in providing incentives to bank managements to operate prudently. Governments also need to consider making appropriate changes to legislation, such as the *Winding Up Act*, in order to support a timely closure process.

The authorities, however, are often established with different mandates, some of which are likely to be in conflict. We consider these issues by studying the optimal institutional allocation of such functions.

1.4 What sort of structure for effective financial stability?

We have already set out that there are at least six functions that need to be in place for a system to offer a credible approach to maintaining financial stability:

- Regulation to ensure a set of standards for prudential behaviour and conduct of business.
- Supervision and monitoring of individual institutions to ensure compliance with the standards and to help institutions develop their risk management.
- Oversight of the financial system as a whole to help in the identification of system wide risks, whether from its structure, regulation or external shocks.
- A means of providing emergency support should there be a crisis or sudden lack of liquidity for the system or specific solvent institutions.
- A means of handling troubled institutions effectively so that their problems do not spill over into the system as a whole.
- A means of protecting small depositors so that they have confidence in the banking system and can have continuing access to their funds.
- Including orderly exit.

We suggest 'at least' six because there are related functions falling normally within the ambit of the public sector that also need to be in place. For example, the fundamental structure of the system – currency, payments, clearing, settlement, custody – needs to be resilient and such that it provides the necessary confidence that it will work properly not just in normal times but also in the face of extreme strain. Similarly, monetary and fiscal policies need to be such that people have confidence in the continuing value of their assets. There are wider requirements for clear property rights, the rule of law and so on. Without the wider framework, fine-tuning the arrangements for deposit insurance could be largely a waste of time. People will not believe that the funds will be there if there is a serious difficulty.

However, just because there are six functions to be addressed it does not entail that there have to be six separate institutions to handle them. We can be certain that there has to be a central bank or a monetary authority in almost all cases but beyond that there is considerable choice. In small countries the functions are often concentrated whereas in larger ones this is rarely the case. As Masciandaro, Nieto and Prast (2006) point out there seem to be two main models applied round the world. In the first, banking supervision is also assigned to the central bank but other financial institutions are separately regulated. In the second, there is a single financial supervisor, separate from the central bank. The UK is an obvious example of the second and Spain of the first. However, there are counter-examples, and both the Netherlands and the Irish Republic have gone for combining all these with the central bank.

Deposit insurance sits uncomfortably in this spectrum, as the nature of the arrangements have an important effect on the structure. If the system is simply a pay box then the handling of problem institutions normally lies with whoever is responsible for supervising banks. This can generate a substantial conflict of interest or purpose. A supervisor is normally responsible for the good running of the system and hence problems are in some sense a failure for them, even though the shock that causes the problem may be very external to the system. They thus have an incentive to try to keep the existing institutions going (or encourage 'voluntary' private sector solutions such as an acquisition). This will tend to lead to the perpetuation of the problem, at least for a while, unless someone is clearly responsible for minimising the loss.

In the United States and Canada, for example, there is a clear statement of what that loss is and who is responsible for minimizing it, namely, the deposit insurer. There the loss to be minimized is that of the deposit insurance fund. In these circumstances there will be strong pressure to act early otherwise the deposit insurer could be liable to accusations of failing in its duty when the case is audited after the event. However, in the event that there are likely to be more widespread losses outside the institution concerned it makes sense to widen the minimand to society as a whole. In the US case this option has not been exercised since the introduction of the Federal Deposit Insurance Corporation Improvement Act in 1989, which defines the current system. There are strong requirements on what is necessary in this case; involving agreement from the Federal Reserve, the Controller of the Currency and the Treasury that such a threat to the system exists.

It is arguable (Feldman and Stern, 2006) that in the USA such systemic problems can be avoided but in smaller countries it will tend to be the case that for a bank to be large enough to be internationally competitive and run a cost efficient full service it will tend to be large relative to the economy. Indeed in the case of some countries, Switzerland for example, some banks (UBS and Crédit Suisse) will tend to dwarf the local economy because of the extent of their offshore operations. The difference between the two concerns is important, as minimizing the loss to the insurance fund is something that it is relatively easy to turn into a clear decision-making framework, and in turn to adjudicate after the event. Once the wider concerns are taken into account it becomes rather more difficult to decide how the issues are to be balanced and it becomes more difficult to make the process technical rather than political.

This in turn has implications for the type of institution that can take on the task. Handling the political concerns implies a major institution and might tend to imply that the function needs to be applied by the central bank or unified supervisor, if some way can be found to avoid the conflicts of interests discussed above. If the problem is to be internalized in this manner then the framework within these larger organizations needs to be very transparent and the legislature needs to have some means of checking that the branch responsible for managing problems acts with the necessary expedition. Since exercising the deposit insurance function requires access to information that would be obtainable in the normal course of supervision and close knowledge of the bank's systems a close relationship with the supervisor or joint supervision seems inevitable.

However, the deposit insurer needs to be able to act to minimize losses even if the supervisor (who bears the loss of reputation but not the financial loss) would be prepared to allow the bank to continue. Someone has to be able to make the judgement at that point. There is more than one way to do this, by executive action for example, with the banking licence being revoked or by application to the courts for power to appoint a statutory manager. Whichever way it is done the action has to be immediate otherwise there would be a run on the bank as soon as knowledge of the application got out.

1.5 Structure and organization issues

As Norton (2005) observes, in the majority of IADI (International Association of Deposit Insurers) jurisdictions, the deposit insurer is housed in a separate organization from that of the supervisor/regulator. This trend is even more common among G-8 nations, with the UK being the only one in which the deposit insurer, the Financial Services Compensation Scheme, is not an entirely separate entity from the supervisory agency.[11] The separation of deposit insurance and supervisory functions in Canada and many other G-8 countries is based on the premise that the deposit insurer and supervisor is each likely to approach an intervention decision with separate sets of incentives in mind.

The first incentive is related to the mandate in that the supervisor is likely to be more concerned with maintaining financial stability. Whereas the deposit insurer, especially one charged with a risk or loss minimization mandate, is likely to be more concerned with the potential financial cost a failure could incur. In these respects, a supervisor might be reluctant to close a troubled bank at the point of insolvency, after having considered the disruption to the financial system that could come as a result. A deposit insurer, on the other hand, would prefer an early closure,[12] as such would be likely to minimize the cost of a failure.

The second incentive deals with reputation. Viewed a different way, a deposit insurance organization insures not only all or part of the claims of depositors but the judgment of the supervisory organization. Vesting supervisory and insurance functions in the same organization is less likely to discipline the supervisor than it is to create a moral hazard whereby the supervisor can take intervention decisions with the fall-back that mistakes can be covered by the deposit insurance fund, which they administer. Fairly or not, blame for a failed institution is likely to be placed at the doorstep of the supervisory agency. Hence, a supervisor might consider the reputation of its own organization before closing a bank, leading the supervisor to forbear. A supervisor with the key to a deposit insurance fund might, in turn, be tempted to 'wager' the fund against the odds that the troubled institution might turn itself around; in the event a failure were ultimately to prove more costly than necessary, it would be possible simply to raise premiums or impose levies to account for the difference. On the other hand, reputation incentives are likely to point a deposit insurer in the opposite direction, as a prompt, successfully handled bank closure and payment of insured claims is likely to enhance the reputation of the deposit insurer, not diminish it. Moreover, with the supervisor and the deposit insurer as separate entities, the supervisor can, in the event of a failure, simply direct angry callers to the other organization, alleviating some of the hassle of dealing with a failed bank and, hopefully, inducing earlier closure.

A further reason for separating the functions of supervisory and deposit insurer, which contrasts with the two laid out above, is that a supervisor, charged with minimizing the deposit insurance fund's exposure to loss, might use its regulatory powers with too great a zeal, closing down banks prematurely and impairing the industry with excessive regulation and unnecessary restriction. The result would be a regulatory framework where the balance between financial stability and loss-minimization tilts too far in the latter direction.

1.6 Prompt payment

If deposit insurance is to be effective in avoiding an unacceptable impact on the ordinary small depositor then it has to permit them to have access to their funds without any significant break. (It is one of the four key features of an effective system for handling failure smoothly set out by George Kaufman in chapter 8.) This has strong implications for the relationship between the deposit insurer and the banks. If an insurer is to come to a bank only at the point of insolvency, when it has been placed in administration, sorting out who the depositors are, which of their deposits are insured and to what extent will be a time consuming task. In the Nordic countries for example it is assumed that this process will take up to three months and indeed there is provision in some countries' legislation for extensions.[13] Clearly such a system would be unworkable and lack credibility unless there were at least an interim payout or release of deposits within a matter of days. This imposes not merely strong requirements on the way in which bank computer systems need to be organized but also a clear interaction between them and the deposit insurer so it can act with the necessary speed.

The difficulties this relationship imposes give a strong incentive for deposit insurers to find ways out of the problem. Clearly if another organization will takeover the deposits, even for a consideration, then the problem of addressing each individual deposit holder and arranging some way in which they can get access to their funds is avoided or rather facilitated. In this respect there is a strong incentive to find an acquirer, if not for the whole business, at least for this part of it within a day or two. Clearly, incentives are improved if the deposit insurer or another agency effectively acting on the insurer's behalf is able to encourage such a solution before the point of insolvency. This has implications for the whole process of Prompt Corrective Action and Structured Early Intervention and Resolution as laid down in FDICIA. Only some failures come as surprise to the authorities and the market, usually as the result of fraud. The bank should not be suddenly vulnerable to any particular counterparty or market if the process of prudential supervision has been conducted appropriately. There is thus likely to be a period of time where harsh pressure can be applied to the bank to seek a solution in a context of increasing restrictions on its ability to make the problem worse through taking on new risks or drawing down balances for the benefit of the owners or influential customers.

Minimizing the losses to the deposit insurer means acting before insolvency, not simply afterwards (Asia-Pacific Economic Co-operation, 2004). Minimizing the losses to society at large also involves this early action. Even if such early intervention is either not permitted or not exercised it is possible to devise an approach to insolvency that enables customers to have access to their deposits without a significant break (Mayes, Halme and Liuksila, 2001; Mayes and Liuksila, 2003). This involves the ability to intervene as soon as the deposit insurer or other competent authority believes that the net worth of the bank has reached zero. At that point the value of the existing shareholdings is zero and hence intervention will not deprive shareholders of any rights as their liability is bounded at zero. In the USA it is technically possible for the authorities to intervene when the value is positive but unacceptably low – a capital ratio of 2 per cent – but it is not at all clear whether in practice the intervention can take place that early. The authors argue that it would be desirable if other countries would permit such earlier intervention but accept that it appears that in Europe at least under the interpretation of the rights of shareholders laid down in the Pafitis case that intervening before shareholder value is zero is not likely to be possible.

However, unless public law can be used to intervene even at zero value the problem will be worsened as the point at which insolvency can be successfully petitioned is likely to be later, which will allow the losses to mount. The form of intervention suggested is akin to the formation of a bridge bank by the authorities in the USA. The authorities need to be able to ensure that the vital functions of the bank are kept running without a break and that the rating of the bank does not fall and trigger the close out of a range of contracts. It is difficult to see how this can be done without some form of government or other credible guarantee, such as that which could be offered by a deposit insurer that has access to using the government for the rapid raising of funds or guarantee. In the Finnish case, for example, the deposit insurer has small funds of its own, contributed by the banking system that should be sufficient to cover a small failure. However, it has access to the Government Guarantee Fund in the event of a large problem, so that adequate funding is available immediately to cover the period until the banking sector can finish recapitalizing the fund without threatening the stability of the rest of the banking system. Thus even though this is at one remove (the deposit insurer is run by the Finnish Banking Association) nevertheless the backing that provides the necessary confidence comes from the state.

It is not suggested that any such guarantee should be general but unless there can be a guarantee against further loss, once the authorities have stepped in, it seems difficult to understand why anyone who can withdraw their funds thereafter should not rush to do so – thereby making continuance of the institution impossible. Mayes *et al.* (2001) suggest a simple sequence:

- The authorities step in at a prescribed benchmark and take over the bank.
- They make an approximate valuation of the position of the bank and write down the claims on it, respecting the priority under insolvency, until the point that the bank is returned to solvency (depositors claims can be derogated to a deposit insurance fund if that is the structure of the system).
- They issue a guarantee against any further loss and reopen the bank for trading under their control within the same value day. (Clearly, it is possible to restrict the range of functions that are continued.)

Thereafter, the authorities will need to minimize the further loss and presumably will want to sell whatever activities are viable to another bank as soon as possible. Clearly it is necessary to structure this arrangement in such a manner that potential purchasers will nevertheless want to purchase the bank before it gets to the point of failure. Minimizing the loss to the deposit insurer and to society at large would be achieved by a private sector solution while the bank still has positive value. If buyers think they will do better by waiting until the authorities have written down the claims and assigned the losses then this will encourage allowing the problems to mount. Avoiding this is perhaps best achieved by having the deposit insurer or whoever else is the resolution agency be involved right from the start of any sign of difficulty. They can then consider the whole potential downward path and in the earlier stages put appropriate pressures and constraints on the owners and managers of the bank to encourage early action or develop options.

The important feature of this proposed resolution process is that depositors' access to their balances is maintained through the existing organization. There is no need to identify depositors in detail in order to make a rapid payout. There is no need to transfer the balances to some other organization, with all the attendant computer difficulties this will entail. In the Mayes *et al.* (2001) proposals, as in the scheme currently in place in New Zealand, a haircut is applied to all deposits, if this is needed to bring the bank back to solvency. There is therefore no need to try to distinguish between insured and uninsured deposits. If some of the deposits are insured, then the task of the deposit insurer will be to make good the part of these deposits that has been written down. If that write down is quite small, then the fact that this can take a while will not be as important as depositors have immediate access to the bulk of their funds.

The New Zealand authorities have explicitly addressed the issue of speed. In their 'Outsourcing Policy' (Reserve Bank of New Zealand, (RBNZ), 2005) the banks that have systemic importance have to structure their operation in such a way that the statutory manager can give access to depositors on the day following the failure. This implies a very close relationship with the supervisor – the central bank in this particular case – and the individual banks. Mayes and Liuksila (2003) argue that this treatment should apply to all banks. They suggest that it is difficult to see why depositors should be better treated in the event of the failure of a large bank than in the case of a small one. This would simply result in giving an implicit subsidy to large banks and discourage the opening of new and innovative institutions. In New Zealand there is no explicit deposit insurance, so this implies that in the case of failures of institutions that are not thought to be systemic, depositors would not get ready access to their deposits. This might be thought to pose a problem for the New Zealand authorities, but in practice the number of retail customers covered by non-systemic banks, whose deposits would be covered by explicit insurance in many other systems, is small. The systemic banks have virtually the whole market between them. The remaining deposits are of a size that could be handled by various means of 'implicit' insurance and indeed a purchase, assisted or not, by one of the larger banks would be plausible.

It is difficult to judge where the uniqueness in the system has come from; whether the lack of substantial retail deposits in non-systemic banks is a function of the regulatory system or whether the regulatory system has responded to that reality. In practice it is probably a bit of both. The Reserve Bank was unhappy with the structure of the savings banks as they did not fit the framework of market discipline that the Bank envisaged for having directors properly responsible for the activities of their banks. They, therefore, managed to push through a change in structure that achieved this. The result was first of all amalgamation of the savings banks (with the exception of the one savings bank that is still in existence, Taranaki Savings Bank) and then a takeover of the banks by some of the systemic players.[14] One of the major non-bank holders of retail deposits, the building society system, has also been acquired by the systemic banks and the finance houses, because they do not seek to use the name 'bank', are not supervised by the Reserve Bank and pay a substantial premium for having funds that are clearly not insured. Such finance houses have in fact failed (two failed in 2006, for example) and those lending to them have incurred losses and interruption in the access to their funds. The scale has been generally politically acceptable, although when the Development Finance Corporation (DFC) failed in 1987, there was effectively some intervention as some of the large losers had political power, particularly the Japanese bondholders.

It may seem strange to labour this small country example but New Zealand along with Australia provides the only counter-example among the Organization for Economic Co-operation and Development countries to our suggestion that explicit but limited deposit insurance is likely to be the best way of preserving financial stability. However, that same lack of insurance pushes New Zealand more than other countries into having very effective means of acting early and swiftly so as to minimize losses to depositors labelled bank creditor recapitalization. It therefore also provides lessons in how to achieve swift access to deposits. However, as with many European countries, these tools are fortunately as yet untested. Simply having such effective tools should act as an incentive to the banks to engineer private sector solutions should difficulties emerge as it means that there is no need for a takeover by the authorities.

The New Zealand requirements go further than simply the handling of deposits; they relate to all essential aspects of the bank. Although they relate to the ability of the statutory manager to step in, they also cover the cases of disasters striking service providers or indeed the failure of the parent, as all New Zealand banks of systemic importance are foreign owned. We return to this issue of problems with cross-border banks below. The key issue here is that if the authorities are to be able to step in effectively they have to be dealing with something that is a viable entity in its own right, with a complete set of systems, staff with the ability to use them and a management that actually has control.

It is interesting in this context to observe that the FDIC has found it rarely necessary to create a bridge bank in order to minimise losses and meet the needs of depositors for a speedy payout, despite the fact that they do have the power to create them. Other routes have been found satisfactory if failure has not been avoided by prior action (FDIC, 2006), principally insolvency, sometimes with the sale of the deposits to another institution that can provide the transaction facilities swiftly or by stripping out the impaired assets and making a similar immediate sale. In cases where the decline of the bank has not been precipitate, the negotiations with potential acquirers will have reached an advanced stage by the time of insolvency if they have not already been completed. The negotiations are likely to have revealed what steps the FDIC has to take to make the deposits saleable, when it gets the power to dismember the bank.

The essential issue here, however, is that it is the deposit insurer that is trying to position itself to meet the two objectives of giving depositors rapid access to their funds and minimizing the cost of the arrangements to the fund. Clearly to achieve that combination it has to have prepared the ground in advance otherwise costs are likely to be increased by the need to have a swift payout and the institution would be faced by a conflict of interests that it would be difficult to resolve by any preordained set of criteria. Again this makes it difficult to see how interim solutions are possible. Either the deposit insurer itself has to be fully involved in the process of supervision in normal times or another authority has to act explicitly on its behalf. Thus if an insurer is simply a pay box another authority has to manage the whole process of preparation of systems and knowledge of the bank if a swift payout is to be possible. The same applies to the resolution process. If the deposit insurer is not to provide this function then another authority does. Given that day to day supervision is likely to be more demanding, particularly under the terms of Basel II, it seems very likely that many supervisory authorities will not focus as strongly on having the necessary processes in place for a speedy pay out, as would a deposit insurer dedicated to that task.

As a consequence many deposit insurance systems may not be able to meet the requirement of any adequately rapid pay out to ensure stability. It is therefore likely that in the event of difficulty there will be wider intervention by the state to keep the system stable, either in the form of open bank assistance or from much more widespread guarantees. The example of the Nordic crises at the beginning of the 1990s shows that authorities can act swiftly and effectively in a crisis (Moe *et al.*, 2005). However, the same example shows that it is difficult to get these authorities to take pre-emptive action to head off the crisis in the first place. While standards of supervision and analysis of risks at the individual institution and systemic level are now high by international standards it is not clear that the intervention processes either before or at failure have fully addressed the problems.

1.7 Cross-border banks

Deposit insurance regimes, along with the rest of the system for preserving financial stability, were originally designed in national frameworks. Here there is a close match between the jurisdictional boundaries and the bulk of the activities of the banks being supervised. Where banks operated across borders they did so largely through subsidiaries, which could be treated by foreign countries very much as if they were purely domestic entities. However, this neat framework has become progressively less representative of reality in recent years. Now it is common for banks to operate across borders, sometimes through branches rather than subsidiaries and for them to try to rationalize many of their operations so that liquidity can be pooled and overheads reduced. As a result the supervisors may be in one country and the supervised entity primarily in another. This mismatch means that the authorities in a country may not have effective control over the banks operating there and so cannot necessarily deliver the stability they seek. In the worst case supervisors in one country may be unconcerned because the consequences are trivial, whereas in another the bank may be of major systemic proportions and hence key to the stability of the country.

In the European Union and the wider European Economic Area this mismatch has been institutionalized. A bank, headquartered in one EU/EEA country, may operate directly or through branches in another member state without needing to obtain permission from the local authorities and these activities will be supervised for prudential purposes by the home country authorities and not by those of the host in which it is operating. Conduct of business remains the preserve of the host authorities and in that respect the cross-border bank will have to conform to the legal framework of the country in which it is operating. Deposit insurance follows the same pattern as prudential supervision. Where a cross-border bank operates through subsidiaries the subsidiary will be part of the deposit insurance framework of the host country along with all the domestic banks. Where it chooses to operate through a branch or directly the deposits will be covered by the deposit insurance scheme in the home country. If the home scheme is inferior to that of the host then the bank can take out supplementary insurance through the host country scheme to provide equal protection for its depositors as they would receive from domestic competitors.

The problem that the host country authorities face in the case of branches is that they can no longer run a programme of structured early intervention and prompt resolution but have to rely on the home country to do that. Furthermore, if the extent of foreign ownership through branches is extensive then this part which the host authorities do cover may be of systemic proportions. Indeed, with the integrated structure of many cross-border banks, the idea that the host country can maintain financial stability through supervising the subsidiaries is illusory. They may not be complete independent units and may be effectively run by a management team outside the host country's jurisdiction. Supervisors are thus looking for an international arrangement that means that the foreign supervisors will look after the banks and their component parts to the same effect as they would if they were able to supervise them themselves. This is not a straightforward aspiration where interests are likely to conflict.

This presents a problem for the deposit insurers in both the home and the host countries. While the cross-border bank may have a share of the domestic market that does not excite the competition authorities unduly, when all the branches are added together it may become very large compared to the domestic banking system and indeed to the assets of the country. This makes a credible claim to be offering financial stability rather difficult. This has been addressed by the Swiss Authorities (Hüpkes, 2003), who, because of the size of their largest banks, have realized that they need to place an upper limit on the size of a payout from the deposit protection fund (4bn CHF) for a single event. It makes particular sense given how much of the payout is likely to be to foreigners. At some point the impact on financial stability as a whole in Switzerland will be limited better by a share being borne by the depositors affected than entirely being shifted onto other Swiss depositors, bank customers, tax payers and society at large.

However, the problem for the deposit insurer is not simply that the size of the potential payout may be large relative to GDP but that it may be very difficult to limit the impact because of the ability to control the activities of the bank in other jurisdictions. This can then be compounded by the arrangements that can be made as difficulties increase and ultimately if there should be insolvency. Although the home country takes the lead role both in consolidating the efforts of the individual national supervisors and considering the risk management of the group as a whole this is a difficult exercise to pull together convincingly. It is not surprising therefore that some of the best known problems with banks in recent years have come with the activities in other countries, take the Barings failure for example and the problem with the Allied Irish Banks.

The problem both in difficulty and in failure is one of coordination and the ability to act fast enough. Supervisors are increasingly developing Memoranda of Understanding between them on the exchange of information and cooperation in action, particularly in the event of problems or suspected problems. There is, however, considerable debate about whether these processes are likely to work effectively (Holthausen and Rønde 2004; Vesala, 2006; Srejber, 2006). There will always be an incentive for each country to look after its own interests first and those of others second even if it is doing its best to be equitable. One supervisor may not recognize what information is going to be particularly useful to others if it cannot see the rest of the national picture, which they can. There are likely to be delays and there may be problems of confidentiality. It seems generally accepted that a closer relationship is needed. Vesala (2006) and Mayes (2006) for example advocate the formation of a 'college of supervisors' in the EU/EEA context, where they take joint responsibility for supervision of the whole banking group under the leadership of the home supervisor, all information being placed in a common database to which all have access. Problems will no doubt remain. The deposit insurer is on the receiving end of these.

It is worth reflecting on the approach of the USA to these problems, as initially they restricted cross-border banking and have increasingly moved to federal supervision of cross-border (cross-state) institutions through the Federal Reserve, the Comptroller of the Currency and the FDIC. Trying to legislate against cross-border activity is not compatible with economic efficiency except where there are concerns over monopoly power but some framework consistent with the maintenance of financial stability in each country is required. The EU/EEA could plausibly move to such a supranational level as it has the legal framework to do so but other countries are not so related and it would be difficult at present to see similar arrangements including the even the rest of the OECD. Even in the EU case there is little current pressure. As described in chapter 11 by David Mayes in this book, it requires very considerable similarity in the regulatory cultures to try to have detailed cooperation in supervisory arrangements. Even the Nordic countries that have much in common have significant differences over how prompt corrective action should be conducted and over the powers of the authorities in the event of actual or imminent failure.

This does not bode well for highly workable systems in the near future and indeed Mayes and Liuksila (2003) and Mayes (2006) float proposals for a European Resolution Agency to fill the gap, which Mayes tentative labels EDIC (the European Deposit Insurance Corporation). Such an EDIC would only need to handle cross-border banks that were of systemic importance in at least one country, which would cut down the numbers to perhaps 30–50 institutions (Schoenmaker and Oosterloo, 2006).

However, while supervision is the pervasive activity it is corrective action and action on failure where the worst problems arise. The USA, inter alia, is sufficiently pessimistic about what can be achieved that it operates a policy of territoriality (Baxter *et al.*, 2004) in handling bank insolvency, which means that they simply try to handle the assets and claims that are held in the USA and ring fence them against claims from the rest of the institution. Only when the domestic position is settled would any surplus assets be passed on to whoever is running the international insolvency proceedings for distribution to foreign creditors. Not surprisingly, the EU follows the opposite 'universal' approach and tries to put together a single set of proceedings for the European assets and claims at least. In that way all European claimants will be treated equally irrelevant of country. However, these approaches are both time consuming and expensive, and have not as yet been tried out for any really large complex financial institution.

This basic difference is in addition to the distinction we have already identified between jurisdictions where public law can be used to allow the authorities to step in and apply a swift resolution process that increases the chance of keeping viable parts of the business going and facilitating rapid access for depositors to their funds, and those where private law applies and there may be only limited alternatives to outright insolvency, except of course open bank assistance. However, open bank assistance becomes much more difficult in the case of a cross-border bank as the country making the assistance is likely to have great difficulty restricting the use of the funds to its citizens/territory unless it can manage to ring fence the problem in the way that is done in the USA. However, that immediately means that the group will be dismembered which may not necessarily be the least cost way to resolve the problem as a whole. Joint approaches to assistance agreed among the countries involved will be difficult to organize in a hurry. It thus easy to see financial instability arising not because the institutions are 'too big to fail' in the classical sense but simply because the problem is too difficult to sort out in the time available. That is a clear case of regulatory failure and should be addressed by the authorities.

In these circumstances the deposit insurer is going to be put in a very difficult position. Any attempt at least cost resolution will be heavily constrained. Instead of being a technical issue these insolvencies become a political issue and much of the efforts at improving the arrangements as illustrated in FDICIA for example will be lost.

1.8 The rest of the book

The chapters that follow develop the themes we have discussed in this introduction.

The first group of chapters consider the options for deposit insurance and how particular countries have addressed them. Christine Blair, Frederick Carns and Rose Kushmeider consider the introduction of a deposit insurance system directly. David Walker looks specifically at East Asia and shows that although one might have thought that the circumstances are similar in fact the countries have chosen a variety of approaches to implementing deposit insurance and he explores why these may be appropriate to the particular circumstances. Deposit insurance does not stand alone but forms part of a much wider safety net. The way in which it is structured thus reflects that wider set of arrangements. There is no one size fits all because the structure also needs to be related to the structure of the financial industry that it seeks to insure. In countries such as the USA where there is a variety of financial forms with thrifts, mortgage corporations, banks and other financial institutions it may well make sense to have a variety of sectoral deposit insurers.

Winston Keith Carr considers this issue of the relationships between the components of the safety net directly. His view is that it is important to have clear segmentation of responsibility. Where responsibilities overlap the system can be burdensome for the banks and costly but can easily result not simply in the obvious conflicts but in areas being uncovered as each party assumes that the other is covering it. Nevertheless if all the various functions are not internalized within the same organization, the different organizations need to set up effective ways of working together. In particular the deposit insurer needs much of the ground prepared for it. Deposit insurance is not a substitute for effective supervision but indeed is only viable of there are effective supervisory standards. Insurance can only be provided at realistic premia if risks are in general well managed and the problems that do occur are more due to bad luck than to poor management including the poor management of operational risk and the prevention of fraud.

Although there is a tendency to focus on the systems in the more advanced economies, both because their financial systems are more complex and hence require suitably complex monitoring and because they have a longer history, giving more examples of success and failure, the book explicitly covers the world as a whole. We have already mentioned the discussion of East Asia. Ganiyu Ogunleye takes this further by looking at the specific case of Nigeria. Here there are many problems with the legal framework in which the financial system has to operate. There are problems with the rule of law itself. If problems have to be taken through the courts then it is essential that the processes be carried out sufficiently rapidly and predictably. This point is developed further in the more focused chapter by Pilsun Choi and Dong-Il Kim on South Korea.

However, some issues do seem to transcend the boundaries of the different systems and Lawrence Kryzanowski considers in particular the importance of having a clear objective for the fund in organizing both its general approach and its approach to specific cases. He uses Canada as an example. Kryzanowski's worry is that it is all too easy to get into a cycle of behaviour that exacerbates financial cycles and hence the risk of crisis unless some entity has a specific mandate to worry solely about banking failures and distress and their consequences. Otherwise as time passes, absence of failures will tend to lead to a belief that failures are becoming less likely. The more time elapses since the last serious failure the greater are the accumulated developments in the rapidly globalizing financial system that have not been tested under real world strain. Furthermore the number of people both in the banks themselves and in the supervisory authority who have had direct experience of a serious bank failure will diminish, changing the perception from one of unpleasant job and wealth threatening reality to one of theory. At the same time market participants also become accustomed to acting as if the risks of failure are zero and hence increase their exposures and risks (Guttentag and Herring, 1986).

The combination is dangerous because of the scale of the switch in reactions that will occur as simultaneously people drastically reconsider their exposures and rush for higher quality assets while the management of banks and the authorities struggle in unfamiliar territory to stop the financial system unravelling. This will lead to contagion and a much more rapid decline in the value of the assets of troubled institutions (Kaufman, 1996). Having deposit insurance may of course increase the moral hazard and increased risk taking because of the more limited downside to failure but Krysanowski argues that this can be offset by an appropriate increase in monitoring and supervisory requirements. However, he acknowledges that the position may differ in emerging markets and advanced countries, with the moral hazard more likely in the former.

Canadian history suggests that unless the deposit insurer has a mandate to minimize losses, intervention will come later thereby reducing the loss to the rest of the financial system but increasing it for the deposit insurer. As is typical, those who are better informed get out first. Krysanowski suggests that the Japanese have learnt the same lesson with the prolonged crisis of the 1990s and as a result have increased the mandate and powers of the Deposit Insurance Corporation of Japan substantially. Simply by having more than one organization looking at the information appearing from and about the banks may increase the chance of spotting difficulties early. An element of competition may enhance diligence, although it could lead to over-regulation. Moreover since the deposit insurer has an incentive to act early its inclusion is likely to reduce the risk of forbearance out of fear of revealing regulatory failure on the part of the supervisor.

In the last part of his chapter Krysanowski goes on to list the powers that a deposit insurer needs to ensure its ability to minimize losses. These are very much in line with the suggestions put forward in the rest of the book: well defined mandate, responsibilities and powers; control over membership – both entry and exit – to avoid adverse selection; ability to obtain information to assess risks; adequate powers to close institutions; ability to manage the process of resolution and loss recovery; coordination with rest of the players in the safety net arrangements. All in all this is a strong set of arguments in favour of having a deposit insurer with a mandate to minimize losses rather than simply a pay box.

In a very full chapter, Roy and Flageole look at the more fundamental rationale for the deposit insurance system through its role in helping the working of the whole framework of financial intermediation. Their worry is that in current circumstances there are strong forces encouraging disintermediation and that this will limit the efficient operation of the economy and the encouragement of innovation. The transfer of risk outside the banking system is not necessarily a bad thing, although it does require that those taking on the risk can appreciate it, manage it and ultimately respond in a more stabilizing manner should problems appear. Even securitization allows the banks to exit the system. The authors explore the extent to which this is a real problem by examining the case of Canada. Banking, run well, can act as an effective device for intertemporal smoothing, through providing a flexible lending and repayment programme if conditions become more difficult. Relationship lending provides a better basis for knowledge than through more anonymous market lending. However, the improved range of markets has itself made it possible to trade more of the risk without the need to rely on the banks to do so.

Regulation, including the deposit insurance framework can increase the burden on banks and hence reduce intermediation in the economy. Indeed the lower the levels of risk involved the greater the chance that the costs will exceed the benefits, according to the authors. Furthermore if the regulatory discipline that deposit insurance adds is greater than the market discipline it displaces again the system will be welfare enhancing. The key issue then is to see that the insurance is properly priced so that it reflects the risks and hence acts as a positive incentive towards prudent intermediation as well as insurance. This implies some form of sharing as the gains extend beyond the bank's customers and the financial institutions to the wider (tax-paying) population. Nevertheless the authors conclude that the contribution of regulation to disintermediation is second order compared to that of market forces.

The bulk of the book, however, focuses on the issue of handling bank failures. William Su begins by setting out what the thinking of the members of the International Association of Deposit Insurers (IADI) is on the topic. The survey that underpins the conclusions covers 34 insurers drawn both from IADI members and more widely. It not only includes views on what is important but catalogues the experience of the respondents in using the various techniques for handling bank failure: open bank assistance, purchase and assumption, bridge banks and liquidation. The experiences covered do not include full blown crises episodes, the net cost of the most drastic amounting to only 1 per cent of GDP, which is well within the fluctuations that occur across the normal economic cycle. These can therefore be appraised as standard techniques for handling failures within the framework of financial stability. It is worth recalling however, as reflected in the sample, that the majority of bank failures tend to occur when the economy is facing disadvantageous circumstances. Banks can grow out of problems or more readily find buyers when times are good. Similarly the bad news about the failure will come when the economy is already under some (relative) distress, which affects the political atmosphere in which the insurer is operating. This is reflected in the chapter's conclusion that insurers need to be adequately independent if they are to fend off the understandable pressures from both parliamentarians and the private sector for forbearance that occur in times of difficulty.

However, what is really therapeutic in these responses is that it is regulatory or supervisory failure that is thought to be the second most important cause, only slightly less important than the macroeconomic pressure. This is reflected in the tone of the whole chapter, which stresses the importance of having a proper framework if losses are to be minimized. Much of the important pressure for maintaining financial stability comes from avoiding failures in the first place. Thus the authorities need to balance the costs of restricting the risk against the costs of managing those problems that do occur. The ability of the deposit insurer to do the first of these on its own is strictly limited, although it can exert pressure on those who can. Nevertheless those who wish to improve precautions tread a fine line as they do not want to give the impression to society at large in the process that the system is facing risks of such a magnitude that they should withdraw their funds.

The bulk of the chapter is however directed at what deposit insurers can do within the confines of their own responsibility. Much of this relates to having good governance and tested procedures in place in advance. It is essential that the responsibilities of the various parties before and during a failure are clear, that between they cover all of the required techniques that could usefully and effectively be applied and that they are not in any important sense contradictory. In many respects all these remarks are obvious common sense but the fact that they have to be made suggests that they do not represent the reality in many countries. If the legal framework is inadequate the authorities will not be able to control a failure. It is no help giving somebody the responsibility to handle failures if they do not have the powers to exercise it. If the society itself is fragile it will not be politically possible to take strong action.

Similarly the deposit insurer cannot take the entire burden, particularly if there are systemic elements to the problem. There needs to be a framework including a lender of last resort, government guarantees and adequate international coordination. All of these are themes picked up in the other chapters. Su does not set out to produce a manual for what to do in the case of a failure, simply to define a framework where the chances of success are greater. It emphasizes some of the characteristics we have discussed earlier. Namely, that the trigger points for action over a troubled institution should be prescribed with, preferably, quantifiable benchmarks; that market mechanisms should be used where possible; that depositors should have early access to their funds; and above all that the guiding rules should be well defined. The importance of the experience reflected in these rules is manifest at many junctures but perhaps one of the most obvious is the enjoinder to use experts during the process – this particularly relates to valuation and to the running of any institution that is acquired.

This theme of being prepared is key concept in the chapter by John Raymond LaBrosse and David Walker on contingency planning. What one can usually bet on is that the next problem will be different from previous ones. Therefore it is necessary to have a range of the possible responses not simply in place but tested where possible in some form of simulation. One of the excellent pieces of advice that the chapter offers, by way of illustration, is that should a problem strike it will be necessary to put out a message that informs people and induces calm rather than a rush to withdraw deposits. Such messages can be drafted well beforehand and the blanks filled in at the time. How to exude the right degree of calm authority without in any way misleading people over the exposures they face is an art form. It is country specific. It is essential that all of the parties know who is going to issue such statements as contradiction could be highly counterproductive.

LaBrosse and Walker look at the deposit insurer (or the parts of the system that will act both before and after a problem is revealed) as a risk minimizer. This is a much more comprehensive concept than a loss minimizer, although minimizing losses to the insurer will in itself be part of minimizing the risk, as it too implies prior action. Clearly many of the risks involved are avoidable because they lie in the system of problem prevention and solution itself rather than in the shocks that may strike. Hence simply being well prepared and well organized will reduce the risks of what can go wrong. This can be viewed very much like operational risk in other organizations. One can assess the risks and the costs of reducing them compared with costs of correction if they are realized. The Canadian Deposit Insurance Corporation has also produced a draft paper on how risk within the organization should be treated (Mylrea and Lattimore, 2006).

The relevance of Su's remarks about having a resolution agency that is independent and dedicated to the objective of resolving problems institutions (at minimum cost) is reflected in Choi and Kim's chapter on the Korean experience. There, until the formation of the deposit insurance corporation (KDIC) and its takeover of responsibility for pursuing resolutions, insolvencies remained stuck in the legal system. Prior to this the KDIC was responsible but not able to accelerate the pace of resolutions. The lawyers responsible did not have any incentive to pursue a speedy resolution. Subsequently the KDIC was able to get the courts to appoint its staff as the responsible lawyers and to pursue a policy of trying to realize assets as rapidly as possible so that creditors (including the insurer – and through it public funds) could get earlier payouts on at least part of their claims. Because there were a large number of pending cases KDIC was able to employ a number of methods for realizing assets such as auctions that may not be so readily available for a single institution. On the other side of the scale however, when there are multiple insolvencies, it may be more difficult to get existing institutions to participate in the purchase of the failing institution or a major part of its business in the short run. This tends therefore to encourage dismemberment.

George Kaufman in his chapter offers a four-point plan for getting an efficient resolution of failed institutions where there are no wider systemic concerns in play. He emphasizes the point made earlier, that there are two sorts of losses in a failure. The first, which he describes as a credit loss, is that bank's assets no longer cover its liabilities. The second, which he describes as a liquidity loss, is that the creditors, depositors included, cannot get access to their funds even though these may be written down to cover the credit loss. His four points therefore focus on the word 'prompt' and are very similar in character to those described above in Mayes *et al.* (2001). Step one is to close the bank promptly at a positive minimum value to limit the possible credit loss. Step two is to estimate the recovery value and assign the losses to the various classes of creditors promptly. Step three is the re-opening with full access to insured accounts the following day (and full access by borrowers to agreed credit lines). This latter point is worth emphasising as a credit crunch can be triggered by either borrowers or lenders and not just by the latter. Borrowers can themselves fail if their expected cash flow is interrupted. Even the worry that it may occur will be sufficient as trade credit and other common features of payments can be stopped. Lastly step four is to reprivatize and recapitalize the bank in short order.

This approach clearly reflects what is in operation in the USA, a system which Kaufman himself had an important role in designing through, *inter alia*, the work of the Shadow Regulatory Committee. Kaufman points out the interlocking nature of the various pieces of the scheme. A bank can only be caught early enough for the losses to be small, if the authorities have been involved at earlier stages as it weakened. The provisions of Prompt Corrective Action (PCA) ensure that considerable effort has gone to ensuring a market solution before the point of failure has been reached. This would in itself involve valuations of the assets and provide the opportunity for the deposit insurer, the FDIC, to gain a good working knowledge of the structure of deposits and how to address the insured depositors should failure eventuate. This enables them to act swiftly in many cases and be able to keep the bank open physically, even if it is terminated in legal personality, and reopen as a new entity under FDIC control. At this point the FDIC either has to recapitalize the bank or at least provide guarantees against further loss. The PCA process is also likely to have thrown up the list of other banks that would be interested in buying all or substantial parts of the bank, should it fail, and hence make it possible to have a very rapid resale to the private sector even if the FDIC steps in temporarily.

An interesting feature of this approach, which helps minimize the impact on the financial system, is that, not only can depositors be paid out rapidly by the FDIC, but all the other creditors participating in the insolvency can get a rapid initial payout and access to their funds according to their priority and the valuation that the FDIC has made of the bank's assets and liabilities and hence the extent of the loss. This payout would be in the form of receivership certificates that could then be on sold in the secondary market. In this way, although the debt holders have had to take a credit loss it does not have to be fully compounded by a liquidity loss thereafter. According to

Kaufman the FDIC does not appear to treat the creditors in the same manner in the case of the failure of small banks, where they are forced to wait for a payout, partly as the consequences have little if any implication for the rest of the financial system. The main problem for other countries is that they simply do not have these legal powers – a prima facie case for action.

The chapters by Gulen Atay and David Mayes deal with the need for international coordination if bank insolvency is to be dealt with effectively in banks that run across national borders. Atay points out in particular that the consequences of problems in one market can readily spill over into others, as was evidenced by the Asian crises, even if the actual risks appear far less correlated. Once markets fear a particular type of problem because it has been revealed in one country, they tend to move their assets away from other markets in which the problem might lie, thereby on some occasions triggering unnecessary difficulties.

The international bodies concerned with financial stability are addressing the issue of bank insolvency that might run across borders by drawing up recommendations for the appropriate institutional framework for handling it. The major problems are that insolvency legislation for banks tends to vary quite considerably across countries, particularly in the Asian region which is Atay's main concern. So if they jointly want to handle an insolvency in a cross-border bank each of the parties tends to go about it differently, making coherent and rapid solutions difficult to achieve. However, even before that point, if the legislative frameworks are rather different this will inhibit the development of cross-border banks. There is thus strong pressure for harmonization. Coordination is difficult when objectives differ and when the tools available for restructuring are not the same. Some of what is required is simply a well functioning domestic system but, in an integrated region, some of the relevant information about risks is going to come from partner countries.

Mayes deals with a far more immediate problem of insolvency among banks in Europe that have extensive networks across borders. Here the framework of responsibility for the banking system is still on national lines but in practice national authorities often do not have the power to deliver that stability themselves in the event of failure. They need to look to their partners in the EU and wider EEA, where the banks are headquartered. In the extreme case of Estonia, for example, almost all of the banking system is foreign owned and actions by those banks which could destabilize the Estonian economy, far short of actual failure, would be outside Estonian jurisdiction. Small countries therefore have to accept that the lead supervisor for many banks will lie outside the country and that therefore there needs to be some sort of guarantee that in exercising their tasks they will take the needs of the small country into account. This provides many problems. If losses are to be minimized, whose losses are we talking about? Does it relate to the deposit insurer in the lead country? If this were the case then trying to concentrate losses elsewhere would be the way to run the insolvency. This is clearly not the way to run an economic union.

However, it will be equally difficult for a lead country with nothing serious at stake to organize the continued operation of a bank that is only important in one of the other, host, countries. The issue is not hypothetical, not just because of the high foreign ownership of banks in the ten new member states and elsewhere in the Balkans but also because one of the largest Nordic banks, Nordea, is planning to operate as a single company headquartered in Sweden and with branches elsewhere. Detailed arrangements, including the role of the deposit insurance funds need to be made among the countries affected, as agencies in one country will be responsible for taking decisions about the management of risks, the resolution of banks and the paying of claims in other countries. Fortunately the countries in the region have relatively homogeneous legislative frameworks for handling banks. Nevertheless, as Atay pointed out for Asia, their powers of Prompt Corrective Action and action to intervene and takeover a bank from the original shareholders are both different and in several cases rather weak. This implies that if a large bank gets into trouble it will have to be bailed out as no other adequate mechanisms are in place.

However, such a bail out may itself be implausible if the bank is large or the coordination required considerable. It would be easy for these countries to break all of the four points for effective prompt action laid down by Kaufman. At least in the EU the countries are trying to harmonize and work together as this is a treaty obligation. Elsewhere in the world this is not so true and the self interest of the parties comes first. Ironically the archetypal example is the USA that not only applies territoriality and ring fences the insolvency in its jurisdiction but applies domestic preference in the hierarchy of claims. With territoriality it is only if there is a surplus in the US resolution that funds are made available for the resolution of the group as a whole. There is no pooling of assets before deciding what to do as in the alternative universalist approach practised in Europe. Even within Europe it would be difficult to have joint proceedings where the structures are very different.

Mayes concludes by looking at the case of Australia and New Zealand where regulatory cultures are very different and a separate approach to insolvency in each jurisdiction is the only workable way forward at present, as claimants in the two countires are not treated equally. (Most New Zealand banks are Australian owned and those that are not are mainly foreign owned.) To operate such a separate solution all the subsidiaries or branches need to be viable entities that could operate on their own if there is to be any hope of continuing the business in the event of the failure of a systemically important institution. In the European case such dismemberment will often be impractical, as even where the operations in a host country are run through subsidiaries and not branches, those subsidiaries are not full function organizations that can stand on their own. They are integral parts of the banking group.

Taking all these chapters together it appears that there is still a lot to do. Only a few countries adhere to the principles for prudent risk management and effective failure resolution suggested by IADI. Nevertheless the problem has been realized and the discussions among deposit insurers and between them and the other authorities in their home countries give the opportunity for progress. This book identifies the problems and suggests blueprints for their solution that respect the diversity of economic, financial and regulatory structures round the world. It is to be hoped that they are adopted. The approach of limited explicit deposit insurance advocated in this chapter should be a step towards a better chance of maintaining financial stability – but it is only one part of a comprehensive framework of good economic management, social stability, a strong legal framework, a set of compatible, focused institutions with clear objectives that between them manage the risks and minimize the costs of the fluctuations that are inherent in a vibrant an innovative financial system that is making a strong contribution to economic growth and welfare.

Notes

1 In January 2005 there were 115 countries with a deposit insurance system in operation, pending, planned or under serious study. See IADI, List of Countries, located at: www.iadi.org/html/App/SiteContent/List%20of%20countries%20with%20a%20DIS_MCC%20020206.pdf

2 In this chapter, the word 'bank' is defined to include all forms of financial institutions that accept deposits from the public.

3 According to Alan Greenspan, 'Deposit insurance has played a key – at times even critical – role in achieving the stability in banking and financial markets that has characterized the past almost seventy years. Deposit insurance, combined with other components of our banking safety net (the Federal Reserve's discount window and payment system guarantees) has meant that periods of financial stress are no longer characterized by depositor runs on banks and thrifts. Quite the opposite: Asset holders now seek out deposits – both insured and uninsured – as safe havens when they have strong doubts about other financial assets". See http://banking.senate.gov/02_04hrg/042302/grnspan.htm

4 Looking at this from the opposite point of view one could argue that strong banks are already in a position to take such risks as they feel appropriate and hence the extra support offered by deposit insurance will not really alter anything.

5 The APEC Policy Dialogue on Deposit Insurance concluded that a test of viability is a better method for ensuring that a deposit insurer minimize its exposure to loss.

6 Trust companies in Canada are much like banks in that they accept deposits and make loans. They differ in name from banks which are under federal jurisdiction.

7 J P Sabourin, Chair of the FSF Working Group on Deposit Insurance, presentation at the Outreach Session, Kuala Lumpur, January 2001.

8 It is contested whether having funds necessarily adds to credibility, as they could be appropriated by the government in the event of a crisis. The wider credibility of the governmental system thus matters.

9 The lessons learned from recent financial crises are well documented in the Annex to the Consultation Process and Background Paper prepared by the Financial Stability Forum Study Group on Deposit Insurance (2000) and the Financial Stability Forum Working Group on Deposit Insurance (2001a, p. 7).

10 White Paper entitled 'Enhancing the Safety and Soundness of the Canadian Financial System', Febuary 1995.

11 While the Financial Services Compensation Scheme (FSCS) is a legally separate organization from the UK Financial Services Authority (FSA) and relies on the work of its own staff, its board of directors is appointed by the FSA, and the FSCS has few intervention powers independent of its parent organization. It should also be noted that the Federal Deposit Insurance Corportation directly examines and supervises about 5,250 banks and savings banks, more than half of the institutions in the US banking system (www.fdic.gov/about/learn/symbol/index.html, accessed 24 August 2006)

12 In Malaysia, the newly established Malaysia Deposit Insurance Corporation is working out criteria with the Supervisor (Bank Negara Malaysia) to use non-viability as the trigger mechanism for closure. This 'best practice' should be adopted by others as the capital triggers in many jurisdictions do not always allow deposit insurers to minimize their losses.

13 In Finland, for example, it is possible for the deposit insurer to request a further three-month delay on two occasions. Even the initial three months is an underestimate, as the insurer has 21 days in which to decide whether the circumstances require it to make a payout. It is only after that determination that the three-month period begins.

14 The Auckland Savings Bank exists in name, but is owned by the Australian Commonwealth Bank. Some other Australian owned banks have retained their New Zealand names, Bank of New Zealand and National Bank of New Zealand for example, but other well-known names, such as the Post Bank were rapidly discontinued.

References

Allen, W. and Wood, G.E. (2006) 'Defining and achieving financial stability', *Journal of Financial Stability*, vol. 2(2), pp. 152–72.

APEC (2004) 'Policy Dialogue on Deposit Insurance: Policy Conclusions Paper', June.

Barajas, A. and Steiner, R. (2000) 'Depositor Behavior and Market Discipline in Colombia', IMF Working Paper No. WP/00/214, Washington, DC: International Monetary Fund.

Bartholdy, J., Boyle, J.G. and Stover, R. (2004) 'Deposit insurance and market assessment of banking system stability: evidence from Denmark', *The European Journal of Finance*, vol. 10(6), pp. 567–78.

Baxter, T.C., Hansen, J. and Sommer, J.H. (2004) 'Two Cheers for Territoriality: An Essay on International Bank Insolvency Law', *American Bankruptcy Law Journal*, vol. 58(1), pp. 57–91.

Beck, T. (2003) 'The Incentive Compatible Design of Deposit Insurance and Bank Failure Resolution: Concepts and Country Studies', in Mayes and Liuksila (eds) pp. 118–41.

Bossone, B. (2001) 'Should Banks Be Narrowed?', IMF Working Paper No. WP/01/159, Washington, DC: International Monetary Fund.

Calomiris, C. W. (1999) 'Building an Incentive-Compatible Safety Net', *Journal of Banking and Finance,* vol. 23, pp. 1499–519.

Calomiris, C.W. and Powell, A. (2000) 'Can Emerging Market Bank Regulators Establish Credible Discipline? The Case of Argentina, 1992–1999', NBER Working Paper No. 7715, Cambridge MA: National Bureau of Economic Research.

Canada Deposit Insurance Corporation (CDIC), Annual Reports, 1985, 1986, 1994, 2003.

Caprio, G. and Honohan, P. (1999) 'Restoring Banking Stability: Beyond Supervised Capital Requirements', *Journal of Economic Perspectives*, vol. 13 (4), pp. 43–64.

Caprio, G. and Klingebiel, D. (2003) 'Episodes of Systemic and Borderline Financial Crises', Washington, DC: World Bank Dataset.

Demirguç-Kunt, A. and Detriache, E. (2000) 'Does deposit insurance increase banking system stability?', IMF Working Paper WP/00/03.

Department of Finance (1995) 'Enhancing the Safety and Soundness of the Canadian Financial System', Ottawa, February, pp. 26–27.

Diamond, D. and Dybvig, P. (1986) Bank runs, deposit insurance and liquidity', *Journal of Political Economy*, vol. 91, pp. 401–9.

FDIC (Federal Deposit Insurance Corporation) (2006) 'Bridge Banks'.

Feldman, R. and Stern, G. (2006) 'Managing Too Big To Fail by Reducing Systemic Risk: Some Recent Developments', *The Region*, June, pp. 7–11.

Financial Stability Forum (2000) Working Group on Deposit Insurance, 'A Consultative Process and Background Paper', June, Basel.

Financial Stability Forum (2001a) 'Final Report of the Financial Stability Forum Working Group on Deposit Insurance', September, Basel.

Financial Stability Forum (2001b) 'Structure and Organization', Discussion Paper, Basel.

Garcia, G. (1996) 'Deposit Insurance: Obtaining the Benefits and Avoiding the Pitfalls', IMF. Working Paper 96/83.

Garcia, G. (1999) 'Deposit Insurance: A Survey of Actual and Best Practices', IMF Working Paper No. WP/99/54, Washington, DC: International Monetary Fund.

Garcia, G. (2000) 'Deposit Insurance: Actual and Good Practices', IMF Occasional Paper No. 197, Washington, DC: International Monetary Fund.

Gropp, R. and Vesala, J. (2001) 'Deposit Insurance and Moral Hazard: Does the Counterfactual Matter?', ECB Working Paper 47.

Guttentag, J. and Herring, R. (1986) 'Disaster Myopia in International Banking', Essays in International Finance, no. 46, Princeton University, September.

Hoggarth, G. and Saporta, V. (2001) 'Costs of Banking Instability: Some Empirical Evidence', Bank of England, *Financial Stability Review.*

Holthausen, C. and Rønde, T. (2004) 'Cooperation in International Banking Supervision', ECB Working Paper no 316.

Hüpkes, E (2003). 'Learning Lessons and Implementing a New Approach to Banking Insolvency in Switzerland', in Mayes and Liuksila (eds), pp. 242-71.

Ingves, S. and Quintyn, M. (2003) 'Financial Stability Assessments: Implications for Governance Arrangements', Presented to the IADI Conference on Effective Governance Arrangements, Seoul, Korea, October.

INSOL INTERNATIONAL (2005) 'Bank Insolvency, an International Guide for Deposit Insurers', London, January, p19.

International Association of Deposit Insurers (2006) 'List of Countries', www.iadi.org

Kane, E. and Wilson, B. (1997) 'The Demise of Double Liability as an Optimal Contract for Large-Bank Stockholders' *Proceedings of the 33rd Annual Conference on Bank Structure and Competition*, Federal Reserve Bank of Chicago, pp. 374–89.

Kaufman, G. (1996) 'Bank Failures, Systemic Risk, and Bank Regulation', *Cato Journal*, vol. 16(1), pp. 17–45.

King, M. (1994) 'Debt Deflation: Theory and Evidence', *European Economic Review*, vol. 38, pp. 419–55.

Mantripragada, K. (1992) 'Depositors as a Source of Market Discipline', *The Yale Journal of Regulation*, vol. 9, pp. 543–74.

Masciandaro, D. Nieto, M. and Prast, H. (2006) 'Who Should Pay What for Bank Supervision? Principles, Practices and Determinants', Western Economic Association International Conference, San Diego, 30 June.

Mayes, D.G. and Liuksila, A. (2003) *Who Pays for Bank Insolvency?*, Basingstoke: Palgrave Macmillan.

Mayes, D.G. Halme, L. and Liuksila, A. (2001) *Improving Banking Supervision*, Basingstoke: Palgrave.

Mayes, D.G. (2006) 'Cross-Border Financial Supervision in Europe: Goals and Transition Paths', *Sverises Riksbank Economic Review*, 2006(2), pp. 58–89.

Moe, T. Solheim, J. and Vale, B. (2005) *The Norwegian Banking Crisis*, Oslo: Bank of Norway Occasional Paper 33.

Mølgaard, E. (2003) 'Avoiding a Crisis: Lessons from the Danish Experience', in Mayes and Liuksila (eds), pp. 222–41.

Mylrea, K. and Lattimore, J. (2006) 'Enterprise Risk Management for Deposit Insurers', Canada Deposit Insurance Corporation.

Norton, Joseph J. (2005) 'Global Financial Sector Reform: The Single Financial Sector Regulator Model Based on the United Kingdom FSA Experience – A Critical Reevaluation', *The International Lawyer*, vol. 39(1), p. 52.

Report of the Royal Commission on Banking and Finance (1964), Queen's Printer and Controller of Stationary, Ottawa, Canada.

Reserve Bank of New Zealand (2006) 'Outsourcing Policy', Paper BS11, Wellington: RBNZ.

Sabourin, J.P. (2000) *Designing an Effective Deposit Insurance Structure: An International Perspective*, Federal Reserve Bank of Chicago, December.

Saunders, A. and Wilson, B. (1995) 'Contingent Liability in Banking: Useful Policy for Developing Countries?', WB Policy Research Working Paper No. WPS1538, Washington, DC: The World Bank.

Schinasi, G. (2005) *Safeguarding Financial Stability: Theory and Practice*, Washington, DC: International Monetary Fund.

Schoenmaker, D. and Oosterloo, S. (2006) 'Cross Border Issues in European Financial Supervision', in D. Mayes and G. Wood (eds), *The Structure of Financial Regulation*, London: Routledge, forthcoming.

Srejber, E. (2006) 'Are We Ready to Deal with a Cross Border Banking Crisis in Europe?' Gdansk, May. www.riksbanken.se/pagefolders/25964/060513e.pdf.

Talley, S.H. (1994) 'Deposit Protection and the Spread of Deposit Insurance: Some Guidelines for Developing Countries', WB FPD Note No.12, Report No. 16956, Washington, DC: The World Bank.

Talley, S.H. and Mas, I. (1990) 'Deposit Insurance in Developing Countries', WB Policy Research Working Paper No. WPS548, Washington, DC: The World Bank.

Vaez-Zadeh, R., Xie, D. and Zoli, E. (2002) 'MODIS: A Market-Oriented Deposit Insurance Scheme', IMF Working Paper No. WP/02/207, Washington, DC: International Monetary Fund.

Vesala, J. (2006) 'Which Model for Prudential Supervision in the EU?', in Monetary Policy and Financial Marker Stability, Proceedings of the 33rd Economics Conference, Austrian National Bank, pp. 99–105.
Wheelock, D. (1992) 'Deposit Insurance and Bank Failures: New Evidence from the 1920s', *Economic Inquiry*, vol. 30(3), pp. 530–43.
www.fdic.gov/bank/historical/history/3_85.pdf.
www.fdic.gov/bank/historical/history/.
www.imf.org/external/pubs/ft/wp/2000/wp0007.pdf.
www.norgesbank.no/publikasjoner/skriftserie/33/hele_heftet.pdf.
www.internationalmonetaryfund.org/external/np/speeches/2002/091102.htm.

2

Legal Aspects of the Interests of Depositor Creditors: The Case for Deposit Protection Systems

Andrew Campbell and Dalvinder Singh

2.1 Introduction

The rationale for the regulation of banks is clearly articulated in a whole host of literature and the interests of depositors feature significantly. This literature on banking regulation and supervision refers to the interests of depositors as unsecured creditors and the importance of protecting them from the unique risks banks pose. However, the full implications of such a status have not been fully explored in this literature from the legal perspective and only by referring back to fundamental principles of banking law can the status of being an unsecured depositor creditor be truly understood, so as to ascertain the full extent of their vulnerability when a bank fails.

In this chapter, an attempt is made to go back to first principles to demonstrate the need for some kind of formal bank safety net to protect the interests of depositor to creditors and maintain confidence in the banking system. The funds banks use to undertake their business are predominantly of an unsecured nature provided by individuals and corporations that seek to utilize banks to manage their personal and corporate affairs.[1] The reliance on unsecured deposits by banks is an important source of finance. DeYoung and Rice have found 'about 57 per cent of the banking industry's assets, and 82 per cent of the typical banking company's assets, were financed with deposits in 2003'.[2] It is important therefore to ascertain why depositor interests are vulnerable by analysing the limited assistance general corporate law provides in protecting their interests as unsecured depositor creditors.[3] Indeed it is only by analysing the position of the depositor in the broader legal context that the problem can be fully appreciated. This is for three purposes: first, to articulate what banking business is and the lack of protection corporate law gives to safeguard depositor interests. Second, what priority is given to depositors in the worst case scenario, that is, if the bank was deemed to be in a position of being insolvent and winding up proceedings are commenced. Third, how does deposit insurance assist in compensating depositors.

The traditional common law position of what is banking has focused on the taking of deposits, lending and cheque facilities.[4] The modern business of banking is a much more complex affair in light of the broad range of services it can provide to its customers from deposit taking, lending, investment and insurance.[5] However, it is the business of accepting deposits that has been the traditional focus of prudential regulation and supervision of banks, and deposit insurance.[6] The traditional business of deposit-taking and lending gives rise to a distinct kind of risk: the business activity of borrowing short and lending long can give rise to a lack of available liquid funds at any given time which places a responsibility on a bank to manage its assets and liabilities as efficiently as possible. This is exacerbated with the added burden that depositors can exercise their common law right to demand the deposited money.[7] This can result in what is commonly referred to as a 'bank run', where mass withdrawals of deposited funds leads to a bank either experiencing liquidity problems or, in exceptional cases, being unable to meet its current liabilities and result in it being judged insolvent.[8] The panic that ensues from a bank run can spread to other similar banks as a result of a loss of mass confidence in the banking system, or sections of it, as a result of the risk of contagion.[9] Because of this, formal bank safety nets have been in place to protect confidence in the banking system in the form of lender of last resort arrangements and deposit insurance. A bank failure can disrupt the efficiency with which banks can act as depositories for other people's money from which the cycle of saving and investment is managed, therefore having an adverse impact on the efficiency with which the real economy can function. Notwithstanding the use of formal bank safety nets to maintain confidence it is important that effective regulation and supervision should act as the primary mechanism to ensure banks act prudentially and the number of bank failures is kept at a minimum. This is to mitigate the risk of moral hazard that arises from having bank safety nets. In light of this, bank supervisors that have authorized banks to undertake the business of banking have the responsibility to revoke, restrict, or limit what banks can and cannot do, and can exercise other enforcement sanctions to ensure banks and their management act prudentially or in other words in a safe and sound manner.[10] The impossibility of small depositors being in a position to assess the business of banking and their appetite for risk in light of the asymmetrical relationship between a bank and its customer are other reasons for regulation.[11]

2.2 The bank and customer relationship

The relationship of bank and customer of debtor and creditor was formally articulated in *Foley* v. *Hill* as one of a contractual nature.[12] The facts of the case are relatively simple, *Foley* and others kept an account at the bank for the purposes of managing the financial matters of their business. The bank failed to pay interest for six years as agreed when the account was opened. The appellants sought to claim in account for the interest that should have been paid. The question for the court was whether it could appropriately be heard in equity or in law as they sought special damages which could only be claimed if a fiduciary duty could be established rather than contractual damages from a breach of contract. In order to determine this, the court sought to distinguish the relationship between banker and customer on the grounds that it was one of debtor and creditor and not one of a fiduciary nature where the bank acted for the customer in a capacity of trustee, where 'the trustee for the particular matter in which he is employed ... sells the principals goods, and accounts to him for the money'.[13] The Lord Chancellor in his decision placed reliance on two particular cases to articulate the relationship between banker and customer which is now associated with his decision in *Foley* v. *Hill*. In *Parker* v. *Merchant*[14] the issue was whether money deposited in a bank account was equivalent to 'ready money'.[15] The deposit was considered to be 'a debt due from the banker' to the person making the deposit. In this relationship it is said the bank needs to be in a position to 'be ready to pay an equal amount when called for' rather than in a position to pay the original 'money' back. The Lord Chancellor in *Foley* v. *Hill* reiteraten this and somewhat expanded on the relationship of banker and customer explaining it in the following manner:

> The money paid into the bankers is money known by the principal to be placed there for the purpose of being under the control of the banker; it is then the banker's money; he is known to deal with it as his own; he makes what profit of it he can, which profit he retains to himself... The money placed in the custody of a banker is, to all intents and purposes, the money of the banker, to do with it as he pleases; he is guilty of no breach of trust in employing it; he is not answerable to the principal if he puts it into jeopardy, if he engages in a hazardous speculation.[16]

This rule as enunciated in *Foley* v. *Hill* that the relationship of the bank and customer as one of debtor and creditor, and not one of principal and agent is a key foundation of banking law and is echoed universally in other common law jurisdictions.[17] This contract between the bank and customer is normally governed by the law where the account is held even though the funds themselves are co-mingled across borders.[18] In *Libyan Arab Foreign Bank* STAUGHTON J referred to the position as 'elementary, or hornbook law to use an American expression, that the customer does not own any money in a bank.... Students are taught at an early stage of their studies in the law that it is incorrect to speak of "all my money in the bank"'.[19] In the USA, for example, in *Marine Bank* v. *Fulton Bank*[20] a Supreme Court decision, MILLER J expressed the general point that 'when the money was received, it was to be held as an ordinary bank deposit, it became by virtue of that understanding the money of the [bank] the moment it was received'.[21] The case of *Foley* v. *Hill* was referred to, for example, in *Bank of Republic* v. *Millard*[22] where it was emphasized that the relationship between a banker and depositor is not one of trust and the money credited in a bank account, 'becomes part of its general funds, and can be loaned by it as other moneys'.[23] In Canada, for example, in the *Toronto Dominion Bank*[24] case the principle was reaffirmed. In this case a group of 'investors' claimed *inter alia* the bank breached its fiduciary duty in a case involving guarantees for loans to a number of corporate customers. It was held that no fiduciary duty was owed where information about specific business affairs warranted disclosure to unsecured creditors. In exceptional circumstances however a fiduciary duty did arise where for instance the bank acts in an advisory capacity and the relationship is 'transformed'. [25]

The way Lord COTTENHAM articulated the relationship has not been echoed so explicitly in other cases although the general principle has been.[26] Lord COTTENHAM in many respects attempts to remove any hint of any fiduciary obligation between the bank and depositor in the clearest of terms leaving little ambiguity as to the responsibility of the bank. In *R* v. *Davenport* Lord GODDARD described the impact of *Foley* v. *Hill* as 'explosive' to the idea that the relationship between bank and depositor could be one of agent and trustee.[27] According to Smart, the implications of a fiduciary obligation would have been too onerous a burden for banks and their business as it would have placed a continuous responsibility on them to account for their decisions.[28] The principle also highlights the high degree of discretion the banker has with the way it can use other people's money. The obligation on the banker to pay on demand the sum placed in the account is obviously a curb on this. Nevertheless, the fact remains that the bank does not have to advise customers on how it uses its 'reservoir' of deposited funds and the risks it places them to once the money is in their accounts; as it would have to if an investment product was being bought by a customer in which case a whole host of common law fiduciary rules would govern the sale of such products. Nevertheless some have advocated the adoption of a fiduciary duty on directors to safeguard the interests of depositors.[29] The adoption of such a rule has not been articulated with the practical relationship of banker and depositor being one of debtor and creditor in mind as the obligation would strike at the heart of the universal principle on which banking law is based. The business of banking would then need to be undertaken in the interests of depositors as beneficiaries as is the case in investment business. In addition to this the money deposited would be the money of the depositor. The implications of this would be catastrophic for the banking industry in terms of the compliance costs it would incur and the cost of reconfiguring the way banks undertake their business. The cost implications for depositors would also be a significant issue to consider in light of the way banking would need to be administered. In light of this the position of depositor creditors needs to be analysed further in a broader legal context to ascertain the extent to which their interests are considered in general corporate law.

2.3 Bank corporations and depositor creditors

The implications of the rule in *Foley* v. *Hill* is far reaching to the extent one could safely ask why would an individual place their savings or salaries in a bank for it to place it at whatever risk it thought necessary. This would be a difficult set of circumstances to pallet if it were not for the fact that a bank like any corporation needs to be managed in good faith in the interests of the corporation as whole.[30] In the USA the obligation of directors to act in good faith in the interests of the corporation follows a similar approach.[31] This fiduciary obligation on directors of a corporation is ambiguous as it could quite literally be interpreted to mean that those who are commercially associated with the corporation have their beneficial interests protected.[32] However this obligation is almost exclusively interpreted to refer to the interests of shareholders of the corporation.[33] In the corporate decision making process the shareholders would want to ensure that the directors exercise the appropriate level of care with due regard to their interests.[34] In this respect the directors would have an obligation to disclose to the shareholders the options available which are in the best interests of the company as a whole.[35]

The obligation on the corporation to take into account the interests of creditors is a much more precarious issue to address.[36] It is generally the case that the directors as highlighted above do not owe a duty to creditors if a corporation is solvent.[37] In such circumstances the directors of a corporation are required to discharge their obligations to the corporation 'properly' mindful of the general interests of creditors and their ability to be able to repay its debts.[38] This general duty is interpreted by Keay not to be a direct duty but one 'mediated through the company'.[39] However, this is reversed if the company is experiencing financial difficulties which call into question its solvency. The directors in such circumstances need to be mindful of not trying to steer out of serious difficult circumstances where the corporation is in all intents and purposes insolvent for they could be liable for wrongful trading, that is, continuing in business when they knew there was very little prospect of avoiding insolvency.[40] In these circumstances the directors need to be alert to the fact that the interests of creditors do need to feature at the centre of their decision making rather than the interests of shareholders as is the case when a corporation is solvent. The position is clearly indicated in *Brady* v. *Brady*. Nourse LJ explains in his decision that during the life of the company it is the shareholders interests that are given priority and creditors interests 'ought not to count for very much'. However, the position of shareholders and creditors is reversed in an insolvency situation in which case 'the interests of the company are in reality the interests of existing creditors alone'.[41] For example in the USA *Re Ben Franklin* the officers of the corporation were accused of continuing their wholesale and retail business when it was 'in the vicinity of insolvency' by misrepresenting its financial state of affairs so to continue to attract business. The defendants were held to be in breach of their duty to the creditors in negligence. The courts have established that the obligation of the directors to creditors is 'triggered' when a corporation is insolvent but also if it deems it to be in such financial difficulties that it warrants the directors to consider the interests of creditors in its corporate decision making. As to when the duty should be 'triggered' has been interpreted in a whole host of ways giving rise to the difficulty as to when an obligation arises, namely where a corporation is 'near or in the vicinity of insolvency', 'doubtful insolvency', 'risk of insolvency' and 'financial instability'.[42] These permutations of when an obligation could or could not arise highlight the difficulty of addressing the issue as an outsider looking in to the affairs of a corporation, a position depositor creditors would surely be in.

The position of bank creditor depositors and their right to be paid an equivalent to what has been deposited adds a further dimension to the above analysis. In such circumstances the directors of banks would need to ensure that the bank has the ability to pay depositors on demand a sum equivalent to what is in their account. In contrast to 'normal' creditors banks are not required to seek out depositor creditors. In order to remain in business it will need to balance the interests of shareholders and creditor depositors more than most other corporations would need to, in light of the large amount of funds creditor depositors provide to allow them to undertake their business. The vulnerability of banks, as highlighted above, to a bank run requires directors to ensure any bank failure is managed in an orderly fashion. The courts have been sensitive to this risk peculiar to banks. For example, in *Re Chancery plc*,[43] the directors of the bank sought an administration order from the court on the same day because they could not meet the debts of the bank due the following day. HARMAN J gave the order sought in view of the exceptional circumstances of the case, without proper consideration of the interests of other parties, to avoid the possibility of a bank run if problems about the bank were made public. The order was given in light of the possibility that the bank could potentially work out a solution which could even mean it could potentially 'resume trading as an authorised bank'.[44] A rather optimistic view in light of the fact that once a bank has reached such unfortunate times it is highly unlikely the regulator will authorize those managing it to continue to do so. The one possibility is where a bank is taken over by another bank which would inevitably lead to a restructuring and the loss of the original directors that may be implicated in the demise of the bank.[45]

2.4 Insolvency issues

Having established that the legal relationship between a bank and its depositors is contractual and that it is one of debtor and creditor it becomes necessary to consider, from the legal perspective, what the effect of this contractual relationship is where the bank in which the deposit is placed becomes subject to an insolvency procedure.[46]

It is important at this stage to make a distinction between insolvency and illiquidity. Where a bank is suffering from a liquidity problem but remains solvent on a balance sheet basis[47] it is possible that it may be able to receive emergency liquidity financing[48] from the central bank to enable it to meet its current commitments.[49] In most countries the central bank[50] will be willing to provide this type of assistance to banks that can satisfy the various tests for solvency.[51] The central bank could exercise this function either by open-market operations or by providing loans to individual banks. The central bank intervenes in such circumstances to stabilize market confidence and avoid unnecessary bank failures because of temporary liquidity problems.[52] In this respect the central bank must act decisively and quickly without hesitation, otherwise a panic could be prolonged and could spread into other parts of the financial system which were otherwise unaffected by the original problem.[53]

In the case of a bank the position is further complicated because of the concept of regulatory insolvency.[54] This is where the bank is solvent on a balance sheet basis but fails to meet minimum regulatory requirements. In this situation it still may be possible for the central bank and regulator to use regulatory forbearance and some degree of financial assistance to nurse the bank back to compliance.[55]

However it will often be the case that a bank has gone beyond the stage where emergency liquidity financing or a degree of regulatory forbearance would adequately address the problem and when this happens the insolvency options have to be considered.

2.5 Bank insolvency and liquidation

The liquidation of a bank will be used only as a last resort after all of the possible alternative strategies have been fully explored, and in the context of bank insolvency a number of strategies have been developed in many countries in recent years. In many jurisdictions alternatives to liquidation have been introduced and where these exist their possible use will be considered by the central bank and bank regulator to establish whether liquidation can be avoided. It is beyond the scope of the aims of this chapter to consider bank insolvency procedures in any great detail and what is being focused on here is simply the situation where a bank is unable to meet depositors' demands for repayment of what is due to them. Sometimes an insolvent bank will have to be liquidated but the term 'insolvency proceedings' actually covers a range of possible options including bank restructuring, purchase and assumption transactions and mergers and acquisitions.[56]

Liquidation is essentially the process by which the bank is wound-up and eventually ceases to exist. For a liquidation process to be efficient and effective it must aim *inter alia* to maximize the value of the insolvent entity's estate. However it has to be recognized that where a bank is insolvent it is unlikely that there will be sufficient funds to repay all creditors in full. The liquidator, who in most jurisdictions is appointed by the court,[57] will be given powers under the law to gather in assets and realize them and then pay creditors in the order in which they are entitled. Once the liquidator has completed these tasks the bank will be wound-up.

The main objectives of a bank liquidation will include: (a) the immediate termination of the banking activity of the bank to avoid any increased losses; (b) minimization of disruption to customers; (c) minimization of disruption to the economy (both locally and nationally); (d) maximizing the value of the bank's assets; (e) ensuring the equitable treatment of similarly situated creditors; and (f) ensuring transparency in the process.

Regardless of which type of procedure is to be used, a common feature in all insolvency procedures is the immediate termination of the banking activity of the bank. A complete moratorium on creditor action will come into effect immediately on the appointment of a conservator, receiver or liquidator. This has obvious and important consequences for depositors who will no longer have access to their funds.

Where the laws of a country do not provide any special protection for depositors it is unlikely that they will receive any of what they are owed for a considerable period of time. Even where the liquidation process is efficient there will be a delay of many months before distributions to unsecured creditors will be made and in some cases this could extend to more than a year. Why is this? The liquidator will be under a duty to protect the assets of the insolvent bank and to maximize as far as possible the amount which will be available for distribution. The liquidator will also have to verify that all claims by creditors are legally valid and how much they are for. Where there are thousands of depositors, as well as other creditors, this will be a time consuming process.

In most liquidations the liquidator is not going to be in a position to start making any distributions until the exact financial position of the insolvent estate has been calculated. The liquidator should be given sufficient powers to be able to undertake the liquidation process in the most effective and timely manner and will need legal power to do a number of things including:

1. managing the property of the insolvent bank during the liquidation process;
2. taking measures to protect the bank's assets;

3. to sell property (either by public auction or private sale);
4. to terminate certain contracts;
5. to dismiss employees (but in so doing will have to comply with the labour laws of the country and this may, and often will, include making priority payments to dismissed employees);
6. take action to enforce debts owed to the bank and to avoid certain transactions;
7. to distribute payments to creditors, including depositors, once all claims have been verified.

Because of the possibility of a liquidator facing potential liability for failing to undertake his or her task properly this has led, under many systems, to a liquidation culture to emerge whereby the liquidator will need to go to court for approval of even the most minor action. Understandably there are many disgruntled people in any insolvency situation and it is quite common for liquidators to be blamed for many things, for example disposing of assets at a lower price than might otherwise have been obtained. This has led to the laws in many countries giving very little discretion, if any, to a liquidator. This has the effect of increasing the costs involved in administering the estate and in ensuring that the process is lengthy. While it may be argued that to give more flexibility to the liquidator would be desirable there is no generally agreed international approach to this.

In such a situation the costs involved in administering the process are increased with the inevitable result that ultimately there will be less available for distribution to depositors.

Secured and preferential creditors

Secured and preferential creditors will, under any system of law, rank ahead of unsecured creditors in the liquidation process. Any creditor which holds security for money or property will be able to rely on that security and will, in many cases, be able to do so outside the liquidation process.

Some other creditors will be given priority under the law of the particular jurisdiction. Most commonly this will apply to employees, who will often be entitled to a certain percentage of earnings in priority to other claims, and to such public bodies as the taxation and customs authorities. The approach to the treatment of preferential creditors varies considerably between jurisdictions.

Set-off

The laws on set-off vary considerably among jurisdictions[58] but while its availability is generally considered to be a positive factor in a bank insolvency regime it can have adverse effects on unsecured creditors, including depositors. To illustrate how set-off works consider the situation where A is owed £10,000 by B but also owes B £12,000. If the law allows set-off then on the insolvency of B the two obligations would be set-off against each other with the result that A would only have to pay £2,000 to the liquidator of B's estate. If set-off is not allowed A would have to pay £12,000 to B's liquidator and then make a claim for the £10,000 that is owed.

Where set-off is available it operates outside the insolvency proceedings and therefore acts as a form of priority. Frequently in a bank insolvency it will be the case that there will be inter-bank activity and where one of the banks fails set-off will be applied. While most experts consider this to be something that promotes efficiency and fairness it actually has the effect of working against most depositors (as they will not normally also have a loan with the bank and will not be in a position to exercise set-off) as it will reduce the amount of assets available for the liquidation estate. Where there is no form of depositor protection and set-off is allowed the bank depositor is in an even more disadvantaged position.

2.6 The unsecured creditor

In this part of the chapter three separate situations are addressed. The first is where the law does not provide any special treatment for bank depositors. The second is where depositors are given some degree of priority and the third is where a deposit insurance system is in place.

From the legal perspective all the depositors of a bank will fall into the category of unsecured creditors which means that they will have to take their place in the queue for payment behind the preferred and secured creditors referred to previously. In fact, where the insolvent entity is a bank another problem is that the availability of set-off puts the unsecured creditor in an even weaker position and this also has already been considered.[59] The low ranking of the unsecured creditor will have the effect in a liquidation of depositors being unlikely to be repaid what they are owed by their bank. This inevitably means that depositors will not be paid in full on the liquidation of their bank, and often will receive nothing, unless the law provides for some sort of protection to be made available to them, either in the form of legal priority or an explicit deposit insurance system, or for the government to provide implicit protection.

After taking control of the insolvent bank the liquidator will give notice of the closure of the bank to the public[60] and this should be followed by information relating to the time and place for filing claims against the bank. What then happens depends on the three situations already mentioned:

- Is there a deposit insurance system already in existence?
- Second, is any form of priority given to depositors under the law?
- Third is where depositors are given no special treatment whatsoever.

No special treatment for depositors

Unless there is some intervention by the public authorities,[61] depositors will have to respond to the notice from the liquidator and make a claim against the insolvent estate for the amount that is owed. As previously mentioned this will not be an expeditious process as the unsecured creditors will receive what is available for them only once the liquidator is in a position to do so out of the net estate. In many bank insolvencies there may be little or nothing available for unsecured creditors but this may not become apparent to depositors for a considerable period of time.

The legal position here is straightforward but it does create a number of problems. For example, if there are thousands of depositors with no access to their savings this will have a detrimental effect on the local economy and, if the bank is large enough, have an effect on the national economy. From the legal perspective bank depositors who cannot access their savings may not be in a position to pay what they are legally obliged to pay and may have no alternative but to default on these commitments. This is often the case with payment of rent for the family home. From the social perspective a bank failure can cause much discontent and it is likely that a government would wish to miminize any adverse effects of depositors. For these reasons bank depositors are often considered to be worthy of some degree of special treatment and simply treating them as unsecured creditors with no special treatment is becoming less commom.

Priority for depositors under the law

To alleviate some of the problems associated with the preceding scenario some jurisdictions have limited depositor protection laws that will give some degree of advantage to depositors on the failure of their banks. These will normally provide for deposits up to a certain amount to be treated in a preferential manner. There are two possible ways to do this. The first is to provide a provision in the law that deposits up to a certain figure will be treated as priority claims and will therefore rank ahead of unsecured creditors. The exact positioning of their ranking can vary depending on the approach taken by the particular jurisdiction. Should they rank ahead of employee claims for example?

While this approach is helpful it is not without difficulties. The first is at what level to put the protected ceiling? In most countries this tends to be set at a relatively low level, high enough to avoid immediate financial difficulties but not any higher than that. The second is that while it gives some form of priority it does not expedite the payments process.

A variation on this approach is that in some jurisdictions the liquidator is given legal power to make payments up to the protected level within a specified period of time. This approach helps to ensure that the liquidator can make a distribution quickly without having to wait for the finalization of the estate. Where this happens it will be necessary to provide legal protection for the liquidator against claims from other creditors.

Where there is a deposit insurance system

Where there is an explicit deposit insurance system in place the legal position of the depositor is, in some respects, more complicated than where no protection is provided. In addition to the legal position of the depositor the legal position of the deposit insurance agency also has to be considered.

Where the deposit insurance system covers one hundred per cent of all deposits the position of the bank depositor is straightforward. On making a claim to the deposit insurance agency the depositor will surrender his or her legal rights to a claim against the insolvent bank's estate. What happens in law is that the depositor's claim is subrogated to the deposit insurance agency which will then be able to claim against the estate for the amount of compensation it has made to the depositor. As it will not normally be the case that all deposits are fully covered the legal position becomes more complicated.

There are various possibilities for the level and type of cover to be provided. First, one hundred per cent cover with no upper limit. Second, one hundred per cent cover up to a specified amount with deposits in excess of this receiving no protection.[62] Third, a variation on the above with one hundred per cent cover up to a specified amount and less than one hundred per cent cover from this amount up to another specified amount.[63] This involves the concept of co-insurance where the depositor will have to bear some of the loss. In some schemes co-insurance may apply to all of the deposit. This was the position in the UK before the scheme was recently changed where regardless of how small the amount on deposit the depositor would have to bear a percentage of the loss.[64]

What is the legal position in each of these scenarios? The position in scenario one has already been dealt with. In all of the other scenarios the legal position is more complicated.

There is a need to consider those depositors who have two separate claims. One against the deposit insurer for the protected amount and another against the liquidator as an unsecured creditor for the outstanding amount. While it would be expected that depositors will be compensated expeditiously to the full extent of their entitlement by the deposit insurer[65] they will have a lengthy and probably fruitless wait for payment of any claims by the liquidator. Bank liquidation processes are always complicated and take a considerable time to complete.

2.7 The protection of depositors

The vulnerability of depositors to incur losses post insolvency as examined above gives rise to a need to protect them from such losses through formal means such as the establishment of an explicit deposit insurance system. The consequences of not doing so are potentially extreme with a loss of depositor confidence spreading to other unrelated banks through mass withdrawal of money equivalent to their deposit therefore damaging confidence in the banking system. However, it is generally agreed that an effective system of regulation and supervision is a necessary precondition for the introduction of a system of deposit insurance, as is emergency liquidity financing.[66] Both of these must be in place prior to designing and implementing the legal framework for a deposit insurance system. In this section of the chapter some of the most significant issues relating to the legal framework for depositor protection systems are examined. But before embarking on it it is important to outline the regulation and supervision of banks in the UK and the objectives and principles it is required to conform to when it exercises its responsibilities. It will be important to note a formal responsibility exists in the prudential regulation and supervision of banking to safeguard the interests of consumers in a broad sense both in terms of conduct of business as well as in light of prudential matters where there interests could be undermined.

2.8 The Financial Services Authority (FSA)

The FSA has the overall regulatory responsibility for deposit-taking businesses, investment businesses (encompassing regulation of recognised investment exchanges) and insurance businesses. The Financial Services and Markets Act 2000 (FSMA) amalgamates the central components of previous regulatory regimes, designating a regulatory authority to make rules governing regulated and prohibited activities, authorization and exemption, continuous supervision, enforcement powers and the establishment of an appeal process. The introduction of the FSMA transfers to the FSA the 'regulation of financial services and markets; to provide for the transfer of certain statutory functions relating to building societies, friendly societies, industrial and provident societies and certain other mutual societies; and connected persons'.[67]

The FSA outlines its approach to supervision of regulated firms in its Supervision Handbook in compliance with the FSMA 2000, which places a responsibility on the FSA to put in place 'arrangements' to ascertain if a regulated firm is complying with their statutory obligations and rules and guidance as set out in the Handbooks.[68] The 'arrangements' the FSA puts in place need to be designed with its objectives and principles of good regulation in mind.[69] In accordance with these principles, for example, the onus is on a firm and its senior management to exercise reasonable care to undertake regulated activities in accordance with the requirements. The FSA has put in place a risk-based approach to fulfil its responsibilities of regulation and supervision so that it uses its resources efficiently to mitigate the risks that ensue from the financial services industry to it achieving its objectives.[70]

The advantage of a single risk-based approach is that it avoids the problems associated with having to deal with the findings of different risk-based systems which would be a result of using the previous regimes as it would hinder cross-comparison of the firms. The difficulty of adopting a plurality of systems of regulation is highlighted by Michael Foot, Head of Financial Supervision at the time, as regulators would exercise their responsibilities 'at the boundaries of their industry even when they had an issue which quite clearly related to other industries'.[71] The plurality of criteria to measure the discrete risks the differing regulators had responsibility for would mean that the results would be difficult to compare in the light of the differing objectives. Therefore, armed with a single set of objectives and principles that transcend the processes of regulation and supervision a single risk-based approach should give rise to a more consistent approach. In addition, the FSA has the responsibility of putting in place 'arrangements' to enforce the provisions set out in the FSMA 2000 and Handbooks.[72] These are fleshed out by the FSA in a complex network of handbooks that set out detailed guidance and rules with which regulated firms and approved persons are required to comply in order to protect the interests associated with financial regulation. These are called the Principles for Businesses, Senior Management Arrangements, Systems and Controls, Statements of Principles and Code of Practice for Approved Persons.

The FSA is required to undertake these responsibilities in accordance with the objectives and principles set out in the FSMA 2000, which provides a foundation for the decisions the FSA takes to fulfil its responsibilities.[73] These objectives and principles provide the context for more precise rules and guidance to assist the FSA to undertake its activities with some assurance that it is compliant with them. In many respects the formalization of regulation governing the financial system by the FSA ensures the degree of discretion in regulation is 'confined', 'structured' and 'checked' to avoid an abuse of power.[74] Moreover, the structuring of regulation sheds a significant amount of light on the way the interests of the various parties are dealt with in the financial services industry. The objectives thus provide not only an external but also an internal mechanism to safeguard other stakeholder interests. For example, the second objective (consumer awareness) provides an obligation on the FSA and financial services industry as a whole to raise the public's understanding of the industry and its products.[75] The third objective (consumer protection) provides an obligation on regulated firms and approved persons to exercise the appropriate level of care when dealing with customers.[76] The inclusion of the interests of other stakeholders into the broader corporate decision-making process is said to give rise to a more ethical approach to business, which subsequently enhances a company's reputation. The ramifications of failing to take into account the interests of other stakeholders are suggested to be much wider than simply damaging the reputation of the firm: it can also undermine the overall reputation of the financial system.[77] Thus the interests of the firm and the market are not mutually exclusive but are interdependent, giving rise to a responsibility to undertake business without undermining investor or depositor confidence.

The objectives place a duty of conduct upon the FSA, and this makes it accountable for its decisions in terms of those objectives. Being declared objectives, they are the yardstick measures to determine whether it is fulfilling its responsibilities. This level of accountability is a positive development from that of the previous regime, whose objectives had never received formal statement and could therefore not be the arbiters of its performance quite so easily. In view of the FSA's position in law in this matter, its objectives do not elaborate a list of formal duties it is obliged to fulfil; rather, those objectives are simply expressions of intent. The political process, and the formal practitioner and consumer panels play a significant part in the accountability process.[78]

2.9 The FSA's objectives

In exercising its responsibilities the FSA focuses on the objectives of market confidence, public awareness, protection of consumers and the reduction of financial crime.[79] While the FSA has not purported to place these objectives in order of importance, it is fitting that market confidence is first as it captures a broad range of factors connected with depositor and investor confidence that directly or indirectly include reference to the other objectives. The first two objectives introduce the idea of the financial system, which suggest that they are rather more nebulous, whilst the latter two require regulated firms and persons to take direct responsibility for implementing measures to protect consumers and reduce the incidence of financial crime. These two objectives focus on the integrity of the UK financial system, and their reach extends territorially in light of the fact that financial markets are globally integrated. For example, an incident overseas by a regulated firm could have a negative impact on the reputation of the UK financial system if that regulated firm is permitted to undertake regulated business in the UK. The following section analyses the first three objectives.

The first objective: market confidence

The first objective requires the FSA to focus its attention on the importance of maintaining confidence in the financial system, which includes reference to financial markets, exchanges and regulated activities.[80] This objective is in many respects the mainstay of well-functioning markets in ensuring that depositors and investors have confidence in the financial markets in which they hold their deposits and make their investments. The objective of market confidence provides a broad rationale for possible intervention, whether it is do with, *inter alia*, an individual firm, a sector of the industry or consumer interests. The wide ambit of responsibility with which the FSA is conferred means that it needs to have a strong understanding of what is happening in the domestic and international financial markets so that it can monitor the risks emanating from them and assess how they can impact on market confidence. In order to ensure market confidence, the FSA needs to focus on the quality of those permitted to undertake regulated activities and take necessary action to avert adverse risks undermining the reputation of the industry. In addition to this the FSA may require the regulated firm to rectify its mistakes and pay compensation to restore confidence.

The FSA has the powers to monitor individual markets and firms so it can require measures to be taken by them if it considers this appropriate. For example, during the slowdown in the economy and equity markets in 2002 the FSA focused on the effectiveness of risk management systems in firms to assess how robust they were in such conditions, and called in some cases for improvements.[81] Whereas in its Financial Risks Outlook 2004, the pressure on firms to comply with a myriad of international and European Union measures was considered a risk the financial services industry needed to take seriously given the enforcement implications that arise once implemented into domestic law.[82] However, maintaining market confidence paradoxically does mean that certain firms will be allowed to fail, and depositors and investors need to be aware of that risk otherwise moral hazard could arise in the market place.[83] The FSA has highlighted that its approach is not to put in place a 'zero-failure regime', which would lead to a high level of moral hazard.[84] This normally accrues when formal mechanisms of support such as lender of last resort and deposit protection schemes exist within a system of regulation. The complexity of achieving market confidence requires cooperation between the FSA, the Bank of England and the Treasury, as manifested in the Memorandum of Understanding, due to the interdependence of financial stability, monetary stability and the regulation of financial institutions. For instance, the Bank of England would conduct its own surveillance of the financial markets for the purposes of financial stability so as to form its own understanding of market trends both domestically and internationally.

The second objective: consumer awareness

The second objective of cultivating public awareness is about enhancing the public's understanding of the financial system.[85] The innovative importance attached to this is elevated by its necessity, due to the systemic failure in the pensions and mortgage industries to sell their financial products with the appropriate level of care so that consumers are aware of the risks associated with the products. Therefore it comes as no surprise that the highest proportion of enquires to the FSA have been with regard to pensions and endowment mortgages.[86] The objective is premised on the idea that a consumer who is aware of the risks in various financial products is one who can make good investment decisions. The FSA has placed a considerable amount of regulatory resources into enhancing the level of financial literacy among the general public.[87] The 2005 Consumer Awareness Report highlighted the degree of awareness of what the FSA does and the level of confidence the public had in its work. It highlighted for instance the degree of public uncertainty surrounding the possibility of a financial firm collapsing.[88] The obligations individuals enter into when buying financial services are not normally short term, but rather long-term commitments exposed to changing market conditions which can negatively impact on the value of financial products. Consumers need to be aware of that fact so they can challenge some of the assertions in promotional literature produced by regulated firms but this is ultimately dependent on their level of financial literacy which was affected by their socio-economic background.[89] However, this is not to say that individual consumers have the right simply to challenge financial services companies on the basis that the returns on an investment were not what they expected when markets did not perform as previously expected. The FSA places the responsibility for informing consumers about financial products and the risks associated with them squarely on the shoulders of the regulated firms and approved persons.[90] It emphasizes the importance of treating consumers fairly as part of its governance strategy.[91] In the light of the issues highlighted, specific emphasis has been placed on internal processes to handle complaints at firms. Moreover, enforcement actions have been taken by the FSA against firms when it has serious misgivings about the robustness of their procedures.[92] This involves, for instance, the sale of endowment mortgages. For example, Abbey Life and Scottish Amicable, two major insurance companies, were fined £1 million and £750,000 respectively for, *inter alia*, mis-selling endowment mortgages, and required to pay compensation in the region of £120–160 million and £11 million respectively to those customers.[93] While the fines indicate a strong stance against individual failures, they need to be considered in the light of the overall gap in endowment mortgages, which is in the region of £30–50 billion over the next couple of decades.[94]

The third objective: consumer protection

The third objective is consumer protection, a key rationale for financial regulation.[95] The FSA has put a significant amount of emphasis on consumer protection rather than purely the efficiency of the financial markets, which distinguishes it from the previous regulatory systems.[96] The FSA has indicated that it does not advocate excessive regulation for the protection of consumer interests, although it has increased the scope of its work to cover financial products that were outside its purview to realign the interests of consumers and financial providers, so that the former's interests are dealt with more fairly. But an overemphasis on consumer-related regulations is not appropriate: first, because no amount of regulation is capable of protecting consumers from all risk; and second, a regulatory order should not attempt to attain an objective of absolute protection. Nevertheless, the FSA has certainly attempted to realign the interests of the industry and consumers to deal with the expectation gap that exists between them.[97]

The rationale for more emphasis on consumer protection in financial regulation is necessary considering, for instance, the vulnerability of bank customers as unsecured creditors of banks. The FSA is required to assess the appropriate level of consumer protection. In order to do that it needs to be mindful of the risks associated with individual financial products and the degree of experience and understanding consumers may have of them. This needs to be measured against the general principle of *caveat emptor*. This principle is interpreted to place little more than a broad onus of duty on consumers to take responsibility for their investment decisions.[98] In order to mitigate the risk to consumers, the FSA has devised principles to govern the way regulated firms undertake their business so that they do not undermine consumer interests by treating them unfairly. It places that obligation on both the regulated firm and individual senior management. Furthermore, it has required that regulated firms incorporate consumer interests into strategic plans to achieve compliance.[99] Ultimately, the interests of consumers are formally protected, to a limited extent, with a compensation scheme for losses that may accrue from the failure or closure of a regulated firm. But the consumer still bears a significant degree of risk from the loss, as such schemes only provide 100 per cent compensation up to a certain level. The proportion not recoverable could be claimed through the liquidation process.[100] This form of co-insurance can be called into question on the grounds that the small depositor would find it impossible to assess the extent to which a regulated firm is risk averse.

2.10 The UK Financial Services Compensation Scheme

The move towards a single regulator also brought with it a single compensation scheme to replace the individual compensation schemes that existed pre-FSMA 2000 for the UK financial services industry. The FSMA 2000 simply provides the framework for the compensation scheme.[101] The parameters of the compensation scheme in terms of how it operates and is administered is set out separately.[102] The objectives of a formal compensation scheme, as highlighted by the FSA, are to secure 'the appropriate degree of protection for consumers and maintaining confidence in the financial system'.[103]

The overall management of the compensation scheme is rather complicated. The FSA is not responsible for its administration as the regulator of financial services albeit it is conferred responsibility to set up a compensation scheme.[104] The responsibility for operating and administering compensation is placed on the shoulders of a separate corporate body named the Financial Services Compensation Scheme Ltd (FSCS) which has deemed itself a 'fund of last resort'.[105] The FSCS is conferred the responsibility to operate and administer compensation for accepting deposits, designated investment business, insurance business, insurance mediation and mortgage advice and arranging all regulated by the FSA.[106] However the FSCS, although it has separate legal personality, is not an independent body as such from the FSA with its own rule making powers nor is it placed on an equal footing to the FSA in terms of dealing with issues that may arise in these matters.[107] It is for all intents and purposes reliant on the FSA to confer on it responsibilities that it can effectively exercise and for it not to place an undue constraint on the FSCS to raise sufficient funds to meet the costs incurred in discharging its responsibilities.[108] The FSA and FSCS are required to cooperate with one another in such matters as sharing information and in dealing with matters that will give rise to public scrutiny.[109]

The UK scheme has a narrower remit than some of its international counterparts. Since 1982 the UK has had in place an explicit 'paybox' scheme that confers responsibility to raise funds and compensate those eligible for compensation when a bank is liquidated. The responsibility of deposit insurers can range from a 'paybox' system where the agency has a narrow role to ones where the agency has significant additional functions such as being a regulator and insolvency practitioner.[110] This description includes a myriad of permutations to what the scheme can look like. Regardless of whether one approach is considered better from a policy position one significant factor in deciding on the role of the agency has to be the level of resources, both financial and human, which are available to it. To give a wide role to an organization such as the Federal Deposit Insurance Corporation in the United States is one thing but where resources are limited a paybox may be the only realistic option.

The FSCS on the face of it simply administers a 'paybox' scheme, it is conferred the responsibility of managing the compensation scheme. This requires it to pay compensation when a firm regulated to undertake deposit taking business is put into administration or liquidation, and is 'unlikely or likely to be unable to meet claims against it'.[111] However, in the UK the responsibility of dealing with administration, liquidation and winding up proceedings would fall into the responsibility of accounting firms.[112] In the previous regulatory regime the Bank of England would try to ensure as far as possible the claims made by depositors post bank insolvency were duly meet through the liquidation process to reduce the number of claims on the compensation scheme.[113]

The FSCS will only make compensation payments to those who are eligible and the individual firm is a participating firm.[114] Those eligible are normally individuals for whom it would be virtually impossible to determine the financial status of a bank. The rules and guidance basically indicate an 'individual' is eligible provided it is not *inter alia* an 'unregulated firm', 'overseas financial services institution', supranational institution, 'local authorities', 'collective investment schemes', 'pension funds', 'directors and managers of the relevant person in default', 'body corporate of the same group', 'persons holding 5 per cent or more of the capital of the relevant person in default'.[115] In addition to this list of parties that are not eligible for compensation the FSCS can also determine an individual is ineligible 'if they are of the opinion that they are responsible for, or have contributed to, the relevant person's default' this could potentially include employees that have perpetrated a fraud for example.[116] In this matter it would be reliant on the Official Receiver's opinion in accordance with the UK Insolvency Act 1986.

The UK compensation scheme only compensates those with a protected claim,[117] which would basically mean an individual with an account at a credit institution (deposit-taking institutions).[118] The firm is determined to be in default when the FSA, FSCS or judicial authority determine the participating firm is 'unable to satisfy protected claims against it; or likely to be unable to satisfy protected claims against it'.[119] This requires the FSCS to work with the administrator and liquidator to identify who is in default and ultimately to whom compensation is owed.[120] In addition to this the FSCS would also have to work closely with the FSA as the regulator of financial services. In this respect the FSCS is allowed to assist the FSA when it identifies a firm 'is unable, or likely to be unable, to repay its depositors'.[121]

2.11 The level of compensation

The compensation scheme does not, somewhat controversially, provide 100 per cent compensation to those eligible. The idea that the person insured should share some of the risk is very common in general insurance contracts and some jurisdictions, including the UK, have introduced co-insurance into the deposit protection scheme for bank depositors.[122] In fact when the deposit protection scheme was first introduced in the UK no degree of total protection was provided and all depositors were subject to an element of co-insurance.[123] It was not until 1995 that the level of co-insurance was subsequently reduced,[124] when cover was raised to 90 per cent of the first £20,000 on deposit. All deposits were still subject to an element of co-insurance however. The current scheme has only provided limited 100 per cent cover, this is limited to a relatively modest £2,000. Above this up to £33,000 only 90 per cent of the deposit is protected.[125] Therefore the UK compensation scheme only pays out a maximum of £31,700 to any one individual with a protected claim.

Co-insurance also presents an added problem which is that many depositors will not have their claims paid in full and will therefore continue to be creditors of the failed bank. Where co-insurance applies to the entire amount of deposits then all depositors will be unsecured creditors in the liquidation proceedings. This complicates the process and will normally lead to both additional expenses for the liquidator and to a delay in completing the winding-up process. The presence of thousands of small claims, as was the case in the UK in the BCCI liquidation, is undesirable and where they can be removed from the process, as is typically the case where a reasonably generous level of full cover is provided, as in Canada and the USA for example.

The time scale in which claims are to be processed and compensation paid to the depositor has also raised concerns. The UK position is rather vague on the speed with which a payment of compensation should be made. Under the relevant EU legislation compensation to depositors should be made within at least 90 days of a valid claim for compensation being lodged with the FSCS. This legislation permits an extension to six months in exceptional circumstances.[126] According to the FSCS 'after a firm has been declared in default, we generally aim to pay compensation within six months of receiving a completed application form'.[127] Why it should take so long in the UK is unclear and this approach would appear to be in contravention of the EU Directive. In the USA and Canada, for example, such a lengthy delay would be unacceptable and indeed the FDIC often arranges a transfer of deposits to another bank rather than making payouts to individual depositors. It is able to do this because of its wider role but such an outcome is very unlikely where the agency acts merely as a paybox.

2.12 Funding of the compensation scheme

The way the FSCS funds the compensation is also clearly set out in the Compensation Manual. This deals with issue of who should pay, when they should pay and the amount they should pay.[128] Participant firms, as defined above, are required to finance the respective funds.[129] In some jurisdictions membership is optional and where this is the case it will be necessary to ensure that depositors are made aware of this. In reality even where membership of the scheme is not mandatory it is likely that banks will wish to be members as failure to join may have an adverse effect on the amount of deposits being attracted.

The responsibility of deciding the size of the fund is on the FSCS. It has powers for the fund to finance both *ex ante* and *ex post*. In this respect the FSCS can request a levy which is made up of compensation costs incurred and the costs 'reasonably be anticipated as arising in the 12 months following the levy date.[130] Under an *ex ante* scheme the member banks will be legally required to contribute an amount to the fund so that a fund of sufficient size will be available to meet any payouts. Most countries with explicit schemes have decided that funding should be *ex ante* but a few jurisdictions allow for only a small fund being in existence with the right to demand *ex post* funding from member banks when required. According to Garcia 'funded schemes appear to be more rule-based and offer less discretion for the administrators and less uncertainty for those insured than ex post systems'.[131] Once the target level of the fund has been reached the law will normally not require any further contributions until there is a need.

There are several possible methods of deciding how to levy contributions from member banks. At present most jurisdictions use fixed rate premiums but another possibility is to charge premiums which are risk adjusted. Risk adjusted premiums are becoming more widely used and this trend seems likely to continue. Risk based premiums are the norm in the insurance industry and should, if calculated properly, help to ensure fairness. Large banks often claim to be unfairly subsidizing smaller, and potentially riskier banks where fixed premiums are used.

2.13 Conclusion

An effective system of liquidation for a bank will necessarily provide that all creditors of a particular class are treated in the same manner but the problem facing the bank depositor is that other classes of creditor, preferred, secured and those who can exercise set-off will have an advantage over the depositor who is an unsecured creditor.

Where there is no system of deposit insurance in place and where no legal priority on insolvency is given to depositors the bank depositor is, from the legal perspective, actually in a weak position should the bank experience financial difficulties. Where there is an effective system of regulation and supervision, coupled with a central bank which is willing, in appropriate circumstances, to provide emergency liquidity financing the risks can be minimized but not entirely eliminated.

Most bank depositors will be totally unaware of their legal relationship with their bank. Instead of being a lowly ranking unsecured creditor the average bank depositor is likely to consider the relationship as being one where the bank is actually looking after their savings. As has been seen here nothing could be further from the truth.

Notes

1 *Commissioners of the State Savings Bank of Victoria* v. *Permewan Wright & Co* (1914) 19 CLR 457, 471.
2 DeYoung, R. and Rice, T. (2004) 'How do banks make money? The fallacies of fee income', *Federal Reserve Bank of Chicago, Economic Perspectives,* vol. 28: 4, pp. 34–51, at p. 40.
3 *Space Investments Ltd* v. *Canadian Imperial Bank of Commerce Trust Co (Bahamas) Ltd. And others* [1986] 1 WLR 1072: Lord Templeman – 'If the bank becomes insolvent the customer can only prove in the liquidation of the bank as unsecured creditor for the amount which was, ought to have been, credited to the account at the date when the bank went into liquidation.' (at p. 1074).
4 *Woods* v. *Martins Bank Ltd* [1959] 1 55, 56; *United Dominions Trust* v. Kirkwood [1966] 2 QB 431, 447. For a list of activities, see *Libyan Arab Foreign Bank* v. *Bankers Trust* [1989] QB 728, 749.

5 Cranston, R. (2005) *Modern Principles of Banking Law*, Oxford, Oxford University Press at p. 20.

6 In the UK, for example, accepting deposits is prohibited unless one is 'permitted' to do so by the Financial Services Authority, s. 19 the Financial Services and Markets Act 2000.

7 See for example, *Joachimson* v. *Swiss Bank Corporation* (1921) 3 K B 110, 127: This can be exercised during banking hours.

8 Campbell, A. and Cartwright, P. (2002) *Banks in Crisis: The Legal Response*, Aldershot, Ashgate; Hupkes, E. (2000) *Legal Aspects of Bank Insolvency*, The Hague, Kluwer.

9 *Re Chancery plc* [1991] BCLC 712: The directors' of the bank sought an administrative order from the court on the same day because they could not meet the debts of the bank due the next day. HARMAN J gave the order sought in light of the exceptional circumstances of the case without proper consideration of the interests of other parties to avoid the possibility of a bank run if problems about the bank were made public.

10 Singh, D. (2003) 'Enforcement Decisions in Banking Regulation and Supervision', vol. 4: 4, *Journal of International Banking Regulation*, (2003) 301–19; Singh, D. 'Enforcement Methods and Sanctions in Banking Regulation and Supervision', vol., 4, *International and Comparative Corporate Law Journal* (2002) 307–43.

11 Singh, D. 'Corporate Governance and Banking Supervision' 465–501 in Norton, J. J. Rickford, J. (CBE) with Kleinman, J. *'Corporate Governance Post Enron: A Comparative and International Perspective'* Studies in International Financial, Economic and Technology Law London: BIICL 2006; Cartwright P. (2004) *Banks, Consumers and Regulation*, Oxford, Hart.

12 *Edward Thomas Foley* v. *Hill* [1848] II H L C., 27 1002.

13 Ibid., 1005.

14 *Parker and Merchant* 1 PH 356 cited in *Foley* at p. 1005.

15 Ibid., in general terms ' "ready money" is restricted to the money which a man keeps in his house for current expenses' which is distinguishable from money put in a bank account'. at para., 358. In this case whether or not such money could be referred to as 'ready money' depended on the facts of a particular case and the intentions of the party.

16 *Foley* (above n. 12) at p. 1005–6.

17 For an international perspective on the subject see Cranston R. (1999) *European Banking Law: The Banker–Customer Relationship*, London, Lloyds of London Press. In the EU jurisdictions examined in this work the relationship is simply stated to be one of a contractual nature.

18 *Libyan Arab Foreign Bank* v *Bankers Trust* [1989] QB 728 at p. 746 this follows the ruling in *Joachimson* v. *Swiss Bank Corporation* (above n.7) 3 K B 110, 127; Furthermore, STAUGHTON J '[I]n my view . . . the proper law of a bank's contract is the law of the place where the account is kept. Political risk must commonly be an important factor to those who deposit large sums of money with banks; the popularity of Swiss bank accounts with some people is due to the banking laws of the Cantons of Switzerland. And I have already found, on the evidence of Bankers Trust, that the Iranian crisis was at the back of everyone's mind in 1980. Whatever considerations did or did not influence the parties to this case, I believe that banks generally and their customers normally intend the local law to apply. So I would require solid grounds for holding that the general rule does not apply . . . ' at p. 747.

19 Ibid *Libyan Arab Foreign Bank* p. 748.
20 *Marine Bank* v. *Fulton Bank* 69 U S 252; 17 L Ed. 785; (1864).
21 Ibid., p. 258; see also *Thompson* v. *Riggs* 72 U S 663; 18 L Ed 704; (1866).
22 *Bank of the Republic* v. *Millard* 77 U S 152; 19 L Ed 897; 1869 pp. 156-157.
23 Ibid.; see also *Burton* v. *United States* 196 U S 283; 25 S Ct 243; (1905), at p. 302.
24 *Toronto Dominion Bank* v. *Forsythe* 183 D L R (4th) 616, (2000).
25 *Standard Investments Ltd* v. *Canadian Imperial Bank of Commerce* 30 B L R 193. A fiduciary duty has been found in for example where the customer seeks the advice of the bank: *Woods* v. *Martin's Bank Ltd* (above n.4); *Lloyds Bank* v. *Bundy* [1974] 3 All ER 757.
26 For example, *Joachimson* (above n.7); *R* v. *Davenport* [1954] 1 All ER 602.
27 Ibid., Lord Goddard in *R* v. *Davenport* [1954] at p. 603; See also *National Westminister Bank Plc* v. *Spectrum Plus Ltd and others* [2004] EWCA Civ 670.
28 Smart, P.E. (1990) *Leading Cases in the Law of Banking*, London, Sweet & Maxwell, p. 4.
29 Macey, J.R. and O'Hara, M. (2003) 'Corporate Governance of Banks', April pp. 93–4 http://www.newyorkfed.org/research/epr/03v09n1/0304mace.pdf
30 *Percival* v. *Wright* [1902] 2 Ch 421; *Re Smith & Fawcett Ltd* [1942] Ch 304; *Howard Smith Ltd* v. *Ampol Petrol Ltd* [1974] AC 821, in particular where 'in the interests of the company as whole is interpreted to mean in the interests of 'the company as a commercial entity'. p. 824; In *Brady* v. *Brady* [1988] BCLC 20 Nourse LJ referred the difficulty of actually defining the phrase 'the interests of the company' he suggested it to have a relative meaning to the principles to which it is being considered. Davies, P. (2003) *Principles of Modern Company Law*, London, Sweet and Maxwell at p. 372; see further *Dawson International plc* v. *Coats Paton plc* [1989] BCLC 233. Lord Cullen interpreted the position as directors having only 'one master, the company'; see also *Heron International* v. *Lord Grade* [1983] BCLC 244, where the decisions taken by directors needed only to take into account present rather than future shareholders, at p. 244; *Multinational Gas & Petrochemical Co* v. *Multinational Gas & Petrochemical Services Ltd* [1983] Ch 528. For an examination of the interests of creditors internationally see Keay, A. (2003) 'Directors taking into account creditors interests', *Company Lawyer*, vol. 24: 10 pp. 300–6.
31 See for example *F S L I C* v. *Howard D Huff* 237 Kan. 873; 704 P.2d 372 (1985);
32 According to Lord Cullen in *Dawson International Plc* v. *Coats Patons Plc and Others* [1989] BCLC 233 'the fiduciary duty of the directors was owed to the company, although its exercise involved balancing disparate interests, including those of the company's employees and members'.
33 *Brady* v. *Brady* [1988] (above n.30) at p. 552; See F S L I C (1985) (n. 31 above) it refers to *Sampson* v. *Hunt*, 233 Kan. 572, 665 P.2d 743 where it interpreted the obligation as 'a strict fiduciary duty is imposed on officers and directors of a corporation to act in the best interest of the corporation and the stockholders,' at p. 243.
34 *West Mercia Safetywear Ltd* v. *Dodd* [1988] BCLC 250.
35 *Dawson International Plc* v. *Coats Patons Plc and Others* [1989] BCLC 233.
36 However, the issue of placing an obligation on directors to formally take into account other interests has been cautioned against: Committee on Corporate Governance, *Report of the Committee on Corporate Governance*, London, Gee & Co (1998) (hereinafter the Hampel Report).

1.17; However, a considerable level of attention has been paid to the issue of creditor interests in corporate law. Recently, Keay, A. (2005) 'Formulating a framework for the directors' duties to creditors: An Entity Maximisation Approach', 64, *Cambridge Law Journal*, vol. 64: 3, pp. 614–46; Keay A. 'The Director's Duty to Take into Account the Interests of Company Creditors: When is it Triggered?' *Melbourne University Law Review* (2001) vol. 25: 2, pp. 315–9; Prentice, D. D. (1990) 'Creditor's Interests and Director's Duties', *Oxford Journal of Legal Studies*, vol. 10: 2, pp. 265–77; Sappideen, R. (1991) 'Fiduciary Obligations to Corporate Creditors', *Journal of Business Law*, July, pp. 365–97.

37 In the US case for example see Stilson A.E.C. (1995) 'Re-examining the fiduciary paradigm at corporate insolvency and dissolution: Defining Directors' Duties to Creditors, *Delaware Journal of Corporate Law* 20. 1, pp. 1–122; Lin L. (1993) 'Shift of Fiduciary Duty Upon Corporate Insolvency: Proper scope of directors duty to creditors', 46, *Vanderbilt Law Review*, November, pp. 1485–1524 referred to in *Re Ben Franklin Retail Stores Inc* v. *R Kendig et al.* 225 B R 646; (1998) Bankr. Lexis 1266.

38 *Winkworth* v. *Baron Development Ltd* [1986] WLR 1512, 1516.

39 Keay (2001) (above n 36) at p. 321.

40 s. 214 Insolvency Act 1986.

41 *West Mercia Safetywear Ltd* [1988] 4 BCC 30 where DHILLON J refers to the New Zealand case *Kinsela* v. *Russell Kinsela Pty Ltd* (1986) 4 NSWLR 722, 730 where in a liquidation situation the shareholders interests are 'displaced' by the interests of creditors. The company's assets are then for all intents and purposes the creditors and the not the shareholders at p. 34.

42 This is discussed further below.

43 Re Chancery plc (above n.9) pp. 172.

44 Ibid., 173.

45 *Re Barings Plc and others (No. 3), Secretary of State for Trade and Industry* v. *Baker and others (No. 3)* [1999] 1 BCLC 226; *Re Barings plc (No. 5), Secretary for Trade and Industry* v. *Baker and others (No. 5)* Ch D [1999] 1 BCLC 433.

46 The term insolvency will be used throughout this paper but in many jurisdictions this would be described as bankruptcy. For the purposes of this paper both terms have the same meaning.

47 This term is used to describe the situation where assets exceed liabilities.

48 Often referred to as lender of last resort.

49 For further information on emergency liquidity financing see Delston, R. and Campbell, A. 'Emergency Liquidity Financing by Central Banks: Systemic Protection or Bank Bailout?' in (2005) *Current Developments in Monetary and Financial Law Vol. 3* (Washington, D.C., International Monetary Fund) Chapter 23, and Goodhart, C. and Illing, G. *Financial Crises, Contagion and Lender of Last Resort* (eds) (2002), Oxford, Oxford University Press; Lastra, R.M. (2006), *Legal Foundations of International Monetary Stability*, Oxford, Oxford University Press, pp. 110–47; Singh, D. (2007) *Banking Regulation of UK and US Financial Markets*, Aldershot, Ashgate, pp. 1–20.

50 Or in some cases the Ministry of Finance.

51 Much has been written about the theoretical basis of lender of last resort. That it should only be given to banks that are illiquid but solvent; collateral should be provided; a penalty rate of interest should be charged and that its availability should be discretionary. Many commentators are of the opinion that these requirements are not always followed in modern practice. See Delston and Campbell (above n 49).

52 Ibid.
53 See Bagehot, W. 'A General View of Lombard Street' (excerpts), in Goodhart and Illing, (above n.49), p. 67
54 See Hupkes (above n.8) at p 12.
55 In the APEC policy dialogue on deposit insurance it was found that insolvency was too late in the process for the closure of a troubled bank and that capital triggers were not much of an improvement, given the costs of liquidation. It has been suggested by some that, from the deposit insurer's perspective, that 'viability' is a better trigger for action. In Malaysia, for example, the central bank, Bank Negara Malaysia, and the Malaysian Deposit Insurance Corporation have incorporated in the relevant legislation 'viability' as the closure point. It is as yet unclear as to the exact parameters of 'viability'.
56 For detailed discussions of these methods see Asser, T. (2001) *Legal Aspects of Regulatory Treatment of Banks in Distress*, Washington, DC, International Monetary Fund; Campbell and Cartwright (above n.8) and Hupkes (above n.8). See also the extensive amount of information provided by the United States Federal Deposit Insurance Fund at www.fdic.org.
57 A significant exception to this in the case of bank insolvency is the United States.
58 Despite being such an apparently straightforward concept the laws relating to set-off tend to be very complex and vary considerably between jurisdictions.
59 Set-off is considered later in this chapter.
60 The method by which this should be done needs to be set out clearly in the law.
61 It is always possible that the public authorities may decide to intervene on an implicit basis at this stage.
62 This is the case for example in the United States where the first $100,000 is fully covered.
63 This is the approach taken in the United Kingdom where the first £2,000 is fully covered and then 90 per cent of the next £31,000. So under this system a depositor who has a balance in excess of £2,000 will have to bear some of the loss.
64 While some systems may have co-insurance it is uncommon to find situations where it has been implemented. It was applied, however in the case of the BCCI failure in the United Kingdom.
65 This is not without problems and is discussed later in this paper.
66 For further reading see, for example, Garcia, G. (2000) *Deposit Insurance: Actual and Good Practices*, Washington, DC: International Monetary Fund and Campbell and Cartwright (above at n 8) p. 23.
67 Preamble to FSMA 2000.
68 FSMA 2000 s. 6(1) of Schedule 1; SUP 1: The FSA's approach to supervision, SUP 1.1.2G.
69 SUP 1: 1.1.3G.
70 SUP 1:1.3 G.
71 Foot, M. (2000) Managing Director and Head of Financial Supervision, 'Our new approach to regulation – what will be the difference for firms', FSA, December.
72 FSMA 2000 s. 6(3).
73 FSA, (1997) *Financial Services Authority: an Outline*, October; FSA, (1999) *The Financial Services Authority*, August; FSA, (1998) *Financial Services Authority: Meeting our Responsibilities*, August; FSA, (2000) *A New Regulator for the New Millennium.*
74 Davis, K.C. (1980, c.1969) *Discretionary Justice: A Preliminary Enquiry*, Westport, CN: Greenwood Press, at p. 4.
75 FSA, (1998) *Meeting our Responsibilities*, (above n.73) p. 17.

76 Ibid., p. 17.
77 FSA (2002) 'An ethical framework for financial services', Discussion Paper 18, October.
78 FSA, (1998) *Meeting our Responsibilities*, (above n.73) p. 9.
79 FSMA 2000 s. 2(2); see also FSA, (1998) *Meeting Our Responsibilities*, p. 16–18.
80 FSMA 2000 s. 3(1).
81 FSA, Annual Report 2002/03 at p. 103.
82 FSA, (2004) *Financial Risk Outlook*, at pp. 89.
83 Bank of England, 1997/98 Banking Act Report, *Memorandum of Understanding between HM Treasury, The Bank of England and the FSA*, 37–39 (MoU); The Bank of England, Report and Accounts (1998) at p. 15s. 21 and s 22 of the 1998 Act respectively; Blair, M., Cranston, R., Ryan, C. and Taylor, M. (1998) *Blackstone's Guide to the Bank of England Act 1998*, Oxford, Oxford University Press; See 1998 Act Part III: 'Transfer of Supervisory Functions of the Bank to the Financial Services Authority'.
84 FSA, (2003) *Reasonable Expectations: Regulation in a Non-zero Failure World*, September. FSA, Supervision Manual.
85 FSMA 2000 s. 4(1).
86 FSA, Annual Report 2002/03 at p. 15; For an analysis of consumers and financial services see, Cartwright, P. (2005) *Banks, Consumers and Regulation*, (above n.11).
87 For example, FSA, (2005) *Consumer awareness of the FSA and financial regulation*, July.
88 Ibid., p. 17.
89 FSA, (2000) *Better informed consumers. Assessing the implications for consumer education of research by BMRB*, April.
90 For example, Principle 6, Customers' Interests, Principles for Businesses place a responsibility on the firm to 'pay due regard to the interests of its customers and treat them fairly'.
91 FSA, Annual Report, 2003/04 at p. 26.
92 FSA, Enforcement Manual (ENF).
93 FSA, Annual Report 2002/03, at p. 21.
94 FSA, Annual Report 2003/04, at p. 8.
95 FSMA 2000 s. 5(1).
96 FSA, (1997) *Financial Services Authority: An outline*, (above n.73) at p. 30.
97 Ibid.
98 Davies, H. (1999) Chairman Financial Services Authority, 1999 Travers Lecture, London Guildhall University Business School, 'Building The Financial Services Authority: What's New?', March www.fsa.gov.uk/speeches/1999/march/110311999.htm at p. 4.
99 FSA, 2002/03, (above n.93) p. 104.
100 Campbell & Cartwright (above n.8), at p. 151.
101 Pursuant of s. 212, FSMA 2000, a separate body corporate called the 'Scheme Manager'. The FSMA 2000 provides the 'Scheme Manager' with a number of broad powers: to impose levies on authorized persons (s. 213(3)(b)); to set up different funds to meet the different types of claims (s. 214); to devise provisions relating to insolvency of regulated firms (s. 215); to publish an Annual Report (s. 218); to request information and documents (s. 219); to inspect documents held by the Official Receiver (s. 224).
102 COMP – Compensation Scheme at http://fsahandbook.info/FSA/html/handbook/COMP/INTRO.

103 However the extent to which the scheme achieves this is a moot point when considered in the broader context.
104 COMP 1.1.5G.
105 www.fscs.org.uk/.
106 FSCS sub schemes, www.fscs.org.uk/industry/sub-schemes/.
107 The exception noted is its powers under company law to raise finance see, COMP 1.2.1G and 1.2.2G.
108 Memorandum of Understanding between the Financial Services Authority and the Financial Services Compensation Scheme.
109 Ibid., para., 12.
110 In some jurisdictions the agency has a much wider role and operates not only as a 'paybox' but also as a regulator of banks which are members of the scheme and as a receiver of failed bank. For example, this is the approach taken in the United States where the system has worked well but to give the agency such wide powers is a matter\of concern in some countries. This relates particularly to the fact that a major, and frequently the major, creditor is given a role to play in the receivership process of the failed bank and that this amounts to a conflict of interest. In the United States this system has been in place since 1933 and, in relation to it being both creditor and receiver, this is an accepted state of affairs which is now generally accepted. This role for the agency would not be acceptable on policy grounds in many jurisdictions and in some to give the role of receiver to a major creditor would be illegal.
111 COMP 2.2.1R.
112 This is generally discussed above.
113 *Re Goodwin Squires Securities Ltd* (1983) The Times L R March 22nd 204, 205.
114 COMP 4.2.2R.
115 COMP 4.2.2R.
116 COMP 4.2.
117 COMP 5.3.1R; this may require the individual to assign their rights to the FSCS see COMP 7; COMP 8 deals with the FSCS right to reject an application and with an offer for compensation if for instance irregularities exist with the claim.
118 As defined in the Investment Services Directive; COMP 5.3R & COMP 6.2.1R respectively.
119 COMP 6.3.2R.
120 FSCS sub schemes, www.fscs.org.uk/industry/sub-schemes/accepting_deposits_sub-scheme/.
121 Ibid.
122 For a discussion of the relationship between co-insurance and moral hazard see Campbell (above n.8) and Garcia, G. (2000) Deposit Insurance: Actual and Good Practice, Washington, DC: IMF.
123 The scheme was introduced by the Banking Act 1979. Initially protection was limited to 75 per cent of the first £10,000 and this was raised to £20,000 in 1987 with the Banking Act 1987.
124 See the Credit Institutions (Protection of Depositors) Regulations 1995. This implemented the Directive and came into effect on 1st July 1995.
125 COMP 10.2.3R.
126 COMP 9.2.1R.
127 This is taken from the FSCS's Claiming Compensation Booklet. This can be viewed at www.fscs.org.uk/files/documents/pdfs/jysyumnhiezc.pdf.
128 COMP 13.
129 COMP 13.1.3G.

130 COMP 13.6.1R; There are several possible methods of deciding how to levy contributions from member banks. A formula will be used such as a percentage of total deposits. At present most jurisdictions use fixed rate premiums but another possibility is to charge premiums which are risk adjusted. Risk adjusted premiums are becoming more widely used and this trend seems likely to continue. Risk based premiums are the norm in the insurance industry and should, if calculated properly, help to ensure fairness. Large banks often claim to be unfairly subsidising smaller, and potentially riskier banks where fixed premiums are used.

131 Garcia (above n.122) at p 32.

References

Asser, T. (2001) *Legal Aspects of Regulatory Treatment of Banks in Distress*, Washington, DC: International Monetary Fund.

Bank of England, 1997/98 Banking Act Report, *Memorandum of Understanding between HM Treasury, the Bank of England and the FSA*, 37–39.

Blair, M., Cranston, R., Ryan, C. and Taylor, M. (1998) *Blackstone's Guide to the Bank of England Act 1998*, Oxford: Oxford University Press.

Campbell, A. and Cartwright, P. (2002) *Banks in Crisis: The Legal Response*, Aldershot: Ashgate.

Cartwright, P. (2005) *Banks, Consumers and Regulations*, Oxford: Hart Publishing.

Cranston, R. (2005) *Modern Principles of Banking Law*, Oxford: Oxford University Press.

Cranston, R. (1999) *European Banking Law: The Banker-Customer Relationship*, London: Lloyds of London Press.

Davies, P. (2003) *Principles of Modern Company Law*, London: Sweet and Maxwell.

Davies, H. (1999) 1999 Travers Lecture, London Guildhall University Business School, 'Building the Financial Services Authority: What's New?', March.

Davis, K.C. (1980, c.1969) *Discretionary Justice: A Preliminary Enquiry*, Westport, CN: Greenwood Press.

Delston, R. and Campbell, A. (2005) 'Emergency Liquidity Financing by Central Banks: Systemic Protection or Bank Bailout?', *Current Developments in Monetary and Financial Law Vol 3,* Washington, DC: International Monetary Fund.

DeYoung, R. and Rice, T. (2004) 'How do banks make money? The fallacies of fee income', *Federal Reserve Bank of Chicago, Economic Perspectives,* vol. 28: 4, pp. 34–51.

Foot, M. (2000) Managing Director and Head of Financial Supervision, 'Our new approach to regulation – what will be the difference for firms', FSA, December.

FSA (1997) *Financial Services Authority: an outline*, October.

FSA (1998) *Financial Services Authority: Meeting our responsibilities*, August.

FSA (1999) *The Financial Services Authority*, August.

FSA (2000) *A new regulator for the new Millennium.*

FSA (2003) *Reasonable Expectations: Regulation in a Non-zero Failure World*, September.

FSA Annual Report 2002/03.

FSA (2005) *Consumer awareness of the FSA and financial regulation*, July.

FSA Supervision Manual.

FSA Enforcement Manual.

FSA Compensation Scheme.

FSA (2000) Better informed consumers. Assessing the implications for consumer education of research by BMRB, April.
Garcia, G. (2000) *Deposit Insurance: Actual and Good Practices,* Washington, DC: International Monetary Fund.
Goodhart, C. and Illing, G. (eds) (2002) *Financial Crises, Contagion and Lender of Last Resort,* Oxford: Oxford University Press.
Hupkes, E. (2000) *Legal Aspects of Bank Insolvency*, The Hague: Kluwer.
Keay, A, (2001) *The Director's Duty to Take into Account the Interests of Company Creditors: When is it Triggered?* 25, *Melbourne University Law Review*, vol. 25: 2, pp. 315–39.
Keay, A. (2003) 'Directors taking into account creditors' interests', *The Company Lawyer* vol. 24: 10, pp. 300–6.
Keay, A. (2005) 'Formulating a framework for the directors' duties to creditors: An Entity Maximisation Approach', *Cambridge Law Journal* vol. 64: 3, pp. 614–46.
Lastra, R. M. (2006) *Legal Foundations of International Monetary Stability*, Oxford: Oxford University Press.
Lin, L. (1993) 'Shift of Fiduciary Duty Upon Corporate Insolvency: Proper scope of directors duty to creditors', *Vanderbilt Law Review*, November, pp. 1485–524.
Macey, J.R. and O'Hara, M. (2003) 'Corporate Governance of Banks', April, *FRNBY, Economic Policy Review*, pp. 91–107.
Prentice, D.D. (1990) 'Creditor's Interests and Director's Duties', *Oxford Journal of Legal Studies*, vol. 10: 2, pp. 265–277.
Sappideen, R. (1991) 'Fiduciary Obligations to Corporate Creditors', *Journal of Business Law* July, pp. 365–97.
Singh, D. (2002) 'Enforcement Methods and Sanctions in Banking Regulation and Supervision', *International and Comparative Corporate Law Journal*, Vol. 4: 4, pp. 307–43.
Singh, D. (2003) 'Enforcement Decisions in Banking Regulation and Supervision', *Journal of International Banking Regulation*, Vol. 4: 4, pp. 301–19.
Singh, D. (2006) 'Corporate Governance and Banking Supervision', pp. 465 in Norton, J.J., Rickford, J. (CBE) with Kleinman, J. (2006) *Corporate Governance Post Enron: A Comparative and International Perspective, Studies in International Financial, Economic and Technology Law*, London: BIICL.
Singh, D. (2007) *Banking Regulation of UK and US Financial Markets*, Aldershot: Ashgate (forthcoming).
Smart, P.E. (1990) *Leading cases in the Law of Banking*, London: Sweet and Maxwell.
Stilson, A.E.C. (1995) 'Re-examining the fiduciary paradigm at corporate insolvency and dissolution: Defining Directors' Duties to Creditors', *Delaware Journal of Corporate Law*, vol. 20, pp. 1–122.

Legal references

Bank of the Republic v. *Millard* 77 U S 152; 19 L Ed 897; (1869).
Brady v *Brady* [1988] at p. 552.
Burton v. *United States* 196 U S 283; 25 S Ct 243; (1905).
Commissioners of the State Savings Bank of Victoria v. *Permewan Wright & Co* (1914) 19 CLR 457.
Dawson International Plc v. *Coats Patons Plc and Others* [1989] BCLC 233.
Edward Thomas Foley v. *Hill* [1848] II H L C., 27 1002.
FSLIC v. *Howard D Huff* 237 Kan. 873; 704 P.2d 372 (1985).
Heron International v. *Lord Grade* [1983] BCLC 244.
Howard Smith Ltd v. *Ampol Petrol Ltd* [1974] AC 821.
Joachimson v. *Swiss Bank Corporation* [1921] 3 K B 110.

Kinsela v. *Russell Kinsela Pty Ltd* (1986) 4 NSWLR 722.
Libyan Arab Foreign Bank v. *Bankers Trust* [1989] QB 728.
Lloyds Bank v *Bundy* [1974] 3 All ER 757.
Marine Bank v. *Fulton Bank* 69 U S 252; 17 L Ed. 785; (1864).
Multinational Gas & Petrochemical Co v *Multinational Gas & Petrochemical Services Ltd* [1983] Ch 528.
National Westminister Bank Plc v. *Spectrum Plus Ltd and others* [2004] EWCA Civ 670.
Parker v. *Merchant* 1 PH 356.
Percival v *Wright* [1902] 2 Ch 421.
Re Barings Plc and others (No. 3), Secretary of State for Trade and Industry v *Baker and others* (No. 3) [1999] 1 BCLC 226.
Re Barings plc (No.5), Secretary for Trade and Industry v *Baker and others (No. 5)* Ch D [1999] 1 BCLC 433.
Re Ben Franklin Retail Stores Inc v. *R Kending et al* 225 B R 646; (1998).
Re Chancery plc [1991] BCLC 712.
R v. *Davenport* [1954] 1 All ER 602.
Re Goodwin Squires Securities Ltd (1983) The Times L R March 22nd 204.
Re Smith & Fawcett Ltd [1942] Ch 304.
Space Investments Ltd v. *Canadian Imperial Bank of Commerce Trust Co (Bahamas) Ltd. and others* [1986] 1 WLR 1072.
Standard Investments Ltd v. *Canadian Imperial Bank of Commerce* 30 B L R 193.
Thompson v. *Riggs* 72 U S 663; 18 L Ed 704; (1866).
Toronto Dominion Bank v. *Forsythe* (2000) 183 D L R (4th) 616.
United Dominions Trust v. *Kirkwood* [1966] 2 QB 431.
Winkworth v *Baron Development Ltd* [1986] WLR 1512.
Woods v *Martin's Bank Ltd* [1959] 1 55.

3

Instituting a Deposit Insurance System: Why? How?

Christine E. Blair, Frederick Carns and Rose M. Kushmeider

A sound, competitive banking system is critical to a nation's economic vitality. Banks have traditionally performed the important function of intermediating between lenders and borrowers by using liquid, short-term liabilities to fund relatively long-term, illiquid assets. By providing a liquid savings vehicle for small and large investors alike and by developing specialized skills to evaluate and diversify the risks of their borrowers, banks play an important role – financing opaque risks – that helps fund economic growth. Banks also generally play a central role in a country's payment and settlement systems, and can be an important element in the conduct of monetary policy, which works through financial institutions and markets to affect the economy.

Given the special role played by banks, safety-net arrangements are generally provided by governments for the public policy purposes of promoting economic growth and financial stability. The nature of these arrangements can take different forms, but typically includes some combination of the following: (1) bank access to a lender of last resort; (2) final, riskless settlement of payment system transactions; and (3) prudential supervision of banks. Over the past two decades, another element of the safety net has been added in many countries – deposit insurance.

The number of countries either establishing or considering establishing a deposit insurance system has expanded rapidly in recent years. By 2005, 78 countries had instituted some form of an explicit deposit guarantee programme – up from only 12 in 1974. The 1990s witnessed an especially rapid spread of deposit insurance among developing countries in Asia and Africa and in the transitional economies of Central and Eastern Europe. Additionally, a significant number of countries have modified their systems to better handle potential disturbances among their financial institutions. The rise in the number of deposit insurance systems and the interest in modifying existing systems have led many to question how to structure a deposit insurance system to ensure its viability.

This interest led the Financial Stability Forum (FSF) to undertake a study of deposit insurance practices and resulted in the publication of guidance on deposit insurance (FSF, 2001).[1] The overarching conclusion of that work was that there is no one set of answers to this question for all deposit insurance systems. Rather, each country must consider what it hopes to achieve by establishing a deposit insurance system and whether the system that is established is internally consistent with its goal(s). Circumstances unique to the country will have a significant bearing on what a deposit insurance system can achieve and how the system should be structured. This chapter discusses these issues and provides a series of questions designed to help evaluate the strengths and weaknesses of deposit insurance systems. Emphasis is placed on whether the design features are internally consistent and compatible with the goals of the deposit insurance system.

3.1 Striking the proper balance – concerns posed by the financial safety net

While a safety net can contribute to stability and thereby promote economic growth, it can also generate perverse effects. By providing protection to market participants, a safety net reduces the costs for banks of pursuing riskier strategies and may, therefore, contribute to excessive risk-taking – the moral hazard problem. Moral hazard can be expensive, as evidenced by the savings-and-loan crisis in the USA during the 1980s, the banking problems of the Scandinavian countries during the same period, and the crises in Korea and other Asian countries in the late 1990s. While moral hazard was not the only factor at work in these crises, most would agree that it contributed to the high cost of resolution in each case.

Another potentially perverse effect associated with safetynet arrangements involves the possibility of a divergence between market and regulatory incentives. For example, to the extent that market evolution outstrips the evolution of the regulatory framework, the potential grows for misalignment of market and regulatory approaches to assessing risk. To a large degree, this concern has motivated the discussions on international capital regulation. If a divergence between market and safety-net arrangements is left unattended, this may distort bank investment and lending decisions, resulting in reduced productivity.

A final consideration in designing a financial safety net is the potential burden created on the industry. Banks and their customers may be adversely affected if the safety net interferes with the ability of market participants to adapt to changing circumstances. Given the potential for moral hazard, misallocation of resources and undue regulatory burden associated with arrangements to maintain stability, effective safety-net design involves striking a proper balance. Many of the trade offs that arise in constructing a safety net involve the setting of boundaries for the respective roles of the market and the government.

3.2 Why deposit insurance?

Banks can and do fail. What benefit does deposit insurance add to the safety-net structure? The purpose of deposit insurance varies, but typically involves promoting financial stability and protecting small savers in the case of a troubled or failing bank. First, deposit insurance can enhance financial stability by removing the incentive for bank runs to develop. Bank runs are costly because they interfere with the financial intermediation performed by banks. Credit availability and economic activity can be adversely affected if loans are liquidated prematurely in order to meet depositors' claims. Even if bank runs are not widespread, they can disrupt the communities in which they occur. To illustrate, borrowers who may otherwise receive loans in a more favourable environment may not be funded as banks are forced to maintain high levels of liquid assets. No amount of prudential supervision can provide protection against runs equivalent to the protection deposit insurance provides.

Second, deposit insurance provides a minimum level of protection to depositors against the consequences associated with the failure of a bank. Compared with the operation of a country's general laws of insolvency, deposit insurance guarantees that depositors will receive at least a minimum amount of their funds, irrespective of the quality of the bank's assets and more quickly than would otherwise be the case.

A well-designed deposit insurance system will provide clear incentives for risk monitoring by certain creditors *ex ante* and *ex post*, and will provide a basis for distinctions in the treatment of bank creditors. A related effect of deposit insurance that may be important in some financial systems is that it levels the playing field to a degree for large and small institutions and for public and private institutions. Under a formalised deposit insurance programme, all institutions have access to depositor protection in the amounts specified by the coverage rules.

Finally, the explicit rules of a deposit insurance system will provide transparency and added certainty regarding the resolution process for failed banks. This can be extremely important for maintaining stability when a banking crisis threatens. The orderly closing of a failed bank – revoking or transferring the bank's charter and satisfying the claims of its depositors and creditors – is one of the hallmarks of a country's financial stability.

It is easy to underestimate the value of deposit insurance when times are good. When times are bad, governments often re-evaluate the need for such arrangements. Typically, deposit insurance systems are adopted in the aftermath of severe banking crises or when industry conditions are deteriorating and unstable. Although the basic objectives are not mutually exclusive, the weighting given to them can have important implications for the design features of a deposit insurance system. A weighting toward the financial stability objective implies a system with relatively broad membership and high coverage limits, while a weighting toward the protection of small savers will focus on retail deposits and relatively lower coverage limits. Additionally, there may be other objectives which the deposit insurer is expected to meet.

3.3 Explicit or implicit? – designing a deposit insurance system

Countries face a choice between explicit or implicit deposit insurance. A few countries have tried to establish clearly and unambiguously that they have neither an explicit nor an implicit system, but, in general, countries that do not have an explicit system are assumed to have an implicit one. Creation of an explicit deposit insurance system is an expression of government support for a nation's banking system that reflects a concern about the potential for costly bank runs and the treatment of bank depositors, and that recognizes the importance of transparency in government actions. In the absence of explicit deposit insurance, bank runs are an ever-present threat owing to the fact that banks typically fund illiquid assets with relatively liquid liabilities, thus they cannot quickly return all their depositors' funds to them at full face value. Without deposit insurance, depositors remain uncertain about what will happen to their funds if a bank fails.

Besides promoting financial stability and bringing certainty to depositors about what to expect in the event of a bank failure, explicit deposit insurance has a number of other important advantages compared to an implicit system. An explicit deposit insurance system is rule based – the rules establish a limit to the government's obligations and temper the deposit insurer's ability to make arbitrary decisions. The system specifies that in the event of a bank failure, depositors' claims will be met within certain parameters by a scheme established for that purpose.

An explicit deposit insurance system, however, poses certain risks, primarily, the problem of moral hazard. Establishing such a system will affect depositors' incentives to monitor a bank's risk taking, thus potentially reducing market discipline within the system. The benefits of an explicit deposit insurance system, however, can outweigh its potential costs if well designed. Moral hazard can be mitigated by creating and promoting appropriate incentives including: good corporate governance and sound risk management of individual banks; effective market discipline by shareholders and other uninsured creditors; and strong prudential supervision, including prompt corrective action triggers. Specific design features within the deposit insurance system can also mitigate moral hazard. These elements involve trade offs and are most effective when they work in concert.

3.4 How to design an explicit deposit insurance system

A well-designed and well-understood deposit insurance system contributes to the stability of a country's financial system (FSF, 2001). A well-designed deposit insurance system, however, must be consistent and credible. That is, its goals and structures must be compatible and it must be capable of performing its assigned tasks without creating excessive risks in the financial system or itself failing. To be well understood, a system must be transparent – having rules that delineate compensation limits, the types of obligations covered, the methods for calculating obligations, funding arrangements, and the time frame in which reimbursement will be carried out.

Internal consistency and incentive compatibility

The first step in establishing or modifying a deposit insurance system is for policymakers to determine the goal(s) of that system. The goal(s) of the system must be determined within context of the conditions within the country. Consideration should be given to the level of economic activity within the country; current monetary and fiscal policies; the state and structure of the banking system; and public attitudes and expectations regarding a deposit insurance system. Importantly, the state of the country's legal system and its prudential regulatory and supervisory systems, the licensing or chartering regime and the country's accounting and reporting regimes must be robust if the deposit insurance system is to be effective.[2] Importantly, the deposit insurer must have in place a mechanism for controlling its risk.[3]

Another area that challenges policymakers involves the organizational structure of a deposit insurance system. To the extent that the structure facilitates the organizational and political separation of the deposit insurance system from other government operations, there may be less potential for incentive conflicts that compromise the effectiveness of the deposit insurance programme. For example, some argue that combining the insurance function with the chartering function in the US Thrift industry created incentive conflicts that proved to be a factor in the demise of the Federal Savings and Loan Insurance Corporation.[4]

In general, experience suggests that times of crisis produce political pressures for decisions that may not be in the long-run interest of a sound and efficient banking system. An independent deposit insurer is in the best position to resist such pressures. However, it must be recognized that establishing a separate deposit insurance organization requires careful attention to the balance of power among the banking authorities, given the probable tendency toward conservatism on the part of the insurer. Different structures will be appropriate for different institutional settings but, in general, experience in the USA suggests caution in creating structures with a high potential for incentive conflicts.

Box 3.1 Internal consistency and incentive compatibility

Are the goals of the deposit insurer clearly stated?

Does a process exist for evaluating the extent to which the deposit insurance system is meeting its goals?

Can the deposit insurance system perform its functions within the context of the current legal system?

- If not, what changes need to be made?

Is there an effective licensing or chartering regime for new banks?

Is there a regulatory system that provides strong prudential supervision of those institutions that receive deposit insurance?

Do accounting and financial reporting systems exist?

- If so, do they provide accurate, reliable and timely information on the condition of insured institutions? For example, do they follow agreed-upon accounting conventions for the following: asset valuation, measurement of credit exposures, loan-loss provisions, non-performing loans, treatment of unrealized losses, off-balance-sheet exposures, capital, bank earnings and profitability.
- If not, what changes should be made to improve their accuracy, reliability and timeliness?

Do mechanisms exist for the exchange of information between the deposit insurer and other financial safety-net participants?

Does the deposit insurer have a mechanism(s) for controlling its risk?

- Are insured institutions supervised by the deposit insurer?
  - If not, does the deposit insurer receive timely and adequate information from the institution's supervisor?
- Does the funding mechanism reflect the risks imposed by insured institutions?
- Do coverage levels encourage market discipline?
- Can the deposit insurer minimise its risk of loss through timely intervention of troubled insured institutions?

Does the structure of the deposit insurance system enable the deposit insurer to perform its tasks in a timely and efficient manner?

Design features of an explicit deposit insurance system

To establish a credible and effective deposit insurance system, there must be internal consistency not only between the goal(s) of the system and the country's infrastructure, but also between the goal(s) and the deposit insurance system's design features. The questions developed in this section are intended to evaluate the strengths and weaknesses of a system's primary design features – membership, coverage, funding, public awareness and reimbursement of depositors.

Membership

Criteria should ensure that the deposit insurer will remain viable on an ongoing basis. In determining which institutions should be members of a deposit insurance system, it is important to only include those institutions that take deposits and are subject to strong prudential supervision and regulation. This is necessary to control the potential risk exposure of the deposit insurer.

Explicit rules should exist and membership should be compulsory to avoid the problem of adverse selection. When membership is not compulsory, it is likely that stronger institutions will shun the system, while comparatively weaker institutions will join. The result can be a system whose funding base is insufficiently diversified and potentially insufficient to perform its functions. For the same reasons, compulsory membership should include state-owned banks that take deposits as well as private institutions. Since state-owned banks presumably enjoy an implicit guarantee of their deposits, making membership compulsory removes a potential source of distortion between institutions, thus helping to level the playing field. Similarly, requiring compulsory membership of foreign-owned subsidiaries and branches that take deposits will help to ensure a sufficiently broad funding base for the deposit insurer in many countries and will help to mitigate any competitive advantage foreign banks may have *vis-à-vis* local banks.

Box 3.2 Membership

Which institutions are covered by deposit insurance?
  Is membership compulsory for those institutions?
Does the deposit insurer determine whether a new bank is eligible for deposit insurance?
  If not, is the deposit insurer consulted?
Are foreign banks included in the deposit insurance system?
  If so, how is this accomplished?
Are non-bank financial institutions that offer deposits or bank-like deposits included in the deposit insurance system?
Are state-owned banks included in the deposit insurance system?
  If so, are the banks that are covered by the explicit deposit insurance system competitively viable?
What percentage of financial assets is in institutions covered by deposit insurance?
What percentage of small savers' assets is in institutions covered by deposit insurance?

Coverage

Striking the right balance is critical in establishing the coverage limit for insured instruments. Coverage must be sufficient to prevent destabilizing bank runs, but not so extensive as to eliminate all effective market discipline on the bank's risk-taking. It is important to define in law or private contract what comprises an insurable deposit. In doing so, the relative importance of different deposit instruments should be considered in relation to the deposit insurer's goals. Many systems exclude deposits held by those who are deemed capable of ascertaining the financial condition of a bank and exerting market discipline. Once the scope is determined, the level of coverage can be set. It is important to consider the relationship between the coverage level and the ability of other mechanisms to control moral hazard.

Deposit insurance systems around the world vary widely in the amounts and types of coverage provided.[5] Some systems protect deposits of all types, several exclude inter-bank deposits, and some protect only household accounts, reflecting the different emphasis on stability versus protection for small, presumably less sophisticated, savers. Coverage is limited to less than $10,000 per account in some countries and is unlimited in others, with most systems falling between these extremes. Several countries provide only coinsurance, such as protection for 80 per cent of the deposit account balance. Coinsurance provides an incentive for all depositors to monitor bank risk-taking by exposing them to small losses, but it thereby also provides an incentive for the depositors to run on banks. Institutional and cultural factors doubtless influence the tolerance for risk exposure among depositors, as well as depositor reactions to adverse financial news and economic shocks. Different schemes are likely to be optimal for different countries, depending upon these factors.

Another significant issue in designing a coverage scheme involves the treatment of 'foreign' deposits, which include deposits payable in foreign currency, deposits in domestic branches of foreign banks, and deposits in foreign branches of domestic banks. Again, there is great variety in the treatment of foreign deposits among deposit insurance systems. Most systems that cover foreign deposits protect themselves from foreign-exchange risk in some fashion, usually by making payment only in domestic currency up to the coverage limit. Unlike the case envisioned for the European Union in its current deposit insurance directive, depositors at branches outside a bank's home country cannot usually depend upon receiving the same protection as the bank's home-country depositors.[6] Nor can such a depositor always depend upon receiving the same protection that is available from his country for domestic deposits.

Box 3.3 Coverage

What financial instruments are covered by deposit insurance?
What is the deposit insurance limit and how is this limit applied?
Is the limit consistent with the deposit insurer's goals?
If the basic objective is to ensure financial stability:
Are deposit insurance limits sufficient to meet this goal?
Are basic transactions accounts covered by deposit insurance?
If the basic objective is to provide a minimum level of protection for the majority of small savers:
Is the scope of deposit insurance relatively narrow?
Can the depositors increase their coverage by setting up multiple accounts in an insured institution?
What percentage of depositors is fully covered by deposit insurance?
Is there a mechanism for adjusting the coverage limits as conditions warrant?
Are foreign currency deposits covered by deposit insurance?
If so, does the deposit insurer have a means for controlling its foreign-exchange risk?
What percentage of financial instruments do these deposits represent?

Funding

Sound funding arrangements are critical to the effectiveness of the deposit insurance system and the maintenance of public confidence. Inadequate funding can lead to delays in resolving failed banks, to significant increases in cost, and to the loss of credibility of the deposit insurance system. There are three aspects to funding deposit insurance: whether to establish a fund – that is, the difference between *ex post* and *ex ante* funding; if a fund is established what the appropriate size of the fund should be; and how to assess banks for the cost of deposit insurance.

Ex post and ex ante funding. *Ex post* funding requires member banks to pay premiums only after a failure. Ex post funding may improve inter-bank monitoring as each member bank has an incentive to avoid the costs associated with a bank failure. Because funding is post failure, however, prompt reimbursement of insured depositors may be problematic. Moreover, banks that fail will not have contributed to the cost of their failure.

Ex ante funding refers to the accumulation of a reserve or fund. It provides an opportunity to smooth the premiums paid by banks over the course of a business cycle. An *ex ante* system is funded by all members, including banks that subsequently fail. *Ex ante* systems have the potential to remove capital from the banking system as premiums paid to the deposit insurer cannot be used for other purposes.

> **Box 3.4 Funding: *ex ante* or *ex post?***
>
> What funding mechanisms are available to the deposit insurer?
> Is the deposit insurance system funded on an *ex ante* or *ex post* basis or some combination thereof?
> If the deposit insurance system is funded on an *ex post* basis:
> - Does the deposit insurer have a mechanism to ensure that banks do not engage in excessive risk-taking?
>   - If not, does another financial safety net participant have this authority and, if so, to what extent is this authority viewed as being credible?
> - Does the deposit insurer have access to funding mechanisms other than waiting to collect a post-failure assessment?
>   - If yes, please describe.
>   - If not, how is financial stability promoted?

Establishing a deposit insurance fund. With a stand-alone fund, monies will be available when needed, provided that the premiums charged have reflected realistic assumptions regarding potential losses and other deposit insurance costs. A benefit of establishing a stand-alone deposit insurance fund financed solely through premiums paid by member institutions is that these institutions may perceive a direct stake in the financial health of the insurance system, providing motivation for them to scrutinise deposit insurance operations and maintain industry self-policing. However, in some circumstances, a stand-alone fund may become a tempting target for either expropriation or misappropriation, and policymakers should take this into account. In the absence of a stand-alone deposit insurance fund, there may be political obstacles to obtaining funds when they are needed for deposit insurance purposes.

If a separate deposit insurance fund is created, it is important to question whether there is an appropriate target ratio of the fund balance to total insured deposits. The answer to this question is likely to vary over time, depending upon the strength of the banking industry and condition of the economy. Moreover, a potential function of a deposit insurance system is to spread risk over time as well as across insured parties. Fund 'adequacy' ultimately depends, therefore, upon the goals established for a deposit insurance system.

If maintaining solvency in the face of extreme outcomes were the only consideration, then the choice of a reserve ratio would, conceptually, be reduced to identifying the process that generates insurance losses and selecting the level of protection desired from an appropriate statistical loss distribution. In practice, this task is difficult, involving judgments on the basis of imperfect information about potential losses. The issue is further complicated by considering other relevant factors, such as economic costs associated with the premium volatility that may be required to maintain a given reserve ratio continuously. These considerations raise the possibility that flexibility in choosing a target reserve ratio, as well as determining the appropriate steps to achieve it, may provide better balance among the relevant objectives.

Box 3.5 Funding: deposit insurance fund

For deposit insurance systems funded on an *ex ante* basis:
- Is the size of the fund adequate to handle potential bank losses and enable the deposit insurer to meet its goals? How is this determined?
    - If not: Is there a plan in place for building and maintaining the fund?
        - If yes, describe that plan.
    - What alternative funding arrangements exist in the interim?
- Once the fund is deemed adequate, do insured institutions continue to pay an assessment?
    - If so, is there a mechanism to return or rebate a portion of the fund to its members?
- What systems are in place to ensure that the deposit insurance fund is well-managed?
    - Do sound investment policies and procedures exist?
        - If yes, describe.
        - If not, how is the fund protected?
    - Do sound internal controls and disclosure and reporting systems exist?
        - If yes, describe.
    - Who has disbursement authority over the fund?

Does the deposit insurer have access to supplemental funding mechanisms?
- If not, how does the deposit insurer promote financial stability?

Choosing an assessment system. The deposit insurance system may build and maintain its fund by adopting a flat-rate premium system or one that has variable rates that are either risk-based or differentiated on the basis of individual bank risk profiles.[7] A simple and relatively easy-to-implement system for assessing deposit insurance premiums is to assess all insured institutions at the same rate for their deposit insurance coverage. Such a pricing system is aimed at maintaining adequate financial capacity for the insurer, and leaves the task of controlling moral hazard to the supervisory process and the market. A flat-rate system was employed successfully in the USA for almost 60 years.

Under a flat-rate system, participation of institutions in the deposit insurance programme may need to be compulsory in order to avoid attracting only the riskier entities – the 'adverse selection' problem. A risk-based premium system addresses adverse selection, but to the extent that risk-based premiums may not fully reflect all the risks posed by insured institutions, compulsory membership still may be warranted.

A risk-based premium system may also provide additional control over moral hazard. At a minimum, such a system can create stronger incentives for institutions to avoid actions that may result in a weakened condition. This is true of systems that charge higher premiums based primarily upon deteriorating financial performance. Although such systems can exacerbate banking problems if not designed with care, they function similarly to supervisory sanctions and may be regarded as an additional tool for traditional bank supervision.

Ideally, however, risk-based pricing of deposit insurance would influence bank management decision-making well ahead of supervisory sanctions, providing incentives *ex ante* for institutions to avoid undue risk-taking. To be most effective, such a pricing system must be based upon the current practices of institutions, current market signals regarding changes in the risk profiles of institutions, or other forward-looking factors, as opposed to observed changes in financial condition. To the extent that market information is incorporated, this may limit any divergence between market and regulatory incentives, thereby reducing the distortions associated with deposit insurance. Moreover, attention to market information may reveal inefficiencies or obsolescence in traditional approaches to risk assessment by regulators, and may suggest reforms that would reduce regulatory burden.

Risk-based pricing systems have been adopted by many countries, and some systems – including those in Argentina, Canada and the USA – explicitly attempt to incorporate forward-looking components. However, these systems have not yet been tested through an entire banking cycle and must be considered as still in the experimental stages.

The primary advantage of a flat-rate system is the ease with which assessments can be calculated and administered. The disadvantage is that low-risk banks effectively pay for part of the deposit insurance benefit received by high-risk banks. The disadvantages of a risk-based premium system are that it is difficult to assess risk and such systems require more resources and greater information sharing.

A final consideration with respect to deposit insurance pricing involves the choice of an assessment base. Most deposit insurance systems base assessments on insured deposits, which many regard as most equitable, but estimating the insured component of total deposits may be costly and impractical under some coverage schemes. Moreover, if a depositor preference scheme is in place that applies to all depositors regardless of insurance status, or resolution practices are such that protection often is extended beyond coverage limits, it could be argued that a broader base is more equitable.

Box 3.6 Funding: assessment system

Does the deposit insurance system use a flat-rate premium system?
- If yes, does the deposit insurer have a mechanism in place to control bank risk-taking or impose penalties on banks that take excessive risk?

Does the deposit insurance system use a risk-based or differential premium system?
- If yes, how is bank risk determined?
- Are the rating criteria transparent?

Does the deposit insurer have access to reliable and timely data?

Once a fund reaches its targeted level, do premiums continue to be collected?
- If not, what tools are in place for the deposit insurer to control bank risk?

Is the risk rating of individual banks available to the public?
- If yes, is this a means to impose market discipline?
- Is this compatible with the deposit insurer's goals?

Do measures exist to mitigate the destabilizing effects of imposing potentially high premiums on the banking system?

Communication issues

The deposit insurer must deal with communication issues on at least two levels. First, the public must be made aware of the existence and parameters of the deposit insurance system in order for the deposit insurer to be effective in meeting its goals. Second, the deposit insurer must have access to timely information about the condition of the banking industry and about the likelihood of bank failures in order to be prepared to step in, in the event of a failure.

Public awareness. In order for a deposit insurance system to be effective, it is essential that the public be informed about its benefits and limitations. Experience has shown that the characteristics of a deposit insurance system need to be publicized regularly so that its credibility can be maintained and strengthened.

When well designed, a public awareness programme should achieve several goals, including the dissemination of relevant information about the deposit insurance system.[8] Such information should contribute to building and maintaining confidence in the banking sector. For example, in the event of a bank failure, such a programme can help to disseminate vital information, such as guidance regarding the filing of claims.

In order to reach the public, it is important to focus on bank employees as they are important conduits for providing information about deposit insurance. Ways to reach the public include providing education modules for schools, informational brochures for distribution by member institutions, television ad campaigns, and interactive web-based programmes.[9] In countries where public confidence in the banking system is high and awareness of an existing deposit insurance system is low, special communication strategies need to be deployed to ensure that the stated goals are achieved while public confidence is maintained.

Box 3.7 Public awareness

Does the public understand which financial instruments and what financial institutions are covered by deposit insurance?

If yes, is the deposit insurer the source of this information?

If no, how does the deposit insurer ensure that depositors receive this information and how is the quality of the information monitored?

Is there a standard method for designating which institutions have deposit insurance?

Are depositors aware that they may suffer losses if their deposits exceed the coverage limit or if they are subject to coinsurance when a bank fails?

If foreign-currency deposits are covered, are depositors aware of how these deposits will be paid in the event of a bank failure?

Are depositors aware of when they will receive their funds in the event of a bank failure?

Does the deposit insurer have a system for informing the public of how, when and where they may file claims and receive reimbursement after a bank failure?

Interrelationships

A need for close coordination exists in any institutional setting and information sharing among safety-net participants is essential.[10] When supervision and the deposit insurance function are assigned to different organizations, issues related to information sharing, allocation of powers and responsibilities, and coordination of actions are more complex and need to be addressed clearly and explicitly. When a single organization performs both the supervision and deposit insurance functions the smooth resolution of bank failures is dependent on the existence of clearly defined roles and responsibilities of the respective players within the organization.

Box 3.8 Interrelationships

Is there a formal information-sharing mechanism in place to ensure that the deposit insurer has timely access to the information it needs?
- If the functions are not performed in the same organization, are there clear and explicit information-sharing arrangements in place?
  - If not, does the deposit insurer have a plan for addressing this information gap?
- If the deposit insurance and bank supervisory functions are performed in the same organization, are there clearly defined roles and responsibilities?

Can the deposit insurer collect information directly from the banks it insures?

Reimbursement of depositors

When an insured institution fails, the deposit insurer must provide the public with ready access to insured funds so that stability and confidence in the banking system is maintained. A basic function of all deposit insurance systems is to reimburse depositors promptly for the losses they otherwise would suffer in the event of a member financial institution's closure. The payment of insured depositors in a deposit reimbursement is generally a time-consuming, labour-intensive, methodical process. In developing its administrative practices and procedures a deposit insurer should strive to set operational priorities, focus on depositors' expectations, and emphasize structure over individual functions.

The reimbursement process should be designed to meet the public-policy objectives of the deposit insurance system. Each part of the reimbursement process must work together in a seamless fashion to ensure an efficient reimbursement process. Determining the timing of reimbursement, who should be reimbursed and ensuring that deposit insurance limits are respected are the most crucial steps in the reimbursement process.

A number of conditions, including those involving legal and financial issues and administrative practices, must be in place for a deposit insurer to accomplish its reimbursement function efficiently – that is, to reduce the recoveryrate and time risks for depositors with insured deposits.

Depositors need to know and understand coverage limits, when and under what conditions the deposit insurer will start the reimbursement process, and the deposit insurer needs adequate funding to fulfill its obligations.

Box 3.9 Depositor reimbursement

Is there a clearly stated time frame for accomplishing the reimbursement process?

At what point is the deposit insurer made aware of the possibility that a bank may fail?

- Whose responsibility is it to inform the deposit insurer of a potential bank failure?
- Does the deposit insurer have adequate time to prepare for the failure of a bank once it becomes aware of the possibility?

Is the deposit insurer given access to the necessary data – including deposit account records – when the insurer becomes aware of the possibility of a bank failure?

Is reimbursement of depositors dependent on the liquidation of a failed bank's assets?

- If no, does the deposit insurer have access to adequate funding to meet its obligations under the established time frames?

Does the deposit insurer have consistent administrative practices and procedures which are readily accessible and can be followed by subcontractors, as well as in-house staff?

- If yes, are these practices and procedures setout in a manual that is periodically reviewed and updated?

Does the deposit insurer have adequate computer capabilities to carry out a reimbursement accurately and in a timely manner?

- Can depositors with multiple accounts at a failed institution be identified and their accounts combined for deposit insurance purposes?

Does the deposit insurer have adequate personnel to conduct the reimbursement in a timely manner?

- If no, can the deposit insurer outsource the reimbursement function?

Who makes the decision whether deposits will be transferred to another institution or paid directly to the depositors?

Does the deposit insurer have a process for locating depositors whose accounts have not been satisfactorily discharged?

Is the reimbursement process audited by an independent authority?

Does the deposit insurer play a role in settling the claims of uninsured depositors and creditors?

Closing failing institutions

The orderly takeover or closure of a problem bank typically will involve multiple parties, for instance the banking authority, the central bank, and the deposit insurer (if one exists). The deposit insurer thus must work in tandem with other members of the financial safety net to perform its functions. Rarely will the deposit insurer have authority to close a bank; rather it will only become involved once a bank has closed. In ideal circumstances, there will be transparency in the closure regime and the deposit insurer will be made aware of an impending closure and will become involved before the bank is actually closed. Timely information sharing between the various interested parties is important to help facilitate the failed-bank resolution. The following questions concern the closure process.

Box 3.10 Bank closure process

Once a problem bank has been identified, does a process exist for handling that bank?

Can open-bank assistance be provided? If so, under what circumstances and how is this done?

Can the banking authorities revoke the bank's charter, take over the bank, or transfer the bank's charter to another institution?

- If yes, describe the process.
- If no, is there another legal process in place to close or takeover an insolvent bank? If another legal process exists, please describe that process.

In the process of revoking the bank's charter, taking over the bank, or transferring the bank's charter can (1) the senior managers be removed and/or (2) stockholder positions be eliminated?

- If yes, describe the process.
- If no, and if the depositors and/or creditors are covered by deposit insurance or a government guarantee, how does the government protect its position while senior managers and stockholders remain in place?
- If there is no deposit insurance or government guarantee what safeguards protect the depositors and creditors of the bank?

If there are multiple parties involved in a bank resolution, is there a process in place to ensure timely information sharing?

- If yes, describe the process, including the timing of the information sharing.
- If no, describe any information-sharing plan in development.

Failure resolution

The timely and quick resolution of failed institutions reinforces systemic stability, promotes public confidence in the banking system, and restores liquidity to the economy.[11] The resolution of a failed bank involves disposing of the failed bank's assets and satisfying the claims of depositors and other creditors of the bank. To minimize disruptions associated with bank failures, every attempt should be made to dispose of the bank's assets quickly and cost effectively.

Failure resolution is generally directed by a safety-net participant or a bankruptcy court. Basic resolution options include liquidation of the bank's assets and reimbursement of creditors' claims, or purchase-and-assumption transactions (sale of the bank). Selecting the most suitable resolution option for a particular failure situation requires that several factors be considered. These include: maintaining stability – both in the failed bank's local community and the economy generally; minimizing the volume of assets managed by, or on behalf of, the government; and ensuring that market discipline is not materially weakened.

The bankruptcy/insolvency and other relevant laws of a country may influence the choice of resolution method. Since these laws vary considerably among countries, the use of particular resolution methods may be limited. However, because of the special significance of banks and bank failures, it is important that these laws facilitate an orderly and timely exit of troubled banks.

To determine the final cost of a bank's failure and to be able to evaluate the efficiency and effectiveness of the resolution, there should be policies and procedures in place to complete the process and account for the costs of the failure. This enhances transparency and accountability. Different types of resolutions could yield different end points. For example, a failed bank may be purchased by another bank along with a one-time government payment to the acquiring bank. If there is no outstanding litigation and the government has no further liability, then the resolution would be complete and the total cost of the failure could be calculated in short order.

It should be noted that a lack of funding for resolution initiatives can cause severe problems and impose significant costs to the resolution authority, the government, and ultimately, the taxpayer. Without adequate funding, the resolution authority may select resolution techniques that provide needed liquidity, but ultimately do more harm to the banking system. In addition, if funding is inadequate, delays in resolution activity will likely occur. This creates two fundamental problems, both of which result in higher overall resolution costs. If a resolution authority must delay its resolution of an institution, the asset quality and capital levels of the institution are likely to continue to deteriorate. Second, the cost of funds to the institution is likely to rise. Thus, the longer the resolution is delayed, the more expensive it will be.

In addition, it is important to have an accounting system in place to accurately record the expenses and income from disposing of the failed bank and reimbursing bank creditors. There should also be a legal or administrative process to officially close out the resolution, to extinguish any remaining liability and to create legal finality for the process.

Box 3.11 Failure resolution

What is the process for recovering value from failed bank? Please describe.

Is there a mandate to resolve the failure in the least costly manner?
  If yes, describe.

Who runs the failure-resolution process?

Is the deposit insurer involved in the failure-resolution process?
  If yes, describe the deposit insurer's role(s) and responsibilities.

Are there appropriate accounting procedures in place to be able to accurately determine the final cost of a bank failure?
  If yes, briefly describe the procedures and how they would be implemented.
  If no, are plans being developed? If so, describe.

Is there a point when the creditors' claims on the bank are deemed to be finally settled and the books of the failed institution are closed?

Is there a legal or administrative process to complete or close-out a failed bank resolution?
  If yes, briefly describe the process.
  If no, are there plans to develop a process or request legal authority? If so, describe.

3.5 Concluding remarks

As an integral part of the safety net, deposit insurance systems can help to maintain financial stability, thereby enabling banks to intermediate effectively and support economic growth. As with other components of the safety net, however, deposit insurance can create perverse effects. The potential for problems created by moral hazard, misallocation of resources, and excessive regulatory burden point to the need for an appropriate balance in designing deposit insurance systems. As the FSF Guidance noted, the use of a continuous-improvement process can aid deposit insurers in setting and maintaining that balance.[12] This chapter has reviewed the major features of deposit insurance system design to consider the types of trade-offs that must be confronted in striking a proper balance. The chapter also emphasizes the importance of designing a system that is compatible with the goals established for the deposit insurer – that is, a system that is internally consistent.

There does not appear to be a 'one-size-fits-all' approach for any of the important elements in the deposit insurance system. Institutional, cultural and experiential differences among countries will dictate deposit insurance design. It is apparent, however, that as more deposit insurance systems are established, the harmonization of the different approaches takes on greater importance. Developing guidance for evaluating the effectiveness of deposit insurance programmes will be a major step forward. These efforts should help both existing and new deposit insurers by providing them with internationally accepted benchmarks necessary to build or preserve an effective deposit insurance system.

Notes

1 In 2001, the Financial Stability Forum's Working Group on Deposit Insurance issued its final report, *Guidance for Developing Effective Deposit Insurance Systems* (FSF Guidance), which is intended for the those countries considering the adoption or reform of an explicit, limited-coverage deposit insurance system. The FSF Guidance can be found at www.fsforum.org/publications/publication_19_1.html. For each of the subjects identified in the report there was a corresponding Discussion Paper prepared by the FSF Working Group on Deposit Insurance. These papers can be found at www.fdic.gov/deposit/deposits/international/guidance/guidance/index.html.

2 See FSF (2001) and FSF Working Group on Deposit Insurance (2001), Discussion Paper entitled, *Situational Analysis*.

3 Pay box deposit insurers may have very limited scope to control risks given the nature of their mandates.

4 Prior to the enactment of the Financial Institutions Reform, Recovery, and Enforcement Act of 1989 (FIRREA), the US thrift industry had been regulated at the federal level by the Federal Home Loan Bank System (FHLBS), which chartered federal savings institutions and supervised and insured all thrift institutions. By 1989, the savings-and-loan crisis had left the FHLBS deposit insurer, the Federal Savings and Loan Insurance Corporation (FSLIC) insolvent. As part of the resolution of the savings-and-loan crisis, FIRREA created a new chartering and supervisory agency, the Office of Thrift Supervision (OTS), and a new deposit insurance fund, the Savings Association Insurance Fund (SAIF). Responsibility for insuring thrift deposits and managing the SAIF was shifted to the FDIC. See, FDIC (1997) for a summary of these events.

5 See International Deposit Insurance Survey maintained by the International Association of Deposit Insurers located at: www.iadi.org.

6 The EU Directive on deposit-guarantee schemes provides that home country coverage rules apply wherever a bank operates. See EU (1994).

7 For further discussion of this subject see IADI (2005a).

8 See FSF Working Group on Deposit Insurance (2001), Discussion Paper entitled, *Public Awareness*.

9 For example, the FDIC's web-based Electronic Deposit Insurance Estimator (EDIE) allows the public to calculate the insurance coverage for their accounts at an FDIC-insured institution.

10 For further discussion on this subject see, IADI (2006).
11 For further discussion on this subject, see IADI (2005b).
12 FSF (2001), p.17.

References

European Parliament and the Council of the European Union (1994), Directive 94/19/EC on Deposit-Guarantee Schemes.

Federal Deposit Insurance Corporation (1997) *History of the Eighties: Lessons for the Future. Volume 1, An Examination of the Banking Crises of the 1980s and Early 1990s*, Washington, DC: FDIC.

Financial Stability Forum (FSF) (2001) *Guidance for Developing Effective Deposit Insurance Systems*, Basel: Bank for International Settlements.

FSF Working Group on Deposit Insurance (2001) Discussion Papers, www.fdic.gov/deposit/deposits/international/guidance/guidance/index.html#discussion.

Hoelscher, D.S., Taylor, M. and Klueh, U. (2005) The Design and Implementation of Deposit Insurance Systems. Washington, D.C.: IMF, (Unpublished).

International Association of Deposit Insurers (IADI) (2005a) *General Guidance for Developing Differential Premium Systems*, Basel: IADI.

IADI (2005b) *General Guidance for Resolution of Bank Failures*, Basel: IADI.

IADI (2006) *General Guidance to Promote Effective Interrelationships Among Safety Net Participants*, Basel: IADI.

4

Organizational Design and Positioning of the Deposit Insurance Function in the Financial System Safety Net

Lawrence Kryzanowski

4.1 Introduction

Effective prudential regulation of a country's financial system attempts to balance the protection of the interests of depositors and other creditors with the minimization of the risk to the financial system and the promotion of competition and efficiency. The three functions of liquidity lending, deposit insurance and supervision can reside in one or more entities. For example, these three functions reside in separate entities in Canada (specifically, the Bank of Canada, CDIC and the Office of the Superintendent of Financial Institutions, respectively).

Given the rapid changes in the financial services sector in terms of scale and scope of financial institutions and in global reach and competition, many national governments are continually re-assessing what regulatory changes, if any, are needed to increase regulatory effectiveness and/or decrease regulatory burden/overlap while maintaining the safety, soundness and competitiveness of their financial systems.[1] One such re-occurring theme in these countries is the choice of where to position the function of minimizing deposit insurance (henceforth DI) losses arising from institutional failures. For example, in the Canadian context, an ongoing debate is whether the current organizational design that consists of an entity (CDIC) performing the DI function with a loss minimization (henceforth LM) mandate is superior to having a supervisor (OSFI) perform this function along with its supervisory functions.

Thus, the primary objective of this chapter is to compare the two primary organizational designs for the provision of DI. To this end, we assess how well an organizational design that consists of a deposit insurer independent from the supervisor/regulator with a mandate to minimize its exposure to loss works by examining the Canadian situation. The assessment is benchmarked against the other primary organizational design for the provision of DI: namely, having the LM function for the insurer performed by a supervisor/regulator or monetary authority.

The methodology consists of a critical assessment of the historical development and current status of thought on the role of LM as an objective for a financial system safety net, on whether or not such a LM mandate should be housed within a supervisory entity or within the deposit insurer, and on whether or not an independent deposit insurer is appropriate given current and future challenges to the financial system safety net. Two assessment criteria given primary importance herein are effectiveness in terms of loss experience and efficiency in terms of regulatory burden/overlap.[2]

Three major conclusions are drawn in the chapter. First, a LM mandate appears to be the most effective mechanism to control the moral hazard problem associated with the deposit insurer. Second, the greatest net benefits are achieved, on balance, when the LM mandate is positioned within a proactive and independent deposit insurer. Third, the current organizational design in Canada that consists of a Crown corporation performing the DI function with a LM mandate is superior to the risks associated with a switch to the supervisor (OSFI) performing this function along with its supervisory functions.

The remainder of the chapter is organized as follows. Some of the global challenges that are likely to affect any decision on where to position the DI function in a country's financial system safety net and on the choice of its organizational design are discussed in section 4.2. The role of DI and the LM objective in a country's financial system safety net are reviewed in section 4.3. The arguments for and against each of the two organizational designs for the positioning of the DI function and the LM mandate within a country's financial system safety net are presented and critiqued in section 4.4. To focus the discussion better, the arguments are presented in the context of the Canadian financial system safety net. Some of the powers, instruments and mechanisms required by an independent insurer are discussed in section 4.5. Section 4.6 concludes the chapter.

4.2 Global challenges[3]

Globalization, consolidation, financial engineering and movement towards universal banks

Globalization of capital markets and financial industry consolidation through cross-border and cross-pillar mergers are resulting in a smaller number of banks but a growing number of 'mega' banks. In turn, the capacity of a DI system to fund the failure of these large, complex banks is being reduced. Furthermore, a growing number of these 'mega' banks or conglomerates most likely will qualify for protection as 'too big to fail' under DI or lender of last resort (LOLR) facilities. While the primary purpose of the DI function is to minimize losses to depositors post bank closure, the primary purpose of the lender of last resort (LOLR) function is to prevent the collapse of institutions that are experiencing financial difficulty (generally near collapse). Thus, the LOLR function indirectly attempts to minimize losses to depositors by attempting to prevent bank closure.

While the movement towards universal banks in the absence of firewalls increases the reusability of information within a bank, it also increases the set of risky investments open to banks (Bhattacharya *et al.*, 1998). In turn, this creates larger banks that can exaggerate insurance exposure under the 'too big to fail' doctrine and creates further political frictions against the application of a tough closure policy. Similarly, rapid developments in technology and the increased use of financial engineering to design new and exotic financial products has challenged the ability of regulators and supervisors to monitor the financial system (Furfine, 2001).

Basel II

Basel II represents a significant shift in the supervisory philosophy of large, complex institutions away from the use of pre-set minimum numerical capital standards established by the regulators. The new Accord envisions banks using their own internal risk estimates as inputs to regulator-supplied formulas with the supervisors providing oversight and evaluation of the bank's ability to measure risk.

There are a number of concerns identified in the implementation of a Basel II regime. The first is that processes be identified that ensure that the internal risk estimates of banks be estimated soundly and conservatively. An exclusive reliance on quantitative methods and models will ignore the important role of qualitative elements. Given that judgment is required to assess these qualitative elements, this is better accomplished within a financial system safety net that has a risk-assessing regulatory entity and a deposit insurer with the mandate and capability to minimize its exposure to possible losses in a failure.

The second concern is that a greater degree of complexity and associated burden is unavoidable as banks seek to have capital tailored to their individual risk profiles. This places greater burdens on and increases the judgmental risks faced by regulators. Once again this is better accomplished within a financial system safety net that has a risk-assessing regulatory entity and a deposit insurer with a responsibility for loss minimization. As is the case for the previous concern, the conclusion drawn for this concern is based on a weighing of the arguments and evidence that is presented in section 4.4 of the chapter on whether the insurer should be a paybox or a proactive and independent entity.

The third concern is the need for enhanced coordination in the monitoring and controlling of procylicality, which is the tendency of the capital framework to possibly exaggerate phases of the economic cycle by requiring less regulatory capital in 'good times' and more regulatory capital in 'bad times'. While the maintenance of procylicality is consistent with a LM objective, it is less consistent with other financial system objectives, such as the growth and competitiveness of financial institutions. Thus, by positioning the LM mandate in a pro-active deposit insurer, the point-in-time and through-the-cycle measures of the risk of individual financial institutions will be of primary concern to different participants in the financial system safety net.

Systematic impacts of operational risk

Operational risk is defined as the risk from breakdowns in technology, systems or employee performance (including fraud), and spans a wide range of significant risk exposures to banks. Major operational losses caused by external or internal fraud or breakdowns in internal controls are a common cause of recent bank failures.[4] While operational risk is commonly perceived as being primarily firm-specific, the market-related or systematic component of its impact is growing in importance. Specifically, as the correlations between financial institutions located in different countries increase, operational disruptions are likely to lead to enhanced market volatility and contagion across markets and countries.

Reliance on an overly Bayesian approach to decision making in a supposedly low failure rate regime

A possible and most likely danger is that any decision on whether an insurer should be active or a paybox will be overly Bayesian (that is due to incorrectly inferring the probability and severity of bank failure from currently or most recently observed failures). Specifically, the concern is that government decision makers will conclude that there would be little cost to initiate an insurer as a paybox or to reconstitute an active insurer as a paybox because the expected risks and costs of future failures are low if few failures have occurred in the most recent past and the cost per dollar of such failures has been low.[5] As is the case for most decision makers, government decision makers must guard against the behaviour of agents to either be overly pessimistic or overly optimistic over time.[6] Berger, Kyle and Scalise (2001) provide modest support in favour of a yes answer to all three questions posed in the title to their edited book contribution, 'Did U.S. Bank Supervisors Get Tougher During the Credit Crunch? Did They Get Easier During the Banking Boom? Did It Matter to Bank Lending?'

In addition, behavioural financial economists would argue that after a period of prolonged bank prosperity, bank management will have no basis to calculate the probabilities of a major shock, and may even set the probability as being zero. In turn, this may lead to 'disaster myopia' where banks take greater risks than would be warranted based on objective assessments (Guttentag and Herring, 1986, pp. 2–4). However, banking panics and their consequences have become more severe. For instance, the banking system bailouts in Argentina and Chile required public investments of approximately 55 per cent and 42 per cent of GDP (Caprio and Klingebiel, 1997; Economist, 1999).

4.3 Role of DI and the LM objective in a financial system safety net

The popular perception is that individual banks are more susceptible to failure than other firms and the banking industry is more susceptible to contagion than other industries.[7] Perceptions of the adverse consequences of greater susceptibility to failure at the deposit-taking institution (hereafter referred to as 'banks') level are intensified by the fear that banks invest in opaque assets whose market values are highly volatile, and are often realizable in markets with considerable trading and informational frictions. Similarly, the greater possibility of contagion at the banking industry level heightens the fears of unnecessarily large fire-sale losses caused by 'irrational' runs by depositors on banks (Kaufman, 1996).

Banking theories suggest that banks should be allowed to fund themselves with nontraded demand deposit contracts, and that these contracts should be insured if the banking-related liquidity needs of depositors are sufficiently high (Bhattacharya *et al.*, 1998). Furthermore, deposit insurance can reduce the depth and persistence of severe business downturns by maintaining depositors' access to funds so that they can be reinvested quickly and efficiently in the financial sector (Mason, Anari and Kolari, 2000). If DI provides small depositors with partial access to their funds in the rare event of a bank failure, then this may alleviate political pressures for a fuller government bail out and a more hasty resolution of the bank failure. Both are typically inconsistent with the orderly management of a bank failure at minimum cost.[8]

However, government DI weakens market discipline by reducing the incentives for information acquisition and control by depositors and for banks to bond their ability to repay their depositors.[9] DI may reduce the monitoring efforts of large depositors, who are the most likely and most able to undertake such monitoring, if they believe coverage will be extended to them in times of crisis. This also applies to financial systems without a deposit insurer where system participants believe that a 100 per cent implicit guarantee exists in the case of bank failure. DI may invite banks to seek excessive portfolio risk while keeping lower than optimal liquid reserves. In other words, a bank can shift risk onto its deposit insurer by either increasing its leverage or by increasing the variability of its return on assets.[10] To avoid such risk shifting, a deposit insurer and the regulator must monitor changes in leverage and variability, and take appropriate corresponding actions. Mechanisms to cope with these moral hazards include cash-asset reserve requirements, risk-sensitive capital requirements and DI premia, bank closure policy and industry-based funding.[11]

In the absence of a LM strategy, politicians and regulators tend to create defective incentives for fully evaluating, controlling and disclosing the loss exposure to the public purse (Kane, 1989; Barth, 1991; White, 1991). In turn, these defective incentives expand loss exposures. According to Kane (2003), the lack of timely accountability for the opportunity losses that the tolerance of insolvencies imposes on taxpayers is missing from DI arrangements in most countries. One crucial element in timely accountability is the existence of LM as an objective.

Several studies have compared the opportunity-cost value of DI across countries. Laeven (2002) finds that this value is higher in countries with explicit insurance but that this value disappears in countries with high-quality and well-enforced legal systems. Demirgüç-Kunt and Detragiache (2002) find that DI increases the probability of banking crises in countries with weak institutional environments, and that the probability of having a banking crisis increases with the coverage limit and in having a funded scheme. Hovakimian, Kane and Laeven (2003) find significant risk shifting on average for 56 countries, and that country-specific differences are explained by differences in DI design features and in environmental measures of political repression, economic freedom and government corruption. Specifically, the risk shifting associated with DI is tempered by loss-control features such as risk-sensitive DI premiums, coverage limits and coinsurance, and provides greater risk-shifting opportunities in environments characterized by low political and economic freedom and high corruption.[12] Hovakimian *et al.* also find that explicit DI displaces more private policing than authorities manage to supply, and that leverage and risk-shifting control systems appear particularly strong in Australia and North America. While Hovakimian *et al.* emphasize that Australia (unlike the USA and Canada) has no explicit deposit insurance, the Australian Government is currently planning to introduce such a scheme. Cull *et al.* (2005) find that generous government-funded DI is likely to have a negative impact on the long-run financial development and growth of a country, except for those countries with a well-established rule of law and having supervisors with sufficient discretion and independence from legal reprisals.

Despite the mixed views in the academic literature on the benefits of explicit DI protection, 49 and 32 of the 72 countries for which explicit DI is a crucial component of their safety net have introduced such protection during the past two (1980s and 1990s) and one decade (1990s), respectively (Garcia, 2000). According to Credit Union World (2004), 20 of these systems have been established since 1995, and the introduction of a DI scheme is now firmly on the governmental agendas in both Australia and New Zealand,[13] the only two OECD countries currently without such systems.

4.4 Positioning the DI function and LM mandate in the financial system safety net: the Canadian case

Financial system safety nets are designed to reflect a country's informational, ethical, legal, historical, political and economic environments. As these environments change with time, prudential regulation of the financial system evolves in order to better align the protection of the interests of depositors and other creditors with minimization of the risk to the financial system and the promotion of competition and efficiency.[14] The changes appear to be successful on balance in Canada, since Canada has earned a reputation of having a safe and sound financial system that protects its depositors in a cost-effective manner.

Historical role of the Canadian depositor insurer

The Canada Insurance Corporation or CDIC began in 1967 as a passive or reactive 'paybox' with limited intervention powers. If a member failed and was closed, CDIC simply paid the insured deposits as required. Based on its experience with a number of failures in the 1980s (particularly, the collapse of the Northland Bank and of the Canadian Commercial Bank in 1985) CDIC was given an explicit mandate in 1987 to minimize losses. Subsequent studies acknowledged that the deposit insurer should be given an explicit mandate to minimize losses since the deposit insurer bears direct financial exposure to failures and a potentially costly failure resolution process, is typically the largest creditor in such failures, and may have a lender of last resort role (as is the case for CDIC). As a result, CDIC was given an explicit mandate to minimize losses in 1987. Since adopting this mandate, the cost of providing deposit insurance (DI) has dropped materially and has been reflected in a substantial drop in DI premiums charged annually to members.

Average DI system losses in Canada have dropped from 52 cents per dollar over the period 1967–1987 to 17 cents per dollar for the period after 1987. While not all of this drop can be attributed to the change in CDIC's mandate, it seems reasonable to attribute some material portion of this drop to this change.

This inference is further supported by the findings reported by Kryzanowski and Noiseux (2003) in their examination of bank losses for 29 Canadian chartered bank failures from 1867 through to 1991 in total and differentiated by type of stakeholder for four subperiods that differ in their safety net regimes for note holders, depositors and shareholders. The subperiod 1867–1881 has no protection for note holders or depositors, and poor enforcement of double liability assessments. The subperiod 1883–1899 has note holder protection, no depositor protection, and better enforcement of double liability assessments. The subperiod 1905–1923 has note holder protection, implicit depositor protection provided by the government and the banking industry and coordinated by the CBA, and more stringent enforcement of double liability assessments. The subperiod 1985–1991 has note holder protection, explicit depositor protection by an independent paybox insurer up to 1987 and a proactive insurer thereafter, and no shareholder double liability. The last subperiod only includes one failure (the small regional, Bank of Credit and Commerce, in 1991) after the CDIC was given a mandate to minimize losses.

The findings of Kryzanowski and Noiseux suggest that government and financially troubled banks prolong explicit bank failure in a world with (implicit or explicit) DI provided by a paybox insurer so as to minimize the relative loss to the banking industry of explicit bank failure. Their findings also suggest that the relative loss at a failed bank is higher in a world with paybox deposit insurance and double liability as financially troubled banks prolong the pre-closure period by attempting to recapitalize by continuing their operations. Their findings also suggest that forbearance heightened the losses per dollar of total assets of the failed bank but lessened the losses per dollar of banking industry assets when bank failure was carefully monitored and controlled by the government and the CBA.[15]

Early intervention (including closure) policy mandate of OSFI

In 1996, the federal government introduced an early intervention policy as a means of preserving the safety and soundness of the financial services sector. OSFI received a legislated mandate to take prompt actions to ensure that the problems of deteriorating institutions are resolved, and to close troubled institutions before they become insolvent. The thrust of such early intervention (including closure) policies is to prevent undue losses to depositors by reducing the discretion of the entity (entities) in charge of supervising and closing financial institutions.

In theory, an early closure policy can potentially reduce the monitoring costs and lower the costs of managing financial crises compared to the market discipline of bank runs. Furthermore, by reducing the moral hazard problems associated with bank supervision, an early intervention (especially closure) policy could contribute to the satisfaction of a DI loss minimization (LM) objective. In the absence of large-scale malfeasance or an unusual (large) break in market values, depositors or the insurer suffer no losses if the critical cutoff value for the closure metric (such as the capital-to-asset ratio) is set sufficiently high. Thus, it has been argued that there no longer is a need for a LM objective to be part of the mandate of an insurer such as CDIC.

Bank charter values and regulatory closure policy interact. Higher charter values due to expected rents (for example, from funding-related reputational benefits) can deter risk taking if regulators implement an appropriate closure policy, and an appropriate closure policy can deter moral hazard if banks have sufficiently high charter value (Bhattacharya *et al.*, 1998, p. 760). Unfortunately, means for generating such rents (such as entry restrictions, concentration via in-pillar and expanded banking powers) may themselves be unacceptable to the public.

Not only may tough closure rules not be consistent with the incentives needed for banks to recapitalize but also they may face implementation difficulties due to the reputational concerns of regulators. The evidence indicates that regulators, due to the resulting criticisms, have been reluctant to incur the short-run disruptions and criticisms resulting from early bank closure, especially when the troubled bank is large or when the trouble is widespread in the industry or a region. Furthermore, there is little evidence to suggest that the application of an early intervention (including closure) mandate by the supervisor (such as OSFI) will be stringent enough that it will discipline the *ex ante* asset choices of bank management or that it will prevent regulatory risk-taking or dereliction (discussed more fully below).[16] Furthermore, the success of early intervention rules are hampered by the ability of regulated entities to alter their risk profiles quickly, the reliance by regulators on lagged and noisy regulatory metrics, the informational asymmetry gap that will still exist between the regulator and the regulated when the latter is in trouble, and the many restrictive norms that impede regulatory action. As a result, the actual efficiency of an early closure policy will only be known when this new policy is stress tested by a significant new failure or by evidence that it was responsible for the prevention of a significant bank failure.

Choice of organizational design for the DI function and LM mandate

As noted earlier, two primary organizational designs exist for the positioning of the DI (deposit insurance) function within a country's financial system safety net.[17] The first organizational design is where the deposit insurer performs this function proactively so as to best satisfy a loss minimization (LM) mandate. Under this design, the insurer requires certain powers (as is the case in the USA and Canada).[18] The second organizational design is where the entity mandated with the supervisory function (so-called 'supervisor') performs all DI functions or at a minimum all the supervisory functions associated with a LM objective.[19] If an independent insurer exists under this second organizational design, the insurer acts primarily as a reactive paybox (as in the industry-based scheme in Brazil).

Many deposit insurers have started as payboxes and have or are transforming themselves into proactive insurers.[20] An illustrative non-Canadian example is the Deposit Insurance Corporation of Japan (DICJ), which was established in 1971 as a paybox. Following the collapse of the bubble economy in Japan, there was a significant escalation in the amount of non-performing loans and the number of failed financial institutions in Japan in the 1990s. From 1996 onwards, the government in Japan passed legislation that empowered the DICJ to expand its activities and mandate significantly. In 1999, coverage moved from partial to blanket with a 2000 year-end (subsequently prolonged) reversion date to deal with financial instability (IADI, 2002). To prepare for possible failures when Japan planned to return to a limited guarantee system in April 2005, the DICJ was authorized in April 2002 to conduct on-site inspections of financial institutions (IADI, undated).

The prescription of a 'one size fits all countries' approach for the positioning of the DI function within a country's financial system safety net is not possible due to the importance of informational, ethical, legal, historical, political and economic features that govern the differences in the design and the enforcement of financial contracts across countries.

The Canadian system, for example, has evolved so that the DI function is positioned in a separate entity, which is independent from the regulator and has responsibility for protecting its exposure to loss. Unlike a government department or not fully independent supervisory authority, CDIC as a Crown corporation is insulated to a great extent from inappropriate actual or perceived governmental interference, especially when actions that are necessary but politically awkward need to be carried out. Similarly, the 'arms-length' relationship provided by a Crown corporation insulates the responsible minister and the government from issues such as early closure and the resulting litigation and asset disposal, and the political fallout resulting from these decisions. The CDIC's mandate as deposit insurer is to minimize its exposure to loss while contributing to the stability of the financial system.[21] On the other hand, placing the LM objective within the regulator or government department would create conflicts of interest with the other elements of the regulator's mandate.

Not only are the majority of deposit insurers set up as separate and independent legal entities but the recent international experience in Bulgaria, Hong Kong, India, and Singapore indicates that governments are opting for independent insurers. The government of India recently proposed a new financial sector insurer, the Bank Deposits Insurance Corporation (BDIC), which is to be modelled on the independent FDIC in the USA. One concern was to minimize regulatory overlap between the new BDIC and India's supervisory entity (Sen, 2002). In contrast, the proposed deposit insurance agency for Singapore will essentially be a paybox (MAS, 2004).

Historically, insurers often did not have quasi-regulatory/supervisory powers in advanced countries (FITD, 2001). However, more recently, the mandates and powers of deposit insurers worldwide are being broadened to enhance their effectiveness in failure resolution, and cost minimization.

Arguments for the supervisor performing the non-paybox DI function[22]

Regulatory burden/overlap

While regulatory efficiency should promote the efficient production and delivery of financial services, it should not be the only (or even primary) goal of regulation. Canadian banks devote a material portion of their non-interest expense to compliance with the regulatory burden imposed upon them by the regulatory authorities.[23] It can be argued that these explicit costs should be lower if material overlap exists between the regulator and deposit insurer or if significant scale or efficiency economies are possible from concentrating the provision of all supervision in one regulatory entity. Implicit cost reductions would also be possible if unhealthy agency conflicts not only exist but they undermine supervisory discipline and/or impose excessive and costly burdens on the regulated entities. The later appears not to be the case in Canada, and we examine the former next.

The FSA experience in the United Kingdom, where the Financial Services Compensation Scheme (FSCS) is a legally separate subsidiary of the Financial Supervisory Authority (FSA), suggests that the cost savings from concentration are small or non-existent.[24] Similar savings would be expected in Canada since there is relatively little overlap between CDIC and OSFI that result in direct regulatory burden on member institutions. Incorporating the CDIC standards inside OSFI's guidelines alleviated any overlap and duplication between the standards of CDIC and the guidelines of OSFI. More recently, by repealing the promotion of standards from the mandate of the CDIC, the 23 February 2005 budget of the federal government has eliminated any potential overlap. The merits of this change are unclear since both rule-based and guideline approaches to monitoring bank behaviour have merit, and the potential existence of both adds to the checks and balances within the financial system safety net.

Regulatory accountability

Another argument for concentrating all supervisory functions and the loss minimization function in one entity is that decentralization of such functions diffuses accountability for misguided or failed policy actions or shirking of such responsibility when such happens. The counter argument is that it is more difficult to hold an entity accountable as the numbers of its potentially conflicting objectives increase, and when there is only a single entity because there are no footprints of divergences in *ex ante* judgments to audit *ex post* with only a single entity.

Arguments for a proactive and independent insurer

Diversification of style

Regulators can be viewed as value 'overseers'. Supervisors are concerned with the going-concern values of the financial institutions that they oversee, while proactive insurers are concerned with the liquidation values of the financial institutions that they insure. Thus, while the primary interest of supervisors is on expected scenarios, the primary interest of insurers is on extreme (or tail) scenarios. Since each of these requires different talents and abilities (so-called 'styles') to do well, they are best housed in different entities. This has long been recognized in portfolio management where multi-managers are used to manage pension fund assets, and in the corporate sector where corporate managers and service providers specialize by, for example, ongoing operations, mergers and acquisitions and rehabilitations (that is reorganizations, liquidations and bankruptcies).

Diversification of judgment

The identification and disposition of troubled financial institutions is not a hard science, has a substantial impact on the cost of DI and the stability, soundness and competitiveness of the financial system, and requires considerable judgment. Overseers like managers are subject to a small probability of large errors in judgment caused, for example, by operational risks. Thus, the concentration of all mandates (including LM) in one entity is a managerial policy of putting 'all of one's eggs in one basket and trying to watch that basket closely'. In contrast, by having an independent and proactive insurer, who monitors its exposure, some limited but material diversification in judgment can be achieved. Compared to a concentration strategy, a limited diversification strategy for regulatory oversight should lower the risk of a large error in judgment (for example, due to operational risk). Diversification of judgment is consistent with the notion that 'checks and balances' are a vital part of all vibrant organizational systems.[25]

However, it is debatable how much diversification of judgment occurs when a regulator and an insurer are in close contact with each other and work from a common information base. Thus, some observers argue that more active monitoring by uninsured depositors or other interested parties also should augment regulatory monitoring. To illustrate, Bhattacharya *et al.* (1998) interpret the empirical evidence on US bank and thrift failures as providing 'powerful reasons to seriously consider an expanded role for monitoring by uninsured depositors and a lesser reliance on regulators for disciplining banks'.

Regulatory risk-taking or dereliction

Regulatory risk-taking or dereliction occurs when official supervisors acquiesce to pressure of threatened financial institutions to engage in risky activities ('going for broke') in an effort to continue operating. Having separate entities primarily responsible for supervision and DI, LM better provides differential resistance to political pressures to make decisions that may not be in the long-run interest of a sound and efficient banking system during periods of crisis. According to Kane (2003), such regulatory risk-taking takes the form of insurance against failure and concealment of the risk exposures of the insured institutions and their governmental insurers by accounting dereliction due to the conflicting incentives for regulators.

Regulatory risk-taking or dereliction is tempered by having an independent insurer that is aggressively pursuing a LM objective. This was aptly stated in the Blue Paper (1986) as follows:

> By ensuring that the views and concerns of the deposit insurer and lender of last resort, who have financial exposure to troubled institutions, are given full weight in decisions on the nature and timing of supervisory actions, this approach will strengthen the supervisor's 'will to act'.

The MacKay Task Force (1998) expressed similar sentiments:

> the insurer and the regulator have different purposes that are clearly distinct and should remain so. Further, the insurer and the regulator have different objectives with respect to failing institutions: the regulator's interest is in rehabilitation and the insurer's interest is in minimizing exposure. We believe that there is a healthy tension between these objectives that serves public policy best when they are not combined in a single institution.

Regulatory capture

Due to the lack of incentive payments to regulators and given that their reputational and career interests can leave them more directly answerable to politicians and bankers than to taxpayers and depositors, government regulators have in some past crises been pulled more strongly toward subsidizing deposit-institution operations by avoiding failures than they were toward minimizing the long-run costs to taxpayers of loss exposures (Kane, 2003). Potential solutions have been to either rework public-service incentives to make it less attractive for authorities to help troubled institutions to resist healthy exit pressure or to place the two conflicting objectives in different entities.[26] A mixture of both solutions has been adopted in Canada.

External board members

If the insurer is set up as an independent legal entity (as a crown corporation as is the case for CDIC), then private sector directors can be added to the board of the insurer to bring added expertise, experience and independent judgment into the decision-making process of the insurer. Furthermore, the reputational capital of these external board members is at greater risk when the insurer is set up as an independent legal entity with a more focused mandate centered on loss minimization.

Competition in information gathering and risk assessment

When information gathering and risk assessment are concentrated in one entity, there are no healthy competitive forces to innovate and excel. Furthermore, since monitoring and auditing procedures generally depend upon random sampling, such monitoring and auditing procedures should be more effective in identifying instances of malfeasance when conducted by a greater number of entities using different monitoring activities. Thus, some healthy competition in risk monitoring is likely to foster innovation in risk assessment methods and to prevent regulatory stagnation.

Dealing with different jurisdictions

As in several other countries, OSFI and CDIC have different jurisdictions in Canada. Unlike CDIC, OSFI deals with life and health insurance, property and casualty insurance, pensions operating under federal laws and some credit union centrals. Unlike OSFI, CDIC insures provincially chartered deposit-taking institutions. Maintaining these two separate entities should make it easier to deal with policy and agency conflicts emanating from these differences in their jurisdictions.

Exit resistance and tolerance for forbearance

By design, OSFI and CDIC have different incentive incompatibilities (as discussed above) when dealing with troubled institutions. In turn, these incompatibilities imply that the resistance to the exit of failed institutions (or alternatively, the tolerance for forbearance) will be higher for the supervisor than for the insurer. The maintenance of two separate entities maintains a healthy tension between these two entities. Changing the insurer into a 'paybox' would not only remove this healthy tension but also most likely dwarf the significance of a LM objective in the actual decisions of the supervisor.

Conflicting regulatory goals of industry protection versus industry promotion

The perceived conflict between DI administration and bank supervision is another argument advanced against consolidation of supervisory and LM responsibilities into one entity. The argument is centered on the potential conflicts between a requirement to minimize exposure to loss by, for example, early closure of troubled institutions versus the requirement to promote competition by, for example, maintaining minimal barriers to entry. The counter-argument is that the regulator in the absence of any behavioural biases (especially over-optimism) would not allow the expansion of banking to the detriment of financial stability because the regulator's responsibility to ensure that any expansion is 'prudent' or 'safe and sound' requires the consideration of the interests of depositors. This perceived conflict has been aptly stated by the U.S.A Treasury Department (1991, p. XXI-5) as: 'There is an essential conflict in having a single regulatory agency simultaneously promote and protect an industry.' This potential conflict caused only the reference to 'promoting and otherwise contributing to the competitiveness of the financial system' being removed from the objects of CDIC in 1995 after a major review of its objects and independent status (Canada, 1995).

The theoretical evidence

There are few studies that theoretically examine the allocation of bank regulatory powers between one entity and several entities. Kahn and Santos (2001) find that a single regulator leads to insufficient bank monitoring, bank under-investment in loans and possibly to excessive forbearance. If the insurer has the authority to close banks and last resort lending is insured and the rates on lending of last resort can be pre-specified, then the insurer has strong incentives against forbearance. If such rates cannot be pre-specified, then Kahn and Santos find that both the central bank and the deposit insurer should act as lenders of last resort, and that such lending should be uninsured to reduce the temptation to overlend although this will increase somewhat the temptation of the deposit insurer to forbear. Caldwell (2005) compares the welfare implications of two resolution regimes given a credible closure decision. In the single-entity regime, a meta-regulator supervises, closes and resolves failed banks using an *ex post* efficient resolution criterion. In the two-entity regime, the supervisor closes troubled banks and the deposit insurer resolves the closures on a LM basis. The LM resolution dominates its *ex post* efficient resolution counterpart in the presence of market discipline, and neither regime dominates in the absence of market discipline.

Weighing of the arguments and evidence

No precise cost/benefit analysis is possible given the nature of the arguments and evidence discussed above. Nevertheless, the preponderance of the evidence favours the status quo in terms of the continuation of a role in the Canadian financial system safety net for an independent, loss-minimizing insurer (CDIC). The arguments advanced in favour of returning CDIC to its initial paybox status are much too weak to disrupt a financial system safety net that appears to be working well. Given the uncertainties and potentially unintended consequences associated with a change, a variant of a popular saying, 'if it ain't broke, don't change it', appears to be an appropriate response to the proposals to make such a change. Furthermore, in their attempt to reduce a phantom regulatory burden, legislators 'must always keep in mind that their actions may have unintended consequences, thus making the solution worse than the problem they were trying to correct' (Dodge, 2004).

4.5 Powers, instruments and mechanisms required by an independent insurer

Well-defined mandate, responsibilities and powers

The mandates, responsibilities and powers of the insurer and supervisor need to be well defined. For example, the assignment of responsibilities should reflect the information advantage of each entity given asymmetric information and their primary responsibilities. For an insurer, this is particularly the case for the closure and liquidation of insured institutions.

Compared to a 'paybox' insurer, a 'risk-minimizing' insurer has a relatively broad mandate with correspondingly wider responsibilities and powers. As would be expected, the powers of CDIC until the 23 February 2005 budget of the Canadian federal government included the ability to control membership (entry and exit) from the DI system, the ability to elicit information from its members, and the ability to assess and manage its own risks. OSFI is now solely responsible for the former two functions.

Membership and control over member entry and exit

Membership should be compulsory for all eligible entities to avoid adverse selection, where strong banks would leave the insurance scheme in order to avoid the cross-subsidization of weak banks. The rules for delineating member eligibility should be explicit. Furthermore, banks not covered by explicit DI must not become implicitly insured.

As was the case until recently in Canada, the insurer should have exclusive control over the entry and exit of members into and out of the DI scheme in order to manage the risk of adverse selection.[27] This is necessary to resolve conflicts of interest by protecting the insurance fund from policies of the entity in charge of closing financial institutions if that entity is not the insurer. Also, having the power to exclude banks that are deemed as being inappropriately managed can have a sufficiently strong deterrent effect against inappropriate management.

Role in risk assessment and information elicitation

While risk-sensitive capital requirements and DI premia are regulatory mechanisms to cope with the moral hazards associated with DI, their success depends upon the regulator's ability to observe the risk of banks under its supervision or insurance. Thus, an insurer needs to retain a role in risk monitoring and the elicitation of the requisite information. Proper risk pricing requires a competent assessment of risk from the perspective of the portfolio of individual risk exposures and the individual risk exposures themselves. The insurer must be able to make accurate and meaningful assessments of information dealing with such areas as asset valuations, credit and off-balance sheet exposures, loan-loss provisionings, non-performing loans, unrealised losses, capital adequacy, and bank profitability (FSF, 2001).

The need for a role in information elicitation arises because the information obtained by the supervisor through reporting requirements and any on-site examinations are unlikely to fully satisfy the information requirements of the insurer. If the insurer is to effectively satisfy its LM objective, then the minimum information requirements for independent risk monitoring by the insurer are that the insurer has the authority for supplemental reporting requirements and backup examinations, including the ability to conduct on-site examinations if and when required. Specifically, the insurer must be able to examine institutions whose conditions or activities have changes of a sufficient magnitude to be of concern to the insurer. In Canada, the CDIC had such examination powers until recently, as noted above.

When the deposit insurer has LM responsibilities, the information elicitation methods across entities must be appropriately balanced across the various safety-net participants to ensure that this function is executed in a cost effective manner (Ketcha, 1999). To minimize regulatory burden, well-developed mechanisms need to be in place for information sharing and co-ordination between the insurer and the supervisor.

Power to close a financial institution

The steps necessary to liquidate the business and affairs of a failed bank include the resolution or disposition of the failed bank, reimbursement of insured depositors, liquidation of the assets of the bank, settlement of claims in accordance with applicable laws, and disposition of pending or outstanding litigation.

To minimize the insurance losses of DI, an insurer needs an efficient bank failure resolution system that allows for alternatives in addition to liquidation. In order to avoid moral hazard in the application of resolution alternatives other than liquidation, such as purchase and assumption, an insurer with a minimum cost objective would choose the alternative over liquidation only if it implies a lower expected cost for the insurer. The selected alternative should be the lowest actual cost alternative, on average, if the expectations of the decision-maker are unbiased. In Canada, the CDIC and OSFI have a joint program of early intervention that is formalized in the *Guide to Intervention for Federal Financial Institutions* (OSFI, 2002).

Responsibility for the closure and claims-and-recoveries functions

The LM insurer needs to have the primary responsibility to design and implement the closure regime. Since closure is a judgmental decision subject to considerable error, the insurer needs some flexibility in the implementation of the closure regime design. The role of other interested parties, such as the courts and the supervisor, need to be clarified. Also, the basis for making closure decisions should be fairly explicit and transparent to maintain a high level of accountability of the insurer.[28]

During periods of economic or financial turmoil, markets for collateral assets become thin and liquidations become slow or require a large price discount (Shleifer and Vishny, 1992). Thus, by acting as an asset management company, the insurer can help to mitigate asset price volatility by liquidating bank assets at a controlled, reasonable rate that reduces asset market overhang and increases collateral realizations.[29]

Regulatory coordination

There is a need for coordination among the various safety-net participants or agencies when the insurer is both independent and proactive in order to minimize regulatory burden. However, the challenge in doing so is not to eliminate the constructive tension between the agencies that enhances regulatory awareness and responsiveness to changing market conditions.

There are numerous mechanisms for ensuring coordination between CDIC and the other participants in the Canadian financial system safety net. First, five out of the 11 directors of CDIC are drawn from other safety net participants; namely, the Deputy Minister of Finance, the Governor of the Bank of Canada, the Chairperson of FCAC, and the Superintendent and one Deputy Superintendent of OSFI. The Financial Institutions Supervisory Committee (FISC) and the Senior Advisory Committee (SAC), which have similar cross-agency and departmental representation, facilitate information sharing and policy coordination, respectively. Furthermore, CDIC and OSFI have implemented a number of joint initiatives, such as a 'Guide to Intervention for Federal Financial Institutions' that sets out the roles, responsibilities, options and actions of the two agencies for dealing with supervisory issues and interventions. However, going forward, all assessments of institutions will be against OSFI guidelines as CDIC's *Standards of Sound Business and Financial Practices* has been repealed.

4.6 Conclusion

This chapter examined the historical development and current status of thinking on three major areas concerned with the organizational design for deposit insurance (DI) within a country's financial safety net: namely, the role of loss minimization (LM) as an objective for such a net, the positioning of the LM function in that net, and the various modalities required of the insurer if such an insurer design is deemed appropriate. The assessment methodology placed particular emphasis on the effectiveness of the chosen design in terms of loss experience and its efficiency in terms of regulatory burden/overlap.

The chapter cautioned against an approach that infers the probability and severity of bank failure from the most recently observed failure rate for banks if it is abnormally low or high to decide on the appropriate positioning of the DI, LM function. The capacity of a DI system may be severely tested from the failure of one of the increasing numbers of complex 'mega' banks caused by cross-border and cross-pillar mergers, the movement towards universal banks and regulatory capital requirements that are tailored to the risk profiles of individual banks (Basel II), and the increasing systematic component of the operational risks associated with a greater reliance on more sophisticated technology and financial products. Similarly, the adoption of an early intervention regime by the supervisory entity is unlikely to remove the need for a deposit insurer with a LM mandate due to the many operational and motivational problems associated with the implementation of such a regime.

While views of the benefits of explicit DI are mixed with academics being on average less favourable, DI is a crucial component of the financial system safety net in most countries with the few holdout developed countries firmly considering its adoption. Nevertheless, various moral hazard problems permeate the financial system safety net (for example, in central bank liquidity lending, bank supervision and DI). One such moral hazard problem is that DI can weaken market discipline by reducing the incentives for information acquisition and control by depositors and for banks to bond their ability to repay their depositors. In turn, this may cause banks to seek excessive portfolio risk while keeping lower than optimal liquid reserves given the asymmetric sharing of profits and losses among shareholders and depositors. Another moral hazard problem associated with DI is the lack of timely accountability for the regulators in that they may tend to over rely on forbearance to deal with troubled financial institutions. The most effective mechanism to control this moral hazard problem is to make DI loss minimization one of the primary objectives of the financial system safety net.

The arguments for a paybox status or no independent insurer include reduction in regulatory burden/overlap and improved regulatory accountability. Not only have the regulatory burden reductions from such consolidations in other jurisdictions been difficult to find but also there appears to be little gain in accountability when an entity gains an additional objective that can or is in conflict with its existing objectives.

The arguments for an independent and active insurer with a LM mandate include: some limited additional diversification of style (liquidation versus going-concern value orientation) and judgment (not putting 'all of one's eggs in the same basket'), better control over regulatory risk-taking or dereliction that occurs when official supervisors are pressured into allowing threatened financial institutions to engage in risky activities in an effort to recapitalize, less chance of regulatory capture (where the reputational and career interests of regulators make them more responsive to the interests of politicians and bankers than to taxpayers and depositors), possibility of using the expertise, experience and independent judgements of external board members who have their reputational capital at risk, healthy 'checks and balances' in information gathering and risk monitoring, greater ease in dealing with policy and agency conflicts emanating from differences in jurisdictions, better balancing of differences in resistance to bank exit or of tolerance to forbear, and better means of dealing with the conflicting regulatory goals of industry protection versus industry promotion (that is growth over stability).

Furthermore, a deposit insurer should be independent with an explicit mandate to minimize losses since the deposit insurer bears direct financial exposure to failures, is exposed to potentially costly failure resolution processes, is typically the largest creditor in such failures, and may have a lender of last resort role (as is the case for CDIC in Canada). However, because of an over-riding concern with regulatory burden and the mistaken inference that the probability and severity of future bank failure has moved permanently to a lower level regime based on the extrapolation of most recent experience, legislators may conclude that an independent deposit insurer with an explicit LM mandate is no longer required.

For an independent insurer to effectively discharge a LM mandate, the insurer needs well-defined objectives, responsibilities and powers. These include basic control over member entry and exit to avoid adverse selection and to minimize forbearance and cross-subsidization of weak banks, a supplemental role in information elicitation and risk monitoring to effectively discharge its LM objective and for proper premium risk pricing, the power to close a financial institution using a resolution alternative that avoids moral hazard and is the least cost alternative, and responsibility for the closure and claims-and-recoveries functions in an effort to minimize losses and externalities to markets and other financial system safety net participants. A high level of coordination and information sharing is needed among the various safety net participants without eliminating the constructive tension between the participants that enhances regulatory awareness and responsiveness to changing market conditions. The promotion of standards and guidelines should be placed within the purview of different entities since both rule-based and guideline approaches to monitoring bank behaviour have merit, and the potential existence of both adds to the checks and balances within the financial system safety net.

Notes

1 Consolidation has been on the public policy agenda in the USA since at least 1919 (Beach, 1993). Interestingly, the US government did not include the partial consolidation recommendations for federal bank regulatory agencies contained in the US Treasury Department study (1991) in the passed legislation, 'The Federal Deposit Insurance Corporation Improvement Act of 1991'. The Treasury Department recommendations would have made the US regulatory entities more like their Canadian counterparts, especially if the indirect regulatory authority of FDIC was still material.

2 Not unexpectedly, the need for a similar balance for regulators was recently stated by Dodge (2004) as follows: 'That balance is between maintaining and strengthening the key elements of regulation and supervision that promote appropriate risk management, and the necessity to promote efficiency by keeping compliance costs to a minimum.'

3 Other potential challenges not dealt with herein are failures of internet-based or extensively ATM-based institutions or of holding companies.

4 To illustrate, fraud contributed to eight of the eleven US bank failures in 2002 (Powell, 2003).

5 This was a primary reason for proposing that the deposit insurer for Hong Kong be established as a paybox. The other reason is the small size of the Hong Kong market (Carse, 2002, p. 21).

6 To illustrate, Guttentag and Herring (1986) find that bank managements tend to under-estimate the probability of 'shocks' after long periods of prosperity.

7 Five reasons for greater contagion in banking are found in Kaufman (1994).

8 These comments are based on a collection of public speeches made by Professor Kaufman in New Zealand in 2004. A revised version of these speeches was published in the June 2004 *Reserve Bank Bulletin* at www.rbnz.govt.nz/research/bulletin/2002_2006/jun2004.html.

9 See Saunders and Wilson (1996) for empirical evidence on the role of informed depositors.

10 Carapella and Di Giorgio (2003) find that deposit protection provides bank incentives to engage in riskier lending activities as exemplified by higher average loan rates.

11 Moral hazard occurs when the occurrence of the insured risk increases because the provision of the insurance has diminished the incentives for the insured to avoid the insured risk.

12 In contrast, Carapella and Di Giorgio (2003) evaluate their findings as indicating that a coinsurance provision is not effective in reducing the moral hazard problems associated with bank lending. CDIC introduced a system of risk-based or differential premiums in 1999.

13 The positions of the reserve banks in these two countries differ. The Reserve Bank of Australia sees merit in a limited guarantee of the deposits held by banks, credit unions and building societies in the form of explicit deposit insurance given that many depositors believe that an implicit guarantee already exists (http://au.pfinance.yahoo.com/040930/1/bjd.html). In contrast, the Reserve Bank of New Zealand agrees that partial access to depositors' funds may be desirable immediately after a bank failure, but believes that this is best accomplished through other (unspecified) means than by *ex ante* depositor insurance (www.rbnz.govt.nz/finstab/banking/regulation/0154814.html).

14 Engert (2005) provides a more extensive discussion of the historical evolution of the Canadian financial safety net.

15 These results extend the work of Kryzanowski and Roberts (1993, 1998, 1999) who show that forbearance was a primary determinant of why many Canadian financial institutions survived during the 1920s and the 1930s.

16 In their reputational sequential equilibrium model, Boot and Thakor (1993) find that the regulator's optimal bank closure policy is more lax than is socially optimal. Furthermore, Acharya and Dreyfus (1989) find that forbearance is always

suboptimal when deciding on an optimal closure rule that minimizes the costs to the insurer.

17 We do not consider the case where all safety net functions are given to the central bank.

18 These powers need not be completely formal. For example, in Germany, the private-sector DI agency has narrow formal powers but yields much wider powers in practice (Beck, 2003).

19 Some authors propose that only the insurer may have a legitimate supervisory role (Benston, 1983).

20 Nevertheless, many insurers continue to operate as payboxes. For example, 16 out of 25 insurers operating in European Union countries operated as payboxes in 2005 (Pawlikowski, 2005, p. 22). These include insurers in such countries as Sweden, UK and Netherlands.

21 The promotion of standards of sound business and financial practices was recently removed from its mandate.

22 The agency competition and differential cost arguments given in the US due to the existence of multiple agencies at both the federal and state levels to regulate competing depositor institutions do not appear to have much applicability to the Canadian setting. The example commonly used to support this argument in the US is the S&L regulations in the 1980s that led some commercial banks to become S&Ls.

23 It is estimated that US banks devote an average of about 14 per cent of their non-interest expenses to comply with the regulatory burden (*The Economist, 1994).*

24 Furthermore, according to a recent survey, the level of regulatory burden has actually increased since the creation of FSA. See Financial Services Practitioner Panel Annual Report (2002) and Survey of the FSA's Regulatory Performance Report (2002).

25 Other means, such as industry pressure, litigation and governmental committee oversight, can also be used to check the behaviour of a single supervisory entity.

26 The later solution appears to be easier to implement.

27 Adverse selection occurs when the most failure-prone or risk-loving bankers find it advantageous to enter the banking business because they can take advantage of the DI scheme.

28 This could involve the use of explicit triggers based, for example, on liquidity or balance sheet/market value insolvency.

29 Mason (2002) addresses the efficiency and profitability of these arrangements. Anari (2005) hypothesizes that financial disintermediation during and after the Great Depression in the USA was the result of the slow liquidation of failed-bank deposits.

References

Anari, A. (2005) 'Bank asset liquidation and the propagation of the U.S. Great Depression', *Journal of Money, Credit, and Banking* vol. 37: 4 (August), pp. 753–73.

Acharya, S. and Dreyfus, J.-F. (1989) 'Optimal bank reorganization policies and the pricing of federal deposit insurance', *Journal of Finance* vol. 44, pp. 1313–33.

Barth, J. (1991) *The great savings and loan debacle*, Washington, DC: The AEI Press.

Beach, H. (1993) 'How should bank regulatory agencies be organized?', *Contemporary Policy Issues* vol. 11: 1 (January), pp. 99–107.

Beck, T. (2003) 'The incentive compatible design of deposit insurance and bank failure resolution – concepts and country studies', World Bank Policy Research Working Paper 3043, May.

Benston, G. (1983) 'Federal regulation of banking: Analysis and policy recommendation', *Journal of Bank Research* (Winter), pp. 216–44.

Berger, A.N., Kyle, M.K. and Scalise, J.M. (2001) 'Did U.S. bank supervisors get tougher during the credit crunch? Did they get easier during the banking boom? Did it matter to bank lending?' in F.S. Mishkin (ed.), *Prudential Supervision: What Works and What Doesn't* Chicago, IL: University of Chicago Press for National Bureau of Economic Research.

Bhattacharya, S., Boot, A.W.A. and Thakor, A.V. (1998) 'The economics of bank regulation', *Journal of Money, Credit and Banking* vol. 30:4 (November), pp. 745–70.

Blue Paper (1986) *New directions for the financial sector*, Government of Canada.

Boot, A. and A.V. Thakor (1993). 'Self-interested bank regulation', *American Economic Review* vol. 83, pp. 206–12.

Caldwell, G., (2005) 'An analysis of closure policy under alternative regulatory structures', Banking of Canada Working Paper 2005–11, April.

Canada (1995) *Enhancing the Safety and Soundness of the Canadian Financial System*, Government of Canada, February.

Carapella, F. and Giorgio, G. Di (2003) 'Deposit insurance, institutions and bank interest rates,' Discussion Paper No. 0304-06, Department of Economics, Columbia University, November.

Caprio, G.Jr. and Klingebiel, D. (1997) 'Bank insolvency: Bad luck, bad policy or bad banking?' in M. Bruno and B. Pleskovic (eds), *Annual World Bank Conference on Development Economics* Washington, DC: The World Bank.

Carse, D. (2002) Enhancing deposit protection in Hong Kong. Powerpoint Presentation, Hong Kong Monetary Authority, July 11. Available at: www.info.gov.hk/hkma/eng/speeches/speechs/david/attach/20020711a.ppt.

Credit Union World (2004) *Global trends: Insuring the safety of savings*, Credit Union World 6: 1 (February).

Cull, R., Senbet, L.W. and Sorge, M. (2005) 'Deposit insurance and financial development', *Journal of Money, Credit and Banking* vol. 37: 1, pp. 43–82.

Demirgüç-Kunt, A. and Detragiache, E. (2002) 'Does deposit insurance increase banking system stability? An empirical investigation', *Journal of Monetary Economics*, vol. 49, pp. 1373–406.

Dodge, D., (2004) Research in financial services and public policy – filling the gaps. Remarks by the Governor of the Bank of Canada to the Conference on Financial Services and Public Policy, Toronto, Ontario, April 22.

Economist, The (1994) 'American bank regulation: four into one can go', 330 (March 5), pp. 88–91.

Economist, The, September 4, 1999, p. 71.

Engert, W. (2005) 'On the evolution of the financial system safety net', in *Financial System Review* Ottawa: Bank of Canada, June, pp. 67–73.

FSF, (2001) *Guidance for Developing Effective Deposit Insurance Systems*. Basel, Switzerland: Financial Stability Forum, September.

FITD, (2001) *Survey*. Italian Interbank Deposit Fund.

Furfine, G.H. (2001) 'Banks as monitors of other banks: Evidence from the overnight federal funds market', *Journal of Business* vol. 74: 1, pp. 33–57.

Garcia, G.H. (2000) 'Deposit insurance: Actual and good practices', *IMF Occasional Paper No. 197*.

Guttentag, J. and Herring, R. (1986) 'Disaster myopia in international banking.' Essays in International Finance, No. 46, Princeton University, September.

Hovakimian, A., Kane, E.J. and L. Laeven (2003). *How Country and Safety-net Characteristics Affect Bank Risk-shifting* New York: World Bank Working Paper, February.

IADI (undated) Profile – Deposit Insurance Corporation of Japan. International Association of Deposit Insurers. Available at: www.iadi.org/html/App/SiteContent/Member%20Profile%20DIC%20of%20Japan.pdf.

IADI (2002) 'Transitioning issues for deposit insurance practitioners,' Conference Proceedings, International Association of Deposit Insurers, Switzerland, May 7–8.

Kahn, C.M. and Santos, J.A.C. (2001) 'Allocating bank regulatory powers: Lender of last resort, deposit insurance and supervision.' Bank for International Settlements (BIS) Working Paper No. 102, Monetary and Economic Department, August.

Kane, E.J. (1989) *The S&L insurance mess: How did it happen?*, Washington: The Urban Institute Press.

Kane, E.J. (2003) 'What economic principles should policymakers in other countries have learned from the S&L mess?', *Business Economics* vol. 38:1 (January), pp. 21–30.

Kaufman, G.G. (1994) 'Bank contagion: A review of the theory and evidence', *Journal of Financial Services Research* vol. 8, pp. 123–50.

Kaufman, G.G. (1996) 'Bank failures, systemic risk, and bank regulation', *Cato Journal* vol. 16: 1 (Summer), pp.17–45.

Ketcha, N.J.Jr. (1999) 'Deposit insurance system design and consideration,' Bank for International Settlements (BIS) Policy Paper, November.

Kryzanowski, L. and Noiseux, M.-H. (2003) 'Losses incurred by various groups of stakeholders from Canadian bank failures under different safety net regimes.' Working Paper, Concordia University, Montreal.

Kryzanowski, L. and Roberts, G.S. (1993) 'Canadian banking solvency, 1922–1940', *Journal of Money, Credit and Banking* vol. 25:3 (August, Part 1), pp. 361–76.

Kryzanowski, L. and G.S. Roberts (1998), 'Capital forbearance: Depression-era experience of life insurance companies', *Canadian Journal of Administrative Sciences* vol. 15:1 (March), pp. 1–16.

Kryzanowski, L. and G.S. Roberts (1999) 'Perspectives on Canadian bank insolvency during the 1930s', *Journal of Money, Credit and Banking* vol. 31:1 (February), pp. 130–36.

Laeven, L. (2002) 'International evidence on the cost of deposit insurance', *Quarterly Review of Economics and Finance* vol. 42, pp. 721–32.

MacKay Task Force (1998) *Task force on the future of the Canadian financial services sector: Change, challenge and opportunity*, Government of Canada, Ottawa, Ontario, September 15.

Mason, J.R. (2002) 'A real options approach to bankruptcy costs: Evidence from failed commercial banks during the 1990s,' Wharton Financial Institutions Center Working Paper No. 0220.

Mason, J., Anari, A. and Kolari, J. (2000) 'The stock of closed bank deposits, duration of credit channel effects, and the persistence of the U.S. great depression', Cliometric Conference Presentation.

MAS (2004) *Second Consultation on Deposit Insurance*, P005-2004, Monetary Authority of Singapore, April. Available at: www.mas.gov.sg/masmcm/upload/mm/MM_117FE353_6295_5312_49AAE8F55F3D0AF0__117FE362_6295_5312_493AA08FD5994B7B/Second%20Consultation%20on%20DI.pdf.

Office of the Superintendent of Financial Institutions (OSFI) (2002) *Guide to Intervention for Federal Financial Institutions*.

Pawlikowski, A. (2005) 'The Polish deposit insurance scheme compared to arrangements adopted in other EU countries,' Materialy I Studia, Paper No. 34, Warsaw, June.

Powell, D.E. (2003) *Statement on the New Basel Accord,* Subcommittee on Domestic and International Monetary Policy, Trade and Technology of the Committee on Financial Services of the US House of Representatives, February 27.

Saunders, A. and Wilson, B. (1996) 'Contagious bank runs: Evidence from the 1929–1933 Period', *Journal of Financial Intermediation,* vol. 5: 4, pp. 409–23.

Sen, S.K. (2002) 'New bank deposit insurer to be modeled on US body', *Business Line,* May 14.

Shleifer, A. and Vishny, R.W. (1992) 'Liquidation values and debt capacity: A market equilibrium approach', *Journal of Finance* vol. 47: 4, pp. 1343–66.

US Treasury Department (1991) *Modernizing the Financial System,* February.

White, L.J. (1991) *The S&L debacle: Public policy lessons for bank and thrift regulation,* New York: Oxford University Press.

5

A Survey of Deposit Insurance in East Asia: Post-Asian Financial Crisis

David K. Walker[1]

5.1 Introduction

In most economies banks play the predominant role among financial institutions in intermediating between savers and investors, in the operation of the payments system and the execution of monetary policy.[2] The importance of banks in an economy, the potential for depositors to suffer losses when banks fail, and the need to mitigate 'runs' and 'contagion' risks, have lead an increasing number of countries to establish financial safety nets.[3] These usually include prudential regulation and supervision, a lender of last resort facility[4] and, increasingly, some form of deposit insurance. A deposit insurance system provides explicit – but limited – protection for eligible depositors in the event of a bank failure.[5]

Deposit insurance can be designed to fulfill a variety of goals. However, the most common objectives are to contribute to financial stability and to protect smaller and less financially sophisticated depositors from loss.[6] Without a credible deposit insurance system in place, the possibility exists that depositors might 'run' by removing their deposits from a bank, and/or other banks, in response to difficulties at a single bank.[7]

Nevertheless, it is important to understand that the design of deposit insurance systems generally involves tradeoffs and the potential for introducing distortions into the financial system. The most notable being moral hazard – or the incentive for excessive risk taking by banks or those receiving the benefit of a guarantee of protection. For example, full coverage for all deposits would effect the greatest protection for depositors but at the same time present the greatest challenge for controlling moral hazard. At the other end of the spectrum, very low coverage levels – that do not protect the majority of depositors in the system – would not be effective at curtailing runs and protecting the savings of most depositors. Therefore designers of deposit insurance systems must choose coverage levels which provide adequate protection but which do not create excessive distortions such as moral hazard.[8]

Moreover, even a well-designed deposit insurance system needs to be supported externally by strong prudential regulation and supervision, an effective legal system, sound corporate governance and risk management in banks and appropriate accounting standards and disclosure regimes.

Although deposit insurance is effective at protecting depositors and contributing to stability in most situations, it cannot by itself deal with a systemic financial system crisis.[9] Systemic crises require the combined efforts of all safety net participants to effectively deal with them. Deposit insurance systems are most effective at dealing with single failures or a wave of small failures.[10]

The growth of deposit insurance systems have been particularly noticeable in East Asia, driven by such factors as rapid financial system development, the Asian financial crisis and a general desire to improve depositor protection and financial stability.[11] For example, prior to the mid-1990s, deposit insurance systems were initially introduced in Japan, Korea, the Philippines and Taiwan as a means to protect depositors and contribute to stability during the rapid development of their financial systems. Other economies in this period such as Hong Kong, Indonesia, Malaysia, Singapore and Thailand opted instead to protect their depositors through the use of implicit guarantees and other means.[12] Experience with the Asian financial crisis in 1997 and its aftermath, however, convinced these economies to develop their own explicit limited deposit insurance systems. The People's Republic of China intends to introduce a deposit insurance system by 2007 as part of its financial system modernization plans.

This chapter looks at the growth of deposit insurance systems in East Asia with emphasis on the development of new systems following the Asian financial crisis. The first part of the chapter begins with a brief survey of well-established systems in the region such as the Philippines, Japan, Taiwan and Korea. Section 5.3 examines the Asian financial crisis and its role in spurring the development of new deposit insurance systems. The chapter then describes the key characteristics of new systems in Hong Kong, Indonesia, Malaysia, Singapore and Thailand. Section 5.4 reviews the similarities and differences of the new systems and examines the extent to which they follow good practices in deposit insurance. Section 5.5 reviews work underway in the People's Republic of China on deposit insurance. The chapter ends with a look at opportunities for greater regional cooperation on deposit insurance in East Asia.

5.2 Overview of well-established systems in East Asia

Prior to the advent of the Asian financial crisis, explicit limited deposit insurance was introduced in a number of Asian countries including the Philippines (1963), Japan (1971), Taiwan (1985) and Korea (1996).[13] Vietnam began developing a system in the mid-1990s and introduced its formal scheme in 1999.[14] The following section provides an overview of the key features of these systems including information on their objectives, mandates, governance structures, membership, coverage and funding capabilities.

Philippines

The Philippine Deposit Insurance Corporation (PDIC) was established in 1963. PDIC is a separate legal entity and structured as a government corporation. Its objectives are to protect depositors, promote greater public confidence in banks and foster stability in the banking system. The PDIC's Board of Directors is chaired by the Secretary of Finance with the President and CEO of PDIC serving as the Board's Vice-Chairman. Members of the Board are the Governor of the Central Bank (Bangko Sentral ng Philippines) and two private sector representatives.

PDIC is viewed as a 'risk minimizing' deposit insurer and has been provided with the roles of statutory receiver and co-regulator of banks with its own examination staff.[15] Membership is compulsory for all deposit-taking institutions including domestic branches of foreign banks. Referring to Table 5.1, all deposits (including foreign currencies) up to a limit of P250,000, or about US$4,800, are covered. Banks are assessed a flat-rate premium of 0.2 per cent of total deposits per annum. PDIC has established a Permanent Insurance Fund (PIF) with an initial government contribution of P3 billion.[16] The funds long term target is P90 billion.

Japan

The Deposit Insurance Corporation of Japan (DICJ) was established in 1971 with a mandate to protect depositors, contribute to financial stability and assist in the orderly resolution of problem banks. Coverage at that time was limited to ¥ 1 million (US$8,800) per depositor. The Deposit Insurance Law was amended in 1986 to expand the insurer's function to provide financial assistance for mergers and acquisitions of failed financial institutions. In 1996, the Law was amended again to incorporate a blanket guarantee (to deal with Japan's financial crisis); extend financial assistance beyond payout costs; and, to allow for the collection of a special premium to help finance the blanket guarantee.

In 1998, legislation was enhanced further to allow the DICJ nationalization powers, borrowing authority from the market with a government guarantee and the ability to recover non-performing loans through a newly established subsidiary – the Resolution and Collection Corporation (RCC). The DICJ was allowed to pursue civil and criminal liability of executives of failed banks and discover hidden assets of debtors in cooperation with the RCC. Special measures to deal with intervention in a systemic crisis were added to the legislation in 2000. The DICJ's powers also involve: financial administration, operation of bridge bank assistance and on-site inspection of financial institutions. As of April 1, 2005, demand and time deposits are under a limited guarantee of ¥ 10 million (US$89,000). Unlike demand deposits, deposits for settlement and payment purposes continue to receive a full blanket guarantee.[17]

Table 5.1 highlights the fact that membership in the DICJ is compulsory for all banks, building societies and credit cooperatives. The system excludes foreign bank branches and postal savings banks. However, after the planned privatization of the postal savings system in 2007, postal savings banks will be included as members of the DICJ.

The DICJ is funded by premiums on insured deposits and may borrow from the private financial markets and issue bonds guaranteed by the government. Premium rates are currently 0.083 per cent for general deposits and 0.115 per cent for payment and settlement deposits. A differential (risk-adjusted) premium system is under consideration.

Taiwan

The Taiwan Ministry of Finance and the Central Bank jointly established the Central Deposit Insurance Corporation (CDIC) in 1985. CDIC is responsible for protecting depositors, promoting savings, maintaining an orderly credit system and enhancing the safety and soundness of the financial system. CDIC is governed by a seven-member Board of Directors and has been provided authority to conduct risk assessment. It has been granted a broad range of failure resolution powers and a least cost resolution mandate.[18]

Membership is compulsory for all deposit taking institutions but excludes institutions already covered by foreign insurers. Maximum coverage per depositor per bank is NT$1 million (US$31,000) and excludes foreign currency deposits. Premiums are assessed on insured deposits and a differential premium system is employed. Premium assessments currently range from 0.05–0.06 per cent of insured deposits.

Korea

The Korea Deposit Insurance Corporation (KDIC) was established in 1996 to formally protect depositors of insured financial institutions and to maintain public confidence in the financial system. The system protects deposits at banks, securities companies, insurance companies, merchant banking corporations, mutual savings banks, and credit unions. KDIC has been provided with a wide range of powers to minimize its exposure to losses including risk assessment, joint examinations of high risk (insolvency-threatened) institutions, on-site inspection and investigation of failed financial institutions and failure resolution.

During the Asian financial crisis, Korea introduced a blanket guarantee. This began to be withdrawn in 2001 as financial system stability returned

Table 5.1 Established deposit insurance systems in East Asia

Country	Governance and structure	Membership	Coverage	Funding
Japan (1971)	– DICJ is a separate legal entity. – began life as a 'paybox' but has acquired many elements of a 'risk minimizer' such as a failure resolution mandate and specific examination powers.	– compulsory for all banks, building societies and credit cooperatives. – excludes foreign bank branches and postal savings banks. – after privatization in 2007, postal savings banks to be members.	– ¥ 10 million (US$89,000) for general (demand and time) deposits. – settlement deposits unlimited. – per depositor, per institution. – excludes foreign currency deposits.	– industry funded by premiums on insured deposits. – combined *ex ante/ex post.* – flat rate of 0.083% for general deposits and 0.115% for payment and settlement deposits. – differential premiums planned.
Korea (1997)	– KDIC is a separate legal entity. – 'Risk minimizer' with examination powers and a requirement for least cost resolution.	– compulsory for all domestic banks, foreign bank branches and most other institutions.	– KRW 50,000,000 (US$53,000). – per depositor per institution. – excludes foreign currency deposits. – depositor priority in place.	– industry funded by premiums on deposits. – combined *ex ante/ex post.* – flat rate of 0.1% on bank deposits. – diff. premiums planned.

Table 5.1 (Continued)

Country	Governance and structure	Membership	Coverage	Funding
Philippines (1963)	– PDIC a separate legal entity. – 'risk minimizer' with regulatory/examination powers and a requirement for least cost resolutions.	– compulsory for all deposit taking institutions including foreign bank branches.	– P250,000 (US$4,800). – per depositor, per institution. – includes foreign currency deposits.	– industry funded by premiums on total deposits. – *ex ante* with a current P3 billion fund with capital provided by government. – long-term fund target of P90 billion. – flat rate premium of 0.2%.
Taiwan (1985)	CDIC a separate legal entity. – provided with elements of a risk minimizer including a requirement to use a 'least payout cost' method for failure resolutions.	– compulsory for all deposit taking institutions. – excludes institutions. already insured by foreign insurers.	– NT$ 1,000,000 (US$ 31,000). – per depositor, per institution. – excludes foreign currency deposits.	– industry funded by premiums on insured deposits. – primarily *ex ante*. – diff. Premiums (0.05 - 0.06% of insured deposits).
Vietnam (1999)	– DIV a separate legal entity – 'risk minimizing' deposit insurer.	– compulsory for all banks and credit unions. – excludes foreign bank branches.	– VND 30,000,000 (US$ 2,000). – per depositor per institution. – excludes foreign currency deposits.	– industry funded by premiums of 0.15% on the average balance of personal insured deposits. – primarily *ex ante*. – flat rate premiums (differential system planned).

and comprehensive economic and financial system restructuring was implemented. It has now been replaced by a limited guarantee of 50 million won (US$53,000) per depositor per member institution. The system is funded by premiums collected from member institutions at a flat rate, but differentiated according to the type of institution protected. Premium assessments range from 0.1 per cent of insured deposits for banks to 0.3 per cent for mutual savings banks.[19] A differentiated (risk-adjusted) premium system is being planned for the future.

Vietnam

Vietnam began developing a deposit insurance system in the mid-1990s and established Deposit Insurance of Vietnam (DIV) in 1999. DIV is charged with protecting depositors; contributing to the stability of insured institutions; and, ensuring the safe and sound development of the banking sector. The DIV was given the power to inspect its member institutions and a major role in failure resolutions. Membership in the system is compulsory and banks must pay an annual premium equivalent to 0.15 per cent of the average balance of all insured deposits. If a bank becomes insolvent, individual depositors are entitled to receive up to VND 30 million (US$2,000) from the DIV. Individual account holders over this limit must recover any deficiency through the liquidation proceedings as other creditors of the bank. Deposit insurance is not applicable to foreign currency deposits.

Since its inception, the DIV has made insurance payments (up to the coverage limit) to nearly 3000 depositors at 33 insured institutions. This has worked to reduce the risk of contagion in the system, maintained stability and kept the banking sector under control. According to the DIV, all payments have been funded by the industry so little or no public funds have been used in these resolutions. In order to deal quickly with insolvent banks, the DIV recently instituted a policy of early closure of troubled institutions.[20]

Other established systems in East Asia

As of writing, Brunei, Macau (SAR), Cambodia, Laos and Myanmar do not have formal explicit limited deposit insurance systems. Laos protects depositors with a special fund created by the central bank. Cambodia and Myanmar provide an explicit 100 per cent guarantee from the central bank for all deposits. Macau utilizes depositor priority and supervisory oversight to protect depositors, although it is investigating a limited explicit deposit insurance system.

5.3 Asian financial crisis and the development of new deposit insurance systems

Before the onset of the Asian financial crisis in 1997, no explicit deposit insurance systems were in place in Indonesia, Malaysia and Thailand.

Instead, they relied heavily on implicit protection whereby troubled institutions were generally rescued by the authorities and depositors and most creditors were fully protected. The crisis showed that these arrangement were not only inadequate but that the pervasiveness of these implicit guarantees, combined with deficiencies in supervisory and regulatory framework, exacerbated the crisis. As a result, explicit 100 per cent blanket guarantees, and major financial sector reforms were required, to help stabilize their financial system.

Although the use of blanket guarantees helped provide stability to the countries most affected by the crisis, blanket guarantees can be detrimental if retained too long. This is because they reduce market discipline and introduce significant moral hazard into the financial system.[21] Thus, the IMF and World Bank, as part of a broad package of financial sector reforms, urged Indonesia, Malaysia and Thailand to withdraw their blanket guarantees as soon as financial stability returned and replace them with explicit – but limited – deposit insurance systems.[22]

Due to the severity of the financial crisis in Japan and Korea, these countries were also forced to adopt blanket guarantees in 1996 and 1997 respectively. However, as financial sector stability returned to their economies they have now withdrawn their full guarantees and transitioned back to their limited explicit deposit insurance systems in place before the financial crisis.[23]

The crisis had a less direct impact on Hong Kong, the Philippines, Taiwan and Singapore – no blanket guarantees were introduced as a result of this crisis.[24] The aftermath of the crisis, however, was a period where officials in Hong Kong and Singapore began to review the adequacy of their own financial stability arrangements and look at ways to improve their competitiveness as international financial centres. As a result, both countries undertook a series of financial sector reforms beginning in 1998 which included the development of explicit limited deposit insurance arrangements to bolster stability and add an additional layer of protection for their depositors.[25]

Indonesia

Prior to the Asian financial crisis failed private banks in Indonesia were generally allowed to remain in the system in recapitalized form or otherwise supported by the Bank of Indonesia (BOI). Some banks were closed but all depositors were generally compensated. As an example, Bank Summa was closed and its depositors compensated in the early 1990s.[26]

In November 1997, 16 insolvent small banks were closed as an initial result of the financial crisis. At the same time, the Government announced it would guarantee only small deposits (up to Rp 20 million – then equivalent to US$6,000). This, however, failed to prevent large-scale runs and in January 1998 the Government issued a blanket guarantee covering all Rp and foreign exchange liabilities for all creditors. With the assistance of the IMF, the Indonesian Bank Restructuring Agency (IBRA) was introduced in 1998 and given responsibility for bank resolution and restructuring of insolvent banks.[27] Initially, the administration of the blanket guarantee was shared between the BOI and IBRA. However, from June 2000 onwards, IBRA was given full responsibility.

In addition to the use of blanket guarantees, the BOI continued to provide liquidity support to facilitate the resolution process for troubled banks during the next four years. As stability gradually returned to the financial system, the Indonesian authorities (under the auspices of the IMF and World Bank) began developing a plan for the eventual transition from blanket guarantees to a limited explicit deposit insurance system.[28]

Following a number of years of development, a deposit insurance system was introduced on 22 September, 2005.[29] The Indonesian Deposit Insurance Corporation (IDIC) was established with an initial capital of Rp 4 trillion (US$400 million). It is governed by a six-person Board of Commissioners with three persons from the industry or IDIC employees and one representative each from the MOF, Indonesian Financial Supervisory Authority (FSA) and BOI. The organization's objectives are to protect depositors and promote financial system stability and confidence. The IDIC is deemed an operationally independent institution which is accountable to the President of Indonesia.

The insurer is responsible for failure resolution and payouts and settlement of what are considered non-systemic banks. It can act as a liquidator or nominate a liquidator. All decisions are made by a coordination committee made up of representatives from the IDIC, MOF, FSA, and BOI. A notable feature of the IDIC is that the decision on the type of resolution undertaken will be based on a lowest or least cost to the deposit insurer criteria. Membership is compulsory for all licensed banks and includes foreign bank branches.

With respect to coverage, the IDIC will replace the existing blanket guarantee with a limited guarantee of Rp 5 billion (US$500,000). The plan is to reduce this gradually to Rp 1 billion and then to Rp 100 million (US$11,000) per depositor per institution by March 2007. This coverage limit is expected to protect roughly 98.5 per cent of all individual deposit accounts.

Indonesia's high share of state banks and large number of small domestic banks has caused concerns that the removal of the blanket guarantee may cause abrupt shifts in deposits to state and foreign banks, if not properly managed.[30] Thus, the government decided to provide high levels of coverage for insured depositors in the deposit insurance system and stipulated that systemic banks will continue to receive full blanket protection. Coverage limits will apply on a per depositor per institution basis and will cover demand and savings deposits as well as foreign currency deposits.

Box 5.1 Transitioning from blanket to limited guarantees

According to the Financial Stability Forum Working Group on Deposit Insurance (2001), any country considering transitioning from a blanket guarantee to a limited explicit deposit insurance system should do so as quickly as circumstances permit. Nevertheless, special care must be taken to ensure that some measure of stability has returned to the financial system before transitioning; and, that all necessary structural reforms have been initiated.

Walker and Hoontrakul (2001) caution that the full implementation of a deposit insurance system should only be undertaken when the banking system returns to normalcy and the financial and economic environment is conducive. Otherwise, transitioning could be counterproductive and even lead to increased fragility, capital flight and further exacerbate moral hazard problems. The key questions for policymakers are how to manage the transition process in a timely, orderly and constructive manner and how to design an incentive compatible deposit insurance system.

Of particular concern is that protection for depositors and other creditors is being reduced during the transition process. Therefore, policy makers should pay attention to public attitudes and expectations. In addition, economies with a high level of capital mobility, and/or regional integration, should consider the effects of different protection levels and other related policies. Policy makers need also to consider the capacity of the banking system to fund deposit insurance.

In some transitioning cases, various countries (for example, Indonesia, Japan, Mexico and Hungary) have opted for a gradual removal of blanket guarantees, allowing banks time to adjust to new prudential standards and other reforms. In addition, a gradual transition permits bank managers to be trained in a risk-management culture and gives depositors time to become accustomed to the new arrangements. A major disadvantage, however, is that the transition period might be too long, raising doubts among depositors and creditors about the government's commitment to withdraw the blanket guarantee.

Premiums will initially be set at a minimum 0.1 per cent of banks' insured deposit balances per six-month periods (with a provision to increase it to a maximum of 0.5 per cent per six month period in accordance with a risk-based premium scale which will be fully implemented at a latter date). In practice, the initial rate charged to most banks is expected to be around 0.2 per cent per year and the objective of the IDIC will be to eventually reach a fund target ratio of 2.5 per cent of insured deposits. If additional funds are required, the deposit insurer will be allowed to borrow funds for liquidity purposes from the government.

Malaysia

Bank Negara Malaysia's (BNM) practice prior to the Asian financial crisis was to take over failed commercial banks and market the assets of the failed banks to healthy institutions. In many cases, due to the poor quality of the assets, the acquiring banking institutions reimbursed all depositors of the failed banks with the full assistance of BNM.[31] This created an implicit guarantee among depositors that all their deposits would be fully covered. However, this guarantee covered only commercial banks and finance companies. Other failed institutions, such as deposit-taking cooperatives, were normally liquidated without any compensation to depositors.

Unlike Indonesia and Thailand, systemic bank runs did not occur in Malaysia during the crisis. However, during the latter part of 1997 there was a flight to quality for depositors, which adversely affected several of the weaker banks and finance companies, necessitating BNM liquidity support.[32] The government announced a comprehensive blanket guarantee on deposits in January 1998 to prevent a further shift in deposits and possible bank runs.

In the period 1998–2004, the implementation of bank restructuring and the 2001 Financial Sector Master Plan further strengthened the financial system. It was also in this period that the planning and development of a deposit insurance system was initiated.[33] Since then, the banking system has been restructured and the supervisory and regulatory system updated. Danaharta, Malaysia's bank restructuring agency which played a leading role in the disposal of distressed assets in the financial crisis, completed the bulk of its work and is now being wound down.

The Malaysia Deposit Insurance Corporation (MDIC) was established in August 2005 and became operational on 1 September 2005. Its primary objectives are the protection of depositors and contributing to financial system stability. The MDIC is provided with the additional objectives of reinforcing and complementing the existing regulatory and supervisory system by promoting sound risk management practices; the minimization of regulatory costs; and complying with Shariah Law for Islamic deposits. MDIC is governed by a Board of Directors made up of public and private representatives and managed by a President.[34] The MDIC reports directly to the Minister of Finance.

The deposit insurer's mandate stresses that its function is to minimize resolution costs to the financial system. The MDIC is charged with resolving banks deemed non-viable by Bank Negara (the supervisory authority) and has been granted powers to recapitalize institutions, conduct non-performing loan carve outs, undertake purchase and assumption agreements, and liquidations and payouts to insured depositors. And, regular examinations, other than preparatory exams, will be conducted by Bank Negara.[35] The MDIC has the power to terminate membership in the deposit insurance system.

Membership is mandatory for all commercial banks (including locally incorporated foreign bank subsidiaries but not foreign bank branches) and finance companies. In response to the significant role played by Islamic finance in Malaysia, these institutions are included in Malaysia's deposit insurance system. The maximum coverage level is RM 60,000 (US$16,500) per depositor per institution. Separate protection is provided for joint accounts and trust accounts. Foreign currency deposits are not covered. Islamic and conventional deposits will receive separate but equivalent protection and two separate funds will be created for each sub-scheme.

The system is funded by premiums on insured deposits with the MDIC granted the authority to borrow from the government for liquidity purposes. Premium rates have not yet been determined but the maximum premium rate will be capped at 0.5 per cent of insured deposit liabilities. However, the actual rates imposed are expected to be relatively low given that most problem banks have been resolved and their costs absorbed by the financial system. A differential (risk-adjusted) premium system is expected to be introduced within the first few years of operation. Deposit insurance premiums will be a tax-deductible business expense.

Malaysia's system will also allow depositor liability to a bank to be offset against insured deposit liabilities and depositors will also receive priority over all other unsecured creditors in insolvency. Employees of the MDIC receive legal protection against civil liability for their decisions, actions or omissions taken in 'good faith' while discharging their mandates.

Thailand

Although Thailand experienced a number of financial institution failures prior to 1997, no explicit limited deposit insurance system was created. Instead, authorities dealt with failure resolutions on a case-by-case basis. However, following a series of high profile finance companies failures in the early 1980s, Thailand established the Financial Institutions Development Fund (FIDF) in 1985. The FIDF is administered by the Fund Management Committee, chaired by the Governor of the Bank of Thailand, and funded through bank contributions and interbank and repurchase market borrowings. The FIDF is empowered to provide financial assistance to depositors and creditors. It is viewed as an implicit insurance system since it does not announce *ex ante* the terms and conditions of coverage.[36]

When institutional failures occurred in the 1997 crisis, the financial system was provided with liquidity support by the FIDF but eventually 56 finance firms were permanently closed and most depositors compensated. Nevertheless, by August 1997 blanket guarantees were provided to all creditors in financial institutions in the event of failure. Comprehensive financial restructuring measures were initiated shortly thereafter affecting the legal, supervisory and regulatory systems.

The Financial Restructuring Agency (FRA) was created to provide advice to the MOF on how best to deal with resolving the failed finance companies. As part of these initiatives, a number of private asset management companies were also created to deal with non-performing loans. Eventually a state asset management company was created (that is, Thailand Asset Management Company or TAMC) to deal with the non-performing loan problems and to help viable debtors continue to service their loans. In addition, the Thai government, under advice provided by the IMF and World Bank, initiated the development of an explicit deposit insurance programme to eventually replace the guarantee provided by the FIDF.[37] Further reforms to the system were contained in the 2004 Financial Sector Master Plan which sought to improve financial system stability, efficiency, competitiveness and broaden the accessibility of the financial system for all users.[38]

Thailand has taken steps to establish a deposit insurance system with plans to gradually remove its blanket guarantee over time. For instance, in November 2003, the blanket guarantee for all non-deposit creditors was withdrawn although depositors remained fully protected. On 30 November, 2004, the Cabinet approved a draft law to establish a deposit insurance agency. The law is currently being moved through the legislative process and is expected to be finalized and implemented in 2007 or early in 2008, provided the economic and financial sector environment is conducive.

When this occurs the deposit insurance agency will be established and the process of replacing the existing blanket deposit guarantee with a limited coverage deposit insurance system will commence. At present, it is proposed that the blanket guarantee should be gradually reduced from 50 million Baht (US$1.23 million) per depositor as a first step and then be gradually reduced further to 1 million Baht (US$26,000) by the end of the process. The final coverage limit is expected to cover an estimated 98 per cent of individual depositors and approximately 40 per cent of the value of deposits in the system.[39]

The deposit insurance agency will be provided with a mandate to protect depositors, contribute to financial system stability, assume the task of the liquidator of failed institutions, and minimize costs associated with depositor payouts. It will be a separate legal entity reporting to the Minister of Finance (MOF) and governed by a committee made up of seven persons including representation from the Bank of Thailand (BOT) and MOF.[40] Membership in the system will be compulsory for all banks and finance companies and include foreign bank branches. However, credit unions will not be included in the scheme.

The government is considering granting the insurer the right to demand confidential information from financial institutions in cooperation with the BOT and other financial regulatory agencies. For budgetary purposes, it is envisioned that the agency will not have the classification of a state agency or state enterprise. In keeping with the established practices for supervisory personnel in Thailand, legal indemnification for employees of the agency is expected to be limited.

With respect to funding, the agency would be provided with initial capital of up to 1 billion Baht (US$26 million).[41] The deposit insurer will be allowed to issue bonds but will not be able to borrow from the MOF. Premiums are expected to be set initially at 0.4 per cent of insured deposits, although the deposit insurer will have the authority to raise premiums to a ceiling of 1 per cent of insured deposits. This relatively high premium rate is similar to what the FIDF is currently charging institutions in order to help recover its resolution costs associated with the Asian financial crisis. A differential premium system may eventually be adopted after experience has been gained running the deposit insurance system. The full netting of obligations in an insolvency is expected to be exercised.

Hong Kong

Prior to passing the Hong Kong Deposit Protection Scheme Ordinance in May 2004, depositors were protected primarily through a depositor priority system.[42] As Hong Kong increasingly developed into a major financial centre and most developed economies began adopting deposit insurance systems, it decided to introduce explicit deposit insurance.

Hong Kong's Deposit Protection Board (DPB) is a body corporate with a seven-member board composed of a mix of government ex-officio and private board members. Its mandate is that of a paybox insurer with responsibilities for the contribution (premium) assessment and collection, fund management, depositor compensation (payout) and the recovery of compensation payments from the assets of failed banks. In order to economize on its limited supervisory resources, the DPB performs its functions through the Hong Kong Monetary Authority (HKMA) and reports to the Financial Secretary of the Government of the Hong Kong Special Administrative Region (SAR).

Membership is compulsory for all licensed banks and includes foreign bank branches. This reflects the position of Hong Kong as an international financial centre and the importance of foreign banks in their financial system. Foreign bank branches are exempted if there is an equivalent scheme which covers depositors in the home country. Members of the DPB may be subject to requirements for maintaining assets in Hong Kong.

The coverage limit is set at HKD100,000 (US$13,000) and is estimated to fully cover 84 per cent of individual depositor accounts.[43] Coverage is per depositor per institution with savings, chequing, time deposits and foreign currency deposits booked in Hong Kong being covered. There is separate coverage for special accounts such as joint accounts and trust accounts.

The DPB is funded by contributions collected on protected (insured) deposits. A differential premium system is in place with a range of 0.05–0.14 per cent of protected deposits. The target fund for the DPB is 0.3 per cent of total protected deposits.[44]

A depositor's liabilities to a failed bank will be fully netted or set off against their protected deposits. The board members and those acting on behalf of the DPB will be indemnified and receive legal protection against civil liability when discharging the DPB's mandate in good faith.

Singapore

Singapore began studying a deposit insurance system in 2001 and introduced a deposit insurance system in the latter part of 2005 to provide an extra element of protection for depositors and dispel public expectations of 100 per cent implicit coverage. Due to the small size of its jurisdiction in Singapore, the Monetary Authority of Singapore (MAS) decided to minimize administrative costs as much as possible when designing its deposit insurance system. Thus, the Singapore Deposit Insurance Corporation (SDIC) has been given a paybox mandate with no intervention or resolution powers.[45] The SDIC is a separate legal entity and reports directly to the Minister.[46] Its Board of Directors is made up of both public and private sector officials.

SDIC Membership is compulsory for all full banks (that is, banks allowed to take retail deposits from Singapore residents) and finance companies. Membership includes full foreign bank branches.[47] In terms of coverage, the maximum limit is S$20,000 (US$12,500). Coverage will be per depositor per institution, excluding interbank, foreign currency, and small business deposits. Designated provident funds placed as bank deposits will receive separate protection of up to S$20,000.[48]

Funding of the system is based on the collection of premiums on insured deposits with a differential premium system planned. The differential premium system considered would initially rely on asset maintenance levels and have a range of 0.03–0.08 per cent of insured deposits. It is expected that the differential premium system will in time encompass supervisory ratings as well as asset maintenance levels. A target fund of 0.3 per cent of insured deposits has been set. The deposit insurer may seek access to government funds for emergency liquidity. Presently, Singapore utilizes automatic set-off of mutual obligations in a bank insolvency. As in Hong Kong and Malaysia, employees of the SDIC will receive legal protection from liability while discharging their mandates. According to the governing legislation, depositors (and the insurer) will receive depositor priority in an insolvency.[49]

5.4 Common features, differences and good practices

The following section reviews some of the common features and differences of the new East Asian deposit insurance systems and the extent to which

Table 5.2 New systems being introduced

Country	Governance and structure	Membership	Coverage	Funding
Hong Kong (2005–06)	– DPB a separate legal entity 'paybox model'.	– compulsory for licensed banks. – includes foreign bank branches.	– HKD 100,000 (US$ 13,000). – per depositor, per institution. – includes foreign currency deposits. – depositor priority in place.	– industry funded by premiums on insured deposits. – combined *ex ante/ex post* funding and ability to borrow for liquidity. – target fund (0.3%). – diff. premiums (0.05–0.14% of insured deposits).
Indonesia (2005)	– IDIC a separate legal entity. – 'paybox plus' with a lowest cost resolution mandate and liquidation responsibilities.	– compulsory for all banks. – includes foreign bank branches.	– unlimited to be reduced to IDR 5 billion; IDR 1 billion and finally to IDR 100 million (US$ 11,000). – per depositor per institution – includes foreign currency.	– industry funded by premiums on total deposits. – combined *ex ante/ex post* with govt. borrowing authority. – target fund (2.5%). – diff. prem (0.1–0.6%).
Malaysia (2006)	– MDIC a separate legal entity. – 'pay-box plus' model with a least cost resolution mandate.	– compulsory for all banks, discount houses. – excludes foreign bank branches.	– RM 60,000 (US$ 16,500). – per depositor, per institution, excludes foreign currency deposits. – includes Islamic deposits. – depositor priority in place.	– industry funded with separate assessments for Islamic/ordinary insured deposits. – primarily *ex ante*; power to impose levies and borrow from central bank. – flat rate premiums initially (max rate of 0.5%). – diff. premiums planned.

Singapore (2006)	DIA a separate legal entity. – 'paybox' model.	– compulsory for all 'full' banks and finance companies. – includes foreign bank branches.	– S$ 20,000 (US$ 12,500). – per depositor, per institution. – excludes foreign currency. – depositor priority in place.	– industry funded by premiums on insured deposits. – primarily *ex ante* (target of 0.3% of insured deposits) with power to borrow from the government. – diff. premiums (0.03 – 0.08% of insured deposits envisioned).
Thailand (2007)	DIA a separate legal entity. – 'paybox' model with consideration of a least cost method of depositor payout.	– compulsory for all banks and finance companies. – excludes credit unions and includes foreign bank branches.	– blanket deposit guarantee proposed to be reduced over time to 1 million Baht (US$26,000). – per depositor per institution. – excludes foreign currency. – depositor priority in place.	– industry funded by premiums on insured deposits. – primarily *ex ante* but agency may issue bonds for liquidity purposes. – flat rate premium up to a limit of 1% of insured deposits). – may be replaced by differential system.

the new systems have embraced evolving good practices in deposit insurance developed by organizations such as the International Association of Deposit Insurers (IADI), the organization for Asia-Pacific Economic Cooperation (APEC), the Financial Stability Forum (FSF), and the International Monetary Fund (IMF).[50]

Public policy objectives

All of the new systems formally specify their objectives in legislation with the most common being the protection of depositors and to contribute to financial system stability. Some, such as Malaysia, include additional objects such as the promotion of sound risk management practices and minimizing regulatory costs. Singapore has the objectives of providing extra depositor protection and limiting public expectations of blanket coverage in bank failures.

Mandates and powers

Deposit insurer mandates range from relatively narrow 'paybox' mandates (concentrating on reimbursing depositors of failed institutions) to those encompassing risk assessment and management, failure resolution and direct regulation and supervision. The FSF Working Group (2001a) stresses that there is no single mandate suitable for all deposit insurers. But, whatever mandate is chosen should be formally specified and the powers accorded to the deposit insurer should be consistent with its mandate.

All the systems reviewed specified their mandates in legislation and contain a core paybox component. Singapore and Hong Kong have the most limited systems in terms of mandates and powers, driven by their focus on minimizing administrative costs.

Malaysia and Indonesia have provided more extensive failure resolution powers (and a least cost resolution mandate) to their insurers in an effort to minimize future resolution costs as much as possible. Thailand is considering some form of least-cost resolution approach for its deposit insurance system.

Box 5.2 Summary of key IADI endorsed good practices on building effective deposit insurance systems

- **Mandate and powers**: There is no single mandate suitable for all deposit insurers but mandates need to be formally specified and consistent with powers.
- **Governance**: The sound governance of deposit insurers strengthens the financial system's architecture and contributes directly to financial system stability. An operationally independent

and accountable deposit insurance system, with a clear mandate and which is insulated from undue political and industry influence, provides greater integrity, credibility and legitimacy than entities lacking such independence. The governance framework should also reflect the mandate of the deposit insurer and the governing body should have knowledgeable people.

- **Membership:** Membership should be compulsory and the deposit insurer should have control over entry and exit.
- **Funding**: Member banks should pay for the cost of deposit insurance. There should be *ex ante* and *ex post* arrangements. Deposit insurers should consider the use of differential premiums when they can ensure that the necessary resources are in place to administer the system appropriately.
- **Failure resolution**: Ensuring that a framework exists for prompt corrective action and resolution of troubled banks can reduce the costs to depositors and the deposit insurer, contribute to financial system stability and help reduce the likelihood of an isolated bank failure turning into a financial crisis. Cooperation and information sharing between deposit insurers and supervisory authorities need to be in place before and after a failure.
- **Reimbursing depositors**: It is important to reimburse depositors as quickly and accurately as possible. Preparatory reviews prior to failure are critical.
- **Public awareness**: The public must be informed of the benefits and limitations of deposit insurance on a regular basis.
- **Interrelationships**: Information sharing and coordination mechanisms need to be in place for all safety net participants and unproductive overlap and duplication should be minimized. Formal information sharing arrangements either through legislation, memoranda of understanding, legal agreements or a combination of these techniques are necessary.
- **Legal protection:** Individuals working for deposit insurers and other safety net participants should be protected against legal liability, except in cases of misconduct, for their decisions, actions or omissions taken in 'good faith' while discharging their mandates.
- **Transitioning**: In transitioning from a blanket guarantee to limited coverage, care must be taken to ensure that financial stability has returned; and, policy makers need to understand public attitudes and expectations.

Governance

The IMF, World Bank, APEC and IADI (2005) all stress that sound governance of organizations comprising the safety net strengthens the financial system's architecture and contributes to system stability. Furthermore, operationally independent and accountable safety net organizations, with clear mandates and which are insulated from undue political and industry influence, provide greater integrity, credibility and legitimacy than entities lacking such independence. Independence is helpful for all deposit insurance systems whether they have a simple paybox mandate or more extensive mandates. This guidance also stresses that the governance structure should reflect the public policy objectives and mandate of the insurer.[51] In this regard, all the new systems have adopted a publicly administered model incorporating a Board of Directors structure with both public and private sector representation.[52]

Although the newly established East Asian systems are legally separate organizations, the level of *de facto* independence varies. In Singapore the deposit insurer is accountable to the Minister in charge of the Monetary Authority of Singapore. In Malaysia, the PDIC reports to the Minister of Finance. In Indonesia the IDIC is accountable to the President. Hong Kong's deposit insurer is accountable to the Financial Secretary.

Information sharing and coordination

According to the FSF Working Group (2001a) and IADI Guidance (2005), information sharing and coordination of the activities of the deposit insurer and other safety-net players is extremely important regardless of the insurer's mandate. It is also critical that formal agreements (ideally supported by legislation) be in place between the deposit insurer and other safety-net participants to facilitate information exchange and cooperation. Consideration is given in most of the systems to the use of formal mechanisms to exchange information and coordinate activities. For example Hong Kong, Indonesia and Malaysia have these provisions incorporated into their legislation and appear to be developing standard operating procedures in these areas.

Membership

Compulsory membership has become increasingly common the world over for deposit insurance and in all new East Asian systems. All these systems include their major deposit-taking institutions. Reflecting the importance of foreign banking institutions in their economies, Hong Kong, Indonesia, Singapore and Thailand extend or plan to extend membership to foreign bank branches. The risks of insuring foreign bank branches is generally dealt with in these economies through the use of asset maintenance requirements.

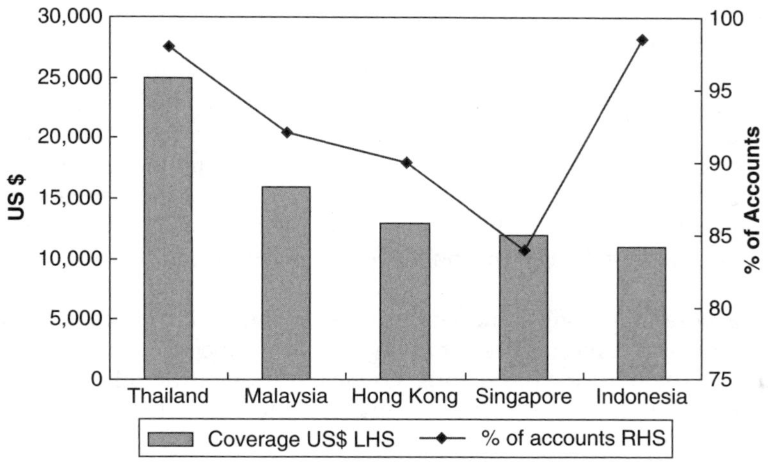

Figure 5.1 New system coverage limits

Coverage

Each of the new East Asian systems cover core demand and saving deposit products. Hong Kong, Indonesia, Malaysia, Singapore and Thailand exclude coverage of non-deposit products and sophisticated depositors. Hong Kong and Indonesia (along with the well established system in the Philippines) are the only systems covering foreign currency deposits. Provident funds placed in bank deposits are covered in Singapore. Islamic deposits receive separate protection in Malaysia from the MDIC.

The maximum coverage limits in the new East Asian systems appear to fully protect the majority of their small depositors (Figure 5.1). The highest proposed coverage level, in terms of the proportion of individual deposit accounts covered, is in Indonesia at 98.5 per cent, followed closely by Thailand.[53] Indonesia's law also stipulates that in the failure of a systemic bank, depositors in these institutions will receive full 100 per cent protection. Although criticized by McLeod (2005) for allowing moral hazard problems to persist, this approach illustrates the overriding concern of Indonesian authorities with ensuring financial stability during the transitioning process. The lowest coverage level (as a proportion of accounts covered) is in Singapore, which covers around 84 per cent of depositors.

Depositors (and the deposit insurer through subrogation) will receive additional protection in Hong Kong, Malaysia and Singapore from the existence of depositor priority in an insolvency.

Funding

According to the FSF Working Group (2001a), member banks should pay for the cost of deposit insurance; there should be *ex ante* and *ex post* arrangements, and deposit insurers should consider the use of differential premiums when they can ensure that the necessary resources are in place to administer the system appropriately. All the new systems meet these good practices. In addition, a number of the systems have introduced target fund ratios. Indonesia has established a target fund ratio of 2.5 per cent of deposits, and both Singapore and Hong Kong envision a ratio of 0.3 per cent of insured deposits as being sufficient for their systems. It should be mentioned that it may take a considerable amount of time for most of these systems to build up the necessary funds to reach these targets.

Singapore and Hong Kong either have or aim to introduce differential premiums and expect to rely heavily on their supervisory system assessments as the basis for the scoring systems. Although the other economies have flat-rate premium systems in use or planned, Indonesia, Malaysia and Thailand have indicated plans to eventually introduce differential systems once they believe they have sufficient experience to implement them effectively.

Failure resolution

Another area where differences have emerged is in failure resolution approaches. Malaysia's MDIC and Indonesia's IDIC have been given a range of powers over failure resolution and accompanying least cost resolution mandates. Malaysia has been provided with the power to conduct preparatory reviews in payout situations. Indonesia's IDIC is subject to a memorandum of understanding with the BOI so that it may conduct preparatory reviews of deposit liabilities or obtain the necessary information from the BOI. Hong Kong's and Singapore's systems are not expected to have any resolution responsibilities as these are expected to remain the responsibility of their respective supervisory authorities. Thailand is considering providing its deposit insurance system with some ability to seek a least-cost method of depositor payouts.

Public awareness

Growing recognition of the importance of public awareness to promote the benefits and limitations of deposit insurance – particularly with respect to facilitating transitioning from blanket guarantees to limited explicit systems – has made this a strong feature of these new systems facing transitioning challenges. Significant resources are being devoted to programmes underway in Malaysia and Indonesia. Public awareness is explicitly noted in deposit insurance statutes in these countries. Thailand plans to implement an extensive public awareness programme to assist in transitioning to its limited explicit deposit insurance system.

5.5 China and deposit insurance

Presently depositors in the People's Republic of China rely on a 100 per cent implicit state guarantee for all deposits. Depositors who have seen their institutions closed have been fully compensated in practice. The distressed assets of the failed institutions are typically acquired by large state-run asset management companies.

In its drive to reform its financial sector, China has announced its intention to introduce an explicit deposit insurance system by 2007. In fact, a special division of the People's Bank of China is now responsible for design and implementation of a scheme. Key objectives so far announced are to introduce fairer treatment among creditors; clarify the management responsibilities for failed banks; protect and compensate depositors in failed banks; and promote nationwide financial reforms.[54]

As development of the scheme progresses, designers of the deposit insurance system will also need to deal with some major financial restructuring issues. For instance, China is in the process of privatizing many of its state banks and this is expected to be a long and involved process. In addition to dealing with the very large state banks, there are approximately 30,000 rural cooperative banks which need to be consolidated in an orderly fashion.[55] Difficult issues will need to be decided such as will deposit insurance be extended to all remaining state banks or only private banks?

The supervisory, legal and accounting regimes in China are also being restructured in an effort to improve the governance and risk management of China's financial system. As an example, China has established a separate supervisor – the China Banking Regulatory Commission – and is developing a new corporate bankruptcy law. The deposit insurance system will need to be consistent with this framework to be effective.

Other questions which need to be addressed are whether the new deposit insurance system will have a limited or extensive risk minimizing mandate; what will be its membership requirements and coverage limits; how will it be funded; how will transitioning to the limited coverage system work; and to what extent will China's deposit insurance system be integrated with that of Hong Kong?

5.6 Regional cooperation

Another issue with deposit insurance in East Asia is regional cooperation. Given that these new deposit insurance systems are being set up at similar times one could ask how the region's insurers could work together more effectively to build their capabilities and deal better with the failure of a bank operating in multiple jurisdictions.

With respect to information sharing and capacity building, a good example of regional cooperation has been made by IADI in setting up an Asia Regional

Committee (ARC) of Deposit Insurers. The Committee has a mandate to reflect regional interests and common issues through the sharing and exchange of information and ideas. Committee members hold regular meetings and conferences throughout the region and have undertaken research into issues such as: transitioning from blanket guarantees to limited coverage systems; developing guidance on failure resolution; and, examining liquidity issues for deposit insurers. Nevertheless, there may be other opportunities to cooperate in the future such as pooling regional information management resources and partnering with other international organizations such as the IMF and Asian Development Bank (ADB) in the further development of their respective deposit insurance systems.[56]

Finally, with the increasing growth in international banking activities, future failures may well occur in entities with more extensive business throughout the region. And, since many of these institution's foreign branches are increasingly covered by host country deposit insurance systems this may become a major issue with the new schemes. Thus, pursuing opportunities for more formal cooperation and information sharing between deposit insurers and supervisory authorities in the region will also contribute to dealing more effectively with bank failures. An example of this could be the development of formal agreements such as Memoranda of Understanding (MOUs) between various deposit insurers and between deposit insurers and supervisory authorities. Areas which could be addressed include: exchange of information on the financial condition and performance of problem banks; coordinating intervention and closure activities; sharing information on deposit liabilities and the dispositions of assets of failed banks.

5.7 Conclusions

Deposit insurance has become well established in East Asia with virtually every economy in the region now having a system in place, being implemented or under serious consideration. A combination of rapid financial sector development, the influence of the Asian financial crises, and a general desire to improve depositor protection and financial system stability have spurred new system development in Hong Kong, Indonesia, Malaysia, Singapore and Thailand.

Although each of these new systems has been designed to meet specific country circumstances, their designers have sought also to adopt evolving good practices in developing their deposit insurance systems. As a result, the systems share similarities in their objectives and design features such as governance, membership, funding and approaches to public awareness. For instance, all the new systems require compulsory membership and will be pre-funded to a large extent from insurance premiums charged to their member banks. Public awareness of the terms and conditions of deposit insurance has been recognized as important and included in the responsibilities of many of the insurers. And, virtually all the new systems are set up as separate legal entities which are operationally independent.

The major differences arise in the areas of mandates and coverage levels. To a large extent this reflects differing country circumstances. For example, Hong Kong and Singapore opted to restrict their deposit insurers to very narrow mandates focused on making payouts to insured depositors in the event of bank liquidation – reflecting concerns with making the most efficient use of their limited supervisory resources. Meanwhile, Indonesia and Malaysia have provided their insurers with broader failure resolution powers and requirements to seek least-cost resolutions. This flows from their recent experience in having to resolve a large number of banking failures and to do everything possible to minimize losses in the resolution process.

In addition to the challenges of building new deposit insurance systems, Indonesia, Malaysia and Thailand are dealing with the special challenge of transitioning from explicit blanket guarantees to limited coverage deposit insurance. In some cases, the development of deposit insurance systems and the removal of blanket guarantees have been postponed due to concerns over the withdrawal of large deposits from banks if these guarantees are eliminated too quickly. As a result, Indonesia and Thailand plan to rely on long transition periods, and at least initially, relatively high coverage limits to make transitioning more acceptable. More stable environments in Hong Kong, Malaysia and Singapore have allowed authorities there to provide more limited coverage.

And, what about future developments in deposit insurance systems in the region? Certainly, one important new development will be what system emerges in the People's Republic of China and what implications this may have on deposit insurance systems in other East Asian economies. Another issue is regional cooperation. Given that these new deposit insurance systems are being set up at similar times one could ask how the region's insurers could work together more effectively to build their capabilities? A good start has been made by IADI in setting up a regional committee of Deposit Insurers to share information and experiences. There may be also other opportunities to cooperate in the future such as pooling regional resources and building partnerships with other international organizations.

Finally, with the increasing growth in international banking activities, future failures may well occur in entities with more extensive business throughout the region. And, since many of these institution's foreign branches are increasingly covered by host country deposit insurance systems this may become a major issue with the new schemes. Thus, pursuing opportunities for more formal cooperation and information sharing between deposit insurers and supervisory authorities in the region could also contribute to dealing more effectively with bank failures.

Notes

1 Mr. Walker is the Director of Policy and International Affairs for the Canada Deposit Insurance Corporation (CDIC). During the past few years he has been providing assistance to a number of Asian economies developing deposit insurance systems.

The findings, interpretations and conclusions expressed in this paper are entirely those of the author and do not represent the views and opinions of CDIC. The author would like to thank Ms. Michèle Bourque and Mr. Guy Saint-Pierre of CDIC, Mr. Goy Siang Boon (Monetary Authority of Singapore), Messrs. Raymond Chan and Gregory Zimnicki (Hong Kong Deposit Protection Board), Ms. Yvonne Fan and Ms. Fiona Yeh (Central Deposit Insurance Corporation of Taiwan), Mr. James Hambric (Bearing Point Indonesia), Mr. David Hoelscher (International Monetary Fund), Dr. Pongsak Hoontrakul (Sasin of Chulalongkorn University), Messrs. Takahiro Hosojima and Yatuka Nishigaki (Deposit Insurance Corporation of Japan), Mr. John Raymond LaBrosse (International Association of Deposit Insurers), Ms. Wai Keen Lai (Malaysia Deposit Insurance Corporation), Ms. Narida Sreshthaputra (Bank of Thailand), Messrs. Ricardo Tan and Antonio L. Panaligan (Philippine Deposit Insurance Corporation) and Dr. Jung Ryol Kim (Korea Deposit Insurance Corporation) for their helpful suggestions and comments. All comments are welcome and should be directed to David K. Walker at [mail to:dwalker@cdic.ca].

2 FSF Working Group (2001a).

3 In this paper the term 'bank' is used to denote all financial institutions which accept deposits from the general public. The term 'run' is defined as a rapid loss of deposits precipitated by fear on the part of the public that a bank may fail and depositors may suffer losses. 'Contagion' refers to the spread of individual bank runs to other institutions.

4 In most economies, the monetary authority typically supplies lender of last resort (LOLR) facilities to troubled banks. LOLR loans are in principle provided to illiquid but solvent banks and at a penalty rate.

5 Implicit deposit protection arrangements exist where depositors believe they will receive full protection in the event of a bank failure. However, most deposit protection arrangements are explicit and stipulate in legislation the rules governing the terms and conditions of protection. Explicit deposit insurance is viewed as being preferable to implicit protection because it reduces uncertainty and risk for depositors and can be helpful in reducing expectations on the part of the public of full government support in the event of a bank failure. Although some argue that a degree of uncertainty can lead depositors to exert greater effort in monitoring banks, in reality most depositors are not capable of doing so and/or do not have the necessary information or incentives to effectively monitor banks. For more information, see: FSF Working Group (2001a) and Garcia (2000).

6 Other less common objectives for deposit insurance include: enhancing competition providing a mechanism to close troubled banks; and ensuring resolution costs are absorbed by the banking industry. See also CDIC (2003) and Garcia (1999).

7 See Diamond and Dybvig (1983).

8 In addition to limiting coverage there are numerous other design features which can help minimize moral hazard including: the use of differential or 'risk-adjusted'

premiums; the introduction of certain forms of co-insurance; and minimizing the risk of loss through early closure of troubled banks.

9 A 'systemic crisis' is defined as a crisis situation which affects and seriously threatens the viability of the entire financial system.

10 See FSF Working Group (2001a).

11 East Asia is defined to include: Japan, Korea, the People's Republic of China, Hong Kong (SAR), Macau (SAR), Taiwan, the Philippines, Vietnam, Cambodia, Laos, Thailand, Myanmar, Malaysia, Brunei, Singapore and Indonesia.

12 In this period Indonesia, Malaysia and Thailand generally relied on implicit guarantees while Hong Kong and Singapore emphasized the protection of depositors through prudential supervision and priority accorded to depositors over other creditors in insolvency law (that is depositor priority). The People's Republic of China relies primarily on state bank guarantees to protect depositors.

13 See: Republic of the Philippines (1963), Deposit Insurance Law of Japan (1971), Republic of China (1985) and Republic of Korea (1996).

14 See Socialist Republic of Vietnam (1999).

15 There are many different types of mandates available for deposit insurance systems. These typically range from so-called pure 'paybox' type of structures to 'risk minimizers'. A 'paybox' insurer mandate is generally focused on paying out the claims of protected depositors after a bank has been closed. Paybox insurers typically do not have intervention and examination powers. Some paybox systems have been given the added responsibility to minimize costs associated with the closure of banks. That is, while they are mainly reactive they may have some proactive features such as access to risk assessment information and they may play a role in decisions on failure resolution. These have been referred to as 'paybox-plus' or 'least cost resolution' systems. Deposit insurers with a full 'risk minimization' mandate are usually required to minimize their exposure to loss and therefore, be proactive in terms of on-going risk identification, assessment and management.

16 See Republic of the Philippines (1963) and PDIC Annual Report (2003).

17 See Deposit Insurance Law of Japan (1971) and the Deposit Insurance Corporation of Japan Annual Report (2004).

18 See Republic of China (1985) and Central Deposit Insurance Corporation (2004).

19 See Republic of Korea (1996) and Korea Deposit Insurance Corporation Annual Report (2004).

20 See Socialist Republic of Vietnam (1999) and Hai (2005).

21 See FSF Working Group (2001a).

22 See Lane *et al.* (1999).

23 See Nanto (1998) and the IMF (2000).

24 In Taiwan, an implied blanket guarantee was avoided in 1997. But the emergence of serious problems with a number of financial institutions in 2001 led to the eventual introduction of a *de facto* blanket guarantee.

25 See HKMA (2002), MAS (2002) and the IMF (2003,2004).

26 See Akhtar (2004).

27 See Ingves (2001).

28 See IMF (2005).

29 The year 2005 also saw the winding down of IBRA after the agency recovered approximately 28 per cent of the US$60 billion in distressed assets it had managed since 1998. The Ministry of Finance set up a temporary unit to deal with remaining failure resolutions until the IDIC becomes fully operational.

30 See Indonesia Ministry of Finance (2004).
31 This happened in the mid-1980s during the failure of 36 deposit-taking cooperatives which were not under the supervision of BNM.
32 See Akhtar (2004).
33 Malaysia Ministry of Finance (2001).
34 See Bank Negara Malaysia (2005) and MDIC Act (2005).
35 A preparatory exam is usually undertaken prior to depositor reimbursement (payout). It is an examination of the books, records and accounts of the bank relating to its deposit liabilities.
36 See Wesaratchakit (2002).
37 See IMF (October 2005).
38 See Thailand Ministry of Finance (2004).
39 See Yuthamanop and Sirithiveeporn (2002).
40 See Pattaya Mail (2004).
41 See Siam Global Associates Law Bulletin (2004).
42 Depositor priority is the granting of preferential treatment to depositors in an insolvency such that their claims (typically unsecured) must be paid in full before remaining (unsecured) creditors can collect on their claims. However, a drawback with depositor priority is that the assets available to depositors are dependent on the liquidation process and there is no certainty that depositors will receive all of their claims. In addition, because of the complexity of the liquidation process, depositors have no clear indication of the speed of repayment of their priority claims. For more information see FSF Working Group (2001b).
43 See Arthur Andersen (2000).
44 Deposit Protection Scheme Ordinance (2005).
45 The scheme become operational in April 2006.
46 See Singapore Deposit Insurance Act (2005) and MAS (2004).
47 Singapore intends to require foreign bank branches to meet asset maintenance requirements (for example, the minimum requirement is 100 per cent of the insured deposit base) to ensure that there will be sufficient assets in Singapore to meet the insured deposit liabilities of the branch.
48 A provident fund is a fund in which an individual contributes a defined per centage of their salary over the course of their working life in order to receive a lump sum or other form of payment for retirement or other purposes. Provident funds can be administered privately or by governments.
49 Depending on the specific arrangements, depositor priority systems have the potential to lower costs for a deposit insurer. However, this can be mitigated to some degree by the ability of lower ranked creditors to collateralize obligations, initiate early withdrawal of funds and other measures at their disposal. For more information, refer to the FSF Working Group Discussion Paper on Depositor Priority (2001).
50 See FSF Working Group (2001a), Garcia (1999, 2000) and IADI (2005).
51 See IADI (2005).
52 By far the most common deposit insurance systems are those administered by governments. Their main advantages are that they provide the full faith and credit of the government and are part of the financial safety net. As a result, they are able to maintain depositor confidence even in times of great financial stress. Government-backed systems also tend to have the advantage of offering a clear legal obligation pay depositors. Many private systems do not provide this degree of legal certainty.

53 Despite the high levels of individual deposit accounts coverage, the actual value of deposits protected is relatively low (that is estimated to be around 40 per cent for Thailand and 38 per cent for Indonesia).
54 See Hatano (2005).
55 See Bekier, Huang and Wilson (2005).
56 See IADI (2004).

References

Akhtar, S. (2004) *Presentation to the IADI Asia Regional Committee: Challenges for Deposit Insurers Post-Banking Crisis Experiences in East Asia*, Manila:Asian Development Bank.

Aliston, L. Grove W. and Wheelock, D. (1994) Why Do Banks Fail?, *Explorations in Economic History*, vol. 31, no. 4.

Arthur Andersen (2000) *Deposit Protection Study for the Hong Kong Monetary Authority - Final Report*, Hong Kong, July 31.

Bank Negara Malaysia (2001) *Financial Sector Master Plan*, Kuala Lumpur.

Bank Negara Malaysia (2005) *Deposit Insurance System Introduced for Enhanced Consumer Protection*, PEN. 09/05/03 (BN), Kuala Lumpur, September.

Baxendale, B. (2005) *Deposit Insurance Programs in Asia*, Federal Reserve Bank of San Francisco, Asia Focus Publication, March.

Bekier, M., Huang, R. and Wilson, G. (2005) 'How to Fix China's Banking System', *McKinsey Quarterly*, no. 1, October.

Canada Deposit Insurance Corporation (2003) *International Deposit Insurance Survey* see,www.cdic.ca/?id=285, Ottawa.

Central Deposit Insurance Corporation (2004) *Annual Report*, Taipei, Taiwan.www.cdic. gov.tw/ct.asp?xItem=863&ctNode=433.

Demirgüç-Kunt, A. and Kane, E. (2001) *Deposit Insurance around the Globe: Where Does it Work?*, Washington DC: World Bank.

Deposit Insurance Corporation of Japan (2003) *Annual Report*, Tokyo. http://www.dic. go.jp/english/e_annual/e_annual_fy2003.html.

Deposit Insurance Corporation of Japan (2004), Annual Report, Tokyo, http://www.dic. go.jp.english/e_annual/e_annual_fy2004,html.

Deposit Insurance Law of Japan (1971) Diet of Japan, Tokyo.

Diamond, D.W. and Dybvig, P.H. (1983) 'Bank Runs, Deposit Insurance, and Liquidity', *Journal of Political Economy* vol. 91: 3, pp. 401–19.

Financial Stability Forum Working Group on Deposit Insurance (2001a) *Guidance for Developing Effective Deposit Insurance Systems: Final Report of the Working Group on Deposit Insurance*, Basel, September.

Financial Stability Forum Working Group on Deposit Insurance (2001b) *Discussion Paper on Depositor Priority and Right of Set off (Netting)*, Guidance for Developing Effective Deposit Insurance Systems, Volume II, Basel, Switzerland, September.

Garcia, G. (1999) *Deposit Insurance: A Survey of Actual and Best Practices*, IMF Working Paper, Washington DC, April.

Garcia, G. (2000) *Deposit Insurance and Crisis Management*, IMF Working Paper, Washington DC, February.

Hai, Do Khac (2005) *Experience of Deposit Insurance Vietnam in Dealing with Bank Failures*, Presentation at the IADI International Conference and AGM, Taipei, Taiwan.

Hatano, M. (2005) *Introductory Remarks to the Deposit Insurance International Forum of the People's Bank of China*, Dalian, China, September.

Hong Kong Deposit Protection Board (2005) *Annual Report*, www.info.gov.hk/hkma/eng/dis/ar0405e.pdf.

Hong Kong Monetary Authority (2002) *Second Public Consultation on Deposit Insurance*, Hong Kong, July.

Hong Kong Special Administrative Region (2004) *Deposit Protection Scheme Ordinance*, 13 May.

Indonesia Ministry of Finance (2004) *Law of the Republic of Indonesia Concerning the Deposit Insurance Corporation*, Jakarta, December.

Ingves, S. (2001) *Bank Crises and Beyond: Lessons Learned in Asia*, International Monetary Fund, Presented at the KDIC Symposium on International Financial Crises and Beyond, Seoul.

International Association of Depositors (2004) *Annual Report 2003/2004*, Basel. www.iadi.org/html/App/SiteContent/IADI%20Final%20AR%202003%202004.pdf.

International Association of Deposit Insurers (2005) *Key Conclusions of the APEC Policy Dialogue on Deposit insurance as Official IADI Guidance*, Basel.www.iadi.org/html/App/SiteContent/IADI%20-%20APEC%20Guidance%20June%202005.pdf.

International Monetary Fund (2005) *Article IV Consultation with Indonesia*, Washington, DC, July.

International Monetary Fund (2005) *Article IV Consultation with Malaysia*, Washington, DC, July.

International Monetary Fund (2005) *Article IV Consultation with Thailand*, Washington, DC, October.

International Monetary Fund (2003) *People's Republic of China: Hong Kong (SAR) Financial Stability Assessment*, Washington, DC, June.

International Monetary Fund (2000) *Recovery from the Asian Crisis and the Role of the IMF*, Staff Paper, June.

International Monetary Fund (2004) *Singapore Financial Stability Assessment*, Washington, DC, April.

Korea Deposit Insurance Corporation (2003) *Annual Report*, Seoul, www.kdic.or.kr/english/annual_report/annual_report.jsp?mkp=06.

Korea Deposit Insurance Corporation (2004) *Annual Report*, Seoul, www.kdic.or.kr/english/annual_report/annual_report.jsp?mkp=06.

Lane, T., Ghosh A., Hamann J., Phillips S., Schulze-Ghattas M., and Tsikata T. (1999) IMF-Supported Programs in Indonesia, Korea, and Thailand: A Preliminary Assessment, occasional paper no. 178, Washington, DC.

Malaysia Deposit Insurance Corporation Act (2005) *Laws of Malaysia (Act 642)*, Kuala Lumpur.

Malaysia Ministry of Finance (2001) *Financial Sector Master Plan*.

McLeod, R.H. (2005) *Indonesia's New Deposit Guarantee Law*, Australian National University, August.

Monetary Authority of Singapore (MAS) (2002) *Working Paper on Deposit Insurance*, Singapore, March.

Monetary Authority of Singapore (MAS) (2005) *Consultation on Draft Deposit Insurance Bill*, Singapore, January.

Nanto, R.K. (1998) *Congressional Research Report (CRS) on the 1997–98 Asian Financial Crisis*, Washington, DC, February.

Pattaya Mail (2004) *Deposit Insurance Institute Set Up Next Year*, vol.12, no. 3, Thailand, August.

Philippines Deposit Insurance Corporation (2003) *Annual Report*, Manila, www.pdic.gov.ph/import/2003-2annualreport.pdf.

Republic of China (1985) *Banking Law of the Republic of China: Article 46*, Taipei.

Republic of Korea (1996) *Deposit Protection Act*, Seoul,.
Republic of the Philippines (1963) *Philippine Deposit Insurance Corporation Charter*, Manila.
Schmidt, R. H. and Wrinkler, A. (1999) *Building Financial Institutions in Developing Countries*, W.P. 45, Johann Wolfgang Goethe-Universitat, Frankfurt au Main, November.
Siam Global Associates Law Bulletin (2004) *Financial Sector Goes Forward with New Deposit Insurance Agency*, vol. 6:(3), Bangkok, Thailand, December.
Singapore (2005) *Deposit Insurance Act.*
Socialist Republic of Vietnam (1999) Decree *No. 89/1999/ND-CP on Deposit Insurance*, Hanoi.
Thailand Ministry of Finance (2004) *Financial Sector Master Plan*, Bangkok.
Walker D. and Hoontrakul P. (2001) 'Transitioning from Blanket to Limited Deposit Guarantees: Thailand Policy Consideration', *Sasin Journal of Management*, vol. 7, no. 2, Bangkok, Chulalongkorn University.
Wesaratchakit, W. (2002) *The Future of Deposit Insurance System in Thailand*, Bank of Thailand Publication, Bangkok.
World Bank Policy Research Report (2001) *Finance for Growth: Policy Choices in a Volatile World*, Washington, DC.
Yuthamanop, W. and Sirithiveeporn, W. (2002) 'Four Year Time Frame Looks Likely To Cover Up To B1M Limit Per Account', *Bangkok Post*, Thailand, October.

6

Financial Disintermediation, Financial Sector Regulation and Deposit Insurance[1]

Jean Roy and Marc-André Flageole

This chapter provides an explanation of how deposit insurance helps in developing the economy and a strong financial sector in particular. But it also reflects on how insurance can lead to disintermediation and hence be counterproductive.

Financial systems around the world are undergoing profound transformations. Financial institutions are growing at a fast pace in size, scope and geographic reach. At the same time, their operations are more and more integrated with financial markets. For banks in particular, the traditional intermediation role of taking deposits and making loans is becoming a less central activity. This evolution raises several questions that this chapter surveys. First it examines the phenomenon of disintermediation. Starting with some clarifications on the concept of intermediation, it discusses the various ways through which disintermediation can occur. It surveys a number of studies that have documented disintermediation in various countries and provides evidence on disintermediation in Canada. It then examines the effects of disintermediation at the micro and macro economic levels. The second part of the chapter looks at the possible causes driving disintermediation. It first examines market forces at work both on the demand and the supply side. Finally, it studies the impact of financial regulation and in particular deposit insurance on disintermediation.

6.1 Disintermediation: concepts, evidence and effects

Concepts of disintermediation

To begin, it may be useful to define intermediation itself. Financial intermediation occurs when a financial institution accepts savings from the public and acknowledges a fixed obligation such as a deposit, a life insurance policy or some retirement income. In turn, in the meantime, these savings are invested in the real economy. The fixed obligation taken towards savers creates a solvency risk that is controlled by the capital of the financial intermediary. Alternatively, providers and users of capital can avoid financial intermediaries and transact directly in financial markets. Thus, financial intermediaries are in constant competition with direct finance as provided by financial markets. Providers and users of capital can also transact directly, without either markets or intermediaries if they are not efficient

This raises the basic question: 'Why do intermediaries exist?' In a world of perfect markets, where there are no transactions costs, every asset is divisible at will and information is free and available to all, there is no rationale for intermediaries. Thus, the simple answer to the existence of intermediaries lies in market imperfections. Through the years, the financial literature has focused in turn on transaction costs (Benston and Smith, 1976), on information costs (Diamond, 1984; Allen, 1990) and more recently on participation costs (Allen and Santomero, 1997). Gorton and Winton (2002) offer an excellent survey of the current status of financial intermediation theory. Up to now, the explanation based on information costs has been the dominant one. According to this view, intermediaries and, especially banks, can exploit economies of scale in screening, monitoring and eventually renegotiating loans. The economic value of bank lending seems to be recognized by financial markets as many event studies have showed that a bank loan announcement is generally followed by an increase in the price of the shares of the borrower (Aintablian and Roberts, 2000).

As financial intermediaries compete with financial markets, it may be useful also to refer to the theory of competitiveness of Michael Porter (1980). According to Porter, a firm has two basic strategies to compete. First, it can try to differentiate itself from its competition. If this is possible, price competition may be less important as the firm has a partial monopoly on the goods or services it is offering. On the other hand, if the firm cannot achieve differentiation then it has to compete on price. To do so, it is critical that it becomes a low cost producer. As many financial services are difficult to differentiate, cost control is a very important factor of competitiveness for financial institutions.

With these concepts in mind, it is now possible to examine disintermediation. Generally, disintermediation occurs when financial intermediaries are less used as a channel to move capital from providers to users. Many distinctions may be made on this broad definition. First, disintermediation can occur either on the liability side, on the asset side or on both sides of the balance sheet of intermediaries. Second, we will argue that disintermediation can occur either *ex ante* or *ex post*. *Ex ante disintermediation* occurs when providers and users of capital decide to avoid the intermediaries altogether and transact in financial markets right from the start. *Ex post disintermediation* occurs when a transaction is first done through an intermediary that decides afterwards to pull out of the transaction. Third, in the case of a bank loan, traditional intermediation implies that the bank funds the loan and assumes the credit risk associated with the loan. With modern financial markets, banks can pull out of these two functions through securitization or the use of credit derivatives. Thus, we might distinguish between *disintermediation of funding* and *disintermediation of risk-taking*. Finally, it may be important to observe the relative extent of disintermediation among the various types of intermediaries. Clearly, in the context of this chapter, the focus will be put on disintermediation as it affects depository institutions. It must be noted that part of the intermediation activity lost or abandoned by depository institutions may just be taken up by other types of intermediaries such as life insurance companies and pension funds. So, it may again be useful to distinguish between *depository institutions disintermediation* and *overall disintermediation*.

Evidence on disintermediation

This section presents evidence on disintermediation in various contexts. It first reviews evidence on disintermediation in selected countries as described in a few representative articles in order to provide a global background for the situation in Canada. Then it shows and discusses several indicators of the evolution of disintermediation in Canada.

Disintermediation in selected countries

Allen and Santomero (2001) study the evolution of financial intermediation in the USA. They show that long term trends are at work. Since 1950, among financial intermediaries, the share of financial assets held by depository institutions has steadily declined from 60 per cent to just above 20 per cent, while mutual funds and pension and retirement funds have grown considerably. Similarly, banks were controlling roughly 80 per cent of commercial and industrial loans in 1960, but accounted for less than 60 per cent in 1999, yielding their market share mainly to finance companies. Surprisingly, banks also lost ground in the market for credit card receivables going from a share of 95 per cent in 1986 to a small 25 per cent share in 1998. At the same time, the per centage of securitized mortgages has jumped from about 10 per cent in 1980 to some 40 per cent in 1998. On the liability side, bank time and savings deposits declined from nearly 100 per cent of fixed-income mutual funds in 1980 to some 70 per cent in 1997. Consequent to this evolution, the relative economic magnitude of traditional bank intermediation has declined, more precisely net interest income less charge-offs as a per centage of financial sector GDP has declined from 0.38 per cent in 1977 to 0.29 per cent in 1997. Offsetting this setback, non-interest income as a per centage of financial sector GDP has risen from 0.09 per cent in 1977 to 0.18 per cent, such that bank value added as a per cent of financial sector GDP has remained essentially constant over the period 1977 to 1997 at 0.49 per cent. Obviously, this has been achieved through a very significant transformation of banks' activities away from traditional intermediation and very much towards risk management which is largely done off-balance sheet.

Schmidt *et al.* (1999) present an international comparison of disintermediation and the role of banks in France, Germany and the UK over the period 1981–1996. They examine both intermediation and securitization ratios to shed light on four hypotheses. Their conclusions are the following. First, their data do not support the hypothesis that there is a general trend toward disintermediation. There is no such trend in Germany and the UK, but there is a 'quite pronounced' one in France. Second, their evidence is consistent with the hypothesis that there is a general trend toward securitization, although the levels and rates of increase differ among the three countries. Third, the data do not support the hypothesis that there is a decline in the role or importance of banks. Similarly to the first hypothesis, there is no such trend in Germany and the UK, but there seems to be one in the case of France. Finally, evidence seems consistent with the hypothesis that 'there is a tendency on the part of banks to reduce more their level of activity as mobilizers of funds from the non-financial sectors more than the extent of their role as lenders' (p.63). They add that 'Thus instead of a simple shift from banks to capital markets we find a trend toward increased specialization by banks in lending operations, with a growing portion of the function of mobilizing savings being left to Non-Bank Financial Intermediaries' (p.63). They note that two interpretations seem possible: either this trend may be economically sound and efficiency increasing or it may reflect that banks are under stress due to increasing costs of funding. To sum up this research, although overall disintermediation and the decline of the role of banks are not supported, the trend toward securitization and the decline of the role of banks as mobilizers of funds from the non-financial sectors emerge from the evidence.

Overall, these two studies lead to a consistent pattern of historical trends in the four countries: namely a relative decline of deposit-taking by banks, a significant growth of securitization and a relative specialisation of banks in lending and risk management. As a complement to the observation of this evolution, it may also be interesting to position Canada in a cross section of countries with regard to these measures of intermediation intensity.(See Table 6.1)

Given this comparison of developed countries, one sees that the top four countries (lowest values of bank assets over market capitalization) are of Anglo-Saxon origin and, with the exception of Great Britain, the three other countries have the three lowest values for domestic assets of deposit money banks relative to their GDP. These countries thus share the characteristic of relying strongly on their financial markets relative to their banking systems compared to other developed countries. In this perspective, even though Canada is not a very finance-intensive country, it is already among the countries having the most market-based financial systems. With

Table 6.1 Banks versus market capitalization (1990s average)

Country	Domestic assets of deposit money banks / GDP	Market capitalization / GDP	Domestic assets of deposit money banks / market capitalization
USA	0.73	0.80	0.91
Great Britain	1.16	1.13	1.03
Australia	0.77	0.71	1.08
Canada	0.66	0.59	1.12
Netherlands	1.12	0.69	1.63
Japan	1.31	0.79	1.66
Switzerland	1.77	0.98	1.80
France	1.02	0.33	3.11
Spain	0.96	0.30	3.20
Germany	1.21	0.24	5.01

Source: Data extracted from Demirgűç-Kunt and Levine (1999, table 5, p. 50); figures are averages over the 1990s.

this information as a background, the next section looks in greater detail at the evolution of disintermediation in Canada.

Disintermediation in Canada

As in the USA, financial intermediation seems to follow long-term trends in Canada. First, we examine the potential shift from traditional intermediaries towards market-based financial institutions and instruments. Second, we evaluate the changes in banks' financial results achieved through traditional intermediation. Third, we discuss the evolution of the financial activities of Canadian chartered banks in recent years. Fourth, we look at the evolution of the structure of the financial intermediation sector as a whole.

Financial intermediaries and markets. First, we observe that assets and loans of chartered banks and insurance companies declined relative to assets and loans of finance companies. In 1988, finance companies assets represented 8 per cent of those of banks and insurance firms while the same amounts account for 34 per cent today (Figure 6.1). Still in 1988, lending by finance companies represented barely 4.5 per cent of lending by traditional intermediaries while by 2003 it is around 14.5 per cent (Figure 6.2).

A second trend appears if we compare investments in mutual funds to traditional deposits in banks. While in 1990, mutual funds value was only 4 per cent of these deposits, it was slightly over 50 per cent by the end of the year 2000 (Figure 6.3). From 1995 to 2003, bank assets also became less important relative to the total value of shares listed on the Toronto Stock Exchange (Figure 6.4). To examine this shift more closely, it seems relevant

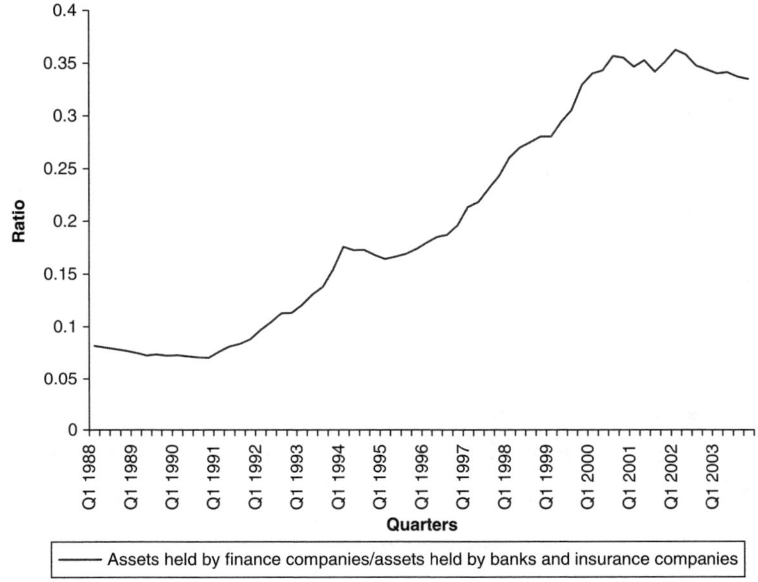

Source: CANSIM.

Figure 6.1 Total assets held by finance companies/total assets held by banks and insurance companies in Canada

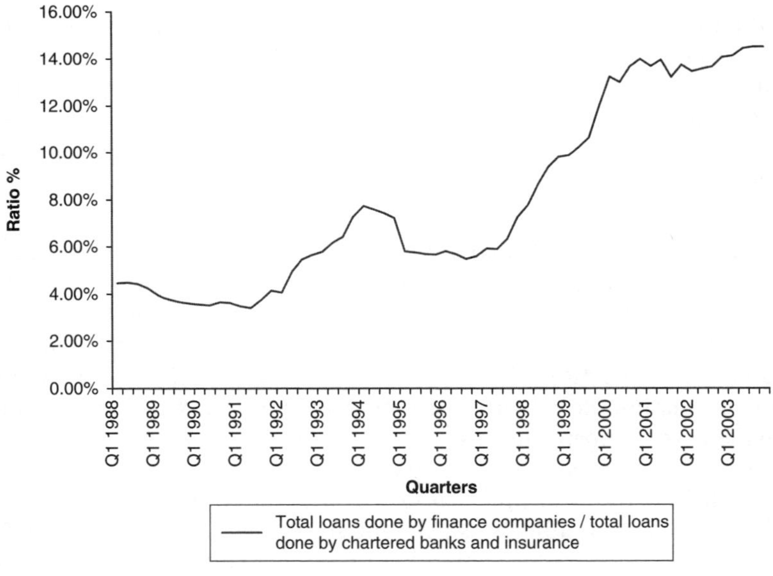

Source: CANSIM.

Figure 6.2 Proportion of total loans in Canada by finance companies versus chartered banks

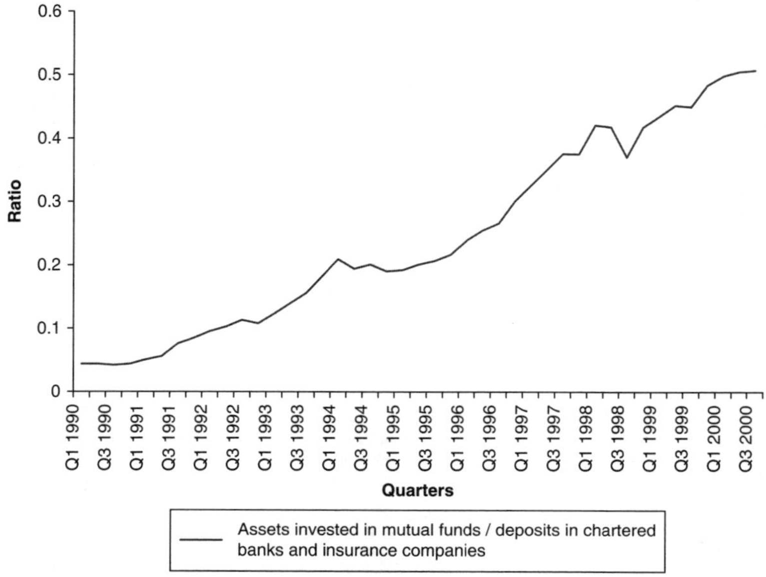

Sources: The Investment Funds Institute of Canada and CANSIM.
Figure 6.3 Total assets invested in mutual funds/deposits in chartered banks and insurance companies in Canada

to link the phenomenon with interest rates of traditional deposits and the rate of return of the S&P/ TSX stock index. While banks deposits declined relative to mutual funds, the stock market yielded higher returns relative to guaranteed certificates (Figure 6.5). Thus, it seems that investors shifted a significant part of their savings away from financial intermediaries into more profitable market based instruments.

Financial performance of chartered banks. Since 1996, net interest income (*revenues from lending minus costs from deposits*) increased steadily, in nominal terms and relative to total revenues of chartered banks. In 1996, net interest income amounted for 11.1 per cent of total revenues while the same ratio is around 25 per cent by 2004 (Figure 6.6). As Allen and Santomero (2001) did in estimating the evolution of intermediation relative to other financial activities, we compare the net interest income of chartered banks to the financial sector gross domestic product. In 1997, net interest income was around 0.30 per cent of financial sector GDP, fell to 0.20 per cent in 2001 and rose back to around 0.36 per cent since then (Figure 6.7). However, this increase seems to be mainly due to a better control of deposits costs. Put differently, interest income of banks did not get significantly higher, only did the net interest income. While the costs of deposits accounted for

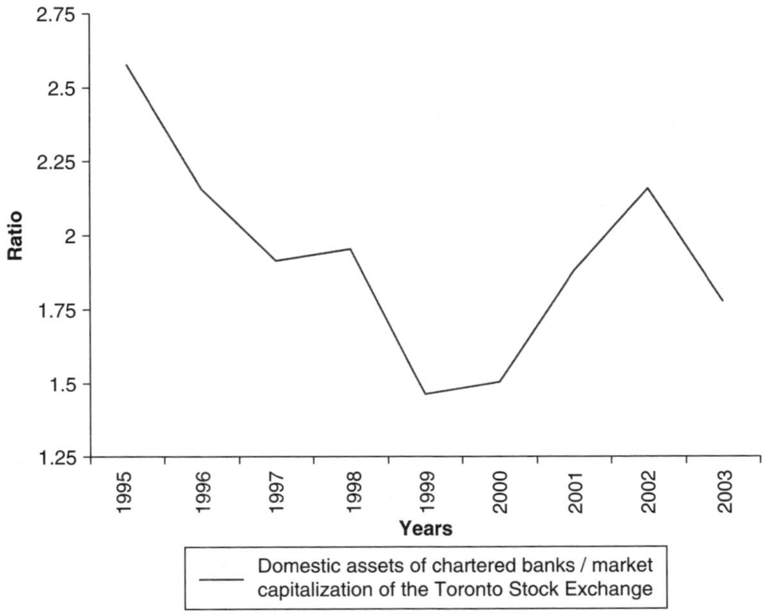

Sources: CANSIM and World Federation of Exchanges.
Figure 6.4 Domestic assets of chartered banks in Canada/market capitalization of the Toronto Stock Exchange

77.5 per cent of lending revenues in 1996, by 2004, they represent only 48.8 per cent (Figure 6.8).

Evolution of banking activities. We examine to what extent Canadian banks restructured their activities away from receiving deposits and granting credit. In 1997, non-interest income of chartered banks was 0.36 per cent of the financial sector gross domestic product while the same proportion was around 0.53 per cent in 2004 (Figure 6.9). This shows that, as it is the case in the USA, income from activities such as risk management or securities' trading now account for a greater proportion of bank revenues in Canada.

We also note a growth in securitization and in the use of credit derivatives for hedging purposes. Using these financial instruments, banks transfer the risk related to their lending activities mainly by reducing their stakes in borrowers and, in turn, in the financial intermediation process. While securitization companies were virtually non-existent 20 years ago in Canada, they now hold a significant share of the credit institutions market. In 1992, their market share was around 2 per cent and grew up to 14 per cent by 2003 (Figure 6.10). Moreover, in 1992, total lending through securitization firms accounted for 2.8 per cent of total lending by chartered banks while this proportion was around 21.1 per cent by 2003 (Figure 6.11). In 1998, the

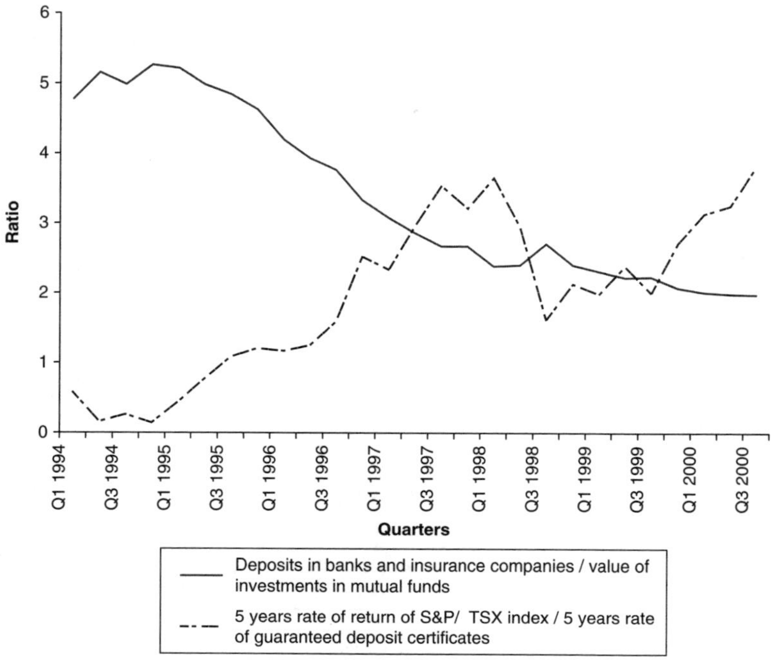

Sources: CANSIM, The Investment Funds Institute of Canada and the Bank of Canada.
Figure 6.5 Comparison of bank and insurance companies deposits decline and increase of stock the Toronto Stock Exchange rate of return

credit derivatives contracts for hedging purposes held by the seven major Canadian banks were worth 325 billions dollars. In 2003, they amounted to 945 billions, an increase of approximately 190 per cent in five years (Figure 6.12).

Evolution of the financial intermediation sector. In addition to chartered banks, intermediation is performed by financial institutions such as insurance companies, credit unions, pension funds or trust and mortgage loan companies. Similarly to banks, these organizations contract a fixed obligation with savers and invest in more or less risky assets. However, savers have typically much less control over the withdrawal of their funds than they have at banks. Table 6.2 shows the evolution of several intermediaries' total domestic assets since 1993.

While Canadian chartered banks seem to have lost ground to market based financial institutions on lending activities, they recently enjoyed the fastest growth within intermediaries in terms of total domestic assets. Since 1993, their assets grew by approximately 150 per cent followed closely by those of pension funds which rose by 120 per cent. Even if intermediaries

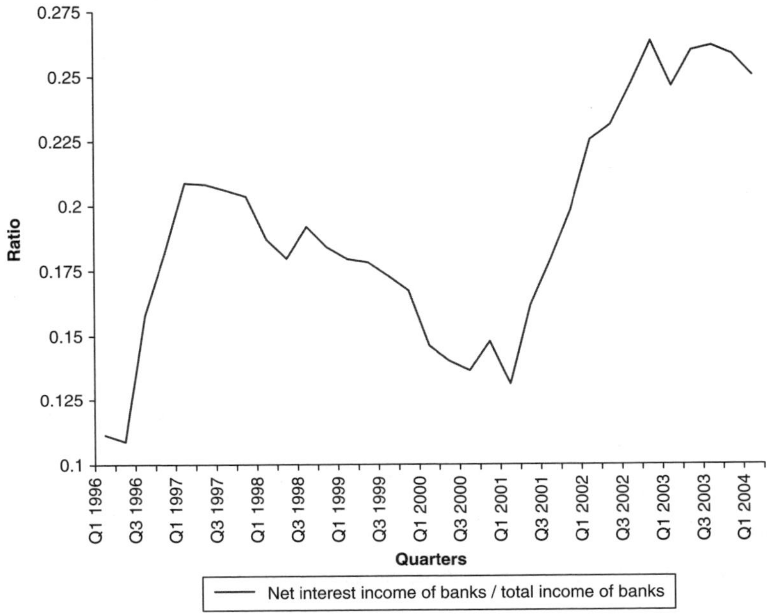

Source: Office of the Superintendent of Financial Institutions.

Figure 6.6 Net interest income of banks/total income of banks in Canada

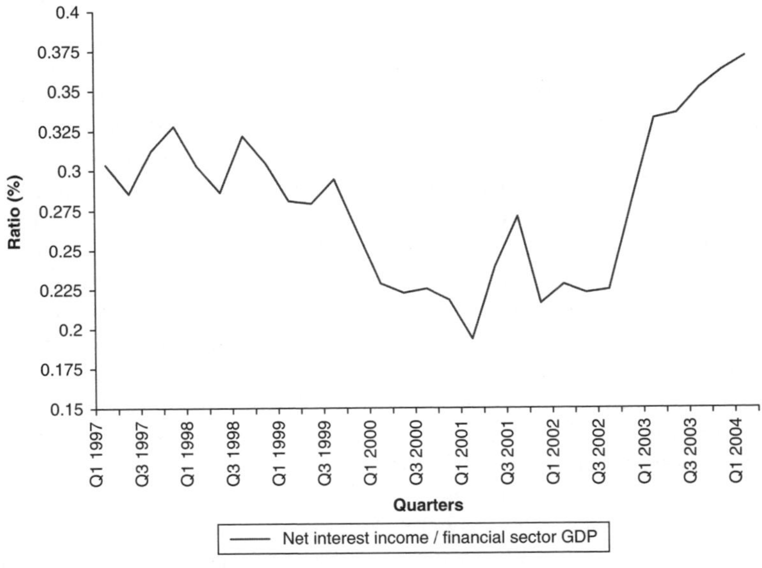

Sources: Office of the Superintendent of Financial Institutions and CANSIM.

Figure 6.7 Net interest income of chartered banks relative to the financial sector gross domestic product in Canada

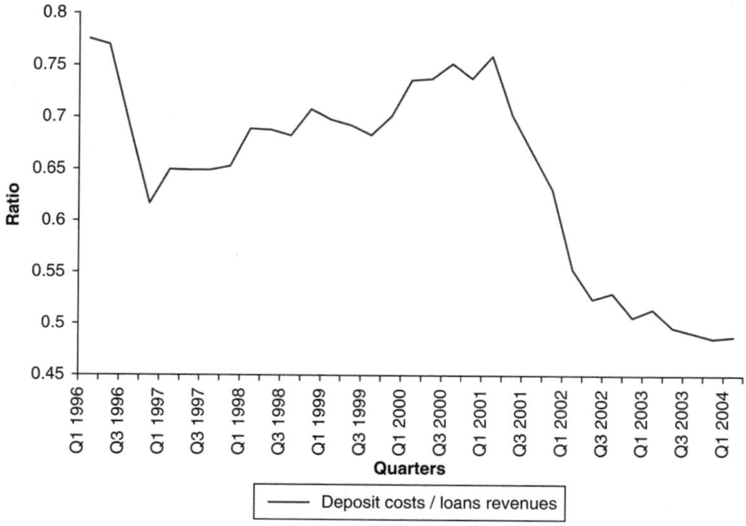

Source: Office of the Superintendent of Financial Institutions.
Figure 6.8 Costs related with deposits in banks/revenues related with loans by banks in Canada

other than banks certainly hold a significant share of the financial intermediation market in Canada, it appears that banks are still the most dominant player not only in nominal figures, but also in relative growth and market share.

On the other hand, it seems that a greater proportion of savings has recently been put in private and public pension funds. In 1993, the assets of these funds represented 43 per cent of chartered banks and insurance companies' deposits. Today, this proportion is around 60 per cent (Figure 6.13). Traditional deposits in banks are losing ground not only to market instruments, but also within the financial intermediation sector.

In sum, both on an *ex ante* and *ex post* basis, and as it appears to be the case in France and in the USA, the Canadian banking sector seems to follow long-term trends towards disintermediation. Compared with finance companies, a lower proportion of loans are now granted by chartered banks and insurance companies. While investments in mutual and pension funds are growing at a fast pace, traditional deposits in banks are flattening. In addition, it appears that lending revenues of the major Canadian banks are not growing significantly and that non-interest incomes are, on the contrary, becoming increasingly important.

Also, we observe a greater usage by Canadian banks of risk transfer instruments such as credit derivatives and securitization. These mechanisms allow financial institutions to reduce their stakes in loans which, in turn, lowers their incentive to intermediate with borrowers as they would otherwise do.

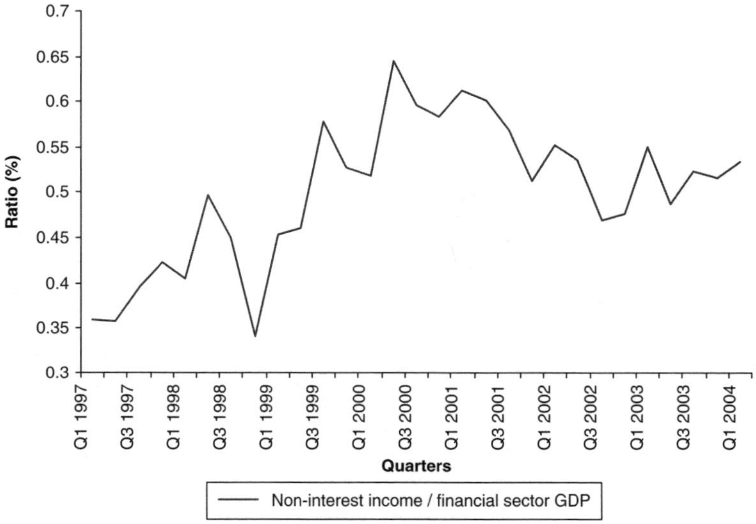

Sources: Office of the Superintendent of Financial Institutions and CANSIM.

Figure 6.9 Non-interest income of Canadian chartered banks relative to financial sector GDP

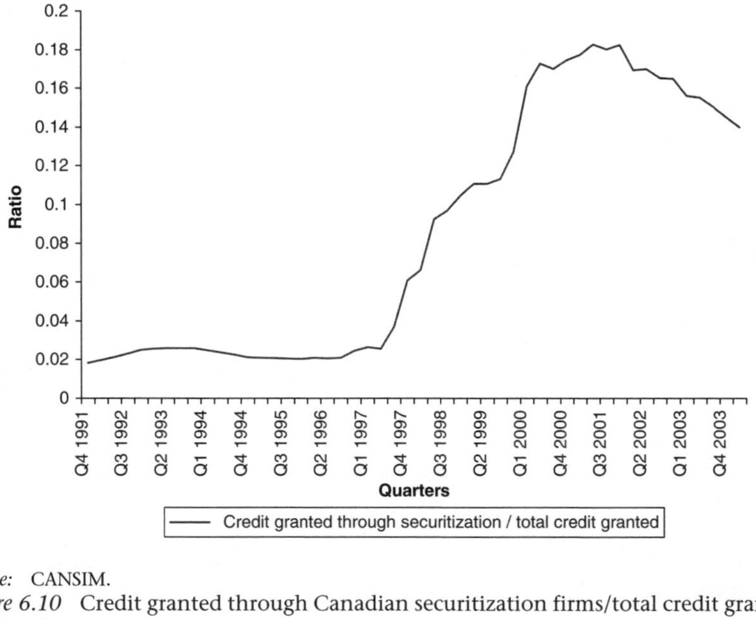

Source: CANSIM.

Figure 6.10 Credit granted through Canadian securitization firms/total credit granted in Canada

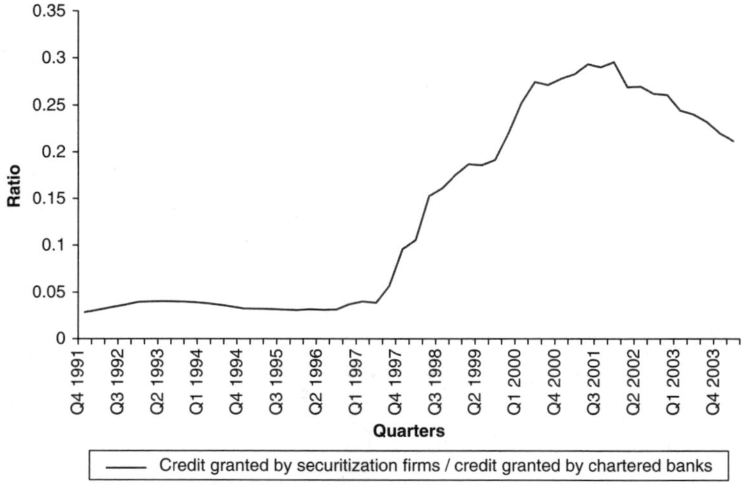

Source: CANSIM.

Figure 6.11 Credit granted by Canadian securitization firms/credit granted by Canadian chartered banks

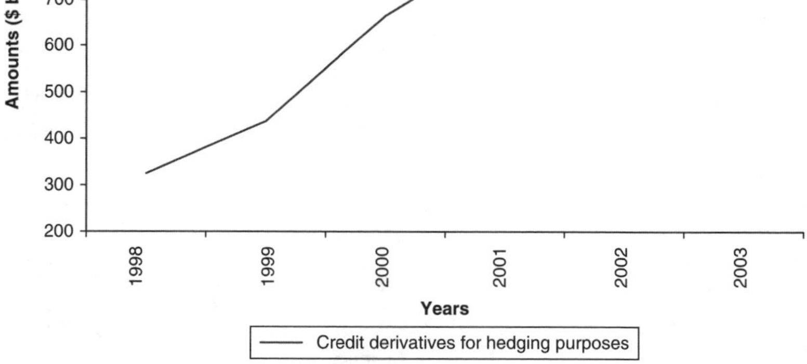

Sources: Annual Reports (1998 to 2003): Royal Bank, Scotia Bank, Bank of Montreal, TD Bank, CIBC, Laurentian Bank, National Bank of Canada.

Figure 6.12 Notional amounts of credit derivatives used by the 7 major Canadian banks for hedging purposes

Table 6.2 Total domestic assets of Canadian financial intermediaries

Intermediaries	Assets 1993 millions $	Assets 2003 millions $	Average annual growth of assets (%)	Market share 1993 (%)	Market share 2003 (%)	Market share evolution (%)
Chartered banks	684, 365	1, 755, 967	9.88	52.58	64.22	11.64
Pension funds	265, 520	584, 206	8.20	20.40	21.37	0.97
Credit unions	86, 871	151, 898	5.75	6.67	5.56	−1.12
Insurance companies	149, 834	230, 886	4.42	11.51	8.44	−3.07
Trust and mortgage	114, 931	11, 161	−20.80	8.83	0.41	−8.42
Total	1, 301, 521	2, 734, 118	7.71			

Source: Data extracted from CANADA'S National Statistical Agency (CANSIM) Statistical data base.

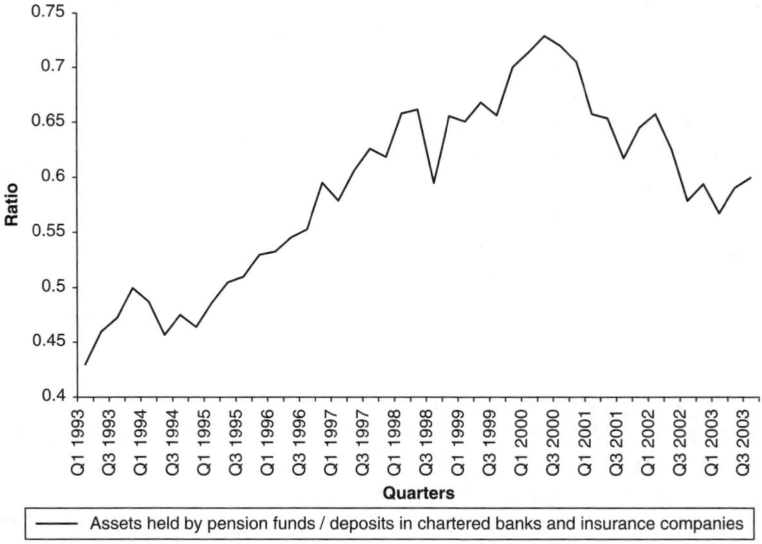

Source: CANSIM.
Figure 6.13 Total assets held by public and private pension funds/total deposits in chartered banks and insurance companies in Canada

In terms of total assets held, Canadian banks have kept a dominant position relative to other financial intermediaries such as credit unions or insurance companies. However, in addition to the impact of market based instruments, savings also shifted away from traditional bank deposits to investments in organisations such as pension funds.

Effects of disintermediation

Disintermediation can be viewed as a shift from a bank-based financial system to a market-based one. An approach to analyze the impact of disintermediation is to refer to the characteristics of the two types of systems that have been identified in the literature. In turn, the disintermediation may have both micro and macro economic effects.

Micro economic effects

The micro economic effects of disintermediation can be analysed mainly by looking at its impact on households (providers of capital) and firms (users of capital).

When households shift their savings from deposits to market instruments, they do so to obtain higher returns and must accept greater financial risk. Obviously, there is an increase in risk simply due to the fact of foregoing deposit insurance. Moreover, households will hold instruments whose rate of return is significantly more volatile. This has been well documented in two articles from Allen and Gale (1995) and Allen and Santomero (2001) that compared the portfolios of households in a bank-based financial system such as Germany with those of households in a market-based financial system such as the USA. In particular, Allen and Gale show that in a bank-based system, banks are able to build reserves and offer a buffer against systematic risk, allowing smoothed rates of return over time. Banks are thus able to provide a mechanism for inter-temporal risk sharing. In the same vein, it has become clear to the observers of financial markets that prices of financial assets fluctuate too much given the fluctuations in cash flows occurring in the real economy. In a bank-based financial system, intermediaries are also able to provide 'noise suppression' and more stable prices. Unfortunately, Allen and Gale note that when banks have to compete with financial markets, they will have to increase the rates of return offered in good times to match the competition and, in doing so will lose the ability to build reserves, smooth interest rates over time and suppress noise. The simple conclusion is that disintermediation may raise the average expected rate of return over time for households but at the cost of a very substantial increase in risk.

As for firms, Allen and Gale contrast the characteristics of bank-based versus market-based systems along four aspects: information, financing, corporate control and diversity of opinion. In bank-based systems, information tends to remain private and confidential, which may be at the advantage of users of capital who better control their disclosure of information. In market-based systems, there tends to be extensive information disclosure which is at the advantage of investors. In general in any system, firms have a definite preference for internal financing versus external financing, whether provided by banks or markets that, as a matter of fact, play only a secondary role relative to the former. This phenomenon is so strong that mergers and acquisitions between corporations may be viewed as 'an informal market for internal funds' (p.202) allowing excess funds generated by 'cash cows' to be channelled directly to 'growth prospects'. In this perspective, this mechanism competes with the financial sector itself in financing firms in need of capital. However, in a bank-based system with less public information available, the market for corporate control cannot work as easily as in a market-based system. Finally, bank-based and market-based systems can be compared regarding the diversity of opinions that they allow. Typically, bank-based systems tend to limit the monitoring and feedback given to a borrower to one or at most a few sources. Market-based systems tend to allow a broad array of analysts to participate in the evaluation of the capital of a firm. In this light, banks would be most suited for traditional industries with well established performance criteria and would be the most efficient solution for monitoring. Markets stimulate heterogeneity of opinions. Hence, they would be most appropriate for innovative economic sectors where performance criteria are still at a development stage. Clearly, the allocation of capital can give rise to two types of mistakes: providing capital to a bad project (type-1 error) or turning down a good project (type-2 error). It is plausible that each type of system has its bias. Specifically bank-based systems tend to be conservative and more prone to type-2 errors whereas market-based systems allow the most optimistic investors to bid up prices and eventually commit more type-1 errors.

Traditional banking is based on long-term relationships with corporate borrowers, an approach that is simply called 'relationship banking' for which Boot (2000) presents an interesting analysis. A long term relationship built on trust between the parties provides many potential benefits. Financing can be more flexible, include more extensive covenants, make more intensive use of collaterals and rates may be more easily smoothed over time. More specifically, a bank can support a firm in times of difficulty if it can reasonably expect to obtain good business in the following good times. Such cooperation between lender and borrower can be shown to be a wealth maximizing strategy for both parties. This being said, relationship banking is not without potential problems: namely they are called the soft-budget constraint problem and the hold-up problem. In the soft-budget constraint situation, the weak borrower abuses the patience of the lender. In the hold-up situation, the lender abuses the captive state of long time good customers. Whatever the balance of advantages and disadvantages, relationship banking is clearly an approach that allow banks to differentiate themselves from 'memory-less' markets. The move towards a market-based financial system seems to induce banks to take a transactional approach towards lending, therefore abandoning to some extent relationship banking.

Finally, although *ex post* disintermediation as it is done through securitization and credit derivatives may have somewhat less marked consequences than *ex ante* disintermediation, it has effects that are basically of the same nature. Following Morrison (2001), banks that resort to these risk transfer instruments lower their stakes in the borrower and, because of the weaker bond have lower incentives to screen, monitor and, if needed, renegotiate the loan. This change in behaviour decreases the economic value of bank loans and thus implies some wealth destruction.

To sum up this section, disintermediation affects firms of the real sector in many different ways. The shift to financial markets implies more disclosure of information and some loss of confidentiality that banks can provide. On the other hand, they may benefit from the feedback of a wider pool of analysts. The market for corporate control may be more active. However, disintermediation whether *ex ante* or *ex post* implies some loss of the benefits that a long term bank relationship may bring, such as patience in difficult times.

Overall, when banks have the ability to build reserves they are able to act as stabilizers and offer, both to providers and users of capital, rates that are somewhat smoothed over the business cycle. When financial markets tend to dominate a financial system, prices and rates of return may react more rapidly to current conditions but more, and perhaps too much, volatility ensues.

Macro economic effects

The macro economic effects of disintermediation can be analysed by looking at its impact on the stability of the financial sector and on the long term growth of the real sector.

The financial sector seems vulnerable to instability whether it is bank-based or market-based. Banks are subject to runs and contagion that lead to crises. Financial markets are prone to bubbles in asset prices that eventually burst. Up to recently, these two types of undesirable events were seen as somewhat different and independent. According to Allen and Gale (2001), this may not be the case. Various incentives in the banking sector may lead to overexpansion of credit which in turn favours speculation and increases in assets prices. Collaterals having increased values, bank can still increase credit. So, for a certain amount of time, the process will feed on itself until the bubble bursts and a fast downward spiral of prices occurs followed by a wave of credit default and, ultimately, a banking crisis. If this interaction between banks and markets is the basic pattern causing financial instability, how is it affected by decreasing intermediation and increasing the role of markets? It is very difficult to say. On the one hand, disintermediation decreases the importance of intermediaries that are by nature inherently fragile. This could be favourable to stability. On the other hand, disintermediation decreases the degree of control held by public authorities on the financial system. Finally, it increases the importance of financial markets, which tend to be volatile. It may be noted that as this phenomenon develops some lightly regulated market participants may become so large as to represent significant systemic risk as the famous debacle of Long Term Capital Management has shown. Still, it remains difficult to predict the net effect of disintermediation on overall financial stability.

As for the effects of the structure of the financial system on the growth of the real sector, a rich literature, both theoretical and empirical, has studied the question. The research team at the World Bank has recently published several papers on the topic, a typical one would be Levine (2000), which does not find any evidence that bank-based or market-based financial systems are associated with greater long term growth. However, the study concludes that the overall development of financial services, in whichever form, is indeed associated with greater growth. In turn the provision of quality financial services is conditioned by a good legal system. Levine thus recommends that public authorities avoid imposing a specific structure to the financial sector and 'focus on the fundamentals: property rights and the enforcement of those rights' (p.38).

Although financial institutions and markets compete with each other and can engage into dysfunctional relationships leading to bubbles and crises, Merton (1995) suggests that they are also complements that have many positive synergistic relationships. First, the interaction of institutions and markets allows for a very active distribution of financial risks that should help every actor to obtain its desired level of risk and an adequately diversified portfolio. Moreover, according to Merton, institutions and markets contribute in some ways to the growth of each other and foster financial innovation. Institutions are able to customize new products for their customers, acting as laboratories to test products on a small scale. If these prove successful, they can be migrated to the markets that standardize them and lower their costs due to high volume. In turn, banks can make use of these products to offer newer services. So, would develop the spiral of financial innovation fostering the dynamic efficiency of the whole system. In this perspective, the structure of the financial sector would naturally develop from the interaction of institutions and markets towards the most efficient one in a given economic and regulatory context. This remark leads us to examine the impact of these two factors on the evolution of the structure of a financial system.

6.2 The potential causes of disintermediation

This second part of the chapter examines the forces that may be driving disintermediation. These can be divided in two broad categories: market forces and effects of public authorities through financial regulation and the requirements of a deposit insurance system.

Market forces

This section examines the potential market forces that may push towards disintermediation. Disintermediation can occur because of changes in either the demand or supply of financial services.

The evolution of demand for financial services

Although the demand for financial services could be studied according to the types of financial services and the sector it originates, the discussion here focuses on the demand for savings instruments by households. The analysis is based on general results of modern financial theory. Portfolio theory states that for every investor optimal or efficient portfolios are composed of some proportion of the safe asset and a complementary proportion of well diversified risky assets, that is, a fraction of the market portfolio. The optimal proportions will depend on risk aversion, which should decline with wealth and the span of the investment horizon. One might also guess that as investors become more financially educated, they should be in a better position to bear risk as they are more able to obtain and understand the relevant information. Finally, the life-cycle hypothesis about saving behaviour states that retirement is the most important motive for saving, such that people accumulate savings while they are working and use their capital to consume when they retire. This theory is fairly basic but it may explain many observed patterns of recent savings behaviour. We argue that over recent decades, the population has on average been better educated, wealthier and that an important part of it (the baby-boomers) are now near retirement, such that they have almost reached the peak of their savings accumulation. If this perception is valid, then it follows that risk aversion may have decreased over the recent past as may the demand for safe assets offered by financial institutions such as banks. However, major changes have also occurred on the supply side that may have had an even greater impact on disintermediation.

The evolution of supply of financial services

Financial services are supplied by financial intermediaries and financial markets that compete for business. Financial intermediaries justify their existence if they can succeed in lowering transaction or information costs for their customers. However, information technology has progressed at a very rapid pace such that transaction costs and information costs have been dramatically reduced. For example, it is estimated that over the last 20 years computer power has increased by a factor of 10,000. The consequences in the financial sector can be illustrated in two contexts. In retail banking the cost of processing a transaction at a branch is approximately US$1 while the cost of an online transaction is approximately US$0.02. Similarly, the cost of a transaction for a customer at a full service broker vary between US$100 and US$300 while costs at an on-line discount broker would be between US$5 and US$30. The internet has also given public access to vast quantities of information thus lowering information asymmetry in the market. With these changes, the rationale for financial intermediation has been very considerably reduced. Several authors document and analyse this evolution namely, Allen *et al.* (2001), Claessens *et al.* (2000), Clemons and Hitt (2000) and Mishkin and Strahan (1999).

Not only has technology decreased the motivation for customers to use intermediaries, it has also provided opportunities for intermediaries themselves to transfer their assets or their risks to the markets through securitization and credit derivatives, thus generating *ex post* disintermediation. The growth of securitization and credit derivatives markets has been nothing less than phenomenal. Cummins (2004) provides a very good analysis of the economic rationale for securitization. He identifies the presence of bankruptcy costs, the ability to improve risk management, the reduction of information asymmetry, the existence of agency costs and the reduction of costs associated with regulation as potential motives for securitization and value creation. Allen *et al.* (2001) summarize the relationship between securitization and disintermediation very well as follows:

> The advent of e-finance technologies furthers the long-standing evolution of the financial services sector from one dominated by financial intermediaries to one dominated by capital markets and financial institutions that hold *marketable* securities as assets. Traditional financial intermediaries transform illiquid, hence non-marketable, assets (e.g. bank loans) into liquid liabilities (e.g. demand deposits). This role has become less important over time as the liquidity of financial assets originated by intermediaries has increased. (p.10)

Furthermore, Morrison (2001) shows that not only does the use of credit derivatives constitute *ex post* disintermediation of risk taking but that it also should decrease the motivation for banks to screen, monitor and renegotiate loans, and hence decrease the certification value of bank loans. This, in turn, should decrease the demand for business loans by firms which will simply prefer to go to the market directly. Thus, rational expectations of firms facing banks that use credit derivatives should lead to *ex ante* disintermediation. It also seems clear that the same line of reasoning applies to business loans that are securitized without recourse.

To sum up, three market forces can be identified as contributors to disintermediation. First, the profile of households may have evolved such as to reduce risk aversion and the demand for safe assets as provided by banks. Second, technology has considerably reduced transaction and information costs thus lowering the barriers to access financial markets. Third, new market instruments such as securitization and credit derivatives have induced banks to transfer their assets or their risks to the market. This in turn is reducing the value of bank loans and, by the same token, the incentive for corporate borrowers to use them.

Financial regulation

This section examines how public intervention through financial regulation and the requirements of a deposit insurance system may affect disintermediation. Before tackling this issue, it is appropriate to recall briefly the objectives of public intervention on the financial system and the means used to implement it.

The rationale and objectives of public intervention on the financial system

There are two major rationales to justify public intervention in the financial system. The first rationale is the externality argument: because the financial system provides capital to non-financial firms, if it became unable to perform this function, the overall economic development of a country would suffer. Thus, financial institutions cannot be managed from the sole perspective of shareholders, because they may have too narrow a view of the benefits and risks associated with their institutions. As a consequence, government could be forced to rescue the system. So, public intervention may also be viewed as a means of protecting tax payers from the cost of a bailout. The second rationale is that households are at an information disadvantage when dealing with financial institutions. Most customers would have neither the knowledge nor the economic incentive to monitor financial institutions adequately. Thus public authorities perform this function for them.

Once public authorities find sufficient justifications to intervene, they tend to pursue a variety of objectives that go beyond the initial motivation. The objectives generally include fostering a safe and sound financial system, ensuring fairness between consumers and suppliers of financial services but also between the various suppliers (the level playing field issue), promoting efficiency in its three forms operational (cost minimization), allocational (risk return optimization) and dynamic (innovation) and finally providing favourable conditions for the growth of the sector. Herring and Santomero (2000) present a similar but slightly different list of the objectives pursued by financial regulation, namely: systemic risk, consumer protection, efficiency enhancement and broader social objectives. Social objectives can be very diverse, such as promoting specific industrial sectors; housing, exports, the provision of essential financial services to low-income customers; or preventing criminal activities using money laundering schemes.

The implementation of financial regulation

To achieve their objectives, public authorities used a wide variety of measures. These measures generally cover allowed activities, entry, exit and ownership rules, risk management and capital requirements, participation to a deposit insurance system, control of the market structure through authorization of mergers and acquisitions and consumer protection rules.

Although public interventions usually target benefits for the society at large or parties outside the financial sector, it is worth noting that in many cases these interventions may also benefit the financial institutions themselves. It can be argued for example that the recent pressure put by the Basel

Committee on Bank Supervision to improve capital adequacy standards has provided the trust to develop advanced risk management techniques that will be beneficial to the internal management of financial institutions. Similarly, measures such as the *Standards of Sound Business and Financial Practices* of CDIC may contribute in limiting the probability of insolvency of each financial institution and to keeping deposit insurance premiums low for all participants. It must be noted that since 1998, total annual premiums collected by CDIC have been reduced from over $534 million to about $100 million currently, the average premium charged on insured deposits having fallen from 17 basis points to around 3. This evolution has certainly contributed to the reduction of the costs of deposits that was mentioned previously and to the parallel improvement of the net interest revenue of banks.

The effects of financial regulation on disintermediation

Although there are many good reasons for public authorities to intervene on the financial sector, some of the measures taken may have unintended consequences. This section analyses how financial regulation may lead to disintermediation.

Restriction to activities permitted. As a first example, the fact that banks cannot under the current Bill C-8 offer auto-leasing services to consumers, while there has been an increasing demand for that service, has taken a considerable part of auto financing away from banks and to finance companies.

Restriction to ownership. Secondly, the current restriction that ownership of large financial institutions is limited to 20 per cent may induce some financial groups to avoid entering the banking market because of their policy of maintaining a high level of control on affiliates.

Consumer protection requirements. Under current bill C-8, large financial intermediaries have to bear with the supervision of the Financial Consumer Agency of Canada and disclose a yearly Public Accountability Statement. These measures imply some operational costs to ensure compliance but also some expenditure to fulfill expectations with regard to the implicit social mandate imposed to financial intermediaries. Again, some financial firms may prefer to operate outside of the framework of intermediation to avoid these costs.

However, it might also be noted that self discipline has become an important force within corporations and financial institutions especially. This is confirmed by the widespread importance taken by corporate social responsibility and sustainability. Although there are many manifestations of this trend, in our opinion, the Global Reporting Initiative stands out. It is a voluntary coalition of firms that has put forward clear and precise guidelines and indicators, some fifty of them, covering the effects of their corporate activities on all their stakeholders. Moreover, it has encouraged specific industrial sectors to develop specialized indicators. Up to now, only the financial sector has proposed specialized social performance indicators. This is mentioned because if the spirit of corporate social responsibility is genuinely implemented in financial institutions, then many aspects of financial consumer protection will be redundant and not binding for them.[2]

Deregulation. Recent deregulation has permitted banks to enter the securities industry and form financial holding companies. This has allowed them to become dominant players in funds management. Some of their previous deposit taking activities have thus been shifted to disintermediated activities. It could be said that part of disintermediation has been internalized within these groups.

Risk management requirements and capital adequacy standards. Jackson (1999) led a study for the Bank for International Settlements on the impact of the capital accord. Among the various questions studied, three are relevant for our purpose, they are:

- Do banks adjust their capital ratios to meet the requirements by increasing capital or reducing weighted assets?
- Have banks artificially boosted their capital ratios by engaging in capital arbitrage?
- Did the introduction of minimum capital requirements for banks harm their competitiveness?

The study obtains the following answers to these questions. First, banks will use the least costly mean to satisfy the requirements and, in some periods, the reduction of loan activity is indeed the chosen approach. It could then be argued that in such times capital standards lead to disintermediation.

The chapter also finds evidence that capital arbitrage, mainly through securitization, was used by some banks. Again, this could be viewed as *ex post* disintermediation induced by regulation. As for the impact on competitiveness, Jackson *et al.* (2002) conclude: 'It is very difficult to draw any firm conclusions from the available studies about the impact of capital requirements on the competitive position of banks' (p.48). Overall, though the effect on the competitive position of banks is still unclear, capital regulation may indeed induce behaviours such as reduction of credit and securitization that are consistent with disintermediation.

Another study by Jackson *et al.* (2002) shows that the 1988 Basel Accord on capital standards delivers a survival probability between 99.0 per cent and 99.9 per cent over a one-year horizon. On the other hand they also show that most banks target and have a credit rating implying a survival probability of 99.96 per cent corresponding to an A- rating by S&P, 'which is considerably greater than the solvency standard implicit in the Basel Accord' (p.967). They move on to explain this behaviour. Their main hypothesis is that such high solvency is required to access the swap market, which has become a necessary tool for risk management. Thus the regulatory capital constraint would be binding only for a relatively small fraction of banks that have below investment grade ratings (3 per cent for Moody's and 8 per cent for Standard & Poor's).

Governance requirements. Following several financial scandals, corporate governance in general is a topic that has attracted much attention. At the international level the OECD has recently updated its 'Principle of Corporate Governance' and the USA has enacted the Sabarnes-Oxley Act. In Canada, this movement has been followed both by public and private organisations. The Department of Finance (2003a) has led a coordinated effort to strengthen the legal and supervisory framework of corporate governance. The Toronto Stock Exchange together with the Chartered Accountants of Canada has revamped its approach to governance. Finally, Canadian firms are also under pressure to improve their governance practices by institutional investors and their newly formed Canadian Coalition for Good Governance (2004). This short and very incomplete list of organizations active with the governance issue is only intended to demonstrate that the interest in the question is broad and the participants numerous.

Still in this general context, the corporate governance of financial institutions deserves special attention for several reasons that relate to their structure, their functions and their responsibilities in society. Financial institutions, and especially depository institutions, are structurally fragile because of their small capital and their vulnerability coming from the transformation of short-term deposits into longer-term loans. This useful social function gives rise to systemic risk. Managers of these institutions if they were to consider the wealth of their shareholders exclusively would neglect this externality. Also, it can be argued that depositors and more generally debt holders are stakeholders whose interests must be taken into account. (Macey and O'Hara) (2003) Finally, inasmuch as there is an explicit or implicit public guarantee of the solvency of depository institutions, public authorities are also stakeholders with a legitimate claim to their governance. Moreover, Allen and Gale (2003) show that in the context of imperfect and incomplete markets a multi-stakeholders approach can lead to superior results.

Thus there is a tradition for financial supervisors of imposing requirements and monitoring the governance of financial institutions. The Bank for International Settlements (1999) issued a report whose purpose was the enhancement of corporate governance in banking organizations. The Department of Finance (2003b) initiated a major consultation on the topic. The Office of the Superintendent of Financial Institutions (2003) issued a 'Corporate

Governance Guideline' the same year. Finally, the Canada Deposit Insurance Corporation has put in place its 'Standard of Sound Business and Financial Practices', containing a very substantial first part (14 elements) devoted to corporate governance and the responsibilities of the board.

This public intervention in the corporate governance of financial institutions raises several questions over its justification and effects. In particular, are the costs associated with governance requirements excessive and leading to disintermediation? First, let us note that several observers still find deficiencies with current corporate governance practices. Montgomery and Kaufman (2003) point out that, in general, the link between shareholders and board members is too weak. It can be argued that the widespread dispersion of ownership of banks stocks in Canada was induced by regulation and contributed to such a weak link and thus that the intervention of public authorities on governance is a natural compensatory measure. Claude Lamoureux (2003), president and CEO of Ontario Teachers' Pension Plan takes the stand that corporate governance will be adequately controlled only by a three pronged approach: legislation, a national securities regulator and 'shareholders banding together' (p.7). Again, the fragmentation and consequent relative weakness of securities regulation in Canada, at least up to now, could also be invoked as a motive for an alternative supervision of the corporate governance of financial institutions.

Let us now turn to the potential costs of the current requirements on the corporate governance of financial institutions. Compliance with governance requirements may involve two types of costs: opportunity costs and operational costs. Opportunity costs are lost benefits due to the constraints that apply on the institution and prevent it from taking otherwise profitable and healthy opportunities. This could also include the lost contribution of potential board members who would decline the office because of the excessive personal liability. Considering the numerous organizations imposing governance requirements on financial firms, it is impossible to isolate the marginal effect on opportunity costs that requirements from OSFI or CDIC may have on financial institutions. Thus only operational costs associated with specific disclosures and examination procedures could be evaluated. We do not have access to these data. However, overall regulatory costs are discussed at the end of this section.

The operational costs may be obvious to regulated institutions, but these may also enjoy significant benefits of which they may be less aware. Gompers *et al.* (2003) conducted an extensive study of the impact of governance on equity prices. They constructed an index based on 24 governance rules and measured it on 1500 large firms during the 1990s. Their conclusions are the following:

> An investment strategy that bought firms in the lowest decile of the index (strongest rights) and sold firms in the highest decile of the index (weakest

> rights) would have earned abnormal returns of 8.5 per cent per year during the sample period. We find that firms with stronger shareholder rights had higher firm value, higher profits, higher sales growth, lower capital expenditures, and made fewer corporate acquisitions. (p.107)

Canadian banks may enjoy such benefits. Lamoureux notes: 'Yes, good governance matters. And more companies are paying attention. The Canadian banks are notable for their responsiveness. They and many large Canadian corporations are listening and have made changes' (p.5). This 'notable responsiveness' may well have been conditioned by prior public intervention. The point here is that good governance may imply some costs, but one should not lose sight of the fact that it also generates benefits that the market itself is ready to acknowledge and value.

Deposit insurance requirements. Deposit insurance contributes positively to the two main objectives of financial regulation of protecting depositors and fostering the stability of the financial system. However, the safety net,[3] of which deposit insurance is a component, creates difficulties of its own, namely the moral hazard problem whereby the shareholders of banks would have an incentive to increase profits by taking on riskier assets given that the cost of most of their liabilities would be fixed. In other words, deposit insurance decreases the effectiveness of market discipline. Thus regulatory discipline has to be put in place to compensate. Regulatory discipline in turn can be implemented through risk-adjusted premiums and monitoring of risk management. As many observers, such as Laeven (2002), believe, the current system of risk adjustment may not totally adjust for risk so that risk monitoring becomes a necessary complement. Following this line of reasoning, the cost of deposit insurance to banks may be viewed as the sum of a variable component, roughly proportional to risk, and a fixed component related to monitoring. It could consequently be argued that the current deposit insurance system creates benefits for depositors and society and costs to banks. The question that is naturally raised is; 'Are there benefits for banks themselves and if so do they exceed the costs?'. Clearly, the answer to this question will shed light on whether deposit insurance implemented as such may contribute to disintermediation or not.

The benefit created for banks by deposit insurance may depend on the benefits created for depositors who may be called to absorb the costs. Let us assume that depositors are somewhat risk averse and that the value of deposit insurance to them is linearly proportional to the risk of the bank. Also, it should be clear that this valuation function runs through zero, as deposit insurance for a bank without risk would have no value. Then a simple break even model of deposit insurance as shown in Figure 6.14 can

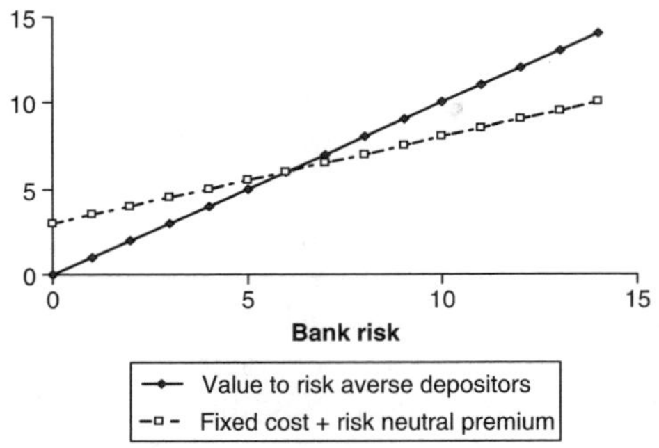

Figure 6.14 Value and cost of deposit insurance

be proposed. Basically, this model suggests that at low levels of risk the benefit generated for depositors would not cover the cost. Then the bank could not pass the entire cost to depositors and shareholders would have to absorb some part of the cost. Beyond some break even level of risk, the value to depositors exceeds the total cost and the bank would obtain an implicit subsidy. Thus, this cost and benefit structure generates predictable behaviour by the banks. To make sure that deposit insurance is not unprofitable to them, they can do several things:

1. shift their level of risk above the break-even level;
2. ask the deposit insurer to decrease the fixed component of costs to lower the break-even point, or;
3. if none of the two previous options are possible, they may consider getting out of intermediation altogether.

This is, admittedly, a very simple model that focuses on the micro-economic effects of deposit insurance. Morrison and White (2004) have a much more elaborate model that focuses on the macro-economic effects of deposit insurance. Not surprisingly, if the major benefit is a collective one then the bulk of the cost should be borne by society at large. Thus, Morrison concludes:

> We have developed a model in which bankers play a socially useful role in monitoring investments to improve their productivity, but where these banking services are subject to both adverse selection and moral hazard. We have shown that in this set-up, deposit insurance is welfare increasing *to the extent that it constitutes a net subsidy to the banking system*. This result runs contrary to the received wisdom that deposit insurance should be

> financed through the contributions of banks and that the objective of the deposit insurance fund should be to minimise losses to the taxpayer. (p.23)

It is clear then that if the model is right and the cost is basically borne by banks, then there would be a wealth transfer from banks and depositors to society, a transfer to which they would naturally object.

Thus both our simple micro-model with the presence of fixed costs and the macro-model of Morrison identify potential reasons for banks to be unsatisfied with the typical deposit insurance scheme. However, both analyses are theoretical and their implications may depend on the exact value of some empirical factors. So now we examine some empirical evidence on the impact of deposit insurance on financial institutions.

Billett *et al.* (1998) have done a very interesting event study to analyse the behaviour of the market and managers of banks around a change of credit rating. Using a sample of 233 change announcements during the period 1990–95, they obtain two significant results. First, banks having a greater proportion of insured deposits before a downgrade suffer less negative abnormal returns, showing that the market takes into account that regulatory discipline (potential increase in premiums) will be softer than market discipline (increase in the risk premium of market debt). Second, the researchers also find that following a downgrade the managers systematically change the financial structure of the bank, using more insured deposits and less market debt. This shows that managers too understand that regulatory discipline is softer than market discipline.

Cull *et al.* (2004) of the Bank for International Settlements have recently published the results of their empirical research on the long term effects of deposit insurance on bank intermediation. Studying 61 countries over the period 1980–97, they conclude that 'generous government-funded deposit insurance might have a negative impact on the long-run growth and stability of bank intermediation, except in countries where the rule of law is well established and banks' supervisors are granted sufficient discretion and independence from legal reprisals'. Clearly, this conclusion is logically equivalent to saying that fairly priced deposit insurance together with adequate supervision is at least neutral, if not beneficial, in the long run to bank intermediation. Both favourable conditions seem to be met in Canada.

Another consideration can be brought to the analysis to show that deposit insurance is not the main driving force behind disintermediation. Indeed, according to Cummins (2004), we observe that *ex post* disintermediation through securitization is developing rapidly in the insurance sector, a sector that is not subject to deposit insurance. Cummins comments however that 'in spite of the potential efficiency gains from securitization, most of the transactions conducted to date have been driven in whole or in part by regulation' (p.43).

Overall regulatory costs. A study of the Board of Governors of the Federal Reserve System (Elliehousen, 1998) estimated that:

> regulatory costs account for 12 per cent to 13 per cent of non-interest expenses (of commercial banks) . . . One case study suggests that incremental regulatory costs were about 6.1 per cent of non-interest expenses. (p.29)

Surely, these levels of costs are very significant for the institutions having to bear them. On the other hand, one can put these costs in relation with the costs of the banking crises that they may contribute to avoid. Several countries that have experienced severe banking crises have had to face losses representing several per centage points of their GDP. In this perspective, regulatory costs, although high in absolute values, appear a very worthy investment in financial stability from the perspective of society at large.

The issue that should be raised is: 'Who should bear the costs?' A principle that would seem fair would be that those parties who enjoy the benefits should contribute to bear the costs. It seems clear that regulation may create benefits for the financial institutions themselves, their customers and society at large (tax-payers). At present it seems that the user-payer approach is interpreted as if financial institutions and their customers are the sole beneficiaries of regulation. This approach is risky as it may overburden financial intermediaries and provide an incentive to move out of intermediation. The analysis of Morrison for deposit insurance, in our opinion, generalizes to financial regulation at large. Part of the costs of financial regulation should be subsidised by taxpayers as they participate to the benefits, and so the pressure that these costs create towards disintermediation would be reduced.

A perspective on public intervention and financial intermediation

Theoretical analysis shows that in the context of imperfect or incomplete markets, regulation of financial intermediaries can increase welfare (Allen and Gale, 2000; Freixas and Santomero, 2002). Similarly, in these conditions a stakeholder approach to governance can achieve results superior to those obtained by governance that focuses solely on shareholders. Thus both theory and empirical wisdom converge on the opportunity of regulating financial intermediaries and monitoring their governance.

Financial regulation, together with a deposit insurance system, creates benefits for users of the financial system, for financial intermediaries themselves and society at large. Because of that, it would seem fair that the direct costs of regulation be shared by all parties enjoying its benefits, which would imply some level of contribution from taxpayers.

On the other hand, many aspects of regulation may constitute a disincentive to financial intermediation. In particular, requirements relative to the capital standard, corporate governance and deposit insurance may seem at face value to impose costly constraints on financial intermediaries. A closer empirical look however has shown that regulatory capital standards are not a binding constraint for most banks, that good governance is demanded by many other parties and is both acknowledged and valued by the market and finally that deposit insurance is identified both by the market and bank managers as softer than market discipline.

This analysis leads us to three conclusions. First, indeed public intervention imposes some costs both explicit and implicit on financial intermediaries that may reduce the level of intermediation. Second, the implicit costs of public intervention may not be as high as some may claim because in several cases other parties are exerting more binding constraints. Third, the explicit costs should perhaps be shared with society at large in order for it to keep the benefits of a healthy level of intermediation.

6.3 Conclusion

Disintermediation has been the central topic of this chapter. First, it was found useful to distinguish various forms of disintermediation. Disintermediation can occur on the asset side or the liability side of the balance sheet of intermediaries. It can be *ex ante* when it is the result of the decisions of savers or borrowers, or *ex post* when it is the decision of an intermediary to pull out of a transaction through the secondary market. In the later case, one can distinguish disintermediation of funding and disintermediation of risk taking. Finally, it may also be useful to keep in mind that disintermediation at depository institutions does not necessarily mean overall disintermediation as intermediation may grow at non-depository intermediaries such as life insurers and pension funds.

The chapter then looked at the empirical evidence on disintermediation, abroad and in Canada. There is strong evidence of a disintermediation trend at depository institutions in the USA and France, but not so in the UK or Germany. In Canada, bank deposits have not grown as much as mutual funds or pension funds as saving instruments. Loans by finance companies have taken a larger share of the market. Banks themselves are increasingly using securitization and credit derivatives and thus disintermediating *ex post*. Nonetheless, banks are doing well both in terms of asset growth and revenues, basically because they have shifted their financial activities towards risk management and fee based revenues.

The effects of disintermediation were analysed by using the literature that compares bank-based financial systems to market-based financial systems, as it can be viewed as a shift from one to the other. At the micro-economic level, it is observed that households have to bear much more risk under a market-based system which may lead to very significant differences in gains for various generations. For firms, a shift towards a market-based system generally means the erosion of the concept of relationship banking. As banks transfer their loans to the market, they lose some incentive to screen, monitor and renegotiate loans, activities that make bank loans valuable. Overall, in a market-based system banks lose some of their ability to build reserves and use these to smooth rates over time for both savers and borrowers. Thus, they lose their capacity to act as stabilizers in the economy and rather transform themselves in access providers to the volatile market.

At the macro-level, it is difficult to predict the effects of financial structure on financial stability. Both banks and markets have their stability problems, banks tend to be subject to runs and crises and markets develop bubbles that eventually burst. The dynamics of these problems is not entirely understood yet, but an appealing theory is that the two sets of problems are interacting. Bank credit would feed market bubbles and market bursts would create extensive credit defaults and banking crises. What would be the effect of reducing intermediation on this process? It is difficult to say. Only one thing is clear: disintermediation reduces the degree of control of public authorities over the financial system. As for the effect of financial structure on growth and development of the real sector, empirical studies have basically found that the structure of the financial system does not matter but its overall level of development does, which in turn critically depends on the quality of the accounting and legal environment. Also, it can be argued that financial institutions and markets interact in a very synergistic way that promotes innovation and dynamic efficiency. If this interaction is presumed to be beneficial, then it will eventually determine by itself an efficient financial structure in the context of its economic and legal environment.

The second part of the chapter examined the causes of disintermediation looking at market forces and the effects of financial regulation and deposit insurance requirements. Market forces may be at play both on the demand and the supply sides on financial services. A number of socio-demographic factors such as education, wealth and age structure of the population may well have decreased risk aversion and consequently the demand for safe assets, such as deposits offered by banks. On the supply side, technology has decreased both transaction and information costs and thus the rationale for intermediation. Moreover, technology and financial innovations have offered intermediaries interesting opportunities to transfer their risks and their assets to the market and thus disintermediate *ex post*. This *ex post* disintermediation reduces the economic value of business loans and naturally leads corporate borrowers to use them less and so contribute *to ex ante* disintermediation.

Financial regulation is extensive as it covers allowed activities, restrictions to ownership, consumer protection requirements, risk management and capital adequacy standards, corporate governance and, for depository institutions, participation in a deposit insurance system. All these create constraints and generate compliance costs for financial intermediaries. The regulatory context may thus lead to disintermediation either because it affects the competitiveness of financial intermediaries negatively or because it creates an incentive for the intermediary itself to move out of intermediation to maximize its profits.

However, a closer look at empirical evidence shows that in many cases regulatory discipline is softer than market or self-discipline, such that for many institutions the apparent regulatory constraints would not be binding. In the particular case of governance requirements, the fragmentation both of the ownership of banks and of securities regulators in Canada are two factors that naturally lead the federal supervisors of financial institutions to play a complementary role. It was also noted that such intervention generates benefits for the financial institutions, as good governance is noticed and valued by the market.

As for the explicit costs, they seem to be very significant but economic analysis suggests that they should be shared by all parties benefiting from the financial stability achieved via financial regulation. This implies that regulatory costs should be borne not only by financial intermediaries and their customers but also by society at large.

The combined analysis of the effects of market forces and financial regulation leads to the conclusion that market forces, specially the evolution of the supply of financial services under the thrust of technological change and financial innovation, constitute the primary factor driving disintermediation. Second, some factors such as the age structure of the population and the size of the recent spread in yield between safe assets and market yields may have added a supplementary cyclical effect to the long term trend. Finally, financial regulation may also have played a role because of the various explicit and implicit costs it imposes on intermediaries. However, this effect appears of second order importance because oftentimes market or self discipline is more constraining. Moreover, the negative effect could still be reduced by a better distribution of the explicit costs.

To conclude, this chapter has tried to examine two challenging questions about the evolution of the structure of the Canadian financial system, namely the identification of the causes and effects of financial disintermediation. Even though a qualitative analysis has been suggested using, as much as possible, the scientific literature and empirical evidence, one must observe that a dynamic theory explaining the evolution of financial systems does not exist yet. In this context, we readily acknowledge that the analysis proposed remains somewhat preliminary and in need of further investigation. The full implications for deposit insurance could then be elaborated.

Notes

1 This chapter originates from a survey paper written for the Canada Deposit Insurance Corporation (CDIC). However, the views expressed are strictly those of the authors.
2 An interesting example of this is the Citizenship report published by Citigroup that goes beyond the regulatory CRA report that this institution has to file, especially in the area of environmental sustainability.
3 The safety net provided to financial institutions is made of several components such as the lender of last resort function of the central bank, the deposit insurance system and the implicit guarantee provided by government for too big to fail firms. All these contribute to the potential moral hazard problem.

References

Aintablian, S. and Roberts, G.S. (2000) 'A Note on Market Response to Corporate Loan Announcements in Canada', *Journal of Banking and Finance*, vol. 24, pp. 381–93.

Allen, F. (1990) 'The Market for Information and the Origin of Financial Intermediation', *Journal of Financial Intermediation*, vol. 1, pp. 3–30.

Allen, F. and Gale, D. (1995) 'A Welfare Comparison of Intermediaries and Financial Markets in Germany and the US', *European Economic Review*, vol. 39, pp. 179–209.

Allen, F. and Gale, D. (2000) 'Banking and Markets', Wharton Financial Institutions Center, Working paper, 2000-44-B.

Allen, F. and Gale, D. (2001) 'Comparative Financial Systems: A Survey', Wharton Financial Institutions Center, Working paper, April.

Allen, F. and Gale, D. (2003) 'A Comparative Theory of Corporate Governance', Wharton Financial Institutions Center, Working paper, 2003–27.

Allen, F. and Santomero, A.M. (1997) 'The Theory of Financial Intermediation', *Journal of Banking and Finance*, vol. 21, pp. 1461–86.

Allen, F. and Santomero, A.M. (2001) 'What Do Financial Intermediaries Do?', *Journal of Banking and Finance*, vol. 25, pp. 271–94.

Allen, F., McAndrews, J. and Strahan, P.E. (2001) 'E-Finance: An Introduction', Wharton Financial Institutions Center, Working paper, 2001–36.

Bank for International Settlements (1999) 'Enhancing Corporate Governance for Banking Organisations', Basel Committee for Bank Supervision.

Benston G.J. and Smith, C.W. (1976) 'A Transaction Cost Approach to the Theory of Financial Intermediation', *Journal of Finance*, vol. 31, pp. 215–31.

Billett, M.T., Garfinkel, J.A. and O'Neal, E.S. (1998) 'The Cost of Market Versus Regulatory Discipline in Banking', *Journal of Financial Economics*, vol. 48, pp. 333–58.

Boot, A.W.A. (2000) 'Relationship Banking: What Do We Know?', *Journal of Financial Intermediation*, vol. 9, pp. 7–25.

Canadian Coalition for Good Governance (2004) Corporate Governance Guidelines for Building High Performance Boards', Ottawa.

Claessens, S., Glaessner, T. and Klingebiel, D. (2000) 'Electronic Finance: Reshaping the Financial landscape around the World', The World Bank, Working paper, September.

Clemons, E.K. and Hitt, L.M. (2000) 'The Internet and the Future of financial Services: Transparency, Differential Pricing and Disintermediation', Wharton Financial Institutions Center, Working paper, 00–35.

Cull, R., Senbet, L. and Sorge, M. (2004) 'Deposit Insurance and Bank Intermediation in the Long Run', BIS Working Papers No 156, July.
Cummins, D. (2004) 'Securitization of Life Insurance Assets and Liabilities', Working paper, The Wharton School, January.
Demirgüç-Kunt, A. and Levine, R. (1999) 'Bank-based and Market-based Financial Systems: Cross-country Comparisons', World Bank, Working paper, Table 5, p. 50.
Department of Finance Canada (2003a) 'Fostering Confidence in Canadian Capital Markets', September, Ottawa.
Department of Finance Canada (2003b) 'Corporate Governance of Financial Institutions', Consultation Paper, Financial Institutions Division, Ottawa.
Diamond, D.W. (1984) 'Financial Intermediation and Delegated Monitoring', *Review of Economic Studies*, vol. 51, pp. 393–414.
Elliehausen, G. (1998) 'The Cost of Bank Regulation: A Review of the Evidence', Board of Governors of the Federal Reserve System, Washington, DC, Staff study no. 171, April.
Freixas, X. and Santomero, A.M. (2002) 'An Overall Perspective on Banking Regulation', Federal Reserve Bank of Philadelphia, Working Paper, February
Global Reporting Initiative (2002a) 'Sustainability Reporting Guidelines', Amsterdam.
Global Reporting Initiative (2002b) 'Financial Services Sector Supplement: Social Performance', November, Amsterdam.
Gompers, P., Ishii, J. and Metrick, A. (2003) 'Corporate Governance and Equity Prices', *Quarterly Journal of Economics*, vol. 188 (1), pp. 107–55.
Gorton, G. and Winton, A. (2002) 'Financial Intermediation', Wharton Financial Institutions Center, Working paper, 02-28, March.
Herring, R.J. and Santomero, A.M. (2000) 'What is Optimal Financial Regulation? A Study for the Government Official Inquiry on the Competitiveness of the Swedish Financial Sector', Wharton Financial Institutions Center, Working paper, 2000–34.
Jackson, P. (1999) 'Capital Requirements and Bank Behaviour: the Impact of the Basle Accord', BIS Working paper no.1, April.
Jackson, P., Perraudin, W. and Saporta, V. (2002) 'Regulatory and Economic Solvency Standards for Internationally Active Banks', *Journal of Banking and Finance*, vol. 26, pp. 953–76.
Laeven, L. (2002) 'Pricing Deposit Insurance', World Bank Policy Research Working Paper 2871, July.
Lamoureux, C. (2003) 'Corporate Governance – Are We There Yet?', Canadian Investor Relations Institute, May, Ottawa.
Levine, R. (2000) 'Bank-Based or Market-Based Financial Systems: Which is Better?', Carlson School of Management University of Minnesota, Working paper, January.
Macey, J. and O'Hara, M. (2003) 'The Corporate Governance of Banks', Federal Reserve Bank of New York, *Economic Policy Review*, April, pp. 91–107.
Merton, R.C. (1995) 'A Functional Perspective of Financial Intermediation', *Financial Management*, vol. 24 (Summer), pp. 23–41.
Mishkin, F.S. and Strahan, P.E. (1999) 'What will technology do to financial structure?', National Bureau of Economic Research, Working paper 6892, January.
Montgomery, C. and Kaufman, R. (2003) 'The Board's Missing Link', *Harvard Business Review*, vol. 81 (3), p. 86.
Morrison, A.D. (2001) 'Credit Derivatives, Disintermediation and Investment Decisions', Working paper, University of Oxford, May.
Morrison, A.D. and White, L. (2004) 'Is Deposit Insurance a Good Thing, and If so, Who Should Pay for It?', University of Oxford, Working paper.

Office of the Superintendent of Financial Institutions (2003) 'Corporate Governance Guideline' January, Ottawa.

Porter, M. (1980) *Competitive Strategy*, New York, Free Press.

Schmidt, R.H., Hackethal, A. and Tyrell, M. (1999) 'Disintermediation and the Role of Banks in Europe: An International Comparison', *Journal of Financial Intermediation*, vol. 8, pp. 36–67.

7

Measures to Promote Effective Interrelationships among Financial Safety Net Participants[1]

Winston Keith Carr

7.1 Introduction

The banking system provides an essential store of liquidity by providing deposits valued at par and payable on demand, and a mechanism to make payments that are essential to completion of financial transactions in the economy. Those functions make the role of a banking system vital for any given country.[2] A well-functioning and efficient banking system underpins a nation's payments system, enhances its savings rate, investment and economic growth, and facilitates financial intermediation.

As the sources of funding of the banking sector are, however, mostly from the public and its capital base is relatively low compared to that of the other industries, there is no guarantee that banks by themselves will strictly control or limit the level of risk exposure as they search out profitable endeavours. At the same time, banks have special characteristics that make them critical to the functioning of the economy and susceptible to financial problems.[3] The nature of possible chain reactions when a bank fails also makes the banking sector very fragile. Thus, governments have decided that banks should be subject to prudential regulation and supervision, and this also briefly explains why the safety and soundness of the financial sector are critical objectives of any government.

It is observed increasingly that fierce competition among financial institutions as well as continuously enlarging operating risk are not only severely testing the banking sector, but these developments are also challenging the financial-sector supervisors, deposit insurers and other related government agencies. Therefore, how to establish strong, efficient and viable financial safety nets is being increasingly recognized in the vast majority of countries.

A country would constitute a financial safety net seeking to promote an efficient and stable banking system and to manage the eventuality of a financial crisis. In most cases, the financial safety net consists of organizations that undertake prudential regulation and supervision, provide a lender of last resort facility, offer explicit depositor protection, a secure payment and clearing system and a clearly defined resolution mechanism to deal with banks in distress.

In September 2001, a Working Group established by the Financial Stability Forum offered for the first time guidance on, *inter alia*, techniques to help promote better interrelationships among safety net participants. The recommendations were contained in a report entitled 'Guidance for Developing Effective Deposit Insurance Systems'. Although the conclusions contained in that report represented a significant breakthrough in the provision of information on this subject, it was soon recognized that further work was needed to provide for detailed and comprehensive guidance from the deposit insurance practitioners' perspective. In May 2002, the IADI was established with a mission to 'contribute to the enhancement of deposit insurance effectiveness by promoting guidance and international cooperation'.[4] As part of its work, IADI undertakes research to provide guidance on deposit insurance issues. Thus, a sub-committee on interrelationship among safety net participants of International Association of Deposit Insurers' (IADI) Research and Guidance Committee was formed to specifically extend the research work in this area.[5]

An examination of interrelationship issues among financial safety net participants, such as the regulator, supervisor, lender-of-last-resort and deposit insurer, and so on, is designed to improve the effectiveness of overall back-up mechanisms and therefore the protection of less sophisticated depositors. This chapter is written from the perspective of the deposit insurer. But in doing so, the contribution of the other participants is recognized in achieving an effective financial sector safety net. This chapter discusses: (1) financial safety nets participants and their responsibilities; (2) coordination among safety net participants; and (3) the importance of information sharing. The final part of the chapter offers some conclusions to help improve co-ordination and effectiveness.

7.2 Financial safety-net participants and responsibilities

The construction of an effective and efficient financial safety net needs to take into account a country's institutional arrangements and they should operate in a fashion that promotes financial stability and be useful in dealing with problem financial institutions in a timely manner, especially during a financial crisis. According to the literature or definition regarding the financial safety net made by some international organizations, the composition of the net is similar in nature.

A BIS Working Paper on 'Deposit Insurance System Design and Considerations'[6] prepared by Nicholas J. Ketcha Jr indicated that the combination of the safety net contains: (1) bank access to a lender of last resort facility; (2) final, riskless settlement of payment system transactions; (3) prudential supervision of banks; (4) deposit insurance. Stefan Ingves, now Governor of the Swedish Riksbank and former Director of Monetary and Financial Systems Department of International Monetary Fund (IMF), also mentioned the three major components of a financial safety net; they are a deposit protection scheme, a lender of last resort facility and effective exit policies for weak financial institutions.[7] In addition, the IADI defines that a financial safety net usually comprises the deposit insurance function, prudential regulation and supervision, and lender of last resort function.[8] It is not surprising, therefore, that most countries have a financial safety net that is composed of a deposit insurance system, a lender of last resort facility, a secure payment and clearing system, prudent financial regulation and supervision, and a mechanism for enabling weak financial institutions to exit from the market.

In the recent survey by IADI we found that some countries (the UK, Taiwan and Korea) have a consolidated financial supervisor, while in some countries, a department of government (generally, the Ministry of Finance or the Treasury) plays an important role in the financial safety net and is usually responsible for financial sector policy, and in some instances, the central bank has the responsibility for supervisory functions (for example, Jamaica, Bulgaria, Jordan, Lithuania, Portugal and Cyprus). The regulatory framework and prudential supervision are designed to promote improved stability performance in the banking system as they attempt to offset the negative consequences of the market failure present in the industry. Prudential regulation and supervision include, *inter alia*, the chartering (for example, licensing) function which imposes capital and character (fit and proper) and disclosure requirements, restrictions on the types of assets that banks may hold and on the activities in which they may engage. Regulation is designed to reduce unwarranted or unmitigated risk taking and supervision to monitor banks to see that they are complying with the regulations in order to ensure the safety and soundness of the banking system.

Central banks play the role of the lender of the last resort and they provide financial support to illiquid but solvent banks so as to curb the spread of a liquidity crisis. We noted from our survey that deposit insurance attends more to equity concerns and offers explicit protection to depositors. According to our findings, all deposit insurance entities described themselves as being integral parts of their respective countries' financial safety nets. It is not surprising, therefore, that a well-designed deposit insurance system will not only safeguard the interests of depositors, but also help to maintain public confidence and enhance financial stability.

Most deposit insurers operate as government agencies but a few (for example, Brazil, Finland and France) operate as private companies. The case of Slovenia is interesting as the depositor protection system consists of the banks themselves. There is no special fund established but only the legal obligation by which banks guarantee payment of deposits. In Japan, besides safety net participants (government and central banks), there is private financial sector's participation in equity, decision-making process and staff.

The survey (Questions 3 and 6, Appendix 7.A.1) also examined mandates and powers. We found that precision on these matters depends on the type of deposit insurer and the public policy objectives. A deposit insurer with the paybox mandate mainly focuses on the collection of levies or premiums and undertakes reimbursement of depositor funds after a bank fails, while an organization with a risk-minimization mandate has more resources and business powers to reduce the risks it faces. These powers may include the ability to control entry and exit from the deposit insurance system, and they could encompass roles and authorities in areas such as risk assessment and management, intervention and failure resolution. Whatever the type of deposit insurer it is, we found that its mandate should be clear and well defined. Moreover, the necessary powers and authorities granted to a deposit insurer should be consistent with the public policy objectives and its specified mandate. If not, it may engender some difficult coordination issues and undermine the stated objectives as a deposit insurer.

Even though there may be restrictions on entry and appropriate prudential regulation and supervision, banks may fail, in one form or another, in all jurisdictions around the world, as in the oft-quoted phrase: 'Banking is essential; banks are not'.[9] In this regard, a well-designed (transparent and understood) mechanism to deal with financial institutions in distress is also necessary. The mechanism should include the institutional and legal framework governing[10] early warning, intervention and the taking of prompt correction action. This framework should consist of clearly defined roles with checks and balances to promote constructive interrelationships among financial safety net participants. If, for example, there is more than one institution dealing with different phases of a resolution, coordination among them assumes even greater significance, because conflicts are inevitable, often relating to differences of opinion or caused by differences in mandates. These conflicts could induce supervisory forbearance and provide room to shift responsibilities or blame to another safety-net participant, and thus impact on financial stability.

The sound governance of organizations comprising the financial safety net strengthens the financial system's architecture and contributes directly to system stability.[11] In reviewing the experience and analysis of financial system assessments, officials from the IMF and IADI found that there are five major elements and they are: independence, accountability, transparency, integrity and stewardship. It was determined that all are equally important and reinforce each other in supporting good practices. Operationally independent and accountable safety-net participants, with clear mandates and which are insulated from undue political and industry influence, provide greater integrity, credibility and legitimacy than entities lacking such independence. Credible safety-net participants are in an excellent position to promote and enforce good governance practices in the supervised institutions. High quality governance in financial institutions, in turn, is a major building block of financial soundness and stability.[12] Specifically, deposit insurers with the responsibility for insured deposits have the same level of fiduciary duty as banks that accept deposits.[13]

In some countries (see Question 5), safety-net participants are independent statutory bodies with their powers, mandates and responsibilities explicitly defined in legislation and in some instances supported by Memoranda of Understanding (for example, Jamaica, Bulgaria and Estonia) as well as special agreements for information sharing and coordination (such as Canada, Hungary, Taiwan and Korea). A number of countries, including Jordan, Slovenia and Trinidad and Tobago, considered that there are areas where the powers and responsibilities of the deposit insurer *vis-à-vis* those of other safety net participants should be better defined. Some of the areas suggested for improvement (see Question 6) include: provision of clearer mandates bolstered by stronger accountability regimes for ensuring that the participants fulfill their responsibilities; the strengthening of corporate governance provisions and improved information sharing through more specific reference in law as to the type of information to be shared and the timing for the receipt of such information.

To sum up, the first step in approaching the matter of interrelationships among safety-net participants is to have a clear understanding of the particular country's institutional arrangements. Then, clarity of the mandates and powers being explicitly defined in legislation, agreements, or Memoranda of Understanding and the compatibility with the public-policy objectives are the keys for determining the role of each participant within the financial safety net. A mechanism for resolution of bank failures should be in place and well-designed. Accordingly, coordination and information sharing are also essential for avoiding the inevitable conflicts and for ensuring an effective safety net especially at a time of having an individual bank failure or even financial crisis. More details concerning coordination and information sharing will be discussed in the following sections. Besides, the sound governance of the safety-net participants is a key element of a well functioning financial safety-net system.

7.3 Coordination among safety-net participants

The composition of a financial safety net and the responsibilities of each of its members were outlined in the previous section. The necessity for close coordination and cooperation among safety-net participants (see Questions 7 to 11) stems from the possibility of conflicting mandates which could undermine the effectiveness of a financial safety net.

We found that these conflicts may appear in such matters as the control function of a banking supervisor and those of a deposit insurer. For example, the banking supervisor has a strong incentive to delay the closing of a bank assuming an indulgent attitude, since this would indicate a failure and could have a negative effect on its reputation and image.[14] Such forbearance may result in increasing the costs to the deposit insurer and hence the government. As well, if the legal regimes are inadequate for supervisors and deposit insurers to fulfill their mandates, the conflicts may also arise, particularly when dealing with bank closures, liquidating assets, and resolving creditors' claims.[15]

Conflicts might also occur between the lender of last resort and the deposit insurer with regard to providing liquidity to a problem financial institution. While the purpose of the former in offering financial accommodation to an individual non-viable bank usually implies the prevention of the systemic crises, some might view resolution of a problem bank as the responsibility of a deposit insurer. Thus, in order to make sure the deposit insurer, equipped with the power of provision of liquidity, appropriately exerts its function, more information should be rendered for its judgment. Coordination and responsibilities also need to be clearly and explicitly addressed in order to enhance the operation and credibility of the overall financial safety net.[16]

Though the precise mechanisms of coordination will obviously depend on each country's institutional set-up, our research showed that, as a first step, there should be a clearly articulated division of powers and responsibilities agreed upon by all the participants to prevent unproductive overlapping and duplication of activities as much as possible.

In normal times, it is clear that agreement as to respective mandates does not have the same level of significance as when there is a banking crisis. However, when failures occur, it could be very difficult for safety net participants to fulfill their respective responsibilities without a clear *ex ante* mandate. Deposit insurance systems may have the capacity to deal with one failure or a number of failures of banks at one time, but they cannot deal with a financial system meltdown or crisis. The location of the function of each financial safety-net participant is important because timing is crucial during a crisis. In order to reconcile potential conflicting mandates a high degree of transparency must be a requirement when establishing the coordination framework to facilitate information sharing and effective communication, so as to handle the banking crisis in an efficient manner.

The survey results demonstrate that coordination mechanisms vary from country to country. In those countries where the deposit insurer is a risk minimizer, we found that there are no significant overlaps between the deposit insurer functions and those of the other safety net participants. This conclusion stems from the fact that the powers of the various agencies are normally clearly defined in law. Where the central bank, supervisory and deposit Insurance functions are contained within one entity (for example, the Netherlands), there is little or no scope for conflicts as they can be resolved internally. Coordination also becomes easier when a single institution has more than one function – such as in Kenya and Cyprus.

Where the possibility of conflict between safety-net participants exists, the survey showed that the following coordination methods are usually adopted: membership of other safety-net participants on the deposit insurance systems' board of directors; use of Memoranda of Understanding (MOUs); specially mandated committees; and, activities undertaken through the deposit insurance licensing process and legal agreements. In the Philippines, for example, the functions and responsibilities of the deposit insurer and the central bank in the areas of examination, monitoring, prompt corrective action, and failure resolution, are defined in their respective charters and/or circulars, rules and regulations and through a Memorandum of Agreement. The boards of both entities prescribe guidelines that may be necessary to ensure that there is no duplication of functions. In Jamaica, by contrast, a statutory committee composed of representatives of the central bank, deposit insurance system, ministry of finance and supervisory authority has been established to facilitate information sharing and to coordinate regulatory policy. In Canada, representation on Board of Directors of the Canada Deposit Insurance Corporation (CDIC) coupled with specially mandated committees designed to consider matters of mutual interest and a 'Guide to Intervention' for federal institutions developed jointly between CDIC and the Office of the Superintendent of Financial Institutions (OSFI) stand as benchmarks for the purpose of enhancing coordination.

In some cases board members of deposit insurance organizations consist of high level representatives from the other financial safety net participants. This is an effective practice as it could help in the coordination and development of different strategies and opinions. It was found that this could help in the decision-making process for important issues related to bank resolution, including intervention and other corrective actions to deal with a problem bank.

7.4 The importance of information sharing

Questions 12 to 16 focused on information sharing issues. We found that effective information sharing can foster better supervision, reduce the regulatory and reporting burden on banks, and facilitate the process of resolution in the case of a bank failure. This is a critical area in the promotion and maintenance of the credibility of the financial safety net.

Depending on its institutional mandate and powers, the need for necessary information by the deposit insurer can vary significantly. In the case of a simple pay-box system, the deposit insurer should have the basic information to calculate the levies or premiums to be paid by member institutions on insured deposits and to reimburse depositors in a timely and efficient manner when required to do so. Such information relates to data on the banks' deposit base, including information on the level of deposits insured and therefore subject to a premium assessment. It may also include details on special products with their insurability, or on the amount of insured deposits held by individual depositors.

A risk-minimizing deposit insurer for the purpose of risk monitoring has, however, a greater need for information given its particular focus. The deposit insurer must be in a position to assess the financial condition not only of individual member institutions, through access to, for example, their financial statements, on-site inspection reports, the value of the bank, but also the entire industry. In addition, the risk minimizer should be able to anticipate the financial troubles of individual banks and deal with them effectively when they arise. Information concerning the value of the bank's assets and the expected time frame for the liquidation process are also needed by the deposit insurer. This requires well-defined roles, responsibilities, information sharing and coordination of activities with the other safety-net participants. When this is accomplished, it can result in a high level of effectiveness and minimization of losses for the deposit insurer and the financial system as a whole.

The nature of the information required by the deposit insurer will vary from normal times to that in a crisis. In normal times deposit insurers need mainly information on premium collection or risk monitoring; however, when there is a bank failure or crisis, more information such as those related to depositor reimbursement or bank resolution or liquidation becomes essential. The survey found that the type and timing of information to be shared may be specified by law, formal agreement or informally.

We found through our research that an important issue arises concerning access to the results of on-site examinations that produce information on the institution's condition not otherwise available. Empirical evidence suggests that, in the majority of cases, the supervisory authority is the primary and most important source of such banking information. Due to its specific powers and responsibilities, the supervisory authority is usually the only safety net agency able to assess accurately and ensure the quality of information provided by financial institutions. Therefore, close coordination of the collection and sharing of information between the supervisory authority and the other safety-net participants becomes an imperative. The available evidence suggests, however, that access of the deposit insurer to examination reports or critical data from such reports differs among the countries surveyed.

Is there a best practice which should be followed? Based on the responses to the survey, the majority of deposit insurers do not have the authority to inspect member banks directly but have the authority to request certain actions or information from the supervisor. Hungary has limited authority while Jordan can do so jointly with the central bank. In the Philippines, the deposit insurer can minimize insurance risks through the conduct of examination of banks. However, this requires prior approval of the central bank's Monetary Board, provided that no examination may be conducted within 12 months from the last examination date. In Mexico, the supervisor is required by law to inform the deposit insurer of the condition of an institution where there is a prospect that intervention may be required. Deposit insurers that can or cannot have access to supervisory inspection reports are about equally divided.

In general, depending on the scope of their specific mandates, deposit insurers may need to supplement information provided by supervisors with certain specific information obtained directly from the insured banks. For example, this could include, for purposes of verification, the level of deposits held for premium assessment and information on specific products and their insurability. However, it is important to balance the need of the deposit insurer to obtain supplemental information against the need not to place an undue burden on the banking industry.

For information to be useful to the deposit insurer, it should be timely, accurate and relevant to facilitate an effective system of ongoing evaluation of individual insured institutions as well as the banking industry as a whole. In many instances, the supervisor is not obliged to respond to the requests of the deposit insurer for information. Examples of exceptions to this are to be found in Canada, Bulgaria, Colombia, Korea, and Albania. There are some deposit insurers which cannot obtain information from the supervisor or other safety net participants, (for example, Trinidad and Tobago) while others (such as Mexico) cannot get information directly from the banks, except what is publicly released. Without obtaining information as they need, deposit insurers cannot fulfill their pre-emptive mandates or responsibilities effectively. Whether a deposit insurer could receive information from its member banks or get access to inspection reports directly, a formal channel of timely and accurate information sharing need to be established.

Certain types of information about individual banks, such as supervisory ratings of individual institutions and customers' accounts, are usually held in confidence. However, no matter if a deposit insurer is a government or privately run entity, it should be able to receive necessary information considering its objective of acting for the public interest. Deficiencies in the flow of information from the banking sector and poor information exchange among the safety-net participants undermine the ability to carry out their mandates. Moreover, rules regarding the confidentiality of information exchanged between safety-net participants should be respected at all times.

7.5 Conclusions

It can be said that 'Banking is essential, but banks are not.' Given the reality that banks will and do fail, it is significant to have in place a well-designed institutional and legal framework governing early warning, intervention, the taking of prompt corrective actions, and finally the resolution of a problem bank to maintain financial stability. The framework should consist of clearly defined roles, and checks and balances to promote constructive interrelationships among financial safety-net participants, as they are essential to an effective deposit insurance system. The more complex the safety-net institutional set-up is, the more relevant the interrelationships issue becomes.

The financial safety net is mainly composed of the deposit insurance system, the lender of last resort, a secure payment and clearing system, prudent financial regulation and supervision, and a mechanism for enabling weak financial institutions to exit from the market. The first step in approaching the matter of interrelationships among safety-net participants is to have a clear understanding of the particular country's institutional arrangements. This will assist with the proper identification of the composition and scope of the financial safety net and provide insights into the potential for conflicts.

The next step is to review their respective functions both in normal times and in a financial crisis. In cases where a single organization performs all of the safety net functions, the smooth resolution of potential tensions will depend on the clarity of mandates and an adequate accountability regime among the relevant departments. Where the functions are assigned to different organizations, issues related to the allocation of powers and responsibilities, coordination of actions among the different functions, and issues related to information sharing become more complex and need to be addressed clearly and explicitly in order to enhance the operation and credibility of the overall financial safety net.

However, one should note that deposit insurance systems are not intended to cope with systemic financial crises by themselves. The resolution of systemic crises requires broad, coordinated government actions. Clear division of responsibilities and effective coordination specified by law are the key elements for a government to handle a systemic crisis successfully and efficiently.

Coordination and cooperation are essential also because conflicts are inevitable. They may arise from a number of reasons, often relating to differences of opinion or caused by differences in mandates. How well these conflicts are resolved will depend on effective interrelationships. Therefore, there should be a clearly articulated division of powers and responsibilities agreed upon by all the participants and explicitly defined in law to avoid or minimize the unpleasant consequences of conflict and to prevent unproductive overlapping and duplication of activities as much as possible.

The need for necessary information by the deposit insurer can vary significantly depending on its institutional mandate and powers but this does not obviate the need for close coordination and information sharing among safety-net participants in all cases. All the required information should be timely, accurate and relevant. In the case of a simple paybox system, the deposit insurance agency should have the basic information to pay off depositors in a timely and efficient manner when required to do so.

A risk-minimizing deposit insurer would however, have greater needs for information given its broader mandate. For example, it must be in a position to assess the financial condition not only of individual member institutions but the entire industry. In addition, the risk minimizer should be able to anticipate the financial troubles of individual banks and deal with them effectively when they arise. The deposit insurer also needs information regarding the value of the bank's assets and the expected time frame for the liquidation process, so as to estimate its net loss after recovery and sufficiency of the deposit insurance fund.

Since the supervisory authority is usually the primary and most important source of banking information given its specific powers and responsibilities, there should be clear guidelines for this entity to share the relevant information with other safety-net participants. Steps must also be taken to ensure that the supervisory authority is obliged to supply the required information.

Deposit insurers may from time to time need to supplement information provided by the supervisory authority with certain specific information obtained directly from the insured banks – for example, the level of deposits held for premium assessment and information on specific products and their insurability. Therefore the necessary arrangements must be put in place to facilitate the deposit insurer gaining access to such supplemental information without difficulty.

Whatever the mandates and powers a deposit insurer is equipped with, they should be compatible with the public–policy objectives. Formal mechanism of information sharing specified by law or formal agreement is important. Apart from or in addition to legislation, consideration should also be given to the formalization of the following coordination and information sharing techniques: membership on deposit insurers' board of directors, use of Memoranda of Understanding (MOUs), specially mandated committees and the deposit insurance licensing process or a combination of these techniques.

Appendix 7A.1

Questionnaire on interrelationships among financial safety-net participants

Mandates and powers

1. In your country, which organizations are considered to be part of the financial safety-net (this might be the deposit insurer, supervisor, central bank, and a government ministry)?
2. What is the institutional arrangement for these organizations?

3. Are the respective powers, mandates, and responsibilities of the various safety-net participants explicitly defined? Where are they defined (this might be in the banking laws of the country, in memoranda of understanding, in informal agreements)? If powers and mandates are governed by informal agreements, do you regard this as satisfactory, or would you prefer more formal arrangements?
4. Does the deposit insurer have the authority to inspect directly member banks? Does the deposit insurer have access to supervisory inspection reports? Which safety-net participant has the authority to decide the liquidation of a bank? And who plays the role of the liquidator or receiver? And what are the interrelationships of the liquidator with other participants in the safety net over the liquidation process? Who decides among safety-net participants, the eligible currencies, accounts and limits of coverage, and has the authority to amend or change any of them?
5. Does the deposit insurer decide independently the investment policy for the reserves? Are there any other safety-net participants who are involved in the investment and reserve allocation policy?
6. In your judgement, are there areas where the powers and responsibilities of the deposit insurer and other safety-net players should be better defined than they presently are? In what areas? In what ways would the effectiveness of the deposit insurer be enhanced?

Coordination of activities

7. In countries where the deposit insurer is a risk minimizer – i.e. with functions going beyond a paybox system – how are the possible overlaps between the deposit insurer's functions and responsibilities and those of other safety-net participants like the supervisor or the entity in charge of the entry and exit decisions addressed?
8. How are the possible conflicts of interest between the entities participating in the safety net and the regulated or supervised entities handled in your country?
9. How are the activities of the various safety-net participants coordinated (examples are membership on each other's boards, specially designated committees, through the process of licensing (chartering) of banks)? Are these arrangements for coordination defined in law, memoranda of understanding or informal agreements?
10. Who are the members of the Board of each organization? Is it possible to have the same person(s) on these different boards?
11. Are there conflicts of interest among the safety net participants?

Information sharing

12. Based on your answer to question 4 (concerning the type of deposit insurer you regard your organization to be – paybox, risk minimizer, etc.) why does the deposit insurer need information?
13. What kinds of information does the deposit insurer in your country obtain from the supervisor or other safety-net participants? What kind of information does the deposit insurer obtain directly from the banks? How is the information obtained by the deposit insurance organization related to its powers, mandates, and responsibilities?
14. If information is obtained from the bank supervisor rather than directly from the banks, is the supervisor obliged to respond to the requests of the deposit insurer within a specified time period?
15. What kind of information about individual banks is held in confidence in your country?

16. Is the sharing of confidential information between safety net members considered in regulation or legislation?

Other interrelationship issues

17. Are there any other issues, not listed above, that should be considered in formulating guidance for deposit insurers regarding interrelationships with other safety net participants?

Appendix 7A.2

Countries responding to the questionnaire:

IADI members

1. Albania
2. Brazil
3. Bulgaria
4. Canada: CDIC
5. l'Autorité des marchés financiers, Québec
6. Colombia
7. Czech Republic
8. El Salvador
9. France
10. Hungary
11. Jamaica
12. Japan
13. Jordan
14. Kazakhstan
15. Kenya
16. Korea
17. Mexico
18. Philippines
19. Russia
20. Sweden
21. Taiwan
22. Trinidad & Tobago
23. USA.
24. Venezuela
25. Vietnam

Non-members

1. Chile
2. Cyprus
3. Estonia
4. Finland
5. Lithuania
6. Netherlands
7. Portugal
8. Slovenia
9. Spain.
10. UK

Notes

1 This chapter was prepared by Winston Carr and it benefited considerably from comments provided by Andrei Pekhterev (Deposit Insurance Agency – Russian Federation), Bakhyt Mazhenova (Kazakhstan Deposit Insurance Fund), Carlos Isoard (Instituto para la Proteccion al Ahorro Bancario – Mexico), Charles Cornut (Fonds de Garantie des Dépôts – France), Daniel Jánossy (National Deposit Insurance Fund of Hungary, David Walker (Canada Deposit Insurance Corporation), Dong-Il Kim (Korea Deposit Insurance Corporation), Hajime Shinohara (Deposit Insurance Corporation of Japan), Ricardo Tan (Philippine Deposit Insurance

Corporation), Roumyana Markova (Deposit Insurance Fund of Bulgaria) who were all members of a subgroup that was established by the International Association of Deposit Insurers to develop guidance to help promote effective relationships among safety-net participants. The author would like to also thank John Raymond LaBrosse, Secretary General, International Association of Deposit Insurers, and Yvonne Fan, Margaret Chuang, Ivory Lin and Fiona Yeh, Central Deposit Insurance Corporation, for their assistance in finalizing this paper.

2 Andrew and Josefsson (2003, p. 10).
3 SEDESA (2003, p. 11).
4 Please see: www.iadi.org/html/Default.aspx?MenuID=294.
5 The paper benefited to a large extent from survey analysis based on a questionnaire to document the experiences of IADI members as well as other financial safety-net participants. A total of seventy six (76) questionnaires were circulated to the thirty four (34) IADI members and forty two (42) non-IADI members. A total of 35 or 46 per cent have responded as shown in Appendix 7.A.2. In addition, the paper drew on relevant literature available on the subject. Approximately one-half of the deposit insurers which responded to the questionnaire, indicated that they had paybox systems, while most of the others described themselves as 'risk minimizers' or 'risk managers' with some business powers or means to reduce risk exposure, with five (5) also having supervisory powers.
6 The paper was issued in November 1999.
7 Ingves and Quintyn (2003, p. 1).
8 Glossary at the IADI website: www.iadi.org.
9 Andrew and Josefsson (2003, p. 10).
10 Ingves, APEC Policy Dialogue on Deposit Insurance, February 2004.
11 Canada Deposit Insurance Corporation (2004, p. 8).
12 Ingves and Quintyn (2003, p. 3).
13 Sabourin (2006).
14 Jaime (2003, p. 107).
15 Financial Stability Forum Working Group on Deposit Insurance – Consultation and Background Paper (2000, pp. 16–17).
16 Central Deposit Insurance Corporation (Taiwan) (2005, p. 76).

References

Andrew, M. and Josefsson, M. (2003) *What Happens After Supervisory Intervention? Considering Bank Closure Options*, International Monetary Fund (IMF) Working paper, January.

Canada Deposit Insurance Corporation (2004) *APEC Policy Dialogue on Deposit Insurance: Policy Conclusion Paper*, Canada, June 25.

Carr, W.K. (2003) *Interrelationships Among Financial Safety-net Players*, presented at International Association of Deposit Insurers (IADI) 2nd Annual Conference, Seoul, South Korea, October 23–24.

Central Deposit Insurance Corporation (Taiwan), (2005) *Deposit Insurance Quarterly Bulletin*, vol. 18: 4, December.

Chen, J. (2005) *Strengthening the Financial Safety Net to Assist in Ensuring the Sound Operation of Financial Institutions: From Viewpoint of Taiwan*, presented at the International Association of Deposit Insurers (IADI) 4th Annual Conference, Taipei, Taiwan, September 27–29.

Financial Stability Forum (2001) *Guidance for Developing Effective Insurance Systems*, final Report of the Working Group on Deposit Insurance, Bank for International Settlements, Basel.

Garcia, G. (1999) *Deposit Insurance: A Survey of Actual and Best Practices*, International Monetary Fund (IMF) Working paper No. 99/554.

Hanc, G. (2003) *Questions on the Design of a Deposit Insurance System: Summary of Responses*, former Chair, Research and Guidance Committee, International Association of Deposit Insurers (IADI), August.

International Association of Deposit Insurers (IADI) website:www.iadi.org/html/Default.aspx?MenuID=294, www. iadi.org.

Ingves, S. and Quintyn, M. (2003) *Financial Stability Assessments: Implications for Governance Arrangements*, presented at the International Association of Deposit Insurers (IADI) 2nd Annual Conference, Seoul, South Korea, October 23–24.

Isoard, C. (2003) Financial Safety Nets: Where We Stand, presented at IDB Seminar, Washington, DC, September 9.

Jaime, J.C. (2005) *New Compendium Based on the Symposia of SEDESA*, February, p. 107.

LaBrosse, J.R. (2004) *Interrelationships and Its Role in Promoting Effective Deposit Insurance Systems*, a presentation to the APEC Policy Dialogue on Deposit Insurance, February 17.

Machinea, J.L. and Rappoport, V. (2003) *Financial Safety Nets and Regional Integration*, presented at IDB Seminar in Washington, DC, September 9.

Sabourin, J.P. (2006) *Corporate Governance Initiatives for Deposit Insurers*, February.

Sabourin, J.P., Isoard, C. Cornut, C. Ogunleye G. and LaBrosse, J. R. (2005) *Promoting Effective Financial Safety Nets*, presented at the Bank for International Settlements, June 27.

Seguro de Depositos Sociedad Anonima (SEDESA) (2003) *IV Symposium on Deposit Insurance: Safety Net Proceedings of Symposium*, April.

Tan, R. M. (2003) *How Deposit Insurers Get the Information to Do Their Job*, presented at International Association of Deposit Insurers (IADI) 2nd Annual Conference, Seoul, South Korea, October 23.

8

Using Efficient Bank Insolvency Resolution to Solve the Deposit Insurance Problem

George G. Kaufman[1]

Deposit insurance in some form or other is a political reality in effectively all countries that have a banking system. But, as many of these countries have experienced, deposit insurance has its economic downside. It encourages both moral hazard behaviour by banks that leads to excessive risk taking and poor agency behaviour by bank regulators that leads to excess forbearance for problem institutions. Both effects increase the probabilities and costs of banking crisis.[2] Provisions to effectively reduce, if not eliminate, these adverse consequences directly by altering the structure of deposit insurance have proven difficult both to design and to implement. Risk-based insurance premiums, coinsurance, restrictions on coverage, and other schemes adopted from private insurance programmes for other types of losses, for example, life, property and casualty, and so on, have not proven very successful either to adopt or to implement. In part, this reflects the fact that deposit insurance is very different from other forms of insurance. Thus, it may be time to focus on alternatives approaches to correcting the moral hazard and principal–agent problems.

Deposit insurance is intended to compensate some or all depositors for any credit losses they may suffer if their banks become insolvent. The smaller the losses, the less important is deposit insurance to the covered depositors and if these losses could be eliminated entirely, so also would the need for deposit insurance. Unlike losses from fires, thefts, accidents, and illnesses, which are largely, although not entirely, outside the control of insurance companies – basically acts of God and exogenous – credit losses in bank insolvencies depend on how quickly after the bank's capital turns negative the bank is officially declared insolvent and resolved. To the extent that the timing of officially declaring a bank insolvent is under the control of bank regulators, the credit losses are potentially under the control of the regulators and largely endogenous. The control is only 'potentially' because it may not be easy for regulators to declare banks insolvent in a timely manner. They require accurate and timely information as well as both the legal tools and the political will to legally close insolvent banks as soon as or even slightly before their correctly measured capital turns negative. But if they are successful in doing so not only would the cost of bank failures be greatly reduced, but deposit insurance becomes effectively redundant and its design becomes relatively less important. That is, efficient insolvency resolution would both lower the costs of bank failure and minimize, if not eliminate, any undesirable side-effects of deposit insurance and may be an easier way of achieving these objectives than operating on deposit insurance structure directly. Premiums would be low and basically required only to fund operating costs and credit losses due to fraud, which by definition is not apparent in the capital measures until it is too late. The regulators' attention can be focused more completely on resolving insolvencies efficiently and permits them to kill two birds with one stone.

The remainder of this chapter outlines a four-point programme for efficiently resolving insolvent banks so that both their credit losses and the widespread fear of bank failures are minimized and deposit insurance becomes benign. Indeed, with efficient insolvency resolution, deposit insurance provides desirable built-in redundancy in case specific resolutions turn out *ex post* not to be efficient and involve losses to depositors, much like airplanes have two or even three brake systems in case the first system fails to produce a fail-safe structure. However, as noted earlier, satisfying these four principles requires that a country has the necessary legal and institutional infrastructure. Because many countries do not have this infrastructure in place, this strategy for developing an efficient deposit insurance structure is feasible only in those countries that do.

8.1 Satisfying the four principles for efficient insolvency resolution

Bank failures produce two potential losses – credit losses and liquidity losses. Credit losses occur when the market (recovery) value of the bank's assets decline below the par value of the bank's debt liabilities on their due dates. Liquidity losses occur when depositors do not receive full and immediate access to the value of their deposits at the insolvent bank and qualified borrowers to their credit lines. Efficient resolution minimizes both costs. All four of the points in the programme for efficient resolution proposed in this paper focus on the term 'prompt':[3]

1. prompt legal closure when the bank's capital declines to some prespecified and well publicized minimum value greater than zero (legal closure rule),
2. prompt estimates of the recovery value and assignment of any credit losses (haircuts) to *de jure* uninsured bank claimants,
3. prompt reopening (for example, the next business day), particularly of larger banks, with full depositor access to their accounts on their due

dates at par value for insured deposits and recovery value for uninsured deposits and full borrower access to their pre-established credit lines, and
4. prompt re-privatization and re-capitalization of the bank in whole or in parts at adequate capital levels.

Because the USA has a separate and unique bankruptcy code for banks in place that permits the four principles to be achieved more easily and many of the provisions were revised in light of a banking crisis – the thrift and commercial banking crises of the 1980s – the chapter analyses these four primarily with respect to banking in the USA.[4] Although US experience may not be representative of all countries, there are sufficient commonalities among banking systems for the US experience to serve as at least a partial model for most other countries.

Prompt legal closure

The Federal Deposit Insurance Corporation Improvement Act (FDICIA) of 1991 introduced a bright line bank closure rule that is triggered when the ratio of book value tangible equity capital to total on-balance sheet assets declines to a minimum of 2 per cent.[5] If not corrected within 90 days (with the possibility of two 90-day expansions), the bank must be declared legally insolvent, closed by the appropriate federal or state regulator, and placed in receivership or conservatorship.[6] Its charter is revoked, shareholder controlling interests are terminated and senior management is changed. If the institution can be successfully resolved before its market value capital declines below zero, losses are confined to shareholders. Depositors and other creditors are fully protected and kept whole, and deposit insurance is effectively redundant. Thus, there would also be no loss to the deposit insurance fund.

However, because the closure rule is specified in terms of book value capital rather than market value, there is no guarantee that the institution will be resolved before its economic capital is depleted or that creditors will be fully protected against losses. As a bank approaches insolvency, book values tend to increasingly overstate market values for assets and understate them for liabilities. They increasingly resemble fiction rather than fact. Thus, market value insolvent banks may be book value solvent and not be legally closed in time with no loss. Nevertheless, specifying a closure rule with a capital ratio that is greater than zero provides important protection against losses due both to the deviation of book from market value and to errors in measuring asset values correctly, including fraud. Credit losses are minimized.

Legal closure according to a well specified, publicized, and credibly enforced closure rule at positive capital has several desirable attributes. There are no surprises. All players know the rules in advance and base their actions accordingly. It treats all depositors and other creditors in the same priority class more fairly. Because banks tend to have a larger percentage of demand deposits and other short short-term deposits and debt than other firms, bad news, impending insolvency, or uncertainty about how creditors would be treated in the event of insolvency typically increase the incentives of those who can withdraw their funds to do so while the bank's assets still have sufficient value to support their claims. Uncertainty thus raises the probability of a run, with the initial runners – at the front of the line – receiving full payment and those unable or unwilling to run – at the end of the line – receiving less. However, the presence of a strong perception of an enforced closure rule at positive capital would greatly reduce the incentive to run. All debt claimants, regardless of the date of maturity of their claims, would know that they would be kept whole. Reducing the incentive for runs also increases the time regulators have to act to deter insolvency or bring about an efficient resolution if the closure trigger is breached.

Banks become insolvent in the USA and need to be legally closed because another provision of FDICIA – prompt corrective action (PCA) – has failed to induce financially troubled banks to turn around before insolvency. PCA established a series of five capital tranches or tripwires ranging down from 'well-capitalized' to 'critically under-capitalized'. Progressively harsher and more mandatory sanctions are applied by the bank regulators on weak financial institutions as their net worth declines through these tranches to discourage their insolvency (Table 8.1). The sanctions are similar to those that the market imposes on firms in non-regulated industries. Sanctions include changes in senior management, reductions in dividends, restrictions on growth and acquisitions, adoption of capital restorations plans and, if the bank is a subsidiary of a financial holding company, loss of its parent's status as a financial holding company with the associated wider range of powers and other privileges. The tranches effectively serve as 'speed bumps' to slow a bank's deterioration and to force regulators to become more involved with troubled banks well before insolvency, so that they may be ready to close them legally when the minimum capital ratio is breached and not be caught by surprise and delayed. Thus, PCA effectively buys the regulators time to act efficiently. For this reason, a legal closure rule is likely to be effective only if it is incorporated in a PCA or structured early intervention and resolution (SEIR) framework.

While PCA has not prevented all bank failures, it has contributed significantly to turning troubled banks around before insolvency and reducing both the number and the aggregate cost of failures.[7] Knowing with certainty that they will be placed in receivership if they breach the minimum capital ratio, banks will either take more timely and decisive actions to avoid insolvency or sell themselves to those who will. However, it is important to note that PCA and a closure rule at positive capital are not intended to prevent all failures. As in other industries, inefficient and/or unlucky banks should be permitted to fail and inept management replaced. But, because the externalities of bank insolvencies are widely perceived to be substantially greater than for

Table 8.1 Summary of prompt corrective action provisions of the Federal Deposit Insurance Corporation Improvement Act of 1991

Zone	Mandatory provisions	Discretionary provisions	Capital ratios (per cent)		
			Risk based Total	Risk based Tier 1	Leverage Tier 1
1. Well capitalized			> 10	> 6	> 5
2. Adequately capitalized	1. No brokered deposits, except with FDIC approval		> 8	> 4	> 4
3. Undercapitalized	1. Suspend dividends and management fees 2. Require capital restoration plan 3. Restrict asset growth 4. Approval required for acquisitions, branching, and new activities 5. No brokered deposits	1. Order recapitalization 2. Restrict inter-affiliate transactions 3. Restrict deposit interest rates 4. Restrict certain other activities 5. Any other action that would better carry out prompt corrective action	< 8	< 4	< 4
4. Significantly undercapitalized	1. Same as for Zone 3 2. Order recapitalization*	1. Any Zone 3 discretionary actions 2. Conservatorship or receivership if fails to submit or implement plan or recapitalize pursuant to order	< 6	< 3	< 3

	3. Restrict inter-affiliate transactions* 4. Restrict deposit interest rates* 5. Pay of officers restricted	3. Any other Zone 5 provision, if such action is necessary to carry out prompt corrective action	
5. Critically undercapitalized	1. Same as for Zone 4 2. Receiver/conservator within 90 days* 3. Receiver if still in Zone 5 four quarters after becoming critically under-capitalized 4. Suspend payments on subordinated debt* 5. Restrict certain other activities		< 2

Note: * Not required if primary supervisor determines action would not serve purpose of prompt corrective action or if certain other conditions are met.
Source: Board of Governors of the Federal Reserve System.

other firms, such failures should occur only at low cost with minimal losses to creditors.

Prompt estimate and allocation of credit losses

Because the regulators should be scrutinizing troubled banks under PCA well before they approach the capital ratio closure trigger, the recovery value of the institution as a whole or in parts should be able to be estimated by them quickly upon legal closure for most banks. If the present value of the estimated recovery value falls short of the par value of the deposits and other debts – that is, the bank's net worth is negative at time of legal closure – *pro rata* losses (haircuts) should be allocated to these claimants in their order of legal priority.[8] In the USA, the FDIC has equal standing with depositors at domestic offices and higher standing than other depositors and creditors. The FDIC stands in the shoes of the insured depositors at domestic offices and is obliged to make them whole. It also shares proportionally in any losses with uninsured depositors at these offices beyond the losses charged first to other creditors and deposits at foreign offices. FDICIA requires the FDIC to resolve the institution at least cost to the insurance fund. This generally implies that the FDIC shares any losses with uninsured claimants. The only exception to the least cost resolution requirement is when doing so is likely to 'have serious adverse effects on economic conditions and financial stability' and protecting uninsured depositors would mitigate or prevent these problems. But invoking this safety valve is not easy and requires among other things the approval of the President of the United States. And should such approval be granted, any losses suffered by the FDIC in the rescue must be repaid promptly by the surviving banks. Requiring at-risk parties besides the FDIC to share in any losses is necessary to minimize moral hazard excessive risk-taking behaviour by banks and to enhance market discipline by reinforcing the *ex post* at-risk nature of *de jure* at-risk claimants. This should, in turn, reduce the number of bank failures.

Prompt re-opening of large banks

Liquidity losses to depositors occur through delayed access to (freezing of) deposit accounts.[9] In effect, demand deposits and other short-term deposits are transformed involuntarily into longer-term time deposits or bonds. Liquidity losses also result when credit lines cannot be relied upon or drawn down to meet business needs. Liquidity losses thus impair the efficient operation of the payments system. When regulators close a bank legally they often also effectively close it physically, at least partially, until funds are recovered from the sale of its assets to start paying depositors on their claims. This delay affects both insured deposits valued at par and uninsured valued at recovery value. Deposit insurance does not protect depositors against liquidity losses, only against credit losses. In many countries the lack of access to deposits and credit lines in bank failures is feared more than actual credit losses to depositors and generates as great, if not greater, adverse externalities.

Because of insufficient information on depositors or recovery values, regulators may find it necessary, at least briefly, to close banks physically when they close them legally, particularly outside the USA. Thus, because of insufficient information about depositors or recovery values, there is considerable pressure on regulators to avoid prompt legal closure of banks. By delaying legal closure, the regulators temporarily avoid liquidity losses. But delay also postpones, at least temporarily, explicitly recognizing underlying implicit credit losses. This can provide additional time for the bank to try to regain solvency and thereby avoid altogether the regulators' unpleasant task of legal closure. But evidence in many countries strongly suggests that, on average, forbearance that permits insolvent banks to continue to stay open and operate under the same ownership and management increases insolvency costs in the long run over what they would have been had the insolvent institution been legally closed promptly. To reduce the incentive for regulators to forbear, FDICIA made prompt legal closure at a minimum positive capital ratio mandatory.

Liquidity losses may be minimized or eliminated entirely by legally reopening the insolvent bank under different ownership and management the next business day. This would provide insured depositors immediate access to the par value of their accounts, uninsured depositors and other general creditors to the estimated recovery value of their accounts on due dates, and borrowers to their credit lines. Thus, legal closure is separated from physical closure.

Prompt payment to depositors and other debt claimants, either directly or through assumption of these claims by another bank, requires an immediate sale of the bank by the FDIC or access to a source of funds. The FDIC may also operate the bank temporarily through a newly chartered bridge bank under its control (statutory management) that assumes most or all of the assets and liabilities of the failed bank, generally at market values. The bridge bank is either capitalized with equity by the FDIC or its deposits are fully guaranteed by the FDIC during its operation until it is reprivatized.

In the USA, the FDIC usually pays insured deposits at the failed bank at par on or close to the next business day. This occurs either through a transfer of the deposits to another assuming solvent bank with an offsetting payment or, less frequently, through a payout. The FDIC can make such speedy payments as they have been monitoring problem banks carefully under PCA and have timely access to the bank's computerized records on eligible insured deposits. In contrast, uninsured depositors and other creditors generally receive receivership certificates, again on or close to the next business day, specifying their claim on the recovery value of the assets. But, they are paid in order of their legal priority more slowly, as proceeds are received from the sale of the bank assets. Unless there is an active secondary market for these certificates, uninsured creditors may suffer liquidity losses when selling the certificates. To maximize efficiency, these depositors should share in any credit losses but not suffer liquidity losses. To achieve this, the FDIC has the authority to make advance payments to these claimants on the basis of estimated or average recovery amounts. If payments are made at the time of legal closure, this procedure is essentially equivalent to not having physically closed the institution. Advance dividends also permit the estimated recovery value of uninsured deposits to be transferred to a newly chartered bridge bank with immediate access by depositors. In bridge banks, borrowers generally maintain access to their existing credit lines. This further reduces any liquidity losses.

Estimates of the recovery value of the funds advanced as dividends tend to be on the conservative side because the FDIC absorbs the loss if it overestimates the amounts eventually recovered. If it underestimates the recovery amounts, it makes additional payments to the claimants later. The FDIC, in its capacity as receiver, can borrow the necessary funds to make advance dividend payments from its corporate capacity, which has access to the FDIC accumulated fund. The FDIC used advance dividends briefly in a number of resolutions in the early 1980s and early 1990s, when it did not fully protect most or all uninsured debt claimants. But probably because most bank failures in the USA since the mid-1990s have involved small banks and often caused by major fraud, the FDIC has not used advance dividends often since. As a result, uninsured claimants have generally experienced liquidity losses.

Use of bridge banks and advance dividends to minimize liquidity losses, especially in combination with the previous principle of preventing or, at least, minimizing credit losses, should eliminate much of the public fear of bank failures. It should permit efficient resolution, particularly of large banks without strong negative reactions by the affected uninsured depositors – who are accustomed to suffering small losses on securities – or having to invoke the idea that some banks are 'too-big-to-fail'. Too-big-to-fail – now known as the 'systemic risk exemption' to the prohibition in FDICIA against the FDIC protecting uninsured claimants against credit losses in bank resolutions – permits the FDIC to protect *de jure* uninsured claimants partially or totally in order to mitigate 'any serious adverse effects on economic activity and financial stability'. The bank is officially failed, but all losses are not shared with uninsured claimants so that the resolution is not least cost to the FDIC.

Prompt reprivatization and recapitalization

FDICIA requires that insolvencies be resolved at least cost to the FDIC. This also reduces losses to depositors at domestic offices, who share the same legal priority. The requirement is generally satisfied best by a rapid sale of bank assets after legal closure. Smaller banks are likely to be liquidated and larger banks sold either as a whole or in large units, frequently after first being bridged. Reprivatization is generally more difficult the longer banks, including bridge banks, are publicly owned. Public ownership of banks is not always rooted in the desire to allocate resources efficiently. Nor do publicly owned institutions necessarily seek to maximize profits. Rather, the intent may be to reallocate funds for socially desirable purposes or for political purposes. Thus, when a government-sponsored bank becomes insolvent, the government is likely to keep the institution in operation regardless of its financial condition, and its return to solvency is likely to be slower. The consequence is that losses are likely to continue and the ultimate costs of resolution to the taxpayer is likely larger than it otherwise would.

To minimize government forbearance and its attendant costs, insolvent banks should be sold to the private sector in whole or parts, as soon as this can be done efficiently. Moreover, the sale should be on terms that provide sufficient capital to ensure that, after adjusting for any guarantees to the buyers, the resulting institution will attain, at minimum, 'adequately capitalized' status, if not 'well capitalized' status, to guard against a quick return to insolvency. Again, because under PCA the FDIC is aware of most pending insolvencies, it can begin the bidder search process for most banks before legal closure occurs and the actual bidding at closure. However, as noted, larger banks may need to be bridged both to reduce liquidity losses and to give the FDIC additional time to sell to the highest bidders without having to resort to fire-sale credit losses or otherwise being forced to unwind the bank inefficiently.

8.2 Legal prerequisites for efficient resolution

To apply an efficient solution strategy to achieve an efficient deposit insurance structure successfully as an indirect byproduct requires not only access to timely and accurate data and the political will of the regulators to use their available tools in a timely fashion to achieve least cost resolution for the insurance fund, the depositors, and the economy as a whole, but also the necessary tools. Depending on the country, these tools may not be available to regulators. The necessary tools would include authority that requires legal closure before a bank's capital is fully depleted and that mandates speedy and irrevocable action to impose pro-rata haircuts on *de jure* uninsured claimants, minimize liquidity losses and sell to the bank's assets. In most countries, including the USA, general corporate bankruptcy codes do not include all or even most of these provisions. To achieve efficient resolutions in these countries it is necessary either to carve out special provisions for banks within the corporate bankruptcy code or to enact a special code for banks (and possibly other types of financial institutions). The latter was the strategy used in the USA.[10]

The US general corporate bankruptcy code provides for a judicial process that grants administrative powers to bankruptcy courts, including the appointment of the trustee, assigns the initiation of bankruptcy to creditors upon a material default, is favourable to debtors and existing management, focuses on rehabilitation of insolvent firms, grants legal standing to all creditors and even shareholders, encourages negotiation among stakeholders that may result in violation of absolute priority, and is open to both *ex ante* and *ex post* judicial appeal. Thus, the code generally produces delayed initiations of bankruptcy until after economic insolvency and lengthy resolutions that delay payments to creditors, delay removal of existing management, and delay cessation of the existing firm as a legal entity. None of these is conducive to efficient resolution and losses to unsecured creditors tend to be large.

In contrast, the US bank bankruptcy code, which is included in the Federal Deposit Insurance Act (FDIA), provides for an administrative process that requires bank regulators to intervene in troubled institutions well before insolvency in order to turn the bank around and failing this to legally close the institution at a minimum positive value of book capital. If the below minimum capital ratio is not corrected within 90 days (with two possible 90 day extensions), the bank's charter is revoked and the bank placed in receivership. Shareholder control is terminated, senior management is removed, and the old entity ceases to operate as a legal entity. The code grants the FDIC strong and exclusive authority to administer the process as receiver, minimize the resolution costs, particularly to the insurance fund, and sell assets with effectively no delays from judicial appeals. Stakeholders other than the FDIC have no legal standing in the process and absolute priority is violated only if it is consistent with least cost resolution or after a multilayered systemic risk exemption to least cost resolution is granted to protect financial stability. Any resulting costs to the FDIC are required to be borne by the other banks, not by the taxpayers. Certainty is maximized.

Although not perfect, particularly in its enforcement provisions, the US code is conducive to minimizing the costs of bank failures and thus to achieving an efficient deposit insurance structure in the process. If a country has or can enact a similar or stronger bank insolvency resolution code, then an indirect approach to minimizing the moral hazard and principal-agent problems and achieving an efficient deposit insurance structure may be easier to apply than a direct approach.[11]

8.3 Conclusions

Efficient resolution of insolvent banks that minimizes adverse externalities and efficient provision of deposit insurance that avoids ultimate high costs from bank failures because of moral hazard, excessive risk taking by banks and poor agency behaviour by regulators are both important goals of public policy. But both are difficult to achieve directly. This chapter argues that these two goals are strongly interrelated and that achieving efficient resolution with no or minimal losses to depositors will achieve efficient deposit insurance as a beneficial byproduct. Deposit insurance becomes redundant, but neither unnecessary nor undesirable. Because improving the efficiency of deposit insurance directly by operating on the structure has proven difficult, doing so indirectly by improving the efficiency of the resolution process may prove easier.

Efficient resolution requires satisfying four principles:

1. Prompt legal closure at positive capital to minimize credit losses,
2. prompt estimate of recovery values and imposition of loss sharing among *de jure* uninsured depositors,
3. prompt reopening of insolvent banks after legal closure to minimize liquidity losses, and
4. prompt reprivatization at appropriate capital levels.

All of these principles focus on 'prompt' and require correct actions by the regulators within a structure of SEIR and PCA. The chapter describes how each of the four principles can be achieved, with primary focus on the USA. Success requires both the political will by regulators and the legal authority and tools for them to take the required actions. The chapter concludes by outlining some of the features that need to be included in the legal system to expedite efficient resolution and thereby also achieve efficient deposit insurance. Of course, the best solution is to avoid insolvencies by maintaining a healthy banking system and using regulatory and market forces to turn around troubled financial institutions before insolvency.

Notes

1 Loyola University Chicago and Federal Reserve Bank of Chicago. This paper was initially prepared for presentation to the International Association of Deposit Insurers Annual Conference, Taipei, Taiwan, September 28–29, 2005. Parts of this paper draw from recent coauthored papers with Robert Bliss (Bliss and Kaufman, 2006) and Robert Eisenbeis (Eisenbeis and Kaufman, 2005).

2 A review of the evidence appears in Barth, Caprio, and Levine (2006).

3 These points were developed in Kaufman (2004a). They are similar to those proposed by Mayes and Liuksila (2003) and by the Reserve Bank of New Zealand (Harrison, 2005)

4 Unlike banks, their parent bank or financial holding companies are subject to the general bankruptcy code.

5 A legal closure rule at positive capital need not represent expropriation of private capital. Shareholders would be paid any residual value that may exist after all higher priority claimants are made whole. The higher the legal closure rule capital ratio, the more likely are shareholders to receive payment. A positive capital legal closure rule may be introduced as a condition of obtaining either a bank charter or deposit insurance. Neither is such a rule in conflict with the misnamed 'too-big-to-fail' (TBTF) concept. At least in the USA, with very rare exception, insolvent banks were eventually failed with shareholders and senior management ousted. Instead, TBTF meant that all depositors and possibly also general creditors at these banks were protected against loss at time of legal closure (Kaufman, 2004c).

6 Regulators may also legally close a bank and place it in receivership for other reasons, including assets insufficient for obligations, unsafe and unsound practices, losses that will deplete capital, and violations of law (12 U.S.C. 1821 (c)(5)), but need not do so. Both Eisenbeis and Wall (2003) and Kaufman (2004b) demonstrate that in fact banks in the USA were legally closed on average well after the market value of their capital had turned negative even after the enactment of FDICIA.
7 See Comptroller (2003) and Salmon *et al.* (2003).
8 Under the Depositor Preference Act of 1993 claims of general creditors, including sellers of Fed funds, and deposits at foreign offices are subordinated to deposits at domestic offices (Kaufman, 1997 and Marino and Bennett, 1999)
9 Kaufman and Seelig (2002), and Kaufman (2004d)
10 The US general corporate and bank bankruptcy codes are compared in Bliss and Kaufman (2006).
11 This paper does not consider which regulatory agency or agencies in a country is the most appropriate to be granted the special resolution authority, for example, the central bank, financial supervisor, or deposit insurance agency. The choice is likely to be country specific and vary from country to country. It is unlikely that one size fits all.

References

Barth, J.R., Caprio, G. and Levine, R. (2006) *Rethinking Bank Regulation and Supervision: Till Angels Govern,* Cambridge: Cambridge University Press.

Bliss, R.R. and Kaufman, G.G. (2006) 'U.S. Corporate and Bank Insolvency Regimes: An Economic Comparison and Evaluation', *Economic Perspectives,* Federal Reserve Bank of Chicago.

Comptroller of the Currency (2003) *Annual Report Fiscal Year 2003,* Washington, DC, November.

Eisenbeis, R.A. and Kaufman, G.G. (2005) 'Bank Crisis Resolution and Foreign Owned Banks', *Economic Review,* Federal Reserve Bank of Atlanta, December.

Eisenbeis, R.A. and Kaufman, G.G. (2006) 'Cross-Border Banking: Challenges for Deposit Insurance and Financial Stability with Particular Attention to the European Union', in, Gerard Caprio, Douglas Evanoff, and George Kaufman (eds), *Cross-Border Banking: Regulatory Challenges,* Singapore: World Scientific.

Eisenbeis, R.A. and Wall, L.D. (2003) 'The Major Supervisory Initiative Post-FDICIA: Are They Based on the Goals of PCA? Should They Be?' in, G. Kaufman (ed.), *Prompt Corrective Action in Banking,* pp. 109–42, Oxford: Elsevier.

Evanoff, D.D. and Kaufman, G.G. (eds) (2006) *Cross-Border Banking: Regulatory Challenges,* Singapore: World Scientific.

Evanoff, D.D. and Kaufman, G.G. (eds) (2005) *Systemic Financial Crises: Resolving Large Bank Insolvencies,* Singapore: World Scientific.

Harrison, I. (2005) 'The Reserve Bank of New Zealand's Creditor Recapitalization (BCR) Project', in, D. Evanoff and G. Kaufman (eds), *Systemic Financial Crises: Resolving Large Bank Insolvencies,* pp. 397–406, Singapore: World Scientific.

Kaufman, G.G. (1997) 'The New Depositor Preference Act: Time Inconsistency in Action', *Managerial Finance,* vol. 23(11), pp. 56–63.

Kaufman, G.G. (2004a) 'Banking Regulation and Foreign Owned Banks', *Reserve Bank of New Zealand Bulletin,* June, pp. 65–74.

Kaufman, G.G. (2004b) 'FDIC Losses in Bank Failures: Has FDICIA Made a Difference?', *Economic Perspectives,* Federal Reserve Bank of Chicago, 3Q, pp. 13–25.

Kaufman, G.G. (2004c) 'Too Big to Fail in U.S. Banking: Quo Vadis?', in Benton Gup (ed.), *Too Big to Fail: Policies and Practices in Government Bailouts*, pp. 153–67, Westport, CT: Praeger.

Kaufman, G.G. (2004d) 'Depositor Liquidity and Loss Sharing in Bank Failure Resolutions', *Contemporary Economic Policy*, April, pp. 237–49.

Kaufman, G.G. and Seelig, S. (2002) 'Post-Resolution Treatment of Depositors at Failed Banks', *Economic Perspectives*, Federal Reserve Bank of Chicago, 2Q, pp. 27–41.

Marino, J.A. and Bennett, R. (1999) 'The Consequences of National Depositor Preference', *FDIC Banking Review*, vol. 12(2), pp. 19–38.

Mayes, D.G. (2004) 'Who Pays for Bank Insolvency?' *Journal of International Money and Finance*, April, pp. 515–51.

Mayes, D.G. and Liuksila, A. (2003) *Who Pays for Bank Insolvency?*, Basingstoke, Palgrave Macmillan.

Salmon, R., Allston, L., McBride, J., Trimper, D., Nelson, E., Barr, D., Almond, B., Hudson, G., Kinser, D. and Robinson, V. (2003) 'Costs Associated with Bank Failures', Working Paper, Washington, DC: Federal Deposit Insurance Corporation, October 10.

9

Contingency Planning: A Practitioner's Guide Drawing from Lessons Learned from Dealing with Bank Failures[1]

John Raymond LaBrosse and David K. Walker

9.1 What is contingency planning?

'Experience may be fine but testing is better. Thinking something will work never takes the place of proving that it will'.[2] NASA did not just launch one Apollo Mission to enable Neil Armstrong to take his first steps on the moon on 20 July 1969.[3] Millions watched those small steps of the commander of Apollo 11 on television but we had to know that there were several practice sessions ('dry runs') and contingency plans were put into place to make that one giant leap for mankind possible.

Simply put, contingency planning is a process whereby an organization undertakes a review of its mandate and powers to assess its capability to manage its business and affairs in an efficient and effective manner. Deposit protection organizations are responsible for making payouts or making sure that depositors have access to their deposits as soon as possible after a bank fails. Thus, a deposit insurer needs to understand the risks it faces and be ready to handle any significant risks that threaten its optimal performance. Without appropriate contingency planning, a deposit protection agency cannot ascertain if it is capable of dealing with the risks inherent in its mandate.

This chapter offers practical advice to deposit insurers to help them prepare for a bank failure. It starts with a brief discussion of moral hazard, examines the different types of mandates of deposit insurers and underscores differences as well as similarities, and then there is a discussion of the risks that are faced by deposit insurers. The lessons learned from the experiences of the Canada Deposit Insurance Corporation (CDIC) are discussed throughout and some conclusions are offered. Appendix 9A.1 outlines an industry supplier perspective for deposit insurers that are organised as 'virtual organisations' while Appendix 9A.2 presents a payout simulation based on an exercise that was performed by CDIC.

9.2 Moral hazard and financial safety nets

It is common in the literature to link the existence of deposit insurance directly to moral hazard. In the absence of deposit insurance, the presumption is that depositors should have sufficient knowledge and information to know the financial condition of the banks with which they deal. Based on that information, it is surmised that they should be in a position to act on that information and move their funds before a failure occurs. In systems that have deposit insurance, it is maintained that the incentive for depositors to exercise such care and caution is taken away and hence moral hazard is created.

Deposit insurance practitioners do not dispute that moral hazard exists but they maintain that it is found in all parts of the financial safety net. Instead, they note that explicit depositor protection arrangements can be used to increase market discipline and thereby reduce moral hazard.[4] Figure 9.1 outlines the prudential regulatory system that exists in Canada. It is, in many ways, typical of what is found in many other counties. Noteworthy are the roles played by the participants. The legislative branch (Parliament) in Canada decided that banks occupy a critical place in the economy and as such should receive special treatment when it comes to legislation, regulation and supervision. Indeed, specific responsibility is given to the federal Minister of Finance to propose measures to set out a prudential regulatory system for federally regulated financial institutions. The Minister then looks to the Department of Finance to provide policy advice on such matters and

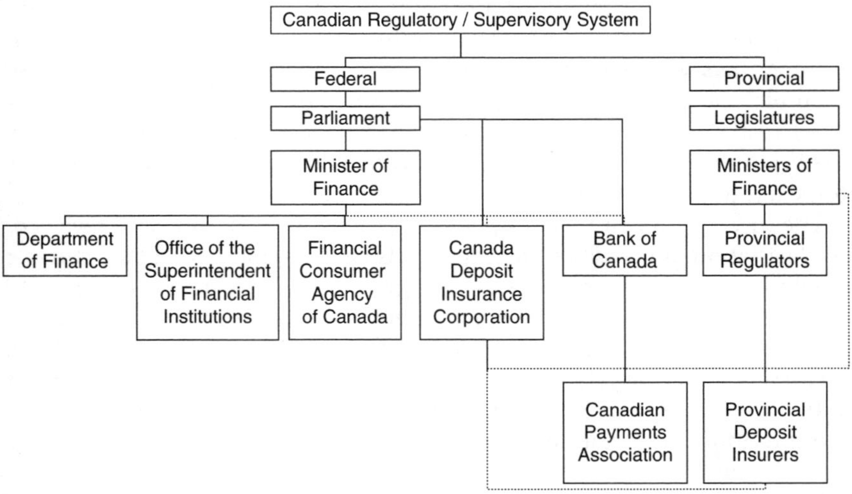

Figure 9.1 The prudential regulatory system in Canada

it, in turn, often draws on the views of the other players in the financial safety net – the Bank of Canada; the Office of the Superintendent of Financial Institutions (OSFI), which is the primary supervisory authority; CDIC; and the Financial Consumer Agency of Canada (FCAC), which is the agency responsible for providing information and overseeing financial institutions to ensure that they comply with federal consumer protection measures. Together, they are responsible for the proper functioning of the financial system. To suggest that moral hazard can be explicitly linked to the existence of deposit insurance seems to be taking the *ceteris paribus* assumption a bit too far.

Having established that moral hazard exists in all parts of the financial system safety net it is therefore incumbent on all the players in the safety net to devise measures to limit its adverse effects.

9.3 Setting mandates for deposit insurance organizations

The public entrusts its funds with banks and they expect to have ready access to their funds even after a bank fails. It is, therefore, necessary for agencies within the financial safety net to engage in contingency planning to ensure that the public can access their funds after a failure and thereby maintain confidence in the financial system to promote financial stability. This is why contingency planning is so important. It involves identifying and assessing the risks an organization faces, assessing the systems, policies and practices that exist to mitigate those risks, and assessing the residual risk to ensure that the level of risk remaining is at an acceptable level.

From recent surveys[5] we know that there are many different types of deposit protection organizations around the world. The mandates range from pure 'paybox' type of structures to 'risk managers'. From a deposit insurer's perspective, there exist a number of risks inherent in mandates. For example, the risk faced by a 'paybox' is different from the risk faced by a 'least-cost' deposit insurer or a 'risk manager'. It is important to start from the beginning – understanding the legislative mandate, the powers, and the roles and responsibilities under which a deposit insurer is established.

The first step of contingency planning, therefore, involves a full review of the legislation under which the deposit insurer is established. A risk manager would be required to mitigate its exposures and would necessarily need to undertake risk assessment and management and have appropriate systems and practices in place to fulfill that function. This is seen by first looking, in Table 9.1,[6] at the relationship between the mandate of a deposit insurer and its powers, interaction within the life cycle of a bank, impact on cost minimization, interrelationship arrangements and the management of those relationships.

Deposit insurers with a pure paybox mandate are largely confined to paying the claims of depositors after a bank has been closed. Accordingly,

Table 9.1 Mandates[7] of deposit insurers in relation to powers, interaction and effectiveness

Mandate	Powers	Interaction within the life cycle a of bank (beginning, midlife, end)	Effectiveness and cost minimisation	Inter relationship issues
Pure paybox	Reactive (e.g. clean-up, liquidation)	Failure	Low	Mainly information sharing
Cost-reducing objective	Mainly reactive, some proactive features (e.g. clean-up but some risk assessment and limited role in failure resolution)	Approaching failure, (but some interaction upon failure)	Low-medium	Requires well-defined roles, responsibilities, information sharing and coordination
Full risk managers	Proactive (e.g. risk identification risk assessment and management)	Beginning, midlife, failure	High	Requires well-defined roles, responsibilities, information sharing and coordination

Source: Canada Deposit Insurance Corporation.

they do not have intervention powers and are mainly reactive. Nevertheless, paybox systems still require appropriate authority, as well as access to deposit information and adequate funding, for the timely and efficient reimbursement of depositors when a bank fails. It should be understood that while the administrative costs associated with a paybox may be low, so is their ability to minimize costs to the financial system.

Some systems have been given the added responsibility to minimize costs associated with the closure of a bank. That is, while they are mainly reactive, they may have some proactive features, such as access to risk assessment, information and they may play a role in decisions on failure resolution. This gives the insurer more of an ability to address costs compared to a pure paybox. Nevertheless, it still requires well-defined roles, responsibilities, information sharing and coordination to be effective at fulfilling its mandate and cost minimization.

Deposit insurers with a 'risk-management' mandate have a very strong incentive to minimize exposure to losses. It must, therefore, be proactive in terms of taking on the risk identification, assessment and management. It will need access to timely and accurate information so it can assess the financial condition of individual banks, as well as the banking industry. It also must anticipate the financial troubles of individual banks and deal with them effectively when they arise. This requires appropriate powers and well-defined roles, responsibilities, information sharing and coordination. When this is accomplished the result can be a high level of effectiveness and minimization of losses for the deposit insurer and the financial system.

Contingency planning is essential for a deposit insurer, especially one that expects to have to deal with the consequences of a bank failure. Failures are costly, and they can be unexpected. Effective deposit insurers must develop contingency plans to deal with the risks they face and to mitigate these risks – there is no substitution for advance preparation. What could cause a bank to fail? What options might be available to respond to such possibilities? These questions need to be answered. And, they need to be answered *before* a problem occurs. Equally important is to break apart the common supposition that the next failure will necessarily resemble the last.[8] This line of thinking is usually wrong, and could be devastatingly so in today's increasingly integrated and internationalized financial environment.

9.4 Managing risks faced by deposit insurers

Managing the risks faced by deposit insurers can best be examined by looking at a specific example. CDIC is a well established deposit insurer with a loss-minimizing mandate. It undertakes contingency planning and its approach focuses on:

- understanding its mandate and powers;
- limiting exposure to loss through early intervention;
- undertaking an assessment of its resources and capabilities – both internally and externally;
- conducting scenario planning and simulations for failures;
- communications;
- attention to the latest development in contingency planning – business continuity planning; and
- documenting lessons learned.

Contingency planning plays a key role in helping to understand the risks faced by a deposit insurer and it is advisable that it be looked at from an enterprise risk management (ERM) perspective. The objective of ERM is to demonstrate that the deposit insurer has identified, understands and is managing its significant risks. Indeed, risk decisions need to be explicitly integrated into strategic day-to-day decision-making, be subject to good corporate governance and be supported by an appropriate control environment. Contingency planning should also help provide assurance to the Board of Directors and senior management of the organization that risks are being identified and managed effectively and efficiently.

Mandate and powers

As noted earlier, a full review and understanding of the mandate, powers and legislation under which a deposit insurer is established is required. We know that deposit insurance systems are difficult to compare as they have varied mandates and powers which depend on their stated public policy objectives. But, it is these mandates and powers that will determine the risks faced by a deposit insurer and its capabilities to address and mitigate those risks.

A risk-manager deposit insurer sets conditions of membership, assesses deposit insurance premiums, and takes necessary insurance action, such as risk assessment and management, and it may impose financial sanctions, cause the termination of a policy of deposit insurance, and engage in early intervention. This form of mandate requires that there be a strong collaborative relationship among safety-net participants, a free flow of information, and a number of checks and balances between the supervisor and deposit insurer. Contingency planning must take all of this into account.

CDIC has a range of powers that can be used to address problems at member institutions from the first incidence of a problem to a formal winding up and liquidation. It is critical to be aware of existing powers and the governing legislation as this creates the framework within which the deposit insurer must work during any situation that may arise. Moreover, contingency planning can help determine what the limitations under the current legislation are and help identify what additional powers could be useful in responding to various hypothetical situations.

Past experience provides a base of strength on which CDIC can draw in exercising judgement about how to deal with future problems. When a member is experiencing serious difficulties CDIC, for example, conducts a 'two-track' analysis. The two-tracks compare the cost of a formal winding-up and liquidation with the cost of CDIC assistance to achieve a going-concern solution (when this is a real option) or an orderly exit of the institution from the market. This approach reflects the fact that CDIC is enjoined to minimize its exposure to loss and that its powers to render financial assistance are to be deployed in order to reduce a loss, or avert a threatened loss. Historically, therefore, CDIC has sought to be satisfied that any assistance provided will likely prove to be, in comparison to a formal winding-up and liquidation, its 'least-cost' solution.

Throughout any intervention one of the deposit insurer's most important needs is for information. CDIC can obtain information about a member from the bank supervisor and the Bank of Canada. CDIC can also conduct a special examination of a member. Special examinations have been targeted at particular aspects of a member's business or used to obtain a more comprehensive evaluation. Obviously, the larger the institution the greater the need would be to focus on the most critical areas of concern.

At a later stage of intervention, in anticipation of a payout, CDIC can conduct a preparatory examination of the deposit liabilities of a member. To do so, it must hold the opinion that a payout is imminent and it requires the Superintendent's concurrence (for a federal institution).[9] At the end stages of an intervention, CDIC can terminate or cancel the policy of deposit insurance of a member and can petition for the formal winding-up and liquidation of an insolvent member.

Coordination of safety-net participants in their activities and functions is critical when intervention to close a troubled bank is required. There are important issues to be clarified, such as how, when and who commences procedures to formally liquidate or restructure the bank. Who pays the cost? What actions should the lender of last resort, the supervisor and the deposit insurer take in concert or individually to ensure that their mandates and obligations are fulfilled? These are important questions that need to be answered before a failure occurs.

Limiting exposure to loss through early intervention

CDIC focuses on the risk of insuring deposits accepted by its members so as to minimize CDIC's exposure to loss in such a manner to act in the best interest of depositors. In contrast, regulators have a mandate to protect the interests of depositors, other creditors and shareholders. The difference in mandates leads to potential differences in the incentive to act in different circumstances. This, not surprisingly, requires that CDIC and regulators share information and communicate effectively. This cooperation is of particular importance given that CDIC does not usually perform audits or examinations of its member institutions. OSFI acts as CDIC's agent in examining the affairs of federally incorporated members annually. Provincially incorporated members are inspected annually either by CDIC or by an agent.

To ensure close coordination and cooperation, the Deputy Minister of Finance, the Governor of the Bank of Canada, the Commissioner of the FCAC, the Superintendent and one Deputy Superintendent of OSFI are full members of the CDIC Board of Directors. In total, they make up five out of the eleven directors. The remaining six directors, including the Chairperson, are from the private sector. Therefore, CDIC decisions requiring Board approval, such as interventions and liquidation of an institution, are made with the input of the public sector directors. This ensures full coordination between the safety-net players that make up the prudential supervisory system.

Information sharing at the federal level is generally facilitated by the Financial Institutions Supervisory Committee (FISC). In terms of policy coordination, CDIC is represented by its Chairperson as a member of the Senior Advisory Committee (SAC)[10] chaired by the Deputy Minister of Finance. The mandate of this Committee is to discuss and establish the policy direction pertaining to the financial services legislative framework in Canada. CDIC and OSFI have also established other mechanisms such as the Guide to Intervention for Federal Financial Institutions depicted in Figure 9.2.

A Strategic Alliance Agreement has been implemented by CDIC and OSFI to enhance the ability of both agencies to perform their mandates efficiently and to coordinate their activities. OSFI and CDIC have established a committee of senior officers to provide a forum for communication with respect to all matters of mutual interest – this is called the OSFI/CDIC Liaison Committee. Issues respecting the activities of OSFI and CDIC are also addressed during regular monthly meetings.

Contingency planning is also very important from a funding perspective and plans need to be in place to deal with future events whatever these might be. The deposit insurer should also look at understanding the criteria under which funding might be required. Since deposit insurers are expected to deal with a bank failure, or a wave of failures, plans need to provide for access to funding to deal with such events. However, it should be noted that deposit insurers are not responsible for dealing with a financial system crisis. That is the role of governments, as deposit insurers do not have access to the level of funding required to deal with a systemic crisis.

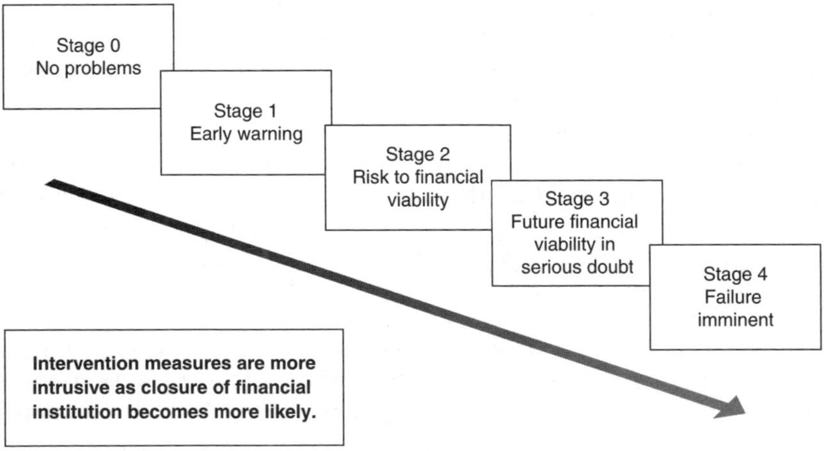

Sources: CDIC and OSFI.
Figure 9.2 Early warning and intervention framework[11] – CDIC/OSFI guide to intervention

Undertaking an assessment of resources and capabilities.

Although each and every failure confronting a deposit insurer will likely pose its own unique challenges, the basic resource framework and structure which guide the deposit insurer's response should already be in place. Nevertheless, contingency planning can help in identifying: what resources are available (internally and externally);[12] determine if there are enough resources to deal with significant risks; and identify if there are serious gaps which need to be addressed. Some of the critical resources which the deposit insurer must evaluate include:

- financial
- human
- communications
- legal/corporate
- technological

One of the most important resources available to an insurer is funding. Sufficient funding and access to funds on a timely basis is critical when dealing with troubled banks. It is generally understood that deposit insurers require a large fund at their immediate disposal to deal with eventual failures. However, the issue of funding is often misunderstood as it is necessary to separate liquidity needs of a deposit insurer to deal with an intervention, such as a payout, and the funding of the eventual losses arising from a bank failure.

Aside from traditional sources, there may be opportunities to find innovative approaches to dealing with liquidity needs and the cost of failures. One example that can be spcited is how CDIC dealt with some failures in the past. CDIC realized that to fund depositor's claims required a large amount of liquidity at the beginning of the failure until distributions were received from the liquidator. CDIC also understood that its losses were affected by the time value of money – the longer it took to recover funds from the estate, the larger were the losses taking into consideration the opportunity cost of investing those funds or the cost of borrowing from the government. It, therefore, looked at different approaches to liquidations and developed a process where CDIC worked with liquidators to put in place a plan whereby the 'good assets' of the failing bank could be tendered quickly. The franchise value (mainly the branches and banking relationships) and deposits would also be transferred by CDIC at the same time to another institution, which had the capacity and capability to undertake such a transaction on the day of the formal liquidation. CDIC also developed a list of criteria under which it would undertake such transactions with institutions.

An important aspect of communications issues is the timeline for dealing with an institution that moves from becoming a 'no problem' to a troubled institution (that is, moving from Stage 0 to another more severe Stage as shown in Figure 9.2). But first it should be remembered that bank supervisors and deposit insurers need a clear separation of their responsibilities as this will help curtail overlaps and provide a clear basis for intervention. In short, this is setting out 'the rules of the game'. Thus, information sharing is a basic need for the proper functioning of the financial system safety net.

Human resources are another critical issue to consider in contingency planning. Having access to the right people – both inside the organization and externally – must be addressed in contingency planning. CDIC, for example, operates a form of a 'virtual organization' (see Appendix 9A.1) which allows it the flexibility to maintain a core staff and then draw heavily on external resources when dealing with a problem bank.

CDIC's past experience in dealing with failures is to some extent captured in a number of legal and corporate precedents that might be utilized in a failure. Thus, it is important to have ready access to copies of past agreements regarding specific transactions. In addition to legal precedents, there are a number of historic Board resolutions that can be very useful. In a crisis the CDIC Board of Directors will be required to act quickly and decisively – there is no time to reinvent the wheel. Consideration should also be given to maintaining a continuous improvement process that allows policymakers the opportunity to implement lessons learned from dealing with problem banks in legislation.[13]

Information technology has become a mission critical resource. In this respect, CDIC has invested heavily in developing independent information technology resources such as risk assessment, evaluation and payout systems.

The role of scenario planning

Failure resolution is a process involving the evaluation of the assets of a failed bank, finding acquirers for all or part of the assets, liquidating the assets, and reimbursing depositors. Effective failure resolution mechanisms help deal with troubled banks early and facilitate orderly resolution options that in turn minimize disruptions and costs. To guide them, deposit insurers will have to assess the answers to two basic questions; first, what type of institution could fail? And second, what might be the circumstances leading to the failure?

As this chapter has demonstrated, contingency planning is looking at different parts of the business and developing workable scenarios in case the problem occurs. But, it must also be assessed from an enterprise wide basis. That is why enterprise risk management (ERM) is receiving the attention it deserves today by deposit insurers and, indeed, it would be advisable for all players in the financial safety net to undertake an ERM assessment.

Every deposit insurer should be well prepared to reimburse depositors when institutions fail. They should also understand the environment in which they operate, and keep abreast of developments in the financial sector. That means understanding new policies, new laws, new products, innovation, new information technology, new approaches to banking such as virtual banking, and cross-border issues that directly affect how deposit insurers manage their business and affairs.

However, contingency planning requires buy in by the board of directors and senior management of the organization since appropriate resources (both human and capital) are required. It must be considered as an investment that will bring benefits in the future. If done right, it also provides the board of directors and senior management with the assurance that the organization is able to demonstrate that it can fulfill its mandate and that the organization is managed efficiently and effectively, and that it is well governed.

At the heart of contingency planning through ERM is the ability to test how the deposit insurer may respond to failures and adverse events. A key component of contingency planning is, therefore, creating scenarios about the types and circumstances which may be encountered. In general terms a simulation allows the insurer to replicate a situation or test the people, processes and technology associated with a particular activity such as a failure scenario (see Appendix 9A.2 for a description of a payout simulation that was conducted by CDIC). It allows the insurer to control the timing, type and nature of a situation and other specific circumstances surrounding it. In addition, a simulation can help to build teamwork for those unfamiliar with the activity; identify gaps in resources, processes and technology that need to be addressed; and determine modifications required to process descriptions, plans and other documentation.

Different simulations have different objectives. They can be of a limited scope, such as those testing a specific process associated with a failure (for example, a payout and liquidation of a small bank), or those involving extensive simulations which could look at all facets of a deposit insurer's operations involved in the failure of a large complex member bank. The basic elements of a scenario plan are: a statement of purpose and objectives; a work plan; a simulation scope and parameters; timing; required resources (for example, human resources, information technology); advance preparation; expected results; and, at the end the process, an independent review and assessment.

While it is not feasible to realistically simulate all aspects and activities of a failure, simulations can be helpful in assessing how existing or new systems and process actually work and can be helpful in uncovering unforeseen factors and problems. At CDIC, they found that such simulations were particularly helpful for their employees given that the last failure was in 1996. Over time, people lose practice in dealing with failures. It should be noted that simulations are not perfect. It is not possible to simulate all facets of an activity; they are costly, and not everything can be planned for as real life always has surprises!

Communications

Coordinated communications plans and activities are an essential element in all cases but more so in the event of a large bank failure. Confidence in the financial system must be maintained from the outset. It is imperative, therefore, that a deposit insurer establish a sound public awareness and communication programme before a failure occurs. A public that is well informed about the terms and conditions of deposit insurance helps to build and maintain confidence in the system. It is critical also to meet with and work out a communication plan among all the key financial safety net players in the event of a problem. For instance, at CDIC they found that:

- communications activities were a 'must-win', particularly during the first 48–72 hours, in order to maintain domestic and international confidence in the system;
- all agencies within the financial safety net must speak in a coordinated fashion, using the same themes and messages;
- all agencies should restrict themselves to their own areas of responsibilities and expertise; and
- all agencies should coordinate their media relations activities and responses with a communications group composed of all the relevant agencies established for this specific purpose.

It has also been found that the media can be your best friend or your worst enemy, depending on how they are treated. Contingency planning must involve developing a communications plan that builds media relationships in good times which can be leveraged in the bad times.

It is vitally important to have a dialogue with depositors after a closure and during a payout. They will want to know when and how they can expect to receive their funds, what they are expected to do to receive their money and whom they can contact to get information. In preparation for the event, it is critical to have a well thought out crisis management communications plan. Some part of the plan can include such things as a 'hidden' website specific to the event and draft news releases.

Business continuity planning

Contingency planning is not just about dealing with bank failures. A deposit insurer must also consider 'business continuity planning' (BCP) to address unexpected events. BCP provides the processes to ensure continuous business operations from a disruptive event (for example, following the impact of a natural disaster). It is made up of two major elements:

- a disaster recovery plan: the plan that provides the processes on how to recover critical business operations from a disruptive event; and
- a business resumption plan: the plan that provides the processes on how to resume business from a disruptive event or transition from the DRP to normal business operations.

There are four phases of CDIC's business continuity planning flow (which have actually been used to deal with an ice storm and an electricity grid failure) and the process flow can best be seen by examining the process depicted in Figure 9.3.

The first phase is the point right after the event and it is the point of an immediate response. It is shortly followed by a period of crisis management where there is a determination of the size of the event – major or minor. Phase 3 focuses on disaster recovery and it should begin within 48 hours with the final phase, business recovery, which should occur not long after that point.

Experience at CDIC has shown that the success factors of a BCP are: having executive sponsorship (covering funding and priority of objectives); business units within the organization developing their own BCP; and, business continuity planning being integrated into ongoing operations of the deposit insurer. It is vitally important to start with a business impact analysis and then develop an infrastructure recovery strategy which should be integrated with contingency planning on a continuous basis.

Lessons learned

Contingency planning is essential for any deposit insurer because failures are costly, and they are often unexpected. Effective deposit insurers must develop contingency plans and conduct regular simulations to keep employees' skills sharp. Equally important is to break apart the common supposition that the next failure will necessarily resemble the last. This line of thinking is usually wrong, and could be devastatingly so in today's increasingly integrated and internationalized financial environment.

Based on the experiences at CDIC, it is important to build relationships with the media in good times so that they can be leveraged in other circumstances. Deposit insurers should also secure a reliable supply of resources (internally or externally) and have a network of suppliers in place. It is important to remember that each problem bank is unique requiring a customized approach, however scenario planning and simulations allow the deposit insurer to test its systems and practices overall. It is vital to be aware of emerging issues and how they may affect future failures (for example, cross-border banks, internet banks, and soon.) as while globalization and technology create many new opportunities, the implications of them can be far reaching and present new challenges.

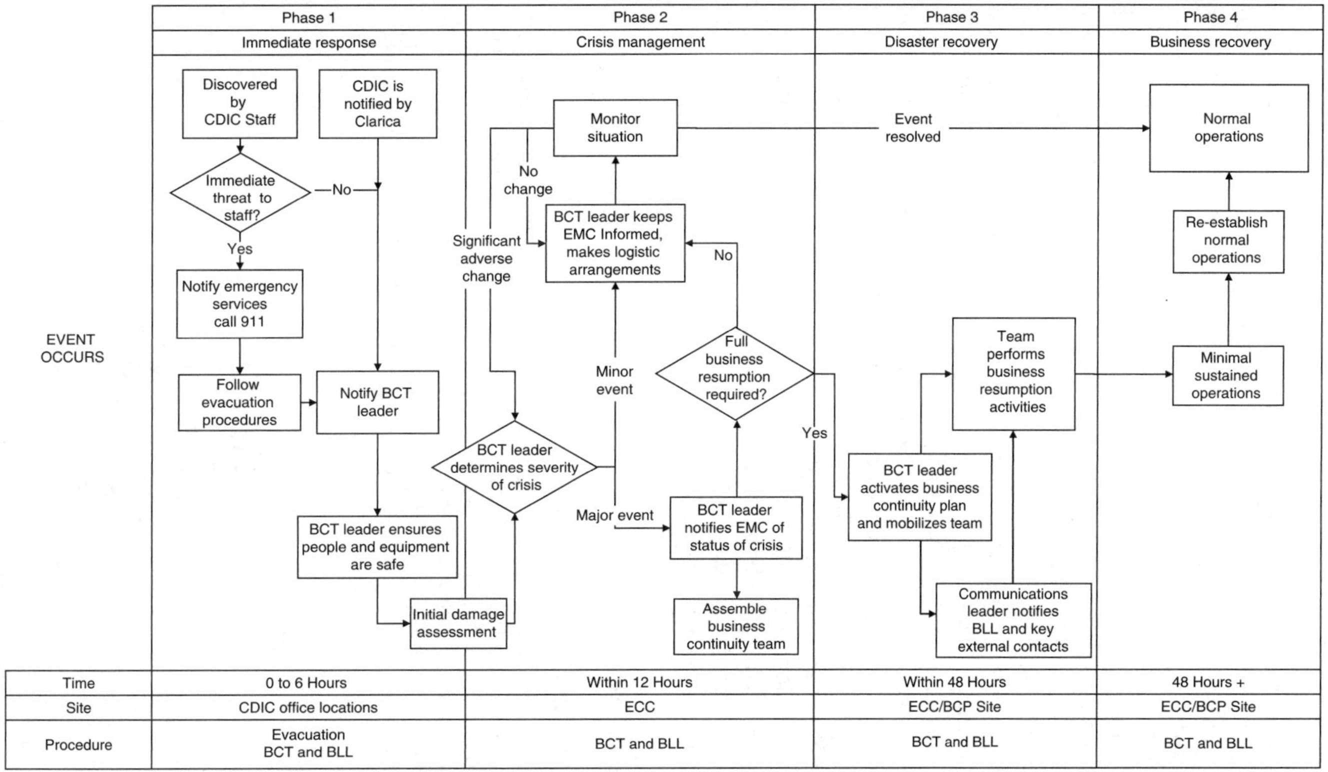

Figure 9.3 Procedure flow for business continuity plan

9.5 Conclusions

This chapter has focused on practical advice to deposit insurers in undertaking contingency planning. It has demonstrated that deposit insurers need to know their mandates and fully understand their roles and responsibilities. In the preparation of plans to deal with failing and problem banks it is highly advisable to set up a team and do contingency planning before it is needed. The underlying expectation should be that the next failure will be quite unlike the last one and attention needs to be given to the establishment of a clear communication process with the other players in the financial system safety net.

Experience has shown that the cost to the financial system of a failure, even just to the deposit insurer, far outweighs the cost of doing effective contingency planning. Having a private sector perspective on a deposit insurance board is a highly valued tool in dealing with problem banks as the market is often a very good source of information concerning new techniques and approaches. Deposit insurers can also look to the private sector and other deposit protection organizations for models of efficiency and practices to help build in good incentive systems.

In conclusion, the CDIC experience has shown that active mandates lead to independence, facilitate innovation, improve accountability, enhance integrity and reduce costs and the investment in contingency planning that was made was worth the cost and effort.

Appendix 9A.1

Industry supplier perspectives[14]

Deposit insurers face many challenges in attracting and retaining qualified personnel. For this reason some organizations have decided to engage the services of outside consultants and professionals, such as lawyers and accountants. CDIC, for example, has been set up as a 'virtual organization' (Figure 9A.1) with access to a large base of expertise and knowledge. In running a virtual organization it is essential to establish relationships and agreements with external suppliers. CDIC has in place processes and

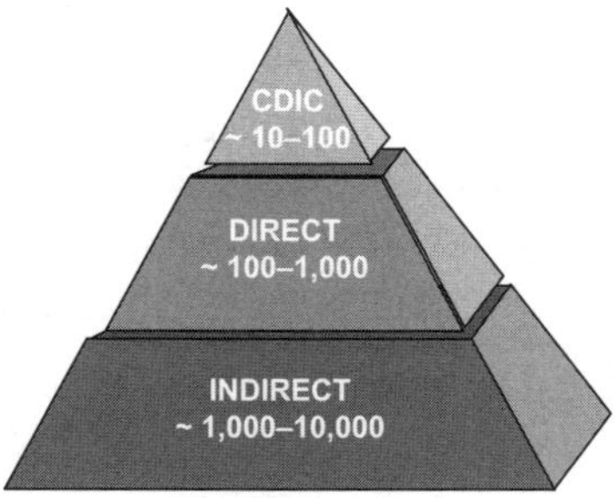

Source: CDIC.
Figure 9A.1 CDIC as a virtual organization – number of positions potentially available

back-up documentation, as well as relationships with various staffing agencies that would ensure the staffing needs of the various functions could be met on a timely basis.

The diagram below represents an idealized sequence for undertaking the liquidation of a significant troubled bank. While possession is an essential first step, all remaining elements of the sequence will likely have to be executed concurrently. Each element is discussed in turn:

Possession

Planning the possession process requires a detailed situation analysis. The questions that need to be answered are: Where are the branches? Where is the controlling mind? What are the liquidator's powers? How will action be coordinated with the Board of Directors, management/Bank Restructuring Committee, banking supervisors and the deposit insurer?

Physical seizure will require implementing a 'day one' procedures manual. Tasks include physically securing properties, dealing with cash and transactions in process/clearing and the recording all assets and liabilities.

Initially, in terms of control of information and communication systems, a lock-down and cut-off is normally required to secure proper backups of information are obtained and to prevent unauthorized initiation of funds transfers, changes to loan balances and so on. Following the implementation of initial procedures, ensuring adequate security over information and communication systems is of key importance, including changing access codes and over-rides.

Realization

The setting of realization approaches requires the liquidator to consider both assets and liabilities. The claims profile will identify priorities, set-off, maturities, deposit insurance entitlements and other guarantees.

Where a sufficient quantity of good quality assets are identified, a 'good bank' strategy may be appropriate, maintaining near-normal operations, perhaps pending a sale/transfer of assets and liabilities. This stage requires the separation of saleable portfolios from nonstandard loans, setting portfolio management strategy and policy, and re-establishing appropriate credit committee and other internal review and control procedures.

For non-standard loans and other assets, and potentially suspect liabilities, a 'bad bank' strategy can be implemented, comprising non-standard asset management policies and asset tracing and collection. In this area insolvency expertise is likely to be important.

Both the good bank and sundry or surplus assets will need to be disposed of *via* an asset sales strategy. This may be partly determined by economic/maximum realization issues and partly by other policy issues, such as deadlines for ensuring liquidity of deposits and the need to minimize systemic risks. However, caution needs to be exercised in combining weak banks as this can lead to increasing rather than decreasing systemic risk. Implementing the asset sales strategy requires various activities, such as: matching saleable asset portfolios with customer deposits, ensuring deficiency coverage agreements are in place and facilitating the sales process and subsequent due diligence, as well as undertaking auctions or securitization.

Under loan administration attention must be focused on funding commitments (contingent), debt maturities, portfolio risks and loan linkages between banks. Restructuring organizations have developed various proprietary software and templates to deal with statements of affairs, loan status and reporting system, litigation management and creditor claims. These reports feed into larger reporting exercises normally required by steering committees, creditors' committees and the courts.

There are many attributes of quality reporting. Use of structured reporting frameworks will ensure appropriate confidentiality together with consistency, timeliness, completeness and accuracy. Also of significance is the proper coordination between banks and regulatory organizations.

In terms of administration and distribution, methodologies need to be developed to deal with such issues as settling foreign exchange claims, updating interest calculations, dealing with powers of attorney and death claim procedures, set-offs and liability verification.

Payment planning comes next, once the claims have been identified, verified and prioritized. This requires management of advertising for claims, the proof of claim process, identifying the best method of distribution, ensuring procedures are in place to facilitate reconciliation of payment account, coordination of debtor/creditor accounts at different banks and dealing with accounts which have been placed on hold.

Claims will come in many types and will normally require differing treatment. Thus, it will be necessary to identify, consolidate and manage various types of claims, including: depositors, creditors, subordinated debt, shareholders; customer trading accounts (both domestic and offshore); counter-parties, letters of credit, traveller's cheques; forward contracts, swaps, options; and contingent claims.

Appendix 9A.2

A payout simulation: results from a simulation performed by CDIC

The scenario outlined in this Appendix involved the imminent closure of a hypothetical institution with only minimal preparations for the specific event on the part of the staff working on the payout team (that is, assuming no preparatory examination is conducted). The simulation was designed not only to test a software payout tool CDIC developed called ROADMAP, but also processes outside of ROADMAP and their links to the application such as interactions with brokerages, deposit brokers, counsels legal opinions, liquidator holds and set-off.

Deposit account aggregation processes were performed both manually and by automation to arrive at an insured and uninsured portfolio upon which a payout could be performed. Historical information was used from preparatory examination files from a previous CDIC member named *Income Trust*.

The simulation was conducted over a three-day period and involved eleven staff members and the exercise was overseen by the CDIC's internal auditor. It included information on over 15,000 depositors and, in some cases, the information was not complete in order to test the verification procedures.

The overall results of the simulation were positive. But, CDIC did find areas on which it could improve in terms of timeliness and accuracy. The main lessons learned were: each payout is unique and requires a customized approach; it is important to secure reliable resources and build a network of suppliers; it is necessary to ensure coordination between accounting, legal, IT and communications; the deposit insurer must determine in advance what is a deposit, and who is the depositor; a consistent application of rules builds confidence and trust; there is a need to involve experienced counsel early on to avoid delays in closure proceedings; the organization must commit to a delivery date and meet it whatever the costs; consideration should be given to using immediate advance payments to reduce pressure on payouts of small balances; and there must be coordination with the liquidator so they know what is needed and when it is required.

Notes

1 The views expressed in this chapter are those of the authors and do not necessarily represent those of the International Association of Deposit Insurers nor the Canada Deposit Insurance Corporation. The chapter is based on a presentation delivered by Jean-Pierre Sabourin, Michael W. Mackey, David K. Walker and John Raymond LaBrosse at the Fourth Annual IADI Conference that was held in Taipei, Taiwan from 27–29 September 2005. The authors are indebted to comments received from Andrew Lee of KPMG.

2 Rules for NASA project managers.

3 A TV camera automatically deployed after Armstrong pulled on a special ring. As he stepped onto the moon's surface he proclaimed, 'That's one small step for man, one giant leap for mankind', see www.historyplace.com/unitedstates/apollo11/

4 Study Group Report June 2000.

5 See IDIS found at www.cdic.ca and www.iadi.org.

6 See INSOL International, Bank Insolvency, *An International Guide for Deposit Insurers*, January 2005, p. 19.

7 There are many different types of deposit insurance systems in operation. Their mandates range from so-called pure 'paybox' type of structures to 'risk minimizers' or 'risk managers'. A paybox insurer is generally focused on paying out the claims of protected depositors after a bank has been closed. They typically do not have intervention and examination powers. Some paybox systems have been given the added responsibility to minimize costs associated with the closure of a bank. That is, while they are mainly reactive they may have some proactive features such as access to risk assessment information and they may play a role in decisions on failure resolution. These have been referred to as 'paybox plus' or 'least cost resolution' systems. Deposit insurers with a full 'risk minimization' or 'risk management' mandates are usually required to minimize their exposure to loss and therefore, be proactive in terms of taking on the risk identification, assessment and management.

8 The first experience in bank liquidation for the Nigeria Deposit Insurance Corporation came on 21 January 1994 when the licences of two merchant banks were revoked. Two other banks were closed the following September, another one was closed in June 1995 and in January 1998 the licences of 26 banks were revoked in one fell swoop. See Bank Liquidation in Nigeria (1994–2004).

9 Federal institution is usually meant to include a bank under the Bank Act or a federally regulated financial institution such as a trust company.

10 The SAC is a policy advisory group which was set up by the Department of Finance in 1976. It meets as needed to discuss policy issues described in White Papers. Mr. LaBrosse was the Secretary to that group for many years.

11 This framework was first presented in the 1995 White Paper entitled 'Enhancing the Safety and Soundness of the Canadian Financial System'.
12 See Appendix 9.A for a full description of how the firm Deloitte & Touche LLP assisted CDIC in the preparation of a payout in the event of a failure.
13 The authors are indebted to Andrew Lee of KPMG for offering this suggestion.
14 This Appendix is drawn from the part of the presentation delivered by Michael W. Mackey, Global Leader, Financial Institutions, Deloitte & Touche LLP.

References

Canada Deposit Insurance Corporation (CDIC), *Annual Report*, Ottawa, Ontario, various issues.

Canada Deposit Insurance Corporation (2003) *International Deposit Insurance Survey*, see:www.cdic.ca??id=285, Ottawa.

Dziobek, C. and Pazarbasioglu, C. (1998) 'Lessons Learned from Systemic Bank Restructuring', April, International Monetary Fund, Washington, DC.

Financial Stability Forum (2000) *Consultation Process and Background Paper of the Study Group on Deposit Insurance*, Basel, Switzerland, June.

Financial Stability Forum Working Group on Deposit Insurance (2001) *Guidance for Developing Effective Deposit Insurance Systems: Final Report of the Working Group on Deposit Insurance*, Basel, September.

Financial Stability Forum Working Group on Deposit Insurance(2001), *Guidance for Developing Effective Deposit Insurance Systems: Final Report of the Working Group on Deposit Insurance*, Volume II, especially Resolution of Failed Institutions, www.iadi.org/html/App/SiteContent/CDIC%20Volume%20II.pdf.

INSOL International, Bank Insolvency (2005) *An International Guide for Deposit Insurers*, January.

International Association of Deposit Insurers (2004) *Annual Report 2003/04*, Basel.

International Association of Deposit Insurers (2005) Fourth Annual Conference, 27–29 September 2005, Session V (b), Taipei, Taiwan.

Presentation of Frank Brown, Deloitte & Touche, and Wayne Acton, Canada Deposit Insurance Corporation, Seminar on Liquidating Financial Institutions at the Asian Policy Conference on Deposit Insurance, 17–18 January 2000, Kuala Lumpur, Malaysia.

Nigeria Deposit Insurance Corporation (2004) *Bank Liquidation in Nigeria (1994-2004).*

White Paper (1995) *Enhancing the Safety and Soundness of the Canadian Financial System, Department of Finance*, February, Ottawa.

10

General Guidance for the Resolution of Bank Failures[1]

William Su

Since its establishment in 2002, the mission of the International Association of Deposit Insurers (IADI) has been to 'contribute to the enhancement of deposit insurance effectiveness by promoting guidance and international cooperation'. As part of its mission, IADI undertakes research projects to provide guidance on deposit insurance issues.

In order to deal in a timely and effective manner with the impact of individual bank failures or systemic banking crisis, many countries are seeking to enhance their mechanisms for dealing with failing or failed banks. Although the responsibilities of deposit insurers for various aspects of the resolution framework vary from country to country, the manner in which failed banks are resolved has a major impact on all deposit insurers.

The objective of this chapter is to develop general guidance for deposit insurers and other safety-net participants interested in establishing or enhancing their mechanisms for the resolution of failed or failing banks. It was prepared by the IADI sub-committee on Developing Guidance for the Resolution of Bank Failures and is designed to take into account different country circumstances, settings and structures.

The guidance developed is based on the judgment of IADI's members and the experiences of deposit insurers involved in the resolution of bank failures. Key sources of information used were the responses from a survey questionnaire distributed by the sub-committee in June 2004. The chapter also draws on relevant reports and other literature available on the subject.

10.1 Key guidance points

The guidance is divided into five parts. The first part addresses general issues; the second part deals with interrelationships among safety-net participants and cross-border issues; the third part looks at the powers accorded to the deposit insurer; part four addresses operational and administrative issues related to resolutions; and the last part deals with specific issues related to the resolution of failing or failed banks.

General issues

1. A strong institutional framework reduces the risk of banking failures or crises and helps minimize the costs of bank failures. Thus, it is recommended that policymakers ensure there is a strong institutional framework in place for the economy and financial system. This should include: sound macroeconomic polices, effective corporate governance, sound banking supervision and regulation (including prompt corrective action), an efficient and effective failure resolution process and a well developed judicial and criminal investigation system. Furthermore, strengthening the institutional framework for bank supervision is of particular importance for deposit insurers with a limited paybox mandate.
2. Effective bank failure resolution requires an operationally independent and accountable deposit insurer, with a clear mandate and that is insulated from undue political and industry influence.
3. The failure resolution powers granted to a deposit insurer should be consistent with its public policy objectives and mandate.
4. The legal system should support the timely and effective resolution of bank failures including situations which pose a systemic risk to the financial system.
5. The use of temporary blanket guarantees and reliance on public funds may be appropriate in certain circumstances.

Interrelationship and cross-border issues

1. The division of duties and responsibilities among safety-net players should be clearly defined and information sharing and coordination mechanisms must be in place for all financial safety-net participants.
2. An explicit statutory mechanism should be set up for dealing with systemic crises and when dealing with 'Too Big To Fail' issues.
3. With the increasing growth in international banking activities there is a need for greater information sharing and coordination between deposit insurers and supervisory authorities dealing with failures across international borders.

Statutory powers accorded to the deposit insurer

1. Deposit insurers should have access to all necessary funding in order to fulfill their mandates.
2. The deposit insurer should have the authority to accept or reject new members and terminate the insurance status of a member bank and coordinate on the timing of termination with the supervisory agency prior to bank closure.
3. The deposit insurer should have the authority to conduct on-site reviews, perform due diligence and have access to depositor records before bank closure.

4. Those working for a deposit insurer and other safety-net participants should have appropriate legal protection while discharging their mandates.
5. Clear legal authority should be in place to allow for the prosecution of the directors, officers, and auditors of failed banks when there is due cause.

Operational and administrative issues

1. Deposit insurers should have appropriate policies and standard operational procedures (SOPs) for all their bank resolution processes.
2. Deposit insurers should have the authority to contract outsourcing services for specialized consultation, evaluation or appraisals (or CPA firms with the capability to assist) in the carrying out an independent valuation of the failing or failed bank.
3. Deposit insurers should undertake an appropriate valuation and follow a transparent sales process for the resolution of failed banks.
4. A deposit insurer should have in place an effective public awareness and communication mechanism to enhance the confidence of the public in the deposit insurance system and the failure resolution process.
5. A code of conduct for employees of a deposit insurer should be in place.
6. A deposit insurer should be provided with the power to investigate, and if necessary, litigate against those parties at fault in a bank failure.

Resolution of failing or failed banks

1. It is important to have in place a rule-based or statutory trigger mechanism for early intervention into the affairs of a troubled bank and for determining whether a bank has failed.
2. A professional, experienced team composed of staff from the supervisor and/or deposit insurer (or outside experts) should assess the viability of a problem bank.
3. In order to be efficient, reliable and credible in handling individual bank failures, the deposit insurer should establish effective resolution policies and procedures.
4. Failure resolution strategies should try to maximize the recovery of the failed bank's assets using a market approach including possible recovery mechanisms that will allow the deposit insurer to benefit from any upside.
5. The rules for managing the liquidation process, reporting duties of the liquidator, legal deadlines and distributions to creditors should be well defined and documented.

10.2 Resolution of failed banks: issues and survey results

In order to assist with the development of guidance on the subject of the resolution of failing or failed banks, the Research and Guidance Committee of IADI prepared a detailed survey questionnaire. The survey collected information from a wide range of countries and different types of deposit insurers and financial system safety-net arrangements.[2]

The deposit insurers who responded ranged from those which could be classified as primarily paybox types (with a mandate focused on paying out depositors claims when a bank fails) to 'risk minimizers' or non-paybox type deposit insurers with wider mandates providing them with the means to better control the risks they face.

In this chapter, the term 'resolution' is defined as a disposition plan for a failed or failing bank, which is directed by the responsible safety-net authority and is generally designed to fully reimburse or protect insured deposits under the principle of minimizing costs to the deposit insurer. Typically, the resolution costs of a deposit insurer may contain the amount that the insurer's obligation to insured deposits exceeds net recoveries on the institution's assets.

Some of the key areas addressed in the survey included: the incidence and costs of bank failures and systemic crises; the factors responsible for failures; the roles and responsibilities of deposit insurers and other safety-net participants in resolutions; the pros and cons of various resolution methods and approaches to asset disposition of failed banks; information sharing and coordination mechanisms; and valuable insights from the actual experiences of deposit insurers in handling resolutions and asset dispositions.

In general, the survey results confirmed the prevalence of consolidation and conglomeration in banking through both internal expansion and mergers and acquisitions. Banking industry concentration continues to increase in most countries. According to the questionnaire responses among 34 countries, five countries had a concentration ratio of 93 per cent of assets for their top five largest banks and the average concentration ratio in 25 countries was more than 30 per cent.

Another finding of the survey was that banking crises are quite common. Twenty four out of the 34 respondents indicated they had had some form of banking crisis or major failures over the last ten years. It also appears that the trend for increasing concentration in banking is raising the risk exposure of deposit insurers and other safety-net participants to individual bank failures and potential systemic crises. Thus, when dealing with bank failures it is important for safety-net participants to understand the issues of both individual bank failures and failures which could result in systemic crises.

In dealing with systemic banking crisis, the role and responsibility of every financial safety-net participant, including the deposit insurer, supervisor and central bank, are very important. Based on the responses to the questionnaire, most deposit insurer (DI) respondents were administered by a government or a public agency. Only four deposit insurers were privately administered. The insurers in ten countries could not be characterized as

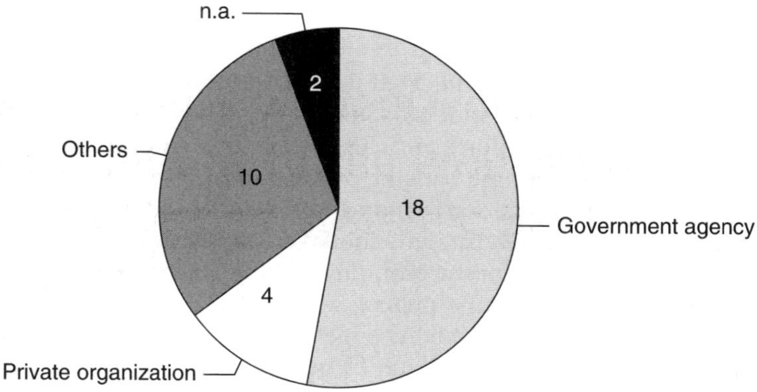

Figure 10.1 Organization of DI

primarily government or private, but have characteristics of both systems (Figure 10.1). For more detailed findings and the sub-committee's analyses of the survey results, please refer to Appendix 10A.1

10.3 Guidance for the resolution of failed banks

The following guidance on the resolution of bank failures was developed after careful analyses of the results of the survey questionnaire and the experience and judgement of IADI Members. Not all deposit insurers have failure resolution as part of their mandates. However, for those insurers with a responsibility for failure resolution the following guidance is aimed at enhancing their mechanism for the resolution of failed banks and provides a better mechanism for checks and balances among financial safety net participants. The guidance is divided into five parts. The first part addresses general issues; the second part deals with interrelationships among safety-net participants and cross-border issues; the third part looks at the powers accorded to the deposit insurer; part four addresses operational and administrative issues related to resolutions; and the last part deals with specific issues related to the resolution of failing or failed banks.

General issues

This section sets out guidance on general issues related to building a strong institutional framework for the deposit insurance system to function within. A suitable framework includes sound corporate governance, an effective supervisory, regulatory, accounting and transparency regime, and a well-developed legal system. All of these features have a major influence on the environment in which the deposit insurance system functions and help to control the risk exposure of the deposit insurer.

A strong institutional framework reduces the risk of banking failures or crises

The responses to the survey indicated that in addition to economic downturns and other external shocks, some of the most important factors responsible for banking failures and crises were: unsound financial regulation/supervision and unsound banking practices, inappropriate risk management at banks, poor corporate governance and a weak legal framework. Thus, it is recommended that governments should ensure there is a strong institutional framework in place for the economy and banking system. This should include sound macroeconomic polices, an effective corporate governance regime, strong and effective banking supervision and regulation (including a prompt corrective action approach to intervention), reliance on market discipline, efficient failed-bank resolution processes, and an effective judicial and criminal investigation system. Strengthening the effectiveness of bank supervision is particularly important for deposit insurers who are limited to a paybox mandate.

An effective deposit insurance system requires sound corporate governance

The sound governance of the deposit insurance organization strengthens the financial system's architecture and contributes directly to system stability. The four major elements comprising sound governance of organizations are: independence, accountability, transparency and integrity. All are equally important and reinforce each other in supporting good governance practices. The sound governance of the deposit insurer can be enhanced by regular internal and external reviews of its governance practices.

Independence helps a deposit insurer avoid unwarranted political and industry interference and forbearance

Effective bank failure resolution requires an operationally independent and accountable deposit insurer, with a clear mandate and that is insulated from undue political and industry influence. This provides a high level of integrity, credibility and legitimacy and reduces the incidence of political interference and forbearance in resolutions.

The mandate, responsibilities and the failure resolution powers granted to a deposit insurer should all be aligned

The powers granted to a deposit insurer should be consistent with its public policy objectives and mandate. If a deposit insurer is given a mandate to deal with the resolution of failed banks in a least cost manner, it should be provided with the necessary powers and authorities to do so. This includes the power to decide upon the appropriate resolution approach, the ability to undertake preventive measures (such as inspections) before a bank fails in order to control its risk exposure.

The legal framework should support the timely and effective resolution of bank failures including situations which may pose a systemic risk to the financial system

An appropriate legal framework should be in place to support the resolution of failed banks and to provide authority to the deposit insurer and supervisory authorities to minimize or mitigate damage to the financial system from a systemic crisis. This should include prompt corrective action measures to contain banking crises and avoid contagion. As well as in some cases providing for exceptions to least cost resolution requirements when dealing with systemically important banks.

The use of temporary blanket guarantees and reliance on public funds may be appropriate in certain exceptional circumstances

Provision of blanket guarantees and the injection of public funds may be necessary if the deposit insurer's funding resources are insufficient to handle a large bank failure or a systemic crisis has occurred. However, moral hazard and market discipline problems should be considered when using blanket guarantees and public funds. Therefore, their use should be restricted to exceptional circumstances and be provided on a temporary basis. If public funds are to be used then it is important that the shareholders of the failing/failed bank should bear losses.

Financial stability and social order are important goals

The confidence of the public in the financial system is an important objective for an effective deposit insurance system. Deposit insurers and other financial safety-net participants should always consider the need to maintain financial system stability and confidence when dealing with the resolution of failed banks. A top priority for deposit insurers should be to focus on protecting the interests of insured depositors via efficient and effective resolution of failed banks.

Interrelationship and cross-border issues

This section sets out guidance on interrelationship management and cross-border issues when dealing with the division of duties and responsibilities among financial safety-net participants in the resolution of failing or failed banks.

The division of duties and responsibilities among safety-net players in a failing/failed bank resolution should be clearly defined

Clear accountability and the division of duties and responsibilities among financial safety-net participants are necessary in order to effectively handle failing or failed banks. A formal division of duties and responsibilities can be reached by legal arrangement, contracts or administrative regulation. The clear legal division of duties and powers to declare whether a bank has failed and determine the bank resolution method is important for all financial safety net participants involved in resolutions.

Information sharing and coordination mechanisms must be in place for all financial safety-net participants

Formal information sharing and coordination mechanisms or arrangements need to be in place between the deposit insurer and the other safety-net participants for handling failing or failed banks – and especially in cases involving a systemic crisis. If prompt corrective action triggers are a part of the intervention process then the deposit insurer should be given access to information to quickly assess the potential impact of the bank failure on its fund.

An explicit statutory mechanism should be set up for dealing with systemic crises

No financial safety-net player by itself can deal effectively with a systemic banking crisis. An explicit statutory mechanism needs to be in place to allow the financial safety net participants to work together in handling a systemic banking crisis. This should include a clear division of work and duties, rules defining what is and is not a systemic crisis and a clear intervention framework for dealing with bank failures and resolutions.

Clear statutory mechanisms for dealing with 'too big to fail' issues should be established

A clear statutory mechanism for dealing with 'too big to fail (TBTF)' issues is very important when determining resolution principles and procedures. An explicit statutory mechanism should include a definition of TBTF and provide guidance on the resolution cost implications of various options. The resolution of failures involving financial holding companies should also be included in the TBTF framework.

Cross-border coordination mechanisms should be established among international financial safety-net players

With the increasing growth in international banking activities there is a need for greater information sharing and coordination among international deposit insurers and supervisory authorities dealing with failures across international borders. Cross-border mechanisms can be established by formal contracts, agreements or arrangement within international organizations.

Statutory powers accorded to the deposit insurer

The statutory powers in this section could be shared between the different authorities of a country according to the regulation applicable in each country.

Deposit insurers should have a deposit insurance fund and a statutory target for the fund

In order to maintain financial stability and enhance public confidence, the deposit insurer should have access to necessary funding which may include a fund and a statutory target ratio for the fund. There should also be a clear timetable for the deposit insurer to achieve its funding goals.

The deposit insurer should have the statutory authority to accept or reject new members and terminate the insurance status of a member bank and coordinate on the timing of termination with the supervisory agency prior to bank closure

In order to control its risk exposure and control moral hazard, the deposit insurer should have the authority to accept or reject new members and terminate the insured status of a member institution if, prior to closure, it is engaged in unsafe and unsound banking practices, severe management problems or fraud. When deciding to terminate the insured status of a bank, the deposit insurer should coordinate its activities with the supervisory agency, so as not to have adverse implication on the banking system.

The deposit insurer should have the authority to conduct on-site reviews, perform due diligence and have access to the records of depositors before bank closure

In order to effectively execute a smooth resolution, a deposit insurer should have the authority to conduct on-site appraisals, conduct due diligence on the assets and liabilities of failing bank, or have access to the records of depositors in a bank prior to bank closure.

A deposit insurer should have a statutory mechanism in place for dealing with a systemic banking crisis

In order to cooperate with other financial safety net participants in dealing with a systemic banking crisis, consideration should be given to introducing an emergency statutory rule that would allow for the introduction of a temporary blanket guarantee and/or suspension of least cost resolution requirements involving the use of public funds.

A deposit insurer's employees should have appropriate legal protection when dealing with bank resolutions

Those working for a deposit insurer and other safety-net participants should have appropriate legal protection while discharging their mandates. Specific provisions in legal protection should include granting statutory immunity to individuals from civil and criminal liability for their decisions, actions or omissions taken in good faith, except in case of gross misconduct, in the normal discharge of their legal responsibilities, as well as covering legal costs for those indemnified under appropriate circumstances.

Clear legal authority should be in place to allow for the prosecution of the directors, officers, and auditors of failed banks when there is due cause

There should be a clear and explicit legal system in place for the prosecution of officers, directors, managers and internal or external auditors of a failed bank when there is due cause. Such mechanisms can lower the costs associated with resolutions and create incentives for the better governance of banks.

Operational and administrative issues

This section sets out guidance on operational and administrative issues for deposit insurers or other financial safety-net participants involved in handling bank failures.

Appropriate policies and standard operational procedures for resolutions should be introduced

Deposit insurers should have appropriate polices and standard operational procedures (SOPs) for their bank resolution procedures. This should include reimbursement of depositors, purchase and assumption transactions, open bank assistance, and use of bridge banks etc. All SOPs should be reviewed periodically in order to update and revise them in tune with changing circumstances.

Use of outsourcing by the deposit insurance system in situations where internal resources are insufficient

Deposit insurers should have the authority to contract outsourcing services for specialized consultation, valuation or appraisals in carrying out the independent valuation and sales of assets and liabilities of the failing/failed bank or payment processes. The process of selecting outsourcing vendors should be transparent and well managed.

Undertake appropriate valuation and follow a transparent sales process for the resolution of failed banks

A deposit insurer should undertake a appropriate process for the appraisal of the value of a failed bank and follow an open and transparent process for the disposition of assets of a failed bank.

A deposit insurer should have in place an effective public awareness and communication mechanism to enhance the confidence of the public in the resolution process

A deposit insurer should, on a regular basis, communicate to the public the terms and conditions of deposit insurance coverage and the approach it takes to the resolution of failed banks.

A code of conduct for employees of a deposit insurer should be in place

Employees of the deposit insurer or other safety-net participants should follow an appropriate code of conduct and confidentiality provisions with respect to failure resolution. Good codes of conduct include prevention of conflict of interest pertaining to the discharge of their duties and the responsibilities of the employees.

A deposit insurer should be provided with the power to investigate and if necessary litigate against those parties at fault in a bank failure

The power of investigation into alleged officers, directors, managers, auditors and related parties of the failing/failed bank can help improve recoveries for an insurer and can mitigate moral hazard problems by providing strong incentives against malfeasance.

The resolution of failing or failed banks

This section sets out guidance on resolution methods for failing or failed banks.

Have in place a rule-based or statutory trigger criterion for intervening in the affairs of a problem bank

It is important for the deposit insurer or other financial safety net participants to set up a rule-based or statutory trigger mechanism for early intervention into the affairs of a troubled bank and for determining whether a bank has failed. The trigger criteria should involve either quantitative or qualitative measures. The quantitative ratios should include measures such as regulatory capital and asset quality. Qualitative indexes should include measures of management quality and any material breaches of standards of sound business and financial practices, violations of regulatory requirements, or the inability of a bank to fulfill its obligations resulting from the claims of depositors.

A professional evaluation team should assess the financial viability of a failing bank

A professional, experienced team composed of staff from the supervisor and/or deposit insurer or outside experts should be created to assess the viability of a problem bank. The evaluation criteria should be based on issues such as market value. If 'workout' plans with a specific timetable are required by supervisors, the plans submitted by the failing bank should be well designed, approved and followed up by the financial supervisory agency and/or deposit insurer.

Effective resolution policy and emergency mechanisms to handle individual bank failures should be established

In order to be efficient, reliable and credible in handling individual bank failures, the deposit insurer should set up effective resolution policies and procedures. These should include how to apply least-cost resolution methods, how to handle the systemic repercussions of the failure of large bank, how to avoid the disruption of banking services in a particular market or region, and what kind of emergency alternatives should be used if conditions deteriorate more quickly than expected.

Try to maximize the recovery of the failed bank's assets using a market approach

The deposit insurer is typically the largest creditor in a failure after subrogation. Therefore, it should try to maximize its recoveries by selling the assets of the failed banks through appropriate legal means and the use of real estate agents and other market mechanisms including possible recovery mechanisms that will allow the deposit insurer to benefit from any upside.

Market principles and mechanisms should be relied upon as much as possible in resolution transactions

It is a good practice for the deposit insurer to resolve failed banks using market mechanisms and principles. This can include approaches which:

- Obtain support or assistance (for example, risk sharing) from other financial safety net participants before commencing a resolution process.
- Build in a transparent approach to resolutions which encourages all potential purchasers to participate.
- Ensure high standards in the internal and external auditing associated with the resolution process.
- Where possible, employ mark-to-market approaches in the appraisal process.
- Use experienced professionals to expedite deal related transactions efficiently.
- Resolution approaches should be both effective and efficient (that is, cost-effective) rather than relying solely on seeking the lowest cost method.

Set up incentives for facilitating market mechanisms in resolution

If market-based processes are likely to be successful there needs to be system-wide statutory incentives for their use. Some examples are:

- Tax incentives: to facilitate mergers and acquisitions and bad debt write-offs.
- Administrative incentives: to reduce compliance costs, enhance debt recovery or insolvency registration.

Ensure efficient and effective insured depositor reimbursement

A top priority for deposit insurers is that there be focus on protecting the interests of insured depositors via efficient and effective reimbursement processes. Examples of efficient and effective depositor reimbursement procedures are:

- Shorten as much as possible the period between the revocation of a bank's licence and the actual reimbursement process.
- Continuous disclosure of information to the public during the reimbursement process and liquidation. This should include keeping depositors informed about the details and timeframe of their reimbursement.
- The deposit insurer should be able to audit the data-processing systems used to assess deposit records and gain access to the failed bank's depositor records before bank closure to speed up the reimbursement process.
- The legal rules regarding objects and items to be withheld and set-off, as well as guiding subrogation should be well defined.
- The deposit insurer should set up partial payment procedures in cases where insured depositors are in need of their funds urgently before the actual reimbursement.

Guiding rules of liquidations should be well defined

The rules for the liquidation process, reporting duties of the liquidator, legal deadlines and distributions to creditors should be well defined and documented. Other factors influencing the recovery in liquidation should also be well controlled and managed, including the depositor's priority ranking, legal deadlines, set-off rules, the collateralization of claims and the litigation exposure of the deposit insurer during liquidation procedures. Furthermore, the guiding subrogation rules of the deposit insurer should be well defined.

Appendix 10A.1: Survey results

In general, the survey results confirmed the prevalence of consolidation and conglomeration in banking through both internal expansion and mergers and acquisitions.

Banking industry concentration continues to increase in most countries. According to the questionnaire responses among 34 countries, five countries had a concentration ratio of 93 per cent of assets for their top five largest banks while the average concentration ratio in 25 countries was more than 30 per cent.

Another finding of the survey was that banking crises have been quite common. Twenty four out of the 34 respondents indicated they had had some form of banking crisis or major failures during the last ten years. It also appears that the trend to increasing concentration in banking is raising the risk exposure of deposit insurers and other safety-net participants to individual bank failures and potential systemic crises. Thus, when dealing with bank failures it is important for safety-net participants to understand the issues of both individual bank failures and failures which could result in systemic crises.

In dealing with systemic banking crisis, the role and responsibility of every financial safety-net participant, including the deposit insurer, supervisor and central bank is very important. Based on the responses to the questionnaire, most deposit insurer (DI) respondents were administered by a government or a public agency. Only four deposit insurers were privately administered. The insurers in ten countries could not be characterized as primarily government or private, but shared characteristics of both systems (Figure 10.1).

Countries confronting a banking crisis or individual bank failure

Except for Portugal and Cyprus, most countries surveyed had confronted a banking crisis or individual bank failures. Over the last ten years, 19 countries had suffered from a banking crisis. The earliest and most recent crises among the sample countries occurred in 1990 and 2003 respectively.

Net resolution cost

Among the 19 countries which responded to questions on resolution costs, the minimum resolution cost was US$709,000 and the maximum was US$162 billion with an average of US$20 billion. As to resolution costs as a percentage of one year's GDP for a country, the lowest ratio was 0.002 per cent for Hungary and the largest was 35.8 per cent for Jamaica, with an average of 5.5 per cent. For those countries with high net resolution costs,[3] the costs to the economy and financial stability were extremely high. This illustrates the importance of strengthening the effectiveness and efficiency of banking supervision, regulation and the resolution of bank failures.

Macro and non-macro factors causing a banking crisis or individual bank failure

Referring to the macro factors[4] causing a banking crisis or individual bank failures, economic recession was the most common reason cited (18 countries), followed by the presence of an unsound financial regulatory/supervisory system (15 countries), financial deregulation (13 countries), and political issues (5 countries). As for bank failure specific non-macro factors,[5] the reasons cited were, in order: unsound banking practices, inappropriate risk management, poor corporate governance and management fraud or embezzlement[6] (Figure 10A.1, 10A.2).

Improvements made after the banking crisis or the bank failure

The improvements made[7] by governments in 34 countries after a banking crisis or bank failures were in top down order: the introduction of safe and sound banking

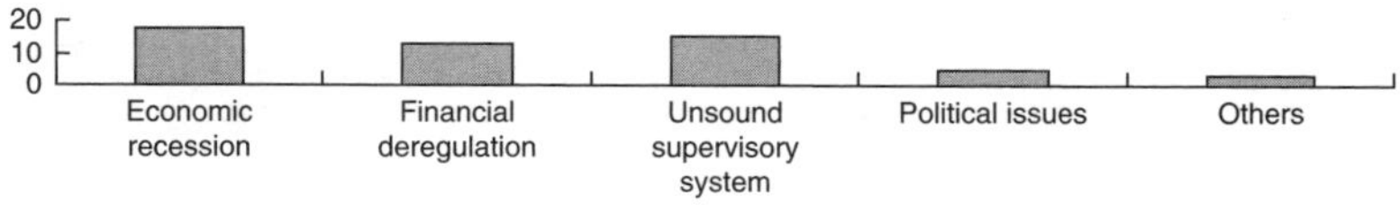

Figure 10A.1 Macro factors causing the banking crisis or individual bank failure

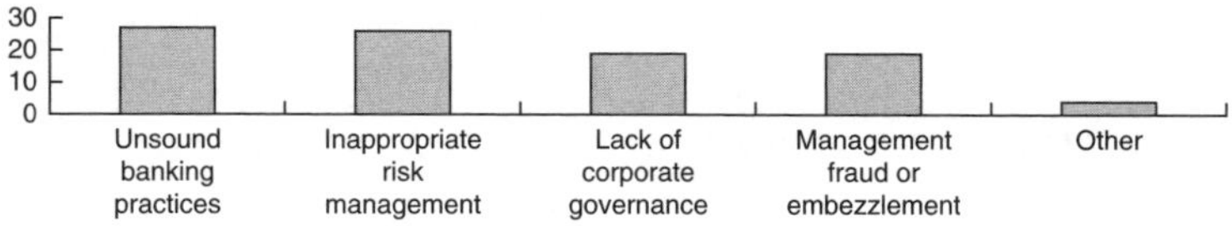

Figure 10A.2 Non-macro factors causing the banking crisis or individual bank failure

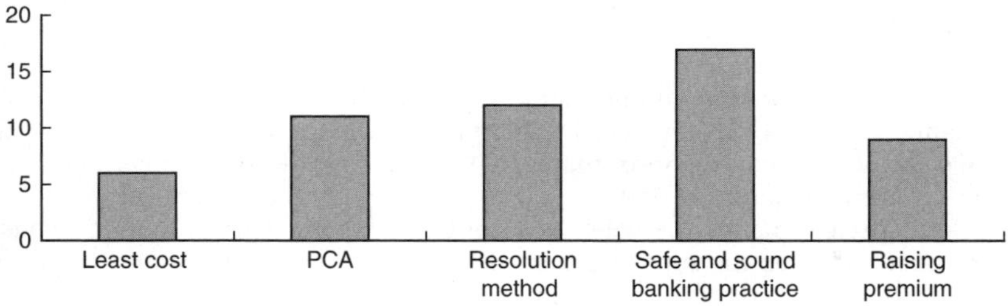

Figure 10A.3 Improvement made after banking crisis or failure

practices, improved bank resolution methods, prompt corrective action (PCA), raising deposit insurance premiums and/or adopting differential premium systems, and the introduction of least cost resolution practices (Figure 10A.3).

Resolution powers and mandates in dealing with individual bank failures

Major actions taken within six months prior to bank closure

According to the survey results, the deposit insurer or supervisory agency can take the following major actions within six months prior to a bank closure[8] (Figure 10A.4):

1. Request the failing bank to submit a recapitalization or improvement plan (11 countries).
2. Arrange for the appraisal of assets and liabilities of the failing bank (7 countries).
3. Place the failing bank into conservatorship (7 countries).
4. Others: some countries responded that the deposit insurer or supervisory agency should first make sure that the bank is insolvent and then properly arrange for the appraisal of the failing bank's assets and liabilities (such as in the Philippines and Cyprus). In other countries the deposit insurer or supervisory agency can take actions when allowed or empowered by their central bank such as in the Netherlands and France.

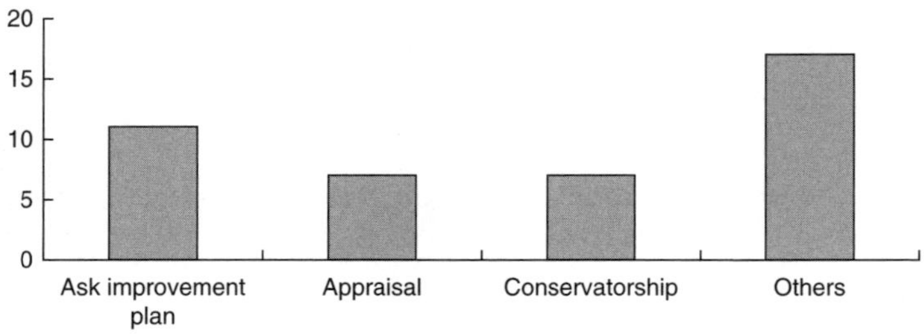

Figure 10A.4 Major actions taken within 6 months prior to bank closure

Prompt corrective action (PCA) and the legal authority to declare bank failure

There were 15 countries surveyed which had a rule-based or statutory approach for early intervention and resolution (for example, PCA).

1. Assessing viability: Responsibility for assessing the true value of a failing bank (for example, its net worth or financial viability) was given to the supervisory agency in 26 countries, accounting firms (that is CPA) in 4 countries, and the deposit insurer in 4 countries (Figure 10A.5).
2. Criteria used to determine whether a bank has failed (Figure 10A.6): 18 countries have adopted the supervisory on-site examination[9] criteria and 2 countries use a liquidation criterion to determine whether a bank has failed. However, no country which responded to the survey had adopted market value criteria for valuation.
3. Declaration of bank failure (Figure 10A.7): the banking supervisory agency in 19 countries was responsible for the declaration of a bank failure. The central bank in seven countries; and the deposit insurer in three countries were granted the legal power to declare whether a bank has failed or is insolvent. The remaining countries responded that these powers reside in their court system.
4. Liquidity assistance: In the case of bank runs or a liquidity crisis, the central bank is responsible for providing urgent liquidity assistance to failing banks in 12 countries surveyed. In four countries both the central bank and deposit insurer are responsible for providing urgent liquidity assistance to failing banks.

The power to determine bank resolution methods

1. The determination of resolution methods: responsibility for this function lies with the banking supervisory agency in 15 countries, the deposit insurer in 11 countries, and the central bank in seven countries. The remaining countries responded that it was their court system which was granted this power.
2. On-site appraisal: in only 13 countries the deposit insurer has the authority to conduct on-site appraisal or due diligence for a failing or problem bank in connection with determining resolution options before a bank is closed.
3. Major source of resolution: while in the process of handling a bank failure resolution, the major source of liquidity for paybox type deposit insurers are their deposit insurance funds. For non-paybox insurers the sources of liquidity support were generally more diversified.

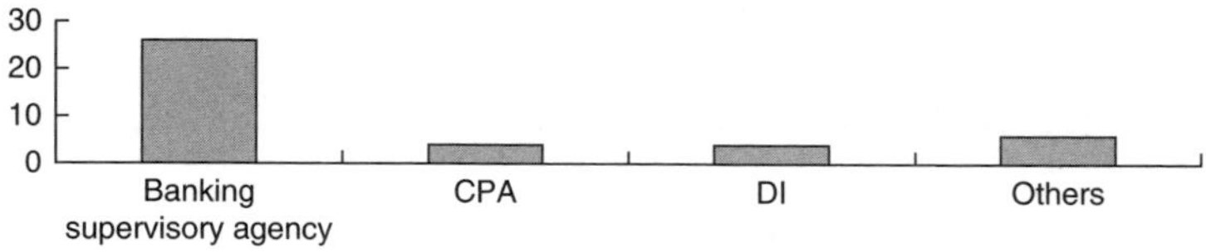

Figure 10A.5 The organization responsible for assessing the value of failing bank

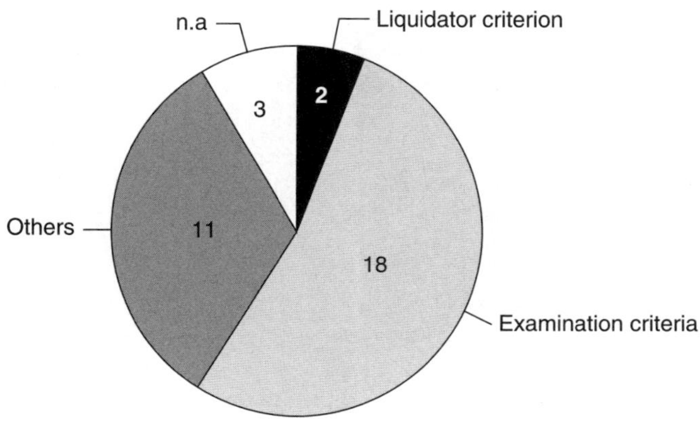

Figure 10A.6 Criteria used to determine whether a bank has failed

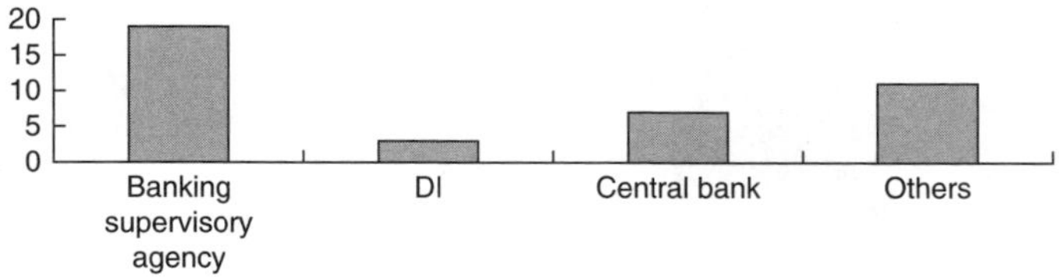

Figure 10A.7 Organization with power to declare bank failure

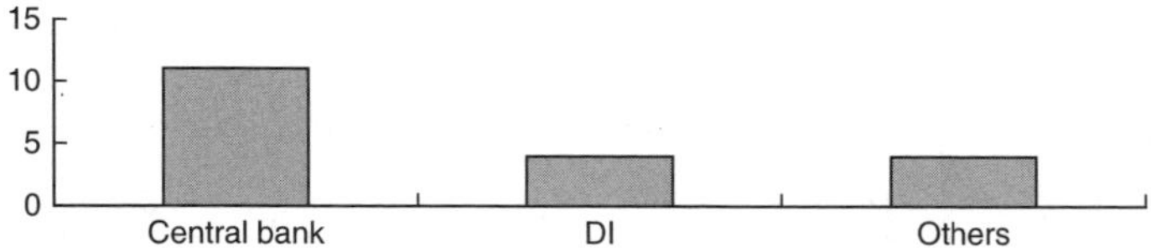

Figure 10A.8 Organization responsible for providing urgent liquidity assistance

Formal coordination mechanism

In dealing with bank failures, 18 countries have a formal coordination mechanism by law, contract or agreement among financial safety net participants (including the deposit insurer), while 15 countries have no formal mechanisms. (Figure 10A.10).

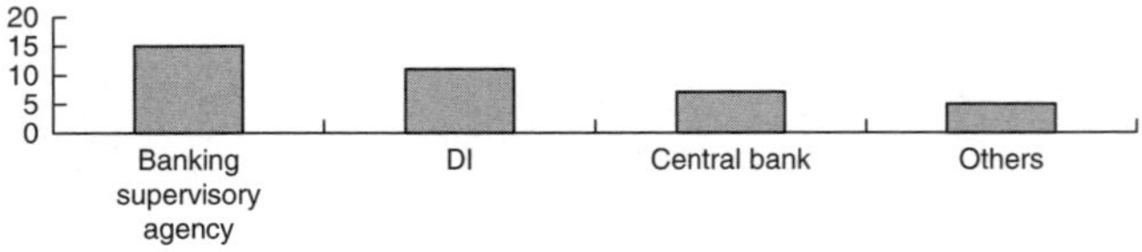

Figure 10A.9 Organization has the power to determine bank resolution method

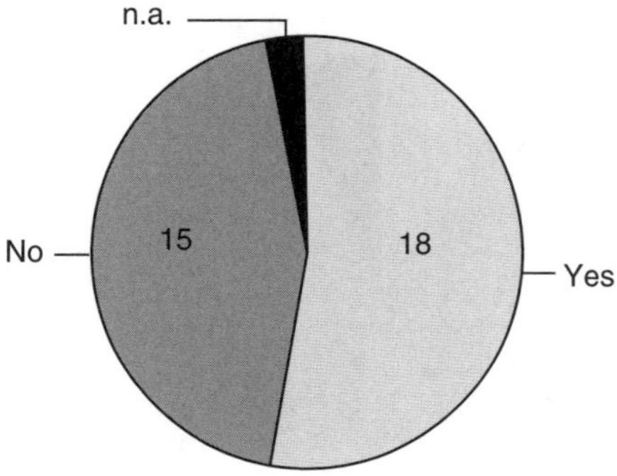

Figure 10A.10 Having coordination mechanism in dealing with bank failures

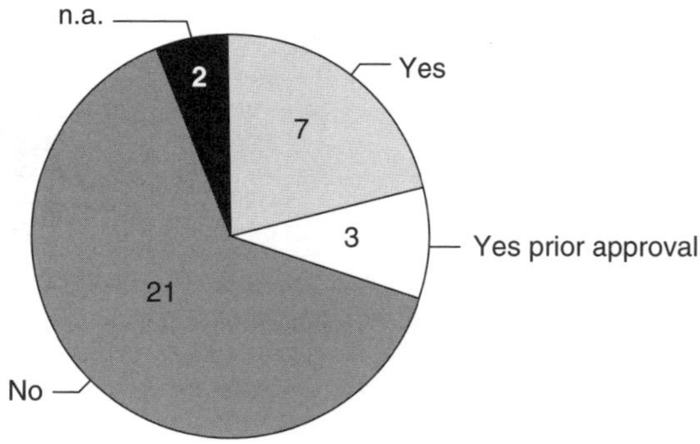

Figure 10A.11 DI has the authority to terminate the insured status

Financial holding companies and their responsibilities for their bank subsidiaries

Financial holding companies (FHC), or financial institutions acting as a subsidiary of a financial conglomerate, were allowed in 24 countries surveyed. However, there were only seven countries where the parent company was required to guarantee the liabilities of a failed bank subsidiary by statute, contract or agreement. In 20 countries, the resolution mechanism for the failed bank subsidiary of a FHC or a financial conglomerate was the same as that for a non-FHC individual bank failure.

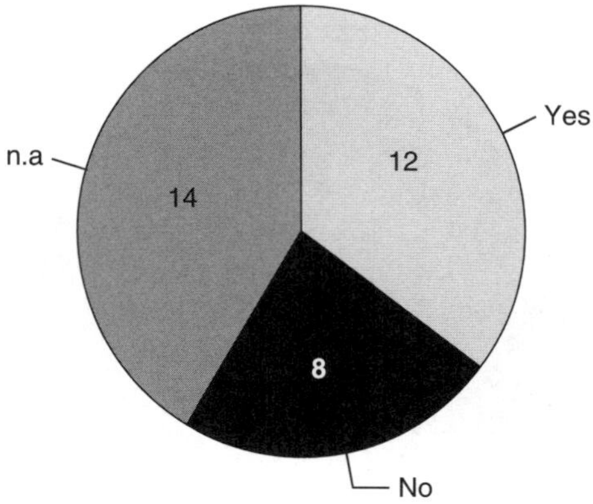

Figure 10A.12 DI provides protection after termination of the desposit

The termination of the insured status of a member bank

Only in seven countries did the deposit insurer have the authority to terminate the insured status (that is membership) of a failing bank before closure (Figure 10A.11). In these cases, the deposit insurer was required to publish a notice of termination of a bank's membership. After terminating the insured status of a member bank, the insurer in 12 countries continued to provide protection to depositors within a period of time ranging from (Figure 10A.12) one year (Taiwan) to two years (Canada: Autorité des marchés financiers (Québec).

Resolution options for bank failures

The major resolution method used for paybox type deposit insurers in resolving failed banks was the reimbursement of insured depositors. Deposit insurers with a loss minimization mandate were generally required to adopt some form of least-cost resolution principle and they may decide on the appropriate resolution method. The resolution methods[10] available for deposit insurers in resolving failed banks were as follows (Figure 10A.13):

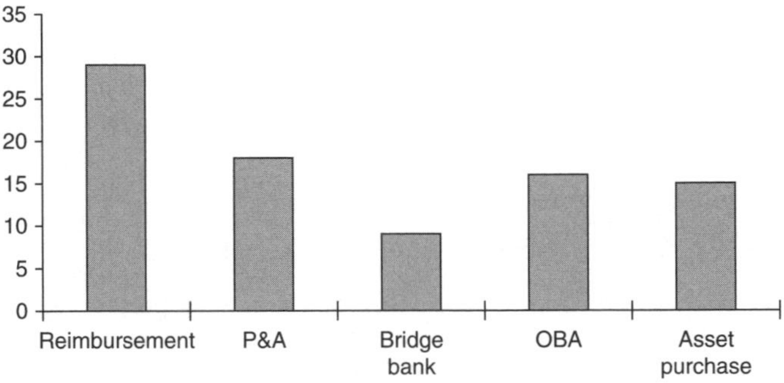

Figure 10A.13 Resolution methods

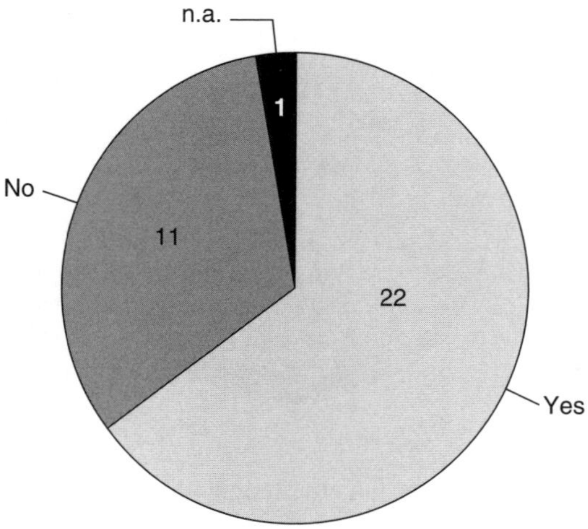

Figure 10A.14 Having SOP for reimbursement

Reimbursement (payout) of insured depositors

A depositor reimbursement or payout resolution may be accomplished by the deposit insurer directly paying depositors their insured balances or by transferring the accounts to another bank that makes the insured balances available to the depositors. The bank is often closed (license or charter extinguished) and the assets and uninsured claims are transferred to a receiver for liquidation and settlement.

The reasons for adopting reimbursement

According to the survey responses, the main reasons for adopting reimbursement (payout) in 29 countries were:

1. The prompt and timely reimbursement of insured depositors can help prevent a contingent systemic crisis.
2. The court's decision on forcible bank liquidation, or a wind-up order has been made.
3. To incur a least-cost resolution as well as less confusion associated with a failure compared with other alternatives.
4. The payout method was preferred over other resolution methods after considering the impact of other resolution options on the deposit insurance fund and the stability of the financial system.
5. No other option: there is no franchise value of the failing bank.

The characteristics of the reimbursement

The characteristics of the reimbursement process in 29 countries were as follows:

1. Most countries (22 countries) have a standard operational procedure (SOP) for the reimbursement of insured depositors (Figure 10A.14).
2. According to statute, contract or agreement, the time limit from the date of the bank closure to actual reimbursement was usually not over six months, and the shortest time limit was one week in the USA (Figure 10A.15). But, according to

actual experiences the average period from the date of bank closure to depositor payout was over six months in four countries surveyed (Figure 10A.16). This indicates that the actual reimbursement period can be longer than the legal statute.

3. According to the survey responses, deposit insurers in ten of the countries can gain access to the deposit records of failed banks before bank closure. In 12 countries access can only be obtained at the time of bank closure and in the remaining 12 countries only after bank closure. This suggests that if a deposit insurer can gain access early to depositor records, it may have greater influence on the expedition of the actual reimbursement process (Figure 10A.17).
4. In cases where the insured depositors are in need of urgent liquidity (that is, their funds) before the completion of the actual reimbursement, ten countries provided their deposit insurers with the option of making advance payments.

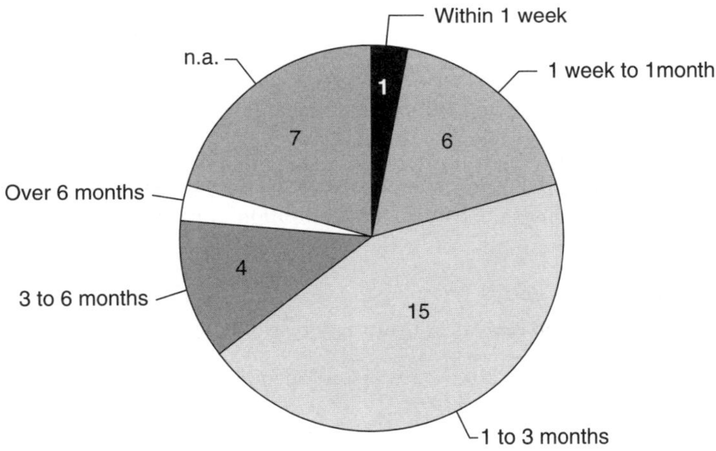

Figure 10A.15 Statutory time limit of reimbursement

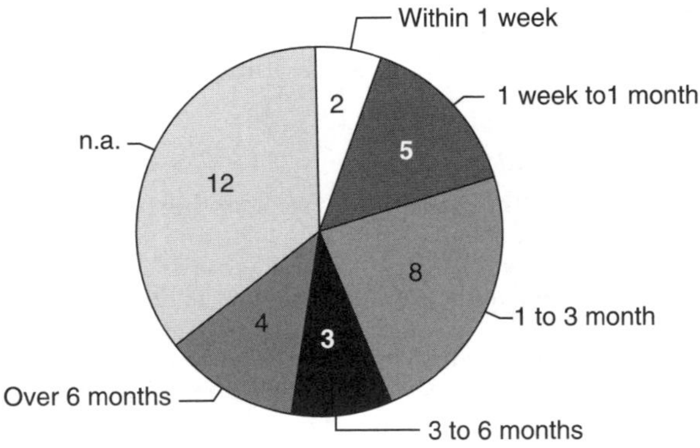

Figure 10A.16 Actual average period of reimbursement

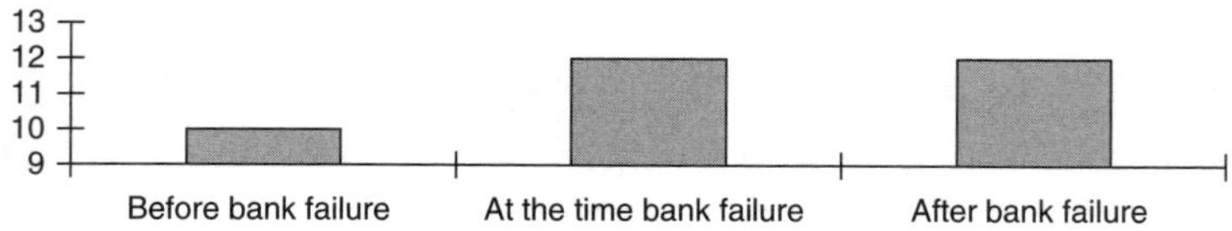

Figure 10A.17 Time to gain access to deposit records

Purchase and assumption (P&A)

A purchase and assumption transaction or resolution is one in which a healthy bank or group of investors assume some or all of the obligations, and purchase some or all of the assets, of the failed or failing bank. Some of the key findings of the survey on P&A resolutions were:

Reasons for adopting P&A

According to the response, the main reasons for adopting a P&A resolution in 18 countries are as follows:

1. When the cost for adopting P&A is less than the estimated loss arising from a payout.
2. P&A is considered to be less disruptive compared to a payout.
3. P&A is considered to be in the best interests of the bank's depositors and would aid in the reconstruction of the bank or the disposition of its assets in an expeditious manner.

Characteristics of the P&A

The characteristics of the P&A in 18 countries are as follows:

1. Most countries still do not have a standard operational procedure (SOP) for P&A transactions.
2. Most countries adopt a whole bank P&A or a P&A with optional asset pools when handling failed banks.

Bridge banks

The term bridge bank refers to a temporary bank established and operated by the deposit insurer to acquire the assets and assume the liabilities of a failed bank until a final resolution can be accomplished. Some of the key findings of the survey on bridge bank resolutions were:

Reasons for adopting a bridge bank

According to the responses, the main reasons for adopting bridge bank in nine countries are as follows:

1. A bank with an attractive franchise is in danger of failing before acquirers can be found.
2. To maintain daily operations of a failed bank.
3. In cases where liquidator is reluctant to proceed with the formal liquidation because either the failed bank is too large (so no adequate funds are available for reimbursement) or there is not enough time to market the bank's assets to potential acquirers.
4. When the number of failed financial institutions are very large and the failures have occurred during a short period of time.

Characteristics of bridge banks

The characteristics of the bridge bank in nine countries are as follows:

1. Only three countries have standard operation procedure (SOP) for bridge bank transaction.
2. There is a capital requirement for a bridge bank in some countries, like Colombia and Japan[11], while there is no capital requirement in the USA and Korea.
3. For three out of six responding countries, the bridge bank continued to be a member of the deposit insurance system.

Open Bank Assistance (OBA)

The term Open Bank Assistance (OBA) refers to a resolution method in which an insured bank in danger of failing receives assistance in the form of a direct loan, an assisted merger, or a purchase of assets. Some of the key findings of the survey on OBA resolutions were:

Reasons for adopting OBA

According to the responses, the main reasons for adopting OBA in 16 countries were as follows:

1. If the failure of a bank poses an extremely serious threat to the stability of the financial system and local and/or national economies.
2. The cost of providing OBA may be less than the potential losses arising from a deposit payout.

Characteristics of OBA

The characteristics of the OBA in 16 countries were as follows:

1. There is a standard operational procedure (SOP) for OBA in only six countries surveyed (Figure 10A.18).
2. In nine countries, the deposit insurer or supervisory agency will dispatch a new management team or require a restructuring plan prior to providing OBA to a failing bank.
3. In some countries like Spain, Canada, Venezuela and Mexico, the failing bank is required to take a capital deduction (for example capital adjustments for large losses) prior to receiving OBA.
4. There did not appear to be any maximum duration requirement for OBA in some countries.

Asset purchases

The reasons for adopting asset purchases

According to the responses received, the main reasons for adopting asset purchases in 15 countries were as follows:

1. As a way to minimize resolution costs by maximizing future recoveries.
2. As part of the financial restructuring of the failed bank.
3. A result of the reduction in the realizable value of assets resulting from a deterioration in asset quality or a situation where the receivables from asset sales are severely affected. Thus, it is essential to be able to provide for fresh earning assets, which can be source of income.

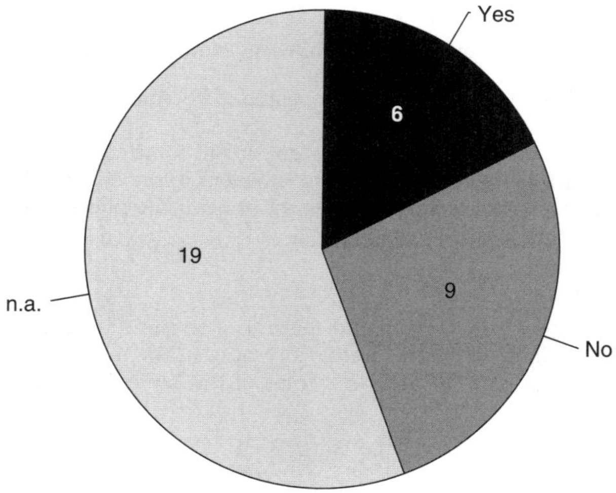

Figure 10A.18 Having SOP for OBA

The characteristics of asset purchases

The characteristics of the assets purchased in 15 countries were as follows:

1. The deposit insurer or the supervisory agency was granted authority to purchase assets from failed banks in most countries.
2. The deposit insurer or the supervisory agency in most countries did not establish another subsidiary or joint asset management company to purchase the asset from the failed banks, except for Japan, Canada and Autorité des marchés financiers (Québec).

Actual experience in handling bank failures

Actual experience

Actual experiences in the past ten years for depositor reimbursement (payouts). According to the responses, these were the main findings regarding depositor reimbursement experiences:

1. The number of cases: in 16 countries surveyed the use of depositor reimbursement varied from 1 to 165, with an average of 19 instances (with the median of 4 instances).
2. The average asset size of failed banks: in 12 countries, it varied from US$0 to US$0.9 billion; the average asset size was about US$0.2 billion (with the median of US$34 million).
3. The average duration for each reimbursement: this varied from 1 to 120 months in 7 countries, the average was 40 months (with the median of 24 months).

Actual experiences in the past ten years in P&A

1. Number of cases: in 10 countries, it varied from 1 to 180, with an average of 30 (with the median of 3).

2. Average asset size of failed banks: in 6 countries it varied from US$0.2 to US$11 billion with an average asset size of about US$3 billion (with the median of US$0.6 billion).
3. The average duration for P&A transactions varied from 4 to 24 months with an average of 14 months (the same for the median).

Actual experiences in the past ten years for bridge banks

1. Number of cases: in 2 countries the cases varied from 1 to 7, with an average of 4 (the same for the median).
2. Average asset size of failed banks: in one country for US$6 billion.
3. Average duration for each resolution: in one country for 48 months.

Actual experiences in the past ten years for OBA

1. Number of cases: in 9 countries this varied from 1 to 22, with an average of 10 (with the median of 11).
2. The average asset size of failed banks: in 4 countries it varied from US$1.2 billion to US$37 billion with an average asset size of about US$13 billion (with the median of US$7 billion).
3. Average duration for each instance of OBA: in 3 countries it varied from 3 to 48 months with an average of 20 months (with the median of 11 months).

Comparison among each resolution experience

The following chart (Figure 10A.19) compares the actual experiences with different types of resolutions during the past ten years. It indicates that P&A resolutions were adopted the most frequently followed by depositor reimbursement.

The average asset size in an OBA resolution was the largest followed by bridge banks (Figure 10A.20). Bridge bank resolutions involved the longest average duration (Figure 10A.21). From this analysis, most countries appear to have adopted P&A for larger bank failures and this method involved the shortest resolution time frame. The OBA resolution approach was generally used in very large bank failures and depositor reimbursement was utilised for relatively small bank failures. Therefore, the deposit insurer should have a clear-cut policy (including the time-span) in place in dealing with resolution methods for failing or failed banks.

Strengths and weaknesses of resolution options

According to the 34 countries' responses to actual experiences in handling bank failures, each resolution method had the following strengths and weaknesses:

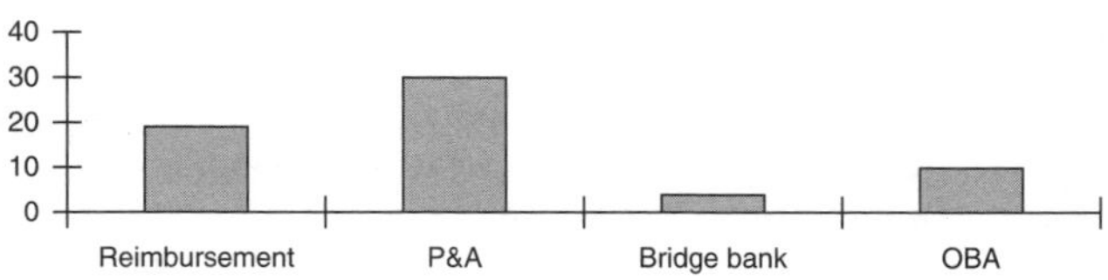

Figure 10A.19 Average failure resolution cases in the past 10 years

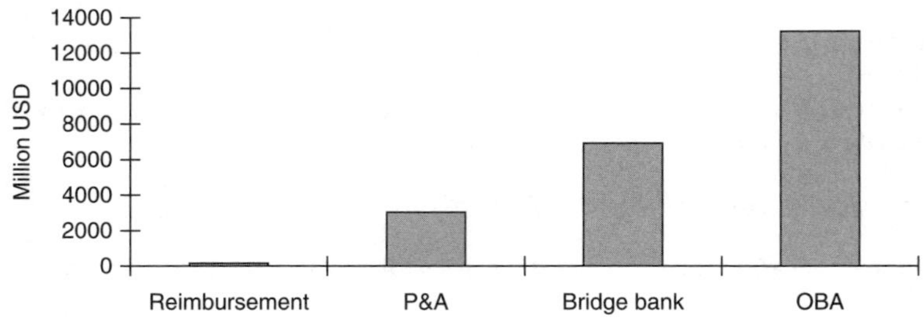

Figure 10A.20 Average asset size of bank failure in the past 10 years

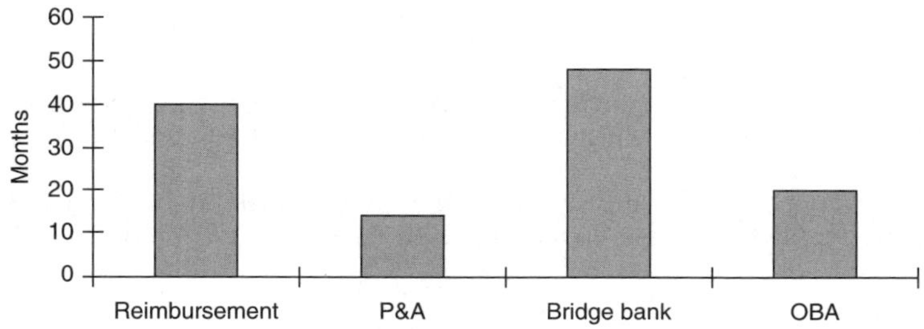

Figure 10A.21 Average duration of each resolution in the past 10 years

Deposit reimbursement

The strengths:

1. It can take care of depositor needs and help minimize the social and economic costs of bank failures.
2. It guarantees the fair treatment of depositors and increases confidence in the banking system.
3. It is especially effective in terms of weeding out 'unwanted' banks in a system with 'too many' non-viable banks.
4. Depositors are compensated based on the amount of accumulated deposit contributions they have in banks (up to the coverage limit).

The weaknesses:

1. All the functions of a failed bank must be given up; the failure of a particular bank is public knowledge which could lead to a crisis in confidence affecting all banks.
2. It limits the discretionary power of the deposit insurer.
3. It may take a long period of time to affect a reimbursement and there is the concomitant risk for employees of the deposit insurer (who may not receive legal protection) of being held personally liable for the losses of uninsured creditors.

P&A

The strengths:

1. It can preserve the functions of the failed bank and maintains the relationship of the depositor with the bank. Thus, it preserves confidence in the system.
2. It often covers all depositors, the timing of cash obligations can be stretched out, and it may preserve some jobs of the failed bank.
3. It is often the least expensive and disruptive resolution approach may not require any additional funds from government finances.
4. It can minimize market disruptions since transference of assets can be executed in a very short period.
5. It allows customers access to their deposits and they do not suffer any shortcomings in service.

The weaknesses:

1. It may be difficult to find an assuming financial institution when economic circumstances or the banking system is weak.
2. It may increase a country's costs of resolving failed banks and could reduce market discipline.
3. If all depositors are covered, it may diminish the significance of deposit insurance limits and could lead to depositors negotiating coverage levels.
4. Private investors are typically not interested in acquiring an insolvent bank; therefore in order to attract an acquirer new funding must be injected into the institution from either the government or the deposit insurer.
5. The insurer faces an arduous task of facilitating the early valuation of assets and liabilities of the failing institution as it endeavours to maintain secrecy. And, not all P&A transactions involve acquiring all deposit liabilities so that not all (100 per cent) of depositors are always fully protected.

Bridge bank

The strengths:

1. It is often better than a P&A in terms of timely resolution and the preservation of the functions of the failed bank.
2. It can make depositors and creditors of financial institutions more confident.
3. The establishment of a bridge bank can provide the insurer with more time to find the right acquirer and prospective acquirers to assess the value of the bank from which they can base their bids.

The weaknesses:

1. It may increase costs incurred by the deposit insurer or the government. This is because the deposit insurer or the government becomes the owner of the failed or failing bank and later must sell it thus, incurring additional resolution expenses and administrative costs.
2. It may be costly for the deposit insurer as it can require more time and effort to set up a bridge bank than other resolution options. In the absence of the right acquirer or in the absence of bidders, completing the resolution process may take longer than would be ideally required.

3. This method may be applied simply to 'buy time' for the supervisory authority and could lead to lengthy delays and costs for the final resolution of the problem bank.

OBA

The strengths:

1. It may resolve the liquidity problems of failed financial institutions, stabilize the confidence of depositors and financial conditions, and avoid a systemic banking crisis.
2. Investors are required to bring in fresh capital to share in the costs of rehabilitating the failing institution.

The weaknesses:

1. The insurance fund may be eroded more quickly and within a shorter time period than with other alternatives.
2. It could induce 'moral hazard' and possibly protect those private agents who contributed to the failure of the bank.
3. It can reduce market discipline and may promote 'too big to fail' problems.

Partial payment

Partial payments are made to cover the immediate living costs and other expenses of depositors, and soon, in a financial institution that has been subject to an insurable contingency, when it is anticipated that insurance payments or the reimbursement of insured deposits will not begin for a considerable length of time.

The strengths:

1. Partial payment provides temporary relief to the distressed depositor. In the case of a depositor with unresolved issues, partial payment up to the resolved amount may mitigate the risk faced by the insured depositor.
2. It forces depositors (small and large) to be more diligent when choosing a bank (all depositors are responsible for a part of their deposits).

The weaknesses:

1. Depositors are not fully reimbursed at one time.
2. It may create unnecessary excess burden on the IT systems and thus delay the whole process, endangering the completion of the payment within statutory time frame.

Advanced payment

The strengths:

Payment to uninsured depositors in advance, prior to liquidation of the failed institution, provides depositors immediate returns on the uninsured portion of their deposits.

The weaknesses:

1. Advanced payment in itself is not a resolution method
2. The amount of payment depends on the conservative valuation of the failed institution; the risk of overestimation is still present.

Gaps in current laws or practices dealing with individual bank failures

The following suggestions are from the respondents of the questionnaire in order to improve the effectiveness of the resolution process:

Changes should be made in mandates and powers

These are some suggestions from respondents for deposit insurers or supervisory agencies to improve the resolution of failed banks:

1. The deposit insurer should have onsite supervisory powers.
2. The deposit insurer should have due diligence power (for example, preparatory examination).
3. The deposit insurer should have the power to withdraw the insurance status of an institution (termination).
4. Laws should be amended to strengthen the independence and the inspection power of the deposit insurer, and to establish a coordinating mechanism between the deposit insurer and the supervisory agency.
5. Provisions regarding the resolution of insured depository institutions that were suspended from operations should be supplemented to accelerate the process of resolution.
6. The deposit insurer should have independence in determining its own administrative expenses budget.
7. The insurer needs more powers in the context of a prompt corrective action programme in order to assess a failing bank's potential impact and take action to resolve the failed bank.

Changes should be made in funding and in the reimbursement of insured depositors

1. Sufficient funds should be available for the deposit insurer to promptly deal with unsound (failed) financial institutions.
2. It would be helpful for a deposit insurer to have the legal capacity to effect deposit transfers between institutions for reimbursement purposes (that is, arrange for institutions to make reimbursements to depositors and other bank creditors in the name of the deposit insurer, for the guaranteed obligations of another institution).
3. The period between revocation of the licence and the initial date of reimbursement needs to be shortened.

Changes should be made if P&A, OBA, assets purchase and other methods adopted

1. The deposit insurer should have disposal options related to P&A transactions, such as to sell assets in pools; to manage the failed bank's property; to credit a healthy bank which wishes buy-out or assume the business of the failed bank or part of its business.
2. The insurer or supervisory agency should have access to sufficient funding resources to provide OBA for a large bank confronted with a financial problem.
3. The deposit insurer should have mandates for direct asset management.
4. Proper guidelines need to be in place to ensure that the insurer correctly determines who gets paid, how much and when, and that the partial payment of one party should set a precedent that others may demand partial payment as well.

Other suggestions

1. The deposit insurer needs more discretionary powers in resolutions; for example, it should have the right to follow the least-cost method, OBA options etc.
2. There needs to be a clearer definition of 'too big to fail' and the specific procedures to follow in the case of such banking problems.
3. Deposit insurers have some legal constraints (regarding different options). Reaching a fair resolution must take the following issues into consideration: the minimization of total resolution costs, delays in reimbursements, the maximization of asset recoveries, and the negative effects on the financial sector of various resolution options. Some of above components are tangible and others are intangible (for example, social costs), which means that a thorough cost-benefit analysis should be undertaken.
4. The insurer should be empowered to select the appropriate resolution method for any bank failure. This includes the right to undertake preventive measures and/or inspections in the bank prior to failing. These suggestions can result in decreased social costs associated with bank failures and increased public trust in the banking system.
5. The deposit insurer's capital should be enhanced and deposit insurer should be more independent.

The main differences between paybox type and non-paybox type of deposit insurance system with respect to resolutions

According to the questionnaire results, there were 16 deposit insurers with a primarily paybox type mandate. There were 18 insurers with a non-paybox mandate which typically involved powers to control their insured risk exposure to some extent. This section provides some comparisons between these two types of insurers and how they deal with failure resolutions.

1. After a banking crisis or a bank failure, those countries with primarily paybox type deposit insurers had to rely heavily on enhancements to the supervisory and regulatory system to promote safe and sound banking practices. However, those countries with non-paybox type deposit insurer were able to adopt more widespread improvements in their banking infrastructure and supervisory practices. For example, initiatives such as the adoption of safe and sound banking practices, least cost resolutions, PCA, enhanced failed bank resolution methods, raising premiums or adopting differential premium system and so on.
2. In actions taken by the deposit insurer within 6 months prior to bank closure, the non-paybox deposit insurers were able to take more actions towards addressing failing banks. For example, they were allowed to require a recapitalization or improvement plan, to arrange for appraisal of assets and liabilities, and to place failing banks into conservatorship.
3. PCA issues: only 2 countries with paybox-type insurers have a rules-based or statutory approach for early intervention and resolution (for example prompt corrective action). But, numerous non-paybox deposit insurers have such mechanisms in place.
4. On-site appraisal issues: only 2 countries with a paybox deposit insurer have the authority to conduct on-site appraisals or due diligence of the failing/problem banks in connection with resolutions. But, most countries with non-paybox deposit insurers have been granted this authority.

5. Sources of funding: while handling bank failures, paybox insurers generally utilize their own funds for liquidity purposes. However, non-paybox deposit insurers generally have access to more sources of liquidity such as their insurance fund, the central bank and other financial institutions and so on.
6. Government as the guarantor of the deposit insurers borrowings for resolution purposes: only three countries with a paybox insurer had governments which acted as guarantors when their insurers issued bonds or borrowed money from the central bank or other financial institutions for resolutions. But, in most countries with non-paybox deposit insurers governments acted as guarantors when the insurer borrowed money for resolutions.
7. Termination power: only four paybox deposit insurers had the authority to terminate the insured status of a failing bank before bank closure. But, a number of non-paybox insurers were given the authority to terminate the insured status of their members when warranted.
8. Resolution methods: almost all the paybox deposit insurers made use of the reimbursement (payout) resolution method. But, non-paybox deposit insurers used other resolution methods in addition to payouts such as purchase and assumption transactions, open-bank assistance, asset purchases, bridge banks and so on.
9. Resolution cost principle issues: for insurers with a paybox mandate the main objective is to minimize payout costs. However, for those with a non-paybox mandate more choices were available such as the use of least-cost resolution objectives and methods, the optimal cost method, straight payout cost approaches and so on.
10. Timing of access to the deposit records: most paybox deposit insurers have access to the deposit records only after the banks are closed. But, for most non-paybox deposit insurers access to the records of depositors is granted before or at the time of banks closure or at the most a few days after closure.

Systemic banking crisis

Resolution powers and mandates in dealing with systemic banking crises

1. Statutory mechanism: among 34 countries, only seven countries had statutory mechanisms for handling a systemic banking crisis.
2. The definition of a systemic banking crisis used by most respondents included reference to the bank in question having a large national or regional market share (for example, exceeding 8 per cent-10 per cent or having a major influence on the economy or a financial system or regional economy and financial system. Or, if the resolution of a failing bank were conducted on a least cost basis and this would cause serious adverse effects on economic conditions or financial stability then it would be considered a systemically important bank.
3. Authority to decide: in cases where a bank closure were deemed to have systemic implications, the central bank was provided with authority in eight countries, the banking supervisory agency in eight countries, and the deposit insurer in two countries.
4. Funding source: the government and the central bank were the main funding sources for handling systemic banking crises.

Methods considered resolving a bank with systemic implications

The following are the methods considered by the respondents' government or deposit insurer to resolve a bank with systemic implications.

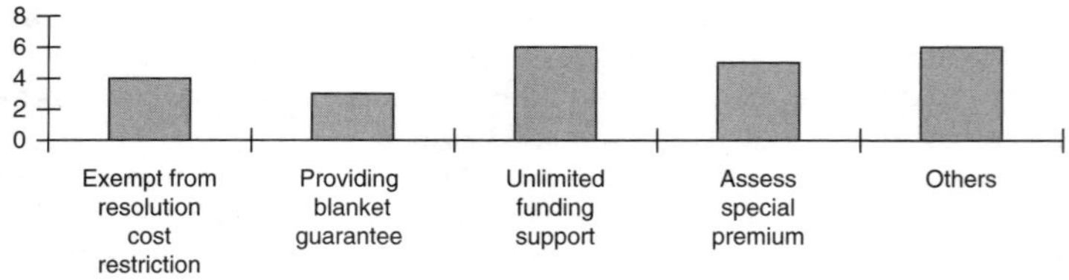

Figure 10A.22 Special regulation for deposit insurer in handling systemic banking crisis

1. Bridge bank transactions.
2. By P&A or bridge bank method, instead of direct payout.
3. Financial assistance.
4. Set up a fund to solve the banking crisis and individual bank failures.
5. By means of the adoption of special legislation.

Special regulations for a deposit insurer

According to the respondents here is a list of special regulations for the deposit insurer in handling a systemic banking crisis:

1. Four countries were exempted from resolution cost restrictions.
2. Three countries provided a blanket guarantee.
3. Six countries had unlimited funding support from the government or central bank.
4. Five countries assessed special premiums after a banking crisis.
5. Six countries responded to 'others': there was no special regulation.

Funding sources for handling systemic bank crises

According to the responses, the funding sources for handling systemic bank crises were as following:

1. Government special budget appropriations: 13 countries.
2. Issuing bonds: eight countries.
3. Central bank: 17 countries.
4. IMF, World Bank: three countries.
5. Others: eight countries.

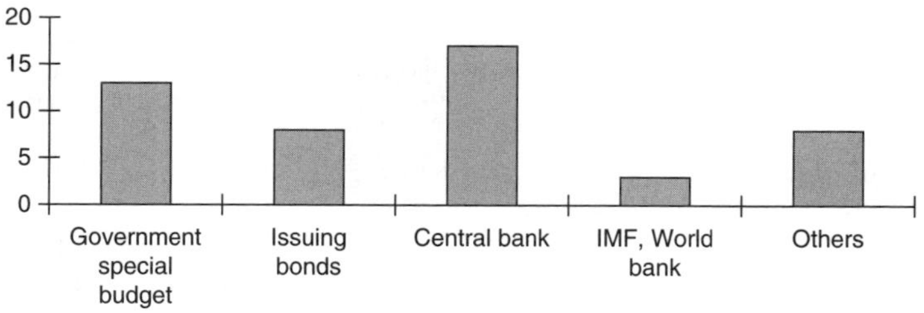

Figure 10A.23 Funding sources for handling systemic bank crisis

Gaps in the current law or practice in dealing with systemic banking crises

These were some suggestions from respondents to improve effectiveness when dealing with systemic banking crises:

1. The government or its authorities should be well empowered, with respect to regulatory powers, to promptly issue the necessary measures to contain a banking crisis.
2. In order to avoid a financial crisis and to maintain an orderly payment system, there should be recognition that in some situations rules which require that the cost of providing financial assistance to a failing bank be less than the cost of a payout need to be removed or suspended to deal with these types of systemic situations.

Cross-border issues

According to the survey, there were nine countries that had confronted the case of cross-border insolvency of a deposit-taking international institution. Only three countries responded to having relevant substantive laws to deal with such a cross-border insolvency issue.

Appendix 10A.2: Net resolution cost[a] in past ten years

Countries	Net resolution cost in past 10 years (USD)[b]	Percentage of GDP[c]	Base of GDP[d]	Main resolution method
Colombia	2,810,000,000	4.00%	2002 GDP	Reimbursement, Bridge bank, OBA
El Salvador	68,000,000	0.50%	–	–
Hungary	709,000	0.00%	2000 GDP	Reimbursement
Czech Republic	2,430,800	0.50%	–	Reimbursement
Russia	3,100,000,000	0.18%	1999 GDP	–
Brazil	20,400,000,000	2.70%	1995,1996,1997, 3-year average GDP	–
Japan	162,000,000,000	3.60%	2003 GDP	P&A
Canada	3,500,000,000	0.40%	–	Reimbursement, P&A
France	15,800,200	1.00%	–	Reimbursement,
Taiwan	2,640,000,000	0.93%	2001 GDP	P&A
Estonia	4,010,820	0.07%	1998 GDP	Reimbursement, P&A
Mexico	57,300,000,000	13.60%	1998 GDP	Reimbursement, OBA
Philippines	923,000,000	0.25%	1997–2001, 5-year average GDP	Reimbursement, P&A,OBA

(Continued)

Countries	Net resolution cost in past 10 years (USD)[b]	Percentage of GDP[c]	Base of GDP[d]	Main resolution method
Jamaica	2,630,000,000	35.80%	–	–
Korea	82,300,000,000	13.59%	2003 GDP	–
Venezuela	4,690,000,000	11.00%	–	Reimbursement, P&A,OBA

Notes: [a] The estimated net resolution cost refers to the costs borne by the deposit insurer, government, or others, minus proceeds received from asset disposition.
[b]The related currency was exchanged to USD based on the rate of September 16, 2004.
[c]The percentage of GDP was calculated and provided by questionnaire respondents and real GDP figure of each country was not provided.
[d]The base of GDP was provided by questionnaire respondents. Some countries used 3 or 5 years average GDP, while most countries used specific one year GDP.

Appendix 10A.3: Number of countries responding to questionnaire

Members

1. Brazil
2. Bulgaria
3. Canada: CDIC
4. Canada: Autorité des marchés financiers (Québec)
5. Colombia
6. Czech Republic
7. El Salvador
8. France
9. Hungary
10. Jamaica
11. Japan
12. Jordan
13. Kazakhstan
14. Kenya
15. Korea
16. Mexico
17. Philippines
18. Russia
19. Sweden
20. Taiwan
21. Tanzania
22. USA
23. Venezuela
24. Vietnam

Non-members

1. Chile
2. Cyprus
3. Finland
4. Estonia
5. Lithuania
6. Netherlands
7. Portugal
8. Slovenia
9. Spain
10. U.K.

Notes

1 Prepared by the IADI Subcommittee on Resolution of Bank Failures Research and Guidance Committee. The author would like to express his heartfelt gratitude

to all respondents who had the patience to complete the entire questionnaire on the Resolution of Bank Failures, as well as the members of the Subcommittee on the Resolution of Banks Failures, Research and Guidance Committee, International Association of Deposit Insurers (IADI). He particularly extends his gratitude to Mr David Walker (Canada Deposit Insurance Corporation) and Mr John Raymond LaBrosse (International Association of Deposit Insurers) for their remarkable comments and enlightenment. Besides, he would like to thank his colleagues for providing valuable assistance, including Mr Crown Chen, Ms Fiona Yeh, Ms Fu-ling Chiang, Mr Harrison Hwang, Ms Margaret Chuang, and Ms Yvonne Fan. Any errors are author's alone.

2 A total of 76 questionnaires were distributed on 3 June 2004, of which 34 were circulated to IADI members and 42 were circulated to non-IADI members. Thirty-four responses were received representing a 45 per cent response rate. Among the 34 respondents, 15 deposit insurers could be classified as primarily paybox types and 19 deposit insurers were classified as primarily non-paybox type deposit insurers or risk minimizers. The collected questionnaires were reviewed for completeness and logic and were processed by SPSS statistical software.

3 Regarding denominator GDP, some countries use the certain year GDP and the Philippines uses the 5-year average GDP.

4 This was multiple-choice.

5 This was multiple-choice.

6 If we need to define the relations among, 'unsound banking practices', 'inappropriate risk management' and 'poor corporate governance', one could say that 'inappropriate risk management' & 'poor governance' are the forms of 'unsound banking practices'.

7 The answer to the question was a multiple-choice.

8 The answer to the question was a multiple-choice.

9 The supervisory on-site examination criteria refer to the general appraisal methodology used by supervisory agency when conducting the on-site examination towards financial institutions. Liquidation criterion refers to the appraisal methodology used by liquidators to access the recovery value of a financial institution on a liquidation basis.

10 The answer to the question was a multiple-choice.

11 In Japan, a bridge bank's capital requirement is stipulated in the banking law, ¥1 billion capital at minimum to every bank.

References

Basel Committee (2000) *Supervisory Guidance on Dealing with Weak Banks*, Bank for International Settlements, April.

Bennett, R.L. (2001) *Failure Resolution and Asset Liquidation*, FDIC Banking Review, vol.14(1), pp 1–28.

Canada Deposit Insurance Corporation (2004) *APEC Policy Dialogue on Deposit Insurance: Policy Conclusions Paper*, Canada, June.

Federal Deposit Insurance Corporation (1998) *Managing the Crisis: The FDIC and RTC Experience 1980-1994*, FDIC, Washington, DC, August.

Financial Stability Forum (2001) *Guidance for Developing Effective Deposit Insurance Systems, Final Report of the Working Group on Deposit Insurance*, Basel, September.

Isoard, C. (2004) 'Handling Systemic Financial Crisis And Interrelationship Among Financial Safety Net Players,' paper presented at International Association of Deposit Insurers (IADI) 3rd Annual Conference, Brunnen, Switzerland, October 26–7.

Mackey, M. (2004) 'Disposition of Problem Financial Institutions/Non-performing Assets based on Market Mechanisms,' paper presented at International Association of Deposit Insurers (IADI) 3rd Annual Conference, Brunnen, Switzerland, October 26–7.

Nigeria Deposit Insurance Corporation (1997) *Bank Deposit Insurance in Nigeria,* Umoh, P.N. (ed.), NDIC, Nigeria.

Ogunleye, G. A. (2004) The Exit Mechanism And Resolution of Problem Financial Institutions, paper presented at International Association of Deposit Insurers (IADI) 3rd Annual Conference, Brunnen, Switzerland, October 26–7.

11

Responsibility without Power: Two Solutions to the Problem of Foreign-Owned Systemic Bank Branches [1]

David G. Mayes

As the process of economic integration has progressed small countries have increasingly found that their banks are foreign owned. This poses a potential problem for both prudential financial supervision and the maintenance of financial stability in those countries and thus potential costs both for deposit insurance and society at large. In most countries around the world the host country retains responsibility for supervising banks operating within its territory, even though they are foreign owned. However, responsibility for the parent bank and indeed the financial group or holding company will lie with the lead or consolidating supervisor in the home country, with whom the host will need to cooperate and share information. Under Basel 2, particularly Pillar 2, this cooperation is enhanced and the consolidating supervisor will be responsible for agreeing group-wide risk management procedures. In the EU/EEA, however, this host country responsibility only applies if the foreign-owned bank runs its operations through a subsidiary. If it chooses to operate directly or as a branch then the home country is responsible for supervision (and deposit insurance, subject to a topping up provision).[2] However, there is no matching migration of responsibility for financial stability; that remains firmly with the host country. This is *prima facie* a recipe for a serious difficulty should the system come under strain.

While the scale of branch operation remains small this may appear to be a limited problem, as the failure of the branch would not lead to a systemic event and the exposures of different foreign owned banks operating through branches may not be particularly correlated. However, the Nordic–Baltic countries and Finland in particular, face the prospect that much of their banking system may be operated as branches of foreign banks. Nordea, the most cross-border of the large European banks has announced that it intends to take advantage of the European Company Statute and operate as a single entity, headquartered in Sweden with branches in Denmark, Estonia,

Finland and Norway. As is clear from Box 11.1 (see p. 274) it is a systemic bank in all of these countries, in some cases more so in the host than the home country. This raises two immediate questions:

- will the host country authorities have enough information about their banking system that they feel they can convincingly maintain systemic stability?
- will the host country authorities be able to do enough to maintain stability should a problem occur?

However, the problem is symmetric. The home country, although well informed, is responsible for a bank, most of whose operations are in other countries. Could it handle an event that is systemic both at home and abroad? Switzerland, for example, has already recognised that its deposit insurance fund might be exposed to unsustainable pressure in the event of a serious problem with UBS or Crédit Suisse and has placed a cap on the payout.[3] Normally a systemic bank is regarded as one which is in some sense 'too big to fail'[4] but in these cross-border cases we may have banks that are in some sense 'too big to save'. Considerable thought has gone into the handling of cross-border banks, both in normal times and in a crisis, not least through the two Brouwer reports in the European context (EFC, 2000, 2001), but the proposals, while identifying the issues clearly, fall well short of what will be required in the more extreme examples of interdependence. There is a danger that problems with such banks might be too difficult to sort out in time and in that sense (too big to fail). Indeed one of the recommendations in Brouwer *et al.* (2003) is that the authorities should 'buy time' by offering some form of support to the institution but how they should agree to do that and what form that should take beyond the emergency liquidity assistance that central banks can offer is not spelt out. This is a recipe for a systemic problem unless it is sorted out in advance.

Clearly in the Nordic–Baltic case the authorities need to cooperate and are well on the way to sorting out a solution. Because of the structure of their economies and their financial regulatory systems, it is likely that their interests will be reasonably well aligned in a systemic event and that it is unlikely that the home country will not face a systemic problem at the same time as the hosts even if the intensity is different. However, we are discussing just one bank and there is no reason why this symmetry should apply to all cross-border banks. Home and host could easily have differing interests under imminent or actual default. Handling the problem is assisted in the EU/EEA case because of the requirement for equal treatment of all depositors and other creditors and the common pool approach to the distribution of the assets under the principle of universality. If the home country could apply territoriality or otherwise discriminate against the creditors and depositors in the host country then such an arrangement would not work. This is clearly the case in New Zealand, where the majority of banks are Australian owned and Australia operates domestic depositor preference.[5]

In this case, the authorities have to work out how to apply territoriality in a satisfactory manner so that they can handle systemic events separately. Indeed New Zealand has gone rather further in recognizing the need to have an entity that can be self-sustaining in the host country. Although New Zealand now insists that systemic banks be locally incorporated (something the EU/EEA countries cannot do) it has gone much further with what is described as an Outsourcing Policy (RBNZ, 2006). This requires that all systemic banks must be structured so that they can continue in operation without a break even if a major external service provider fails. To a large extent this means that they have to be able to operate on their own (or with other providers) even if other parts of the banking group were to fail. This limits the degree to which banks can integrate but apparently in the Australasian environment the ability to consolidate Australian and New Zealand functions has been quite limited – rather less than the banks originally hoped. More importantly in the present context, the 'outsourcing' requirements mean that were the bank to fail, the authorities could also step in and keep the bank running as an entity in New Zealand without a break in business. This ability reflects not just the outsourcing policy but the powers of the Reserve Bank in the event of failure, whereby it can step in and appoint a statutory manager who can make a summary valuation, write down the claims so the bank returns to solvency and stay open with a guarantee against further loss under administration. These powers are also different from those that prevail in most of the EU/EEA countries and are an important contribution to having a credible means of handling problems of potentially systemic proportions without threatening financial stability.

These moves in New Zealand towards ensuring a workable solution for ensuring financial stability in the face of a problem in a foreign owned systemic bank have generated some opposition among the banks, which has been reflected in concerns at the political level.[6] As a result, Australia and New Zealand are engaged in discussions which could move them more towards an EU/EEA solution whereby both countries' interests both for individual creditors and depositors and for systemic stability are jointly and equitably taken into account both in avoiding problems and in solving them. In the Nordic–Baltic case the move is in a sense in the opposite direction, as in the current EU/EEA framework the joint arrangements for avoiding and correcting these problems are not sufficiently workable to provide adequate comfort that systemic level events will be handled adequately and that the national authorities can deliver their obligations to financial stability. While the two approaches may not meet in the middle this chapter explores the lessons they have to offer each other in resolving the difficulty.

The structure of the chapter is therefore as follows. Section 11.1 sets out the nature of the problem faced by the authorities in the Nordic–Baltic region by the case of Nordea and extends this more widely to the handling of other cross-border banks across the whole of the EU/EEA. In particular, it sets out an approach which argues that the only way to have satisfactory procedures in place in advance to handle bank distress in a way that will not threaten the financial stability of the countries concerned is to have adequate cooperation on all of the stages of regulation and supervision, from normal times, through poor performance, non-compliance and the need for prompt corrective action, right down to the procedures for handling exit themselves. Unless the early stages of correction, finding a private sector solution and early intervention work well and minimize the potential demands on public funds, the prospects for avoiding a systemic crisis will be weak. Section 11.2 then sets out the lessons that can be learned from the New Zealand approach, which is effectively based on the assumption that cross-border coordination will be difficult and hence the host country has to have in place a regime where it can handle the threat of a systemic event, whatever the level of successful international cooperation. The final section offers some reflections.

11.1 Putting together a framework

In many countries the framework for financial regulation, supervision, the treatment of problems and the handling of systemic events has been put together in a series of steps, rather than being the result of a single process of careful design. In particular, major changes have tended to be the result of unfortunate experience, be it the Savings and Loan crisis that led to FIDICIA in the USA, or the Nordic crises. The rethink in Australia with the Wallis Commission (1997) is rather more unusual, although a number of European countries, such as Ireland and the Netherlands, have changed their structures in recent years without any immediate pressures. The decision by Nordea to move to adopting the European Company Statute is therefore a welcome opportunity to rethink aspects of the system without the pressures of an imminent, current or recent crisis. In this case what we need to rethink is how a system designed primarily for a closed national environment, where the ownership and management of the banks, location of their borrowers, depositors and creditors, and the wider systemic impact on taxpayers and society at large all fell within the same jurisdiction, should be extended to one which is primarily cross-border.

It is not just a matter of whether the hopefully rare (nonexistent) systemically important crises can be handled satisfactorily in prospect but whether the whole framework of joint operation from bank regulation, registration and supervision, through to prompt corrective action and resolution will operate well. Handling difficulties involves the painful process of allocating losses and unless the authorities are convinced that the procedures for avoiding and minimizing the losses were satisfactorily handled by the other administrations involved with the cross-border banks in question they will find agreement on burden sharing at the time difficult. In a crisis there is no time for fundamental argument and the process of initial resolution at any rate needs to take place within the settlement 'day' on which the failure becomes known to the authorities.[7] It is therefore essential that the opportunity for a set of recriminations over whose fault the problem is and a debate over fair distribution of losers and beneficiaries is minimized. As has been emphasized before, the earlier in the process the authorities can intervene and hence the smaller the losses, the easier it will be to resolve debates over equity.[8] If the position is up in the air this is unlikely to be 'constructive ambiguity' but a threat to the viability of deposit insurance schemes and recipe for a crisis rather than for its avoidance.

The authorities who are between them facing possible systemic outcomes from problems in a particular bank need to be convinced that the framework will function well in all circumstances, which we can effectively divide into five for the purposes of analysis:

1. Normal times when the bank is regulatorily compliant and performing competitively in the market.
2. Difficult times, when, although the bank is regulatorily compliant, it is underperforming in the market.
3. Problems, when the bank has become undercapitalized and the authorities require action if the bank is to remain in business.
4. Systemic events, when although the bank is itself regulatorily compliant its viability is affected by outside shocks to the system.
5. Actual or imminent default when the bank can no longer continue in normal operation and the authorities have to step in.

Most of the discussion, both in practice and in the literature, focuses on Case 1, whether in the organization of supervision under Basel 2 or across Europe.[9] However, this is not the most difficult area to sort out. With some exceptions we discuss shortly, this is well on the way to agreement in the case of Nordea. Similarly the arrangements for handling system-wide shocks are also well advanced. The Eurosystem has had a Memorandum of Understanding on how to organize Emergency Liquidity Assistance since 2003 and the Nordic banks are clear on how the responsibilities go and how they coordinate in the event of market problems, whether they are in the payments system or other parts of the infrastructure. They have conducted joint simulation exercises for the handling of such cross-border problems. The remainder are less well addressed at the cross-border level, although for different reasons.

For ease of exposition, we take these five steps in turn.

Normal times

A cross-border bank, even though operating through branches, has problems of compliance with host country regulations, particularly in the areas of tax and conduct of business. The issue of prudential regulation is, however, much more straightforward in the EU/EEA. Here compliance is the responsibility of the consolidating supervisor, who will be the home country authority – in Nordea's case, Sweden. It is for the Swedish Finansinspektionen to work out with the other supervisors how it wants to run the new structure of supervision to come into force after 2006 and a working group already exists, which in any case has the task of working out how to handle joint supervision under Basel 2. The Swedish authority could in theory just employ its own local staff, presumably recruited from among the ranks of the newly unemployed supervisors in the other countries, since being able to speak the local language and having some experience are essential. The other authorities would then only gain access to information about Nordea officially through what the Swedish authority disclosed under the present or some new MoU. Thus although the Finnish authority remains responsible in its charter for the stability of the financial system it would be only supervising half of the banking activity (given that some (non-systemic) foreign banks already operate through branches).

To operate systemic responsibilities realistically in the host countries it will be necessary to have the same sorts of information available on Nordea that they have on their own home country banks. The Finnish authorities have suggested that the way to do this is to have a 'college' of supervisors under Swedish leadership who have access to a common database (Vesala, 2005), an idea also promoted by the European Financial Services Round Table (2004). Thus the supervisors from the various countries would be jointly responsible for the supervision of Nordea and through the common database would have access to information on the other parts of the group as well as those within its own national boundaries. This would actually increase the information available but would make it more relevant from the point of view of assessing stability. There are other options through agency agreements and the like but some form of voluntary closer arrangement than that laid down under the current home-host rules in the EU will be required if the systemic concerns are to be satisfied. As Vesala (2005) points out, the practical differences between a bank operating as a subsidiary and the same bank operating as a branch are likely to be small and hence having a substantial change in supervisory arrangements between the two circumstances does not *prima facie* seem logical. If the change is necessary for the branch arrangement then it was probably also necessary for the subsidiary arrangement or, conversely, if the arrangements for the subsidiary structure were satisfactory little change is needed for a switch to branch status. The EU legislation introduces an artificial divide.

Exactly the same argument applies to the home country supervisor. It needs to be fully informed of the risks and trends in the markets of the host countries where the cross-border bank has significant exposures. The joint access to information needs to be two-way – and timely in the sense that all have access to the information at the same time.

Although there has been substantial regulatory convergence among the different countries involved with the systemic risks associated with Nordea, assisted by the work of CEBS, this will represent a step up in the level of regulatory competition, with consumers being able to make a very real choice between banks from different regimes. There is no discussion of creating a new Nordic-Baltic level supervisory authority, although that might be the most straightforward way to address a common issue. Given the size of the region this would not be larger than some regulators that already exist in Europe. To some extent this is because there is no great wish to spend considerable effort creating regional institutions when there may be changes at the European level. However, creating a European supervisory authority, even if it were only to have a coordinating or monitoring role, has not been actively discussed outside the academic literature (Schoenmaker and Oosterloo, 2007). The bigger the difference in regulatory and supervisory practices then the more difficult it is for there to be a joint regulatory arrangement or a delegation of responsibility from one regime to the other. In the EU/EEA as a whole some of the differences are still substantial.

There are still a number of wrinkles to be sorted out before an agreement can be reached, one of which relates to deposit insurance. Although all of the EU/EEA members have to have deposit insurance up to a certain minimum standard under the Deposit Insurance Directive, [10] there is a wide range of options that govern how that can be organized, what the coverage should be beyond the minimum in terms of types of account, size of deposit, whether the scheme is industry owned, how quickly it pays out, what extent it is funded, whether contributions are risk-based – the list is long. The conditions of the Nordic and Baltic countries are by no means the same (Sigurdsson, 2003, Appendix, pp.158–62). A bank operating in another EU country can apply to join the local fund to top up its insurance to the locally prevailing level to avoid being at a competitive disadvantage. (There is no corresponding opportunity to worsen it except through choice of corporate form.) Who is responsible for deposit insurance matches the responsibility for supervision, so Nordea would need to switch to the Swedish scheme. [11] However, under current rules that would involve making new contributions to the Swedish scheme, as it is not possible to withdraw the contributions to the other funds and transfer them. Not surprisingly Nordea would like the rules changed and the current review of the Deposit Insurance Directive (European Commission, 2005) might eventually offer such an opportunity.

It is also worth noting that since deposit insurance is intended to provide comfort to depositors outside the institution in trouble, so that there are not runs on healthy banks that cause a systemic crisis, depositors themselves have to be convinced that the home country is going to offer that protection if the primary cause of the problem is in a domestic institution. Thus the deposit insurer would need to be offering credible protection against the consequence of events outside its control. Where that is a large exposure, there could be doubts and people might fear the ex post imposition of a cap along Swiss lines, for example.

Box 11.1 The Nordea case

The Nordea Banking Group, which is currently headquartered in Sweden and has banks in Norway, Denmark, Sweden and Finland, branches in other countries including Estonia, Poland, Singapore and a branch in New York, an investment services arm and an insurance company, is planning to take advantage of the European Company Statute after it comes into force in October 2004 and operate as a single bank based in Sweden with branches in all the other countries by some time in 2006. This is likely to be the first such move by a major international bank and will be a substantial departure from the traditional parent and subsidiary model, even though that itself is rather poor description of the way many international financial services are organized complex groupings. Nordea is clearly of systemic importance. As at March 2004 it had a 40 per cent share of the Finnish banking market, 25 per cent of the Danish, 20 per cent of the Swedish and 15 per cent of the Norwegian. Its share of the insurance markets was somewhat smaller: Finland 35 per cent, Denmark 20 per cent, Norway 9 per cent and Sweden 6 per cent.[12] (It also had a 9 per cent share of the Estonian banking market but only 2 per cent of the insurance market, the latter being clearly of less than systemic proportions.)

The current framework for supervision and the treatment of the solvent bank is straightforward. Each of the constituent banks is supervised by the authorities in its country of location (host) and the group is supervised in Sweden. The same applies to the parts of the insurance arm, although in Finland, at any rate, it is a separate supervisor. However, beyond that the structure becomes more complicated. Nordea Bank (Finland) has the branch in New York and the branch in Estonia.

There is thus overlapping responsibility. In the New York case the branch is supervised by the Finnish authority (Rahoitustarkastus), the New York Fed and New York state authorities. All are involved in on-site inspections. In the Estonian case the position changed on 1 May 2004 when Estonia joined the EU. Up till then the position was similar to New York with overlapping supervision. Now Estonia, in theory, has no role in prudential supervision but in practice Rahoitustarkatus has agreed with Finantsinspektsioon in Estonia that the latter will continue in its previous role, effectively as its agent, until the wider arrangement is put in place. (Conduct of business regulation is still a national concern and hence the supervisory authorities would continue to have some role under any arrangement.)

Poor market performance

Ideally, poor market performance by a bank would be sorted out by normal market forces – market discipline. Its market price would fall, it would lose business and ultimately it would be bought by a competitor. However, once we get to banks of systemic size they are already pushing the limits of concentration in the market and it is unlikely that their immediate competitors would be allowed to purchase them outside a crisis even if they could raise the funds to do so. It would have to be a large bank that was not currently a major player in the markets where this cross-border bank operated that could step in. How possible this would be is somewhat debatable and as recent events have shown, there are difficulties buying in to some European countries, Italy in particular.[13] To some extent, of course, the pressure on the bank will come through the existing shareholders as they see their returns waning and through the management who see the chance of losing their jobs increasing. Stakeholders in the bank need both to be able to monitor effectively how the bank is performing and to take action if they regard performance as inadequate.[14] It is also debatable whether the amount and relevance of information publicly available permits this, despite the role of ratings agencies and subordinated debt markets.[15] Market discipline as the result of extensive public disclosure is the second pillar of the New Zealand framework after the control of registration of banks. Insofar as it does not work well it puts increased pressure on the supervisory authorities who will always be at one remove from the market and hence will tend to be slower and less efficient in the task.

There has not been an extensive debate in Europe or in the Nordic-Baltic region in particular about whether the forces of market discipline are adequate. Margins are relatively high in a number of the Nordic countries (Bank of Finland, 2005; Koskenkylä, 2004), which suggests that perhaps this is not the case, although it may assist in the creation of strong banks.

Emerging problems

One of the consequences of FIDICIA in the USA has been that there is clear path of Prompt Corrective Action (PCA) as part of a sequence of Structured Early Intervention and Resolution (SEIR) laid down for the authorities should a bank become undercapitalized. On the one hand the bank is given a timetable to recapitalize and on the other there are restrictions on its actions, which limit its ability to take on increased risk and prevent the shareholders from extracting capital from the bank in order to improve their position in the event of eventual closure. As the capital ratio falls so the requirements and restrictions become harsher until the point is reached that the bank has to be closed within 90 days if it becomes 'critically undercapitalized'. This final intervention takes place when the leverage ratio falls below 2 per cent so it is not actually a requirement that the bank be insolvent in the sense that its creditors could not be paid out in full, although this has normally turned out to be the case.

Other countries have similar requirements but they are not normally so transparent nor so mandatory. Furthermore, one of the motivations behind FIDICIA was to restrict the ability of the FDIC to offer open bank assistance (Helfer, 1999),[16] that is, forms of support for the bank that enable it to keep open even though it is not regulatorily compliant. Some European countries, among them Finland, have used open bank assistance in recent years (Moe *et al.*, 2004) and, hence, even though this may now be more difficult, especially since direct subsidies are not permitted in the EU and have been challenged successfully in the cases of Crédit Lyonnais and the German LandesBanken, for example, it is by no means clear that banks believe that such support will not be forthcoming in the future. Indeed, there will no doubt be political pressures for this to occur. Joint rules for PCA are not in place in the Nordic-Baltic region and since different approaches were followed in the Nordic crises it seems likely that one authority would not necessarily act in the same way as another under pressure.

This opens up the opportunity for a dispute if a systemic bank were to reach insolvency, as a host might claim that the home country had not done enough to force recapitalization say by merger and acquisition.[17] If the owners hoped for a bailout they might well resist an acquisition that they would accept if they were more certain that the alternative was that their share value was wiped out entirely.[18] One of the big differences in the European environment is the role of the deposit insurance fund. There is no equivalent of the FDIC. In many countries the deposit insurer is simply a paybox with virtually no staff. The Finnish Deposit Insurer, Talletussuojarahasto, for example, is run by the Finnish Bankers Association, Pankkiyhdistus, it has one part-time employee. (The Swedish Deposit Insurer, Insättningsgarantinämnden, has two employees.) This is somewhat different from the FDIC which has 5,200 employees, even allowing for the 60-fold difference in population or the size of insured deposits or number of banks. The Nordea case is thus somewhat easier to address than other cross-border groupings might be. The German deposit insurance system for example operates more in the form of an industry club (Beck, 2003). Since it is financed by the banks they have tended to try to find a least-cost solution and as a result to find a way to takeover the bank without having to go as far as the costs of insolvency. Such a system can work if the banks in trouble are relatively small compared to the rest of the industry. It largely meets the requirements of a market-based solution although it no doubt favours domestic over foreign acquirers.

Ironically the difficulties are in some respects greater if the cross-border bank is operating through subsidiaries and not branches. Then different authorities are responsible for different parts of the organization, some may prefer one form of resolution to another and try to enforce it in separate proceedings. However, unless the bank is truly divisible in the New Zealand sense, dismemberment may be difficult without promoting just the systemic event it is hoped to avoid. Having a cross-border bank that is operating through branches enforces a prior cooperative arrangement, which probably is a better match for the actual structure of the bank as the opportunity for independent decision under insolvency may be illusory but not fully apparent until it is tried – unsuccessfully.

A second way to try to ensure prompt corrective action is the 'four eyes' principle. In this case both the supervisor and the deposit insurance fund will be examining the bank in difficulty. The deposit insurance fund would be setting up the procedures necessary for an orderly resolution of the bank should the point of insolvency (or other compulsory intervention, such as the 2 per cent leverage ratio in the USA) be reached. The most important aspect of this is trying to get a basis for a rapid valuation of the claims as this will be needed in the first step of resolution. Since the deposit insurance organization may not have the capability for doing this in many European countries, the alternative might be to create a 'resolution agency'. This might be particularly suitable in cases like Nordea. The agency could be bank specific. As is clear from Table 11.1 drawn from Schoenmaker and Oosterloo (2007)[19] the number of such banks is quite small and different groups of authorities need to come to an agreement under a particular consolidator or leader in the home country. The terms of that agreement and the approach to any potential burden sharing, such as the consequences of any guarantees that are to be made with respect to the new entity after intervention, could vary from case to case. The countries involved in the Nordea case cannot wait for Europe-wide agreement otherwise they would run the risk of holding up the restructuring and greater efficiency of the bank for an indefinite period.

One might want to go further and argue for a European resolution agency or even European Deposit Insurance Corporation but their likelihood seems relatively small. The national authorities seem to be quite firmly wedded to their current arrangements. However, having the second authority involved helps align the incentives better. For the supervisory agency there will always be an element of worrying that bank failure is equated with supervisory failure and hence a temptation to delay final action if it is plausible. Moreover the supervisor normally has to balance the interests of a number of groups in society of whom the insured depositors/deposit insurance fund is only one. The central bank is perhaps the obvious alternative choice for siting the resolution agency as its interests are also in bringing the problem to a head early so that systemic problems can be minimized. This could pose a problem where the central bank is also the supervisor, although it need not be so as the New Zealand case illustrates.

System-wide problems

One area were there is little need for discussion is emergency lending by the central bank in the Eurosystem and more widely in Europe. It has been agreed that lending will be on the traditional Bagehotian terms: collateralized, short term and at an above market rate of interest. In the Eurosystem the list

Table 11.1 Categories of banking groups (top 30 EU banks in 2003)

Category	Banking group	h(in %)	e(in %)
European	Deutsche Bank	25	41
	Nordea Group	28	71
	ABN AMRO	28	36
	KBC Bank	40	40
	Fortis Group	44	28
	BNP Paribas	47	25
	Westdeutsche Landesbank	48	43
	HypoVereinsbank	48	33
	Groupe Caisse d'Epargne	50	38
International	HSBC Holdings	24	6
	ING Group	29	24
	Banco Bilbao Vizcaya Argentaria	44	3
	Santander Central Hispano	45	16
Domestic	Dexia	54	37
	Société Générale	56	21
	Dresdner Bank	59	29
	Crédit Agricole Groupe	61	19
	UniCredit	71	13
	Bayerische Landesbank	72	14
	Commerzbank	75	15
	Rabobank	75	9
	Crédit Lyonnais	77	8
	Royal Bank of Scotland	77	5
	Banca Intesa	78	10
	Barclays	80	8
	HBOS	91	5
	Lloyds TSB Group	94	3
	Abbey National	97	3
	Crédit Mutuel	n.a.	n.a.
	Groupe Banques Populaires	n.a.	n.a.

Source: Schoenmaker and Oosterloo (2007).
Notes: 'Home' is defined as a bank's business in its home country (denoted by *h*); 'Rest of Europe' is defined as a bank's business in other European countries (denoted by *e*); 'Rest of the world' is defined as a bank's business outside Europe (these figures are not shown). The three categories add up to 100 per cent. Banks in each category are ranked according to the share of their international business. The abbreviation 'n.a.' means 'not available'.

of eligible collateral has been agreed in advance and in the Nordea case there is already a Memorandum of Understanding among the Nordic central banks that establishes how each lends in the circumstances and how they coordinate. There should thus be only a limited chance of lending to an insolvent institution. In any case the expectation is that such lending will be general to the market rather than to a single institution as the chance of market lending to a solvent institution drying up is small. Similarly this restricts the number of players in the resolution process as the routes to accessing public money will be limited.

This facet of generalized action applies more widely to systemic problems. Many can be addressed by macro-economic policy rather than by intervention in the banking system *per se*. Nevertheless it is clear that if major problems arise more extreme measures are taken whatever the prior rules.[20] It is not at all clear how this might be applied to cross-border banks, especially if the systemic problem is in the host country. A natural reaction of a foreign bank might be to curtail its exposures which in itself would contribute to worsening the crisis. Firms (and households) that might otherwise expect to roll over their lending may find themselves forced to close or to realize their assets prematurely at heavily discounted prices, thereby lowering collateral values and pushing others into imbalance or insolvency – the typical debt-deflation problem (King, 1994).

Failure

The solution to the problem if a bank becomes insolvent or reaches the intervention point depends very much on the powers of the authorities to act. There are strong attractions to having a *lex specialis* or public law under which an Authority such as the supervisor or the deposit insurance agency can step in, as is the case in the USA, Canada, New Zealand, Switzerland[21] and Italy for example, as opposed to having banks subject to a *lex generalis*, private law, as in much of the rest of Europe, including Germany and England and Wales. The *lex specialis* approach in effect transfers some of the judicial functions that need to be applied to the authority, enabling it to act with the necessary speed. However, this in itself is one of the main objections raised by some of those who support the *lex generalis* approach[22] in that those adversely affected may not be given adequate opportunity to defend their position.

In Mayes *et al.* (2001) we argue that an effective exit policy requires all of the previous facets of good regulation and supervision that we have just described to be in place. However, should they be insufficient and the bank still approach insolvency, we argue that the necessary process entails three steps:[23]

- The authorities are required to step in and take control of the bank under the provisions of public law at some prescribed benchmark, with the objective of maximizing the value of the bank/minimizing the systemic cost.
- The administrator who is appointed as a result of the first step summarily values the assets and liabilities of the bank as of time of failure and writes down the claims, respecting the order of priority of claimants under insolvency, so as to return the bank to 'economic solvency' (non-negative net worth). This would involve the wiping out of the claims of the existing

shareholders first and probably the subordinated debt holders but how much further the write off would have to go is debatable. Even in the case of the largest failure in the USA, Continental Illinois, it was possible to pay out 96 per cent of claims eventually even after allowing for the costs of the insolvency. There are various ways to perform this restructuring, which can in effect transform the claims from debt in the old bank to equity in the new one, as set out by Aghion *et al.* (1992) for example. The important feature is that no party should be worse off than under insolvency. There are some major problems in how such a rapid assessment and restructuring would be made as discussed *inter alia* by Harrison (2004).[24] In particular, it is necessary to avoid any triggering of close out netting in derivatives markets or other contract closures through rating downgrades, otherwise just the systemic event which is being guarded against will occur. Hüpkes (2004) suggests an alternative way of treating the same problem by addressing only what she describes as the systemic functions of the bank in this manner, that is, one whose failure would have systemic consequences.

- The bank reopens for business under the new control/ownership the next 'day' without any material break in operation, with a guarantee against further loss. (This concept is described in the context of the New Zealand approach in the next section.) Thus the operation of the bank continues but the ownership does not.

The rapidity of the process will no doubt result in some errors of assessment that need to be corrected if they have deprived holders of value – this would even apply to the former shareholders if it were discovered that the bank did in fact have positive net worth. However, the transfer of ownership would be irreversible. Errors of overvaluation would have to be borne by the authorities under the terms of the guarantee.[25] The earlier the resolution agency can enter the bank before the point of intervention is reached the greater the accuracy of the assessment is likely to be. Many other preconditions have to be met for this system to be operational, such as clear and reliable auditing standards, freedom from political interference, which apply in the EU/EEA countries but not necessarily elsewhere.

While Mayes *et al.* (2001) argue that fixed mandatory intervention points are needed in order to reduce the risk of forbearance and ensure that there is no delay, the Swiss scheme has implemented a more discretionary approach for exactly the same reasons (Hüpkes, 2003, p. 251). They permit intervention if the authorities in the form of the Swiss Federal Banking Commission (SFBC) deem that there is a threat to depositors' interests. Severe undercapitalization is not the only threat and hence it is possible to intervene in a bank earlier before it gets to the point of zero net worth if the threat seems real enough.

Implementing this scheme for a cross-border bank entails that it needs to be treated as a single entity (common pool) and that an administrator can act rapidly and early. This could not be achieve by a 'committee' approach and entails that one body has to be in charge with a predetermined mandate from the various countries and authorities involved – hence the previous suggestions about a resolution agency or at least a designated authority among those currently involved, preferably with a clear mandate to minimize the loss rather than the more mixed objectives that may face the supervisors. As suggested, the presumption is that this would be an authority based in the home country although it could be in some sense neutral, say, by being a European institution. Clearly it will need to draft in staff from the host countries to deal with the local legal environment, communicate with the claimants in their own language and so on.

11.2 The antipodean approach

Although New Zealand's banks are almost entirely foreign owned, largely with Australian parents (RBNZ, 2005a), New Zealand faces circumstances that differ crucially from the EU/EEA environment. First of all it does not have depositor protection. Second, Australia operates domestic depositor preference so New Zealand depositors would be disadvantaged in a common pool, universalist resolution operated from Australia. If it wants to manage the impact of a closure or other form of resolution it therefore has to go for a territorial approach that will be effective. Hence it is insisting that the banks operating in New Zealand be viable entities in their own right that could be operated independently should the parent group get into difficulty, if they are of large enough size that their failure would be a systemic threat to the New Zealand financial system.[26] This last remark reflects a clear advantage that New Zealand has over its host country counterparts in the EU/EEA in that it can lay down its own conditions for registration of a bank that allow it to operate a credible exit regime.

New Zealand already has had in place, since 1996, a clear regime setting out how problem banks will be treated, which follows very closely the same principles set out in Mayes *et al.* (2001). The Reserve Bank Act empowers the Reserve Bank, as the supervisor, to apply to the courts for the appointment of a statutory manager to take over the operation of an insolvent bank. At the same time the Reserve Bank has made it clear that public money would not be available in the event of such a failure. Over the ensuing years it has made clearer how the process of resolution would be likely to go – assuming that is that prior attempts to get the bank to recapitalize either through an injection from the existing shareholders or agreed outside injection through acquisition have failed.

The RBNZ requires in its policy on 'Outsourcing' (RBNZ, 2005b) that the bank (or a statutory manager) could ensure that:

- The bank's clearing and settlement obligations due on a day can be met on that day.
- The bank's financial risk positions on a day can be identified on that day.
- The bank's financial risk positions can be monitored and managed on the day following any failure and on subsequent days.
- The bank's existing customers can be given access to payments facilities on the day following any failure and on subsequent days.

This requires a 'legal and practical ability to control and execute' these functions. Hence this includes having personnel with the necessary technical and business knowledge and physical access to and control of the required systems and data. There are also requirements to make sure that the bank is managed from within New Zealand and that the New Zealand Board has control over it.

The reason for the use of the word outsourcing is simply that the RBNZ expects that bank groups will want to rationalize their functions as far as is cost efficient across the group and hence want to ensure that while permitting that process they do not expose the New Zealand financial system to any undue threat were some system-provider inside or outside the group to fail.

These arrangements permit the RBNZ to be convinced that in the effect of failure it could continue to have a viable prospect of keeping the systemic banks open under the normal terms of statutory management. However, applying territoriality and dismemberment in this fashion is not perhaps in line with the ideal way in which one might chose the operate the closer economic relations (CER) that Australia and New Zealand have been developing over an extended number of years with a view to creating a single economic market. In recent years there has been developing cooperation with the Australian Prudential Regulatory Authority (APRA). They have a Memorandum of Understanding on information sharing for crisis management purposes[27] and a new Trans-Tasman Council on Banking Supervision has been set up to develop further cooperation. APRA as the supervisor of the banking groups also has the power to conduct inspections of their operations in New Zealand. In 2004 there was a joint committee among the two countries' treasuries and reserve banks and APRA to explore the possibilities for closer cooperation, that consider a model of APRA being the sole supervisor and an enhancement to the prevailing home-host arrangements. The latter was the chosen route. A second committee that reported in February 2005 extended this to consider adding a joint committee to assist in harmonization of regulation and the option of a joint regulator. This led to the formation of the Trans-Tasman Council on Banking Supervision.

While it might appear at first blush that the two countries were good candidates for joint system, they are considerably further apart in the way in which the operate supervision than is the case among the Nordic-Baltic countries. Australia operates a traditional relatively intrusive supervisory approach, with regular on-site inspections. New Zealand on the other hand, with a tradition of more light-handed supervision, opted for a largely disclosure-based regime in 1996, with a requirement for all banks to make a quarterly public disclosure of their structures, recent accounts and balance sheets, peak exposures to related and other parties and so on, with a view to imposing greater market discipline. The banks are, of course, similarly required to be fully compliant with standards well up to the Basel Committee norms. The disclosure regime is a means of enforcing that, with all directors being liable for the correctness of the disclosure, whether they are executive or non-executive. While they can be sent to prison for up to three years for infringements they can also be civilly liable for losses incurred as a result of failures to ensure accurate disclosure. This provides a strong incentive for those who know and can control the activities of the bank to ensure prudence.

Marrying these two systems would not really be possible and the only plausible joint solution would probably be the adoption of a version of the Australian system, given the country's much larger size and need to supervise local banks that are not systemic in New Zealand. This makes an agreement on joint supervision less likely. Whether the same would apply to crisis resolution is also debatable. The current regime is for cooperation while each country tries to deal with its own problems. Any joint approach would require a prior agreement in burden sharing. If the previous supervision is conducted on different bases then it would be more difficult to agree in advance on steps to be taken in the event of difficulty except in very general terms.

11.3 Mutual lessons

The antipodes provide an illustration of how a host country can protect its own financial stability and power to act on systemic problems despite the fact its banking system is foreign owned. This approach is not possible in the EU/EEA because the host country does not have such a control over the registration of banks whose home is elsewhere in the area. Secondly, if the banks choose to operate as branches their supervision and some of the associated safety net also becomes the responsibility of the home country. This creates a serious mismatch with the host country's continuing responsibility for financial stability within its borders. There is thus no choice but to cooperate closely and thoroughly if a jointly acceptable scheme is to be found, probably involving substantial harmonization of the detail of regulation and supervision. While this may be possible for the Nordic-Baltic region and the case of Nordea in particular, this would be much more difficult to extend generally as there are far greater differences between the member states at all stages of the process from registration to exit regimes.

Thus in one sense the antipodes offer a plan B, if it does not prove possible to get the closer cooperation to work well. However, such a plan B would represent a major step backwards for authorities bent on forming a single market. In another sense they show the difficulty of achieving such cooperation. The EU/EEA on the other hand offers the possibility that some measure of closer cooperation may be possible in the Antipodean environment.

What is clear is that the intention of Nordea to become a European company brings to the surface a problem in home-host control that already exists as the material change to the operation of the company is likely to be relatively small, although the legal and taxation problems may be reduced. Moving to a branch structure will to a considerable extent be recognizing the reality of the structure of the company. Although most of the branches are currently incorporated as subsidiaries they are in many cases more dependent and would not meet the outsourcing criteria laid down by the New Zealand authorities. Thus it is largely an illusion that a systemic problem could be sorted out any better before the change in legal structure than it could afterwards. The changes advocated, with greater regulatory harmonization, a more collegial approach to supervision and data sharing, more scope for market discipline, more transparent and agreed PCA, and reform of the laws governing insolvencies so that a single agency can step in early and act swiftly on a predetermined mandate, are thus required already. The great advantage of this occurring in the Nordic-Baltic region rather than in many other parts of Europe is that the greater similarities in procedures and institutions among the countries make a favourable outcome easier to achieve and practical arrangements that voluntarily go beyond the provisions of current EU law more likely.

Notes

1 The normal disclaimer applies, the views expressed are those of the author and do not necessarily coincide with any that may be held by the Bank of Finland, the Finnish Financial Supervision Authority or the Finnish Deposit Insurance Fund. This chapter does not offer a definition of 'systemic', as, although a widely used term, there is no accepted. In present circumstances, therefore, a function of a bank or indeed the bank itself can be regarded as of 'systemic' importance if the authorities appeal to its impart on the wider financial system and confidence in particular in deciding how to handle it.

2 If the host country offers better conditions for deposit insurance the foreign bank can apply to top up its provisions for depositors in that country to that level.

3 See Hüpkes (2003). Although each account is mandatorily insured up to 30,000 CHF in an industry-run scheme, there is a cap on the scheme of a payout of 4bn CHF. The legislation is silent on what will happen at this point but clearly if there were to be any recourse to further funding the taxpayer is the likely source. The Swiss scheme also has depositor preference, with the deposit insurance fund being subrogated to the claims of the insured depositors in a failure. Thus the chances of the fund not be able to collect in full, eventually, from the liquidation are small.

4 Various definitions of 'too big to fail' have been offered, see for example Stern and Feldman (2003), but the key concern is that can be no material interruption in the main business operations otherwise there will be a systemic event. This is set out in the excerpt from the New Zealand arrangements in Section 2.
5 Baxter *et al.* (2004) provides a helpful assessment of the two approaches. However, within the universal and territorial approaches to insolvency procedures there is still quite a wide range of more detailed differences; see Hadjiemmanuil (2003).
6 These concerns and the resulting consultations and reflections are given in a series of papers available on the RBNZ website: www.rbnz.govt.nz/finstab/banking/supervision/.
7 This may simply be overnight rather than the proverbial weekend before the bank has to re-open in its new guise on the Monday morning.
8 In Mayes *et al.* (2001, ch. 8–10) and Mayes and Liuksila (2003, ch. 1), we argue for intervention at the latest when the net worth of the bank is adjudged to be zero and at best at a small but insufficiently positive capital ratio as in the USA.
9 See for example Schoenmaker, and Oosterloo, (2007) and Masciandaro. (2007) for suggestions about how cross-border supervision might be organized.
10 The Baltic states have a derogation and will not reach the EU minimum standard of protection until 2008.
11 Topping up, of course, deletes the neatness of the match between supervisory responsibility and deposit insurance. In theory under the strict interpretation of the home-host relationship, the host country that was providing the top up would not be involved in the direct supervision or have any specific say in minimizing the losses to the fund.
12 All data from Rahoitustarkastus.
13 Most of the discussion has been journalistic concerning the purchase of Antonveneta by ABN-Amro and Banco Bilbao Vizcaya Argentaria's (BBVA) abandoned bid for Banca Nazionale del Lavoro (BNL).
14 Llewellyn and Mayes (2003) identify ten stakeholders who could have the incentive both to monitor and take action to discipline banks through various markets: depositors, managers, borrowers, supervisory agencies, rating agencies, market traders, shareholders, boards of directors, debt holders and employees. See also Bliss and Flannery (2000).
15 Even the new pillar 3 of Basel 2 is not insisting on standards of disclosure that are as relevant as those that have been required since 1996 in New Zealand; see Mayes *et al.* (2001) for a discussion of the disclosure requirements and the Appendix to chapter 7 for an example of a General Disclosure Document (made by Deutsche Bank).
16 Helfer was Chairman and CEO of the FDIC from 1994 to 1997.
17 Hoggarth *et al.* (2002) produce a neat list of the options open for bank assistance.
18 Padoa-Schioppa (2004) argues that peer pressure might be rather successful in the European environment in ensuring that supervisors actually conform to the rules they set themselves.
19 The number is a little greater than the nine 'European' banks shown in the first category in the table but a number less than 20 sounds plausible even allowing for banks with a very uneven country coverage.
20 Moe *et al.* (2004) gives a good range of examples from the Nordic crises.
21 The Swiss system is set out and explained in Hüpkes (2003).
22 See Hadjiemmanuil (2003) for a clear exposition of the issues and arguments in favour of the 'London Approach' whereby the interested parties, assisted by the authorities, have proved themselves able to achieve rapid effective solutions through the courts.

23 See pp.198–255. The detail is not repeated here.
24 Harrison argues that only a limited portion of claims need to be dealt with immediately as most do not mature on the same value day and will not be subject to a disorderly rush for early closure thereafter if the new bank is guaranteed against further loss by the authorities.
25 See Blowers and Young (2003) for a cautious assessment.
26 Large banks are not defined by market share but by absolute size, namely, as those having New Zealand liabilities, net of amounts due to related parties in excess of $10bnNZ.
27 www.rbnz.govt.nz/finstab/banking/supervision/0137035.html July 2003.

References

Aghion, P., Hart, O. and Moore, J. (1992) 'The Economics of Bankruptcy Reform', *Journal of Law, Economics and Organization*, vol. 8, pp. 523–46.

Bank of Finland (2005) *Financial Stability Review*, Helsinki.

Baxter, T. C., Hansen, J. and Sommer, J. H. (2004) 'Two Cheers for Territoriality: An Essay on International Bank Insolvency Law', *American Bankruptcy Law Journal*, vol. 58(1), pp. 57–91.

Beck, T. (2003) 'The Incentive-compatible Design of Deposit Insurance and Bank Failure Resolution: Concepts and Country Studies', pp. 118–41 in Mayes and Liuksila (2003).

Bliss, R. and Flannery, M. (2000) 'Market Discipline in the Governance of US Bank Holding Companies: Monitoring vs. Influencing', Federal Reserve Bank of Chicago Working Paper, 2000–3.

Blowers, B. and Young, G. (2003) 'The Economic Impact of Insolvency Law' pp. 164–79 in Mayes and Liuksila (2003).

Brouwer, H., Hebbink, G. and Wesseling, S. (2003) 'A European Approach to Banking Crises', pp. 205–21, in Mayes and Liuksila (2003).

Economic and Financial Committee (2000) 'Report on Financial Stability', *Economic* Paper, no. 143, European Commission, May.

Economic and Financial Committee (2001) 'Report on Financial Crisis Management', *Economic* Paper, no. 156, European Commission, July.

European Commission (2005) 'Review of the Deposit Guarantee Schemes Directive (94/19/EC), DG Internal Market, 14 July, DGS 001/2005.

European Financial Services Round Table (2004) 'Towards a Lead Supervisor for Cross-border Financial Institutions in the European Union', Brussels, June.

Hadjiemmanuil, C. (2003) 'Bank Resolution Policy and the Organization of Bank Insolvency Proceedings: Critical Dilemmas', pp. 272–330 in Mayes and Liuksila (2003).

Harrison, I. (2004) 'Systemic Bank Crises: Resolving Large Bank Insolvencies', Federal Reserve Bank of Chicago, October 1.

Helfer, R T (1999) 'What Deposit Insurance Can and Cannot Do', *Finance and Development*, March, pp. 22–5.

Hoggarth, G., Reidhill, J. and Sinclair, P. (2002) 'Resolution of Banking Crises: Theory and Evidence', mimeo, Bank of England.

Hüpkes, E. (2003) 'Bank Insolvency Resolution in Switzerland', pp. 242–71 in Mayes, D. and Liuksila, A (2003) *Who Pays for Bank Insolvency?*, Basingstoke: Palgrave.

Hüpkes, E (2004) ' "Too Big to Save" Towards a Functional Approach to Resolving Crises in Global Financial Institutions', Systemic Bank Crises: Resolving Large Bank Insolvencies, Federal Reserve Bank of Chicago, October 1.

King, M. (1994) 'Debt Deflation: Theory and Evidence', *European Economic Review*, vol.38, pp. 419–55.

Koskenkylä, H. (ed.) (2004) *Financial Integration*, Bank of Finland Study A:108.

Llewellyn, D. and Mayes, D. (2003) 'The Role of Market Discipline in Handling Problem Banks', pp. 183–210 in G. G. Kaufman (ed.,) *Market Discipline in Banking: Theory and Evidence*, Amsterdam: Elsevier.

Masciandaro, D. (2007) 'Allocating Financial Regulatory Powers: the Twin Views' in Mayes and Wood (2007).

Mayes, D. (2004) 'Preparing for Cross-Border Bank Failures', *The Financial Regulator*, vol.11(2), pp. 58–63.

Mayes, D. (2005a) 'The Role of the Safety Net in Resolving Large Financial Institutions', Systemic Bank Crises: Resolving Large Bank Insolvencies, Federal Reserve Bank of Chicago, October 1.

Mayes, D. (2005b) 'Who Pays for Bank Insolvency in Transition and Emerging Economies', *Journal of Banking and Finance*, vol.29, pp. 161–181.

Mayes, D. G., Halme, L. and Liuksila, A. (2001) *Improving Banking Supervision*, Basingstoke: Palgrave.

Mayes, D. G. and Liuksila A. (2003) *Who Pays for Bank Insolvency?*, Basingstoke: Palgrave.

Mayes, D. and Wood, G. (2007) *The Structure of Financial Regulation*, London: Routledge

Moe, T. G., Solheim, J. A. and Vale, B. (2004) *The Norwegian Banking Crisis*, Oslo: Norges Bank Occasional Paper 33.

Padoa-Schioppa, T. (2004) *Regulating Finance: Balancing Freedom and Risk*, Oxford: Oxford University Press.

Reserve Bank of New Zealand (2005a) *Financial Stability Report*, May.

Reserve Bank of New Zealand (2005b) 'Outsourcing Policy', Financial Stability Department Document BS11, October 2005, available on www.rbnz.govt.nz, p.2.

Schoenmaker, D. and Oosterloo, S. (2007) 'Cross-border Issues in European Financial Supervision', in Mayes, D. and Wood, G. (2007).

Sigurdsson, J. (2003) 'Small Countries, large Multi-country banks: a Challenge to Supervisors – the Example of the Nordic-Baltic Area', chapter 5 in Mayes and Liuksila (2003).

Stern, G. and Feldman, R. (2003) *Too Big to Fail: the Hazards of Big Bank Bailouts*, Washington, DC: Brookings Institution.

Vesala, J. (2005) 'Prudential Supervision and Deposit Insurance Issues Raised by the European Company Statute', Colloquium on the European Company Statute, ECB, Frankfurt, 23 February.

Wallis Commission (1997) *Financial System Inquiry Final Report*, Canberra: Australian Government Publishing Service, March.

12 Promoting International Cooperation in Resolving Bank Failures

Gulen Atay

12.1 The need for international cooperation in resolving bank failures

Bank insolvency is an issue of public concern. A bank's failure can produce more negative consequences than that of a non-financial enterprise. Most bank liabilities are owed to the bank's depositors. Many are individuals who are unable to mitigate the risk of bank failure and bear the attendant losses. Deposit insurance schemes are adopted to help with that mitigation. However, the results of bank failures can be more far-reaching. Even if there are deposit insurance schemes, these ultimately transfer the insurer's costs to either the state treasury or the banking industry. The loss of public confidence causes interruption of transactions and losses to creditor counter parties in interbank markets, and this in turn may trigger a systemic crisis that endangers the health not only of a national financial system, but the international financial system as well. The threat of international contagion was realized during the Asian financial crises, when the weaknesses of banks and existing bank regulations across the region made the aftershocks of the crises cross borders and ravage Asia's then-booming economies. Consequently, developing a bank insolvency framework goes beyond resolving conflicts between private parties. A key feature of any such framework is to safeguard the stability of the financial system, and, in so doing, to safeguard public interest.

The need for international cooperation in resolving bank failures is even more urgent today, when cross-border banking is part of everyday life. Banks experiencing financial difficulties in one jurisdiction can possibly have operations or interests in another, and such banks, which operate on an international basis, raise novel legal problems and difficulties. Even as markets have grown international, bank regulations are often still nationally based and are vastly different from one another.

12.2 Current steps taken to promote international cooperation in resolving bank failures

In recent years, a number of international and regional organizations and groups have worked on issues relating to bank insolvency. The Financial Stability Forum (FSF) formed a task force on deposit insurance. The Basel Committee on Banking Supervision (BCBS) likewise formed a task force dealing with the supervision of weak banks. The European Union has adopted various directives on the settlement finality and securities settlement systems; the reorganization and winding up of credit institutions; and on financial collateral arrangements.

As a result of the lessons learned from past resolution of bank failures – especially since the occurrence of the Asian financial crises – much work has been, and is being done, in the area of identifying the appropriate legal, institutional and regulatory frameworks for addressing bank insolvency. Equally important are the increasing efforts devoted to building an international consensus accepting the identified regulatory frameworks appropriate to addressing bank insolvency. International organizations have provided technical assistance and published studies on frameworks for managing systemic banking crises;[1] the legal and institutional underpinnings of the International Financial System;[2] and principles and guidelines for effective insolvency and creditor rights systems.[3] In 2002, the World Bank, the International Monetary Fund, the Bank of International Settlements, the Financial Stability Institute, BCBS and FSF formed a Global Bank Insolvency Initiative. The Initiative is in the process of identifying the appropriate legal, institutional and regulatory framework for addressing bank insolvency and building an international consensus to accept the framework.

The Asian Development Bank (ADB) has been a pioneer in assisting in general insolvency and secured transactions reform in its developing member countries and in the region. Immediately after the Asian financial crises, an ADB regional technical assistance project analyzed insolvency and business reorganization frameworks across 11 Asian jurisdictions. The study proposed recommendations for further reform and became the basis for good practice standards essential to debtor–creditor relations in a sound corporate insolvency environment. While not specifically targeting banking reforms, ADB's experience has been valuable in that it highlighted the importance of developing a regional cooperation framework to address the growing problem of cross-border insolvency.

Cross-border insolvency is concerned with insolvency cases that have commenced in one jurisdiction but which are relevant to other jurisdictions. In the absence of a law or legal process that enables the insolvency administration to be recognized in another jurisdiction, it would be difficult to ensure that the debtor's affairs are dealt with as a whole and in a coordinated way. The focus of cross-border insolvency efforts is the promotion and development of appropriate enabling legislation in as many countries as possible. ADB's study on cross-border insolvency has identified several obstacles to setting up regional cooperation mechanisms to recognize foreign judgments in insolvency cases and assist the resolution of cross-border insolvency cases.[4] To address these obstacles, the ADB study recommends that the application of cross-border insolvency laws should be subject to at least a real prospect, if not a guarantee, of reciprocity. It finds that foreign trade and investment is likely to be more attracted to countries that take account of foreign interests and involvement in the local economy in the context of cross-border insolvency.

Where a case involves the reorganization of an enterprise – a bank, for example – that has significant interests in two or more jurisdictions, such a case would require courts in different countries to act in unison so that effective orders may be made simultaneously. This may mean simultaneous hearings in the courts involved. Some elements to be considered are:

1. At what level and in what circumstances may any communication between the courts occur;
2. Where the courts' languages are different, is there a clear and unambiguous understanding of what one jurisdiction may be attempting or implementing;
3. Do the judges, parties and representatives from different jurisdictions have a common or mutual understanding of the pertinent concepts that apply generally or particularly to the case; and
4. Are there differences in the practice and procedure of affected jurisdictions with respect to an application for interim, urgent relief in a cross-border case?[5]

Failure to be aware of, or address any of these elements, may prevent the successful resolution of cross-border insolvency cases and lead to systemic financial crises.

ADB continues to hold regional meetings of key stakeholders to discuss not only the strengthening of national insolvency frameworks but also the consideration of ways of cooperating in cross-border insolvency within the region.

12.3 Challenges in promoting international cooperation in resolving bank failures

The benefits of regional integration to the banking and financial sector are difficult to realize because of a number of obstacles, most, if not all of which are related to the same factors that cause bank failure. First, there is a general underdevelopment of banks and other financial institutions. There is a limited supply of market instruments and investment opportunities.

There is also limited demand for financial instruments, and low savings ratios and returns on financial instruments are endemic. Second, there is little harmonization of banking regulations and practice within the region. Third, the varied stages of development of the region's countries limit each country's capability to develop telecommunications and information networks that could facilitate and strengthen links and cooperative ventures of a regional scope between banks and other financial markets. How can these obstacles be overcome? The first and second obstacles are being overcome at present by economies that are focusing on domestic policy reforms. Such reforms are modelled on identified best practices and are increasingly becoming more harmonized throughout the region. Consensus must be built in certain areas in order to ensure gradual harmonization of national legal and institutional frameworks in resolving bank failures. Let me discuss a few issues where I believe consensus building is necessary in order to build international cooperation in resolving bank failures.

The legal and institutional framework in general

While there are a variety of ways and authorities that deal with bank insolvencies in different jurisdictions, a bank insolvency regime always includes the following steps: initiating the insolvency proceedings; either taking over or supervising the administration of the bank; undertaking operations relating to the bank's restructuring; liquidating insolvent banks; and paying off insured depositors. To be effective, a bank insolvency regime must clearly and comprehensively specify in the relevant law the powers and responsibilities of all relevant agencies. A dispute resolution mechanism available to all the relevant agencies involved in bank insolvency proceedings will help sort out problems that might arise because of overlapping jurisdictions between such agencies or duplication of functions – all of which should ultimately be avoided.

In some jurisdictions, there is no special distinction between bank insolvency proceedings and those that are applicable to corporate insolvency cases. What is important in designing a framework to address bank insolvency is to determine whether or not the country's existing corporate insolvency laws, insolvency courts, and the skills of the judges can handle the specific issues that differentiate bank insolvency from corporate insolvency.[6] If these institutions have the capability to respond to bank insolvency problems as effectively and efficiently as would a country's banking regulators, then there would be little reason to recommend the design of a new banking insolvency framework. It may be advisable, however, to create special rules that facilitate bank resolution. Moreover, the law must take into account the special role that banking regulators play in bank insolvency proceedings.[7]

Bank regulators must be empowered to implement bank insolvency rules independently, and shielded from political pressure and influence of the market. Laws that guarantee security of tenure, limited grounds for dismissal, autonomy in the disposition of the relevant banking authority's budget, can promote bank regulators' independence.[8] At the same time, there should be sufficient safeguards that guarantee legal accountability to prevent any abuse of power by such regulators.

Laws that facilitate the exchange of information and coordination among all regulators and authorities that deal with insolvent banks are essential to securing bank resolution expediently.[9] This is important not only domestically, but also regionally, as insolvent banks may operate in several jurisdictions. The authority in each jurisdiction would need to coordinate information and action with its counterparts in order to facilitate the smooth resolution of insolvency-related issues that may arise.

Assumption of control of insolvent banks, restructuring and liquidation

Insolvent banks are placed under the control of either a court-appointed administrator, the banking authority, or an administrator appointed by a banking authority during the course of insolvency proceedings. The banking authority or administrator assumes management of the bank in order to protect its assets, assess its financial condition, restructure operations or liquidate the bank. The framework that should govern this stage of the insolvent bank's life should be able to do the following: (1) allow the authority or administrator to quickly and decisively respond to the threat of bank insolvency; and (2) allow the authority or administrator to respond to such threat with autonomy and flexibility.[10] The authority or administrator should be selected through a process that ensures its experience and competence in managing a bank. Likewise, the administrator or authority should be authorized by law to pursue the bank's claims, take any necessary steps to protect the bank's assets and defend the bank against any claim.

When bank restructuring – that is, to substantially modify the operation and financial structure of a banking institution to ensure continuity of the bank business – takes place in the context of an insolvency proceeding, it must be done as soon as possible, in a manner that causes the least amount of disruption to the financial system. The authority or administrator in charge of the restructuring process must compare the cost of restructuring with other options.[11] Restructuring operations that minimize restructuring costs should be considered foremost. Laws that govern or permit bank restructuring must ensure that only well-administered institutions remain in business. This limits problems relating to moral hazard.[12] Competition laws are relevant in so far as they ensure that restructuring should not subsidize failure and penalize efficient banks. Coordination between competition authorities and banking authorities may be essential in ensuring the maintenance of competitive conditions. Finally, information about the restructuring process, and the reasons behind important decisions made during the process, should be made public. Public disclosure of all relevant information should occur once the relevant transactions have been completed.

Where restructuring is not feasible, liquidation would be appropriate. To ensure effective bank liquidation, the legal framework should result in the orderly closure of insolvent banks. There needs to be clear and formal rules for placing the insolvent bank in liquidation and terminating bank activities.[13] Protection of assets through an automatic suspension of collections against the bank or other similar mechanisms are necessary for the orderly disposition of assets among all interested parties. Methods of distributing the assets in the most cost-effective way among various classes of creditors are important.

12.4 Legal issues arising from cross-border banking insolvency regimes

Where banks operate, or have interests, in many jurisdictions, insolvency issues take on an even more complex dimension.

For example: should a bank with assets and interests in various jurisdictions become insolvent, should it be reorganized or liquidated as a single entity – that is, all claims against it and its assets, wherever located, would be dealt with in a single reorganization or liquidation process?[14]

Which country will have jurisdiction over bank insolvency proceedings? Should the home country of the bank take jurisdiction? Or should separate proceedings in each jurisdiction take place, on the basis that the proceedings in the home country do not extend beyond that country's borders?[15]

A similar issue is: should foreign bank branches in a jurisdiction other than the home country be wound up as separate legal entities in the foreign jurisdiction? To do so would ensure that local creditors receive preferential treatment over foreign creditors in the disposition of the bank's assets. This practice is allowed today in certain jurisdictions such as the USA.[16]

These are some issues that routinely arise from cross-border banking insolvency cases, and have been addressed, to some degree, by the European Community Directive on the Reorganization and Winding-Up of Credit Institutions. The framework was introduced to apply where a credit institution with branches in other states is found to be in distress and is required to be subjected to insolvency procedures. It aims to promote equal treatment of creditors, through unity and universality in the resolution of bank insolvency. The Directive can serve as a model to explore these and other legal issues arising from cross-border banking, and to respond to the challenges of international banking in Asia today.[17]

12.5 Beyond domestic reforms: a regional financial framework

To complement domestic policy reforms, a regional financial framework can contribute to the stability of the international financial system by preventing bank insolvency, or resolving systemic financial crises brought about or aggravated by bank insolvency, throughout the region. Such a framework can provide a measure of stability throughout the region while national efforts to reform the banking and financial sectors – which take time – are underway. In any case, the growing trade integration in the region will eventually create a demand for a regional financial cooperation framework that can address crisis prevention and resolution.

Mechanisms for crisis prevention would include regional information sharing, policy dialogue, consultation, surveillance and monitoring. The information shared would include data on monetary and exchange rate policies, fiscal positions and debt management, capital flows and external debts, financial system conditions, and corporate sector developments.[18] Such information would allow monitoring capital flows at the regional level to take place. Effective monitoring and surveillance on a regional level would place each country's banking and financial regulators under peer pressure to pursue disciplined macro economic and structural policies that are necessary to ensure stable external accounts and currencies.

In the face of a systemic crisis in the banking sector, a crisis-affected economy's return to sustainable growth could be hastened by regional fiscal resource mobilization.[19] Fiscal resources are needed to recapitalize weak banks, facilitate corporate debt restructuring and strengthen social safety nets. But raising such fiscal resources regionally may be limited by constraints to external financing on market terms. Multilateral banks' resources may also be limited at the time the crises erupt. Consequently, it could be prudent to establish a framework for regional action to mobilize fiscal resources to resolve the financial crises. A regional commitment to provide a large amount of resources to crises-affected countries may help stabilize regional markets and economies and facilitate the recovery process.[20]

It should be noted that there are a number of initiatives that are underway that have increased the level of integration within the region. The Chiang Mai Initiative, for example, has created a network of bilateral swap arrangements among ASEAN countries, People's Republic of China, Japan and the Republic of Korea (collectively, these countries are known as ASEAN+3), to address short-term liquidity difficulties in the region and to supplement the existing international financial arrangements. ASEAN+3 provides a forum where the countries can exchange consistent and timely data and information on capital flows within the participating nations and has established an early warning system to enhance timely and sufficient financial support for crises in the region.

12.6 Conclusion

There are a number of benefits that would result from harmonization of laws and policies and greater regional integration of the banking sector and financial markets. Regional markets offer the banks of member countries the opportunity to expand their business outside of their jurisdictions. This would allow their businesses to extend beyond the limits set by the size of their own domestic markets. Such banks could extend economies of scale, which, in turn, would result in reduced intermediation costs. Regional integration would also provide domestic banks with new sources of funds. This would enhance efficient resource mobilization and allocation within the region. Regional integration could help domestic banks expand and diversify their portfolio, thereby improving their ability to hedge against financial risks that result from volatile movements in exchange and interest rates. A regional framework that serves as a forum to monitor the financial system regionally and provide financial resources quickly at times of banking crises in the region may help strengthen banks and prevent insolvency and systemic crises. These are only some of the strategies we can employ in working toward the strengthening of the region's financial systems and preventing bank insolvency.

Notes

1 See Hoelcher and Quintyn (2003).
2 Bank for International Settlements (2002).
3 World Bank (2001).
4 Some countries fear that recognizing the decisions of another country with respect to the affairs of their own citizens, or persons residing within their jurisdiction, detracts from its independence to regulate its own citizens and territory. In many instances, countries refuse to respond to requests and applications for recognition and assistance when there is no guarantee of reciprocity from the requesting country. Other countries hesitate to consider acquiescing to cross-border insolvency requests, spending time thinking about whether or not cross-border recognition and assistance benefit local or foreign creditors. Others are paralysed by the fear that their inability to deal with domestic insolvency cases makes them unable to apply international insolvency requests. See Harmer and Fischer (2002).
5 Harmer and Fischer (2002).
6 Aguirre (2005), p. 25.
7 European Central Bank (2005), p. 5.
8 Quintyn and Taylor (2004).
9 Mayes (2003), p. 5.
10 Krimminger (2005), p.3.
11 Aguirre (2005), p. 26.
12 *Idem*—. 25.
13 *Idem*—. 31.
14 Campbell (2005), p. 517.
15 *Idem*—.
16 *Idem*—. 519.
17 *Idem*—. 516.
18 Kuroda and Kawai (2003).
19 The importance of being able to access fiscal resources quickly in order to stave off the ill-effects of systemic crises triggered by bank insolvency can be gleaned from the banking crises of 1999 in Turkey. In 1999, notwithstanding the enactment of

a new bank law that allowed rapid intervention into insolvent small and medium sized banks, fiscal problems prevented the government from rapidly resolving the crises brought about by the banks' insolvency. But once the funding was resolved, resolution of insolvent banks proceeded adequately. See Norton (2003).

20 Kuroda and Kawai (2003).

References

Aguirre, E. (2005) '*Legal, Institutional, and Regulatory Framework to Deal with Banking Resolution and Insolvency*', Ministry of Finance, Czech Republic, Prague.

Bank for International Settlements (2002), 'Report of the Contact Group on the Legal and Institutional Underpinnings of the International Financial System: Insolvency Arrangements and Enforceability', Bank for International Settlements, Basel.

Campbell, A. (2005) 'Issues in Cross-Border Bank Insolvency: the European Community Directive on the Reorganization and Winding Up of Credit Institutions', in *Current Developments in Monetary and Financial Law*, vol. 3 International Monetary Fund, Washington, DC.

European Central Bank (2005), 'Opinion on a Draft Law on Insolvency', CON/2005/36, European Central Bank, Frankfurt am Main.

Harmer, R. and Fisher, R. (2002) 'Promoting Regional Cooperation in the Development of Insolvency Reform', Asia Development Bank, Manila.

Hoelscher, D. and Quintyn, M. (2003) 'A Framework for Managing Systemic Banking Crises', Occasional Paper No. 224, International Monetary Fund, Washington, DC.

Krimminger, M. (2005) 'Banking in a Changing World: Issues and Questions in the Resolution of Cross-Border Banks', in *Current Developments in Monetary and Financial Law*, vol. 4, International Monetary Fund, Washington, DC.

Kuroda, H. and Kawai, M. (2003) 'Strengthening Regional Financial Cooperation in East Asia', *Pacific Economic Papers*, Australia, Japan Research Centre, Australian National University, Canberra.

Mayes, D.G. (2005) 'Who Pays for Bank Insolvency in Transition and Emerging Economies?', *Journal of Banking and Finance*, vol. 29:1, pp. 161–81.

Norton, J. (2004) 'A Rule Oriented Matrix Approach', Canada Deposit Insurance Corporation, Ottawa.

Quintyn, M. and Taylor, M.W. (2004) 'Should Financial Sector Regulators be Independent?', *Economic Issues*, No. 32, International Monetary Fund, Washington, DC.

World Bank (2001) 'Principles and Guidelines for an Effective Insolvency and Creditor Rights System', World Bank, Washington, DC.

13

Economic Performance of KDIC's Resolution System

Pilsun Choi and Dong-Il Kim

Since the end of 1997, when Korea faced a financial crisis, a number of financial institutions have gone bankrupt. In this process, the Korea Deposit Insurance Corporation (KDIC) injected massive amounts of funds into bankrupt financial institutions in the form of paying deposits to customers instead of to the bankrupt institutions. In declaring bankruptcy, the court appoints a trustee with its official power. The main business of the appointed trustee is to convert property held by the bankruptcy estate into money and distribute it to creditors. KDIC withdraws the injected public funds through such a credit allotment. Accordingly, the effective recovery of the bankruptcy estate's assets and cost savings are the issues directly linked to the ability to withdraw public funds.

Owing to the characteristics of a bankruptcy estate, however, there are many difficulties in managing the estate effectively. First of all, the possibility that employees left in the bankruptcy estate will make efforts for prompt recovery of assets and cost savings in a situation where the existing management is stepping down is slim. The employees may delay the recovery of assets intentionally, as an early settlement of bankruptcy procedures leads to shortening their employment period.

Moreover, right after the financial crisis, lawyers were appointed as trustees in bankruptcy estates. Some of these trustees were short on financial knowledge and experience, delaying the recovery of assets. There were also other problems, such as the difference in standards on business and supervision by bankruptcy estates and non-cooperation between estates.

Accordingly, to maximize withdrawal of public funds, KDIC began to improve the system of management of bankruptcy estates. The *Public Fund Oversight Special Law* enacted in December 2000 called for appointing the KDIC (corporation) or KDIC executives and staff as trustees for bankrupt financial institutions that received public funds. After the Constitutional Court of Korea decided in March 2001 that the KDIC trustee system is constitutional, KDIC began to participate actively as a trustee in bankruptcy. To improve the system, KDIC has mapped out and promoted various means of maximizing the withdrawal of funds from bankruptcy estates. To help bankruptcy estates reduce expenses, KDIC also established a system which calls for early settlement of estates from which asset recovery has fallen into arrears and where a certain period has passed since bankruptcy.

In this chapter, we estimate the economic effect of the KDIC's efforts for early settlement by participating in a bankruptcy estate as a trustee and enhancing efficiency of asset recovery. The final goal of KDIC's efforts to enhance efficiency of the procedures is to maximize recovery of bankruptcy estates' assets. Accordingly, in this chapter we focus analysis on the increasing effect in dividends produced by bankruptcy estates since KDIC has participated in the estates as a trustee.

In section 13.1, we outline the development of KDIC's participation in bankrupt financial institutions as a trustee since the nation faced its financial crisis. In section 13.2, we explain the concrete methods KDIC has promoted for effective recovery of assets held by bankruptcy estates and early settlement, section 13.3 presents the concept of the discounted dividend rate as an indicator for estimating the economic impact that the KDIC's trustee system attained. In section 13.4 we estimate the economic impact by making use of statistics on dividend payments that bankruptcy estates report to KDIC every month. Section 13.5 concludes this chapter.

13.1 Progress of KDIC's participation in bankruptcy procedures[1]

In the financial industry's restructuring process, rapidly propelled since the end of 1997 when the nation faced a financial crisis, massive amounts of public funds were injected into ailing financial institutions. The public funds were mobilized chiefly from bond issuance by KDIC and the Korea Asset Management Corporation (KAMCO), and were supported in methods of equity participation, contribution and deposit payoffs. As for funds not retrieved from the supported funds, the state coffer had to shoulder the burden in the end. In particular, withdrawal of deposit payoffs and contributions related to bankruptcy estates was more difficult than that of equity participation and asset purchases of financial institutions in operation.

The bankruptcy system refers to a procedure in trial designed to repay debts to all creditors on an equal basis by compulsorily managing a debtor's total assets and converting them into money in the case that a debtor was unable to pay back all liabilities to total creditors, owing to worsened property status. In a case where the court declares bankruptcy on a debtor as the debtor cannot pay back debts, all property possessed by the debtor is to constitute a sort of estate, the bankruptcy estate. In case of declaring bankruptcy, the court appoints a trustee in bankruptcy with its official power simultaneously. The main business of the appointed trustee is to convert property held by the bankruptcy estate into money and distribute it to creditors.

Since the end of 1998, KDIC has exerted its best effort to maximize withdrawal of public funds in earnest. As part of its efforts, KDIC actively participated in the management of bankruptcy estates and sought ways to effectively withdraw public funds by improving the management system of bankruptcy estates.

Propulsion of effective funds withdrawal through an auditor system

KDIC withdraws its contribution and deposit payoffs from bankrupt financial institutions through dividends. Different from financial institutions in business operations, bankruptcy estates needed thorough management and supervision for effective withdrawal of public funds as there were no managerial identities.

In 1998, there was no way that KDIC could effectively carry out bankruptcy procedures. At that time, law experts, including lawyers, were appointed customarily as bankruptcy trustees. Accordingly, KDIC had no institutional equipment or right to withdraw credit, besides its participation in dividends as the biggest creditor under bankruptcy law. To settle the problem, it was desirable for the KDIC as a corporation or KDIC executives and staff to be appointed as trustees in bankruptcy estates: a significant improvement in the system.

At the time, KDIC actively developed a way of using an auditor system under the bankruptcy laws and concentrated its efforts on guiding and supervising bankruptcy estates' activities of withdrawing credit. Namely, it utilized the auditors' business consent right (Article 187) and the estate audit right (Article 172) under the Bankruptcy Law.

In the initial stage, KDIC had to persuade the court and bankruptcy trustees to appoint its staff as auditors. In December 1998, KDIC officials were appointed for the first time as auditors of bankruptcy estates of eight credit unions, including Daegu Hanyeong Credit Union. Since then, KDIC has continuously promoted the appointment of KDIC officials as auditors, despite strong protest by some bankruptcy trustees. As a result, KDIC officials were appointed as auditors of 140 out of 143 bankruptcy estates that held creditors' meetings as of the end of December 1999.

The auditor's business is divided into the consent business, in the course of asset recovery, and the audit business on the appropriateness of the management of bankrupt property. Through these tools, KDIC indirectly participated in the management of bankrupt estates and sought ways to recover holding assets at a proper price and reduce expenditures. Related to corporate debt restructuring, in particular, it demanded readjustment of the applied matters, resulting in additional credit withdrawal of 2.9 billion won in 1999 and 4.1 billion won in 2000. To enhance objectivity and transparency in auditors' decision making, KDIC also mapped out detailed guidelines on the consent business case by case. At the same time, KDIC prepared ways to appraise and improve auditors' business, enhancing efficiency of the business.

Improvement of the appointment system of bankruptcy trustees

We cannot deny that there was a clear limit for the KDIC to participate in bankruptcy procedures under the auditor system, despite its considerable achievements. First of all, there was a limit to enhancing efficiency of fund withdrawal just with the consent and audit businesses, which were nothing but a passive watcher's role. Feeling this limit keenly, KDIC actively sought to take the initiative in carrying out the asset recovery business for whole bankruptcy procedures.

Thanks to the Corporation's strenuous efforts, the appointment system of bankruptcy trustees was finally improved. On 21 January, 2000, Clause 1 of Article 15 of the *Act on the Structural Improvement of the Financial Industry* was revised, making it possible to appoint KDIC executives and staff as bankruptcy trustees. As a result, KDIC arranged a method to propel asset recovery of bankruptcy estates effectively through direct means, not indirectly as through an auditor system.

As a preparatory step before the revision of the law, KDIC selected talented manpower from officials with experience in financial and supervisory businesses and intensively educated them on bankruptcy law and techniques for withdrawing credit. To carry out the business of trustees effectively, it also established a basic plan for the appointment and operation of bankruptcy trustees, creating an estate for successful implementation of managing bankrupt property.

However, even after the revision of the law, the court still appointed lawyers as bankruptcy trustees. As a result, KDIC officials were designated as bankruptcy trustees for a mere 42 out of the total of 229 bankruptcy estates as of the end of 2000. The trend of appointing those other than KDIC officials as trustees was reinforced, so additional improvement in the appointment system of bankruptcy trustees was called for.

Meanwhile, the *Public Funds Oversight Special Law* enacted on 20 December, 2000 stipulates that KDIC or KDIC staff *should be appointed* as bankruptcy trustees, temporarily for five years after the enforcement date of the law, despite other laws and regulations in case effective recovery of public funds is needed for bankruptcy estates that received public funds.[2] With this step, the way was opened for effective management of bankruptcy estate by KDIC.

In January 2001, however, the court requested the Constitutional Court of Korea to make a decision on whether the regulations concerning appointment of bankruptcy trustees were constitutional or not. Accordingly, the implementation of the regulations concerning appointment of bankruptcy trustees was suspended. Fortunately, the Constitutional Court of Korea ruled on 15 March, 2001 that the article concerning appointment of KDIC officials as bankruptcy trustees was constitutional. So, KDIC officials began to

Table 13.1 Major progress in the appointment system of bankruptcy trustees

Jan 21 2000	•	Revision of *Act on the Structural Improvement of the Financial Industry* → KDIC executives and staff were able to be appointed as bankruptcy trustees.
Dec 20 2000	•	Revision of the *Public Fund Oversight Special Act* → For all financial institutions in bankruptcy, including existing bankruptcy estates, KDIC or KDIC staff were able to be appointed as bankruptcy trustees.
Mar 15 2001	•	The Constitutional Court of Korea ruled that the article concerning appointment of KDIC officials as bankruptcy trustees was constitutional → KDIC officials began to be appointed in earnest as trustees in bankrupt financial institutions.

be appointed in earnest as trustees in bankrupt financial institutions. As a result, KDIC officials were appointed as bankruptcy trustees of 452 out of the 457 bankruptcy estates (including liquidated corporations) as of the end of October 2004.

In the meantime, the *Public Funds Oversight Special Law* called for appointment of KDIC staff as bankruptcy trustees for five years on a temporary basis. However, through the revision of the *Depositor Protection Law* in December 2002, which was designed to maximize withdrawal of public funds, KDIC staff were entitled to serve as bankruptcy trustees continuously without limit of period in case of bankruptcy of financial institutions subject to deposit insurance.

Meaning of the improvement in the appointment system of bankruptcy trustees

Korea's bankruptcy law regards the court's supervision of bankruptcy procedures as its major premise. However, it is impossible for the court to cover all details of bankruptcy procedures in practice. Accordingly, the court appoints bankruptcy trustees and recognizes their wide discretion in the recovery of bankruptcy estates.

In the past, bankruptcy trustees, chiefly lawyers, faced a limit in carrying out property management business owing to the number of financial institution bankruptcies since the financial crisis. It was difficult for them to concentrate on the management of bankruptcy estates while simultaneously performing their principal jobs as lawyers. Some lawyers turned trustees entrusted their subordinates with the business because of lack of financial knowledge and experience. Even among bankruptcy trustees, the methods of asset recovery were widely different from individual to individual. In the process, withdrawal of credit was delayed and questions were raised about the speed and effectiveness of bankruptcy procedures. In the case of lawyers turned trustees, they placed more emphasis on the maintenance of creditors' balances rather than on the speedy process of bankruptcy procedures as they had no direct relationship with bankruptcy estates. Accordingly, such ineffective factors as the delay of bankruptcy procedures and the slow-paced withdrawal of funds occurred. Owing to such problems, the necessity was highlighted that KDIC, with its professional knowledge and experience, could preside over bankruptcy procedures rapidly and in a unified way.

Having special or exceptional regulations in appointing bankruptcy trustees related to bankruptcy of financial institutions is not limited only to Korea. We can find similar legislation cases in other countries, including the USA. The Federal Deposit Insurance Corporation (FDIC), which is free from bankruptcy law, possesses a monopoly position and exclusively deals with disposal and withdrawal businesses of bankrupt financial institutions. About 140 years ago, the National Bank Act (1864) granted financial supervisory authorities the right to liquidate financial institutions independently. Such tradition had continued until the revision of the bankruptcy law in 1989, which called for the separation of liquidation of financial institutions from the objects of bankruptcy law. In the course of passing through a series of substantial bank bankruptcies during the period from the latter half of the 1980s to the early 1990s, relevant laws were enacted and revised several times in such a way as to allow the FDIC to exercise various special rights. These rights exceeded those held by general bankruptcy trustees in the case of bankruptcies of financial institutions. In the USA, accordingly, bankruptcy trustees of financial institutions refer to the FDIC in general. Approval or denial of credit and disposal of property-converted money conducted by the FDIC as a bankruptcy trustees is excluded from the object of judicial screening today.

Affected by the USA, Taiwan also granted the Central Deposit Insurance Corporation (CDIC) the right to conduct comprehensive inspection of financial institutions and other various rights necessary for disposal of bankrupt financial institutions. In particular, its deposit insurance law stipulates that the CDIC should be appointed as bankruptcy trustees for bankrupt financial institutions. Along with the USA and Taiwan, Mexico, Venezuela, Jamaica and the Philippines enacted laws to appoint deposit insurance corporations as bankruptcy trustees for financial institutions.

13.2 Efficient asset recovery and early settlement[3]

Efficient asset recovery

The KDIC has set as the principle for asset recovery by bankruptcy trustees that 'the conversion of assets of bankruptcy estates into money should be made at an earlier date at the highest price', (KDIC, 2002, p.32). It simply means the maximization of fund withdrawals from bankruptcy estates.

KDIC established various plans to maximize asset recovery from bankruptcy estates around early 2001 on the occasion of the appointment of KDIC executives and staff as bankruptcy trustees in earnest. According to the analysis of bankruptcy procedures of existing bankruptcy estates the conversion into money was made at a rapid pace within 9–12 months after the bankruptcy but its pace slowed down remarkably after 18 months from the bankruptcy. However, banks and merchant banks showed a slightly different pattern from the general one. In these sectors, the ratio of asset appraisal amount to converted amount showed a steady rise until two years after bankruptcy. The main cause of banks is the slow progress in repayment of guaranty money for leasing branches or loans to bank officials. In the case of merchant banks, the main reasons were the repayment of mid- and long-term credit, including leases, on an instalment basis and diversified sales of securities. To improve the results of conversion into money in this situation, the conversion of assets into money needed to be accelerated within one year after bankruptcy. This could be achieved by advancing the repayment of guaranty money for leasing branches or loans to bank officials by one year and selling mid- and long-term credit and securities at an earlier date.

According to the analysis of the efficiency of expenses, if a certain period passed after bankruptcy, the ratio of expenses to the recovery amount rose at a rapid pace. In general, the ratio of expenses to the recovery amount soared sharply after the passage of 12 months from bankruptcy for banks, 6 months for merchant banks, and 9 months for credit unions. To enhance efficiency of expenses in this situation, it was concluded there was a need to reduce expenses by slashing manpower from one year after bankruptcy and combining the bankruptcy estates in subsequent operations.

Ways to withdraw assets of bankruptcy estates on a step-by-step basis

In viewing the method for effective conversion of holding assets into money mapped out at that time, the KDIC prepared the *Way to Withdraw Assets of Bankruptcy Estates on a Step-by-step Basis*, which aimed at recovering assets of bankruptcy estates at an early date and shortening the existing time for converting assets into money by a minimum of one year. It also established detailed principles on the passage period, types and status of assets and called for recovery of assets according to the rules.

In the initial stage of within one year after bankruptcy, it set the *acceleration of asset recovery* as the most important goal. Based on the principle of asset recovery, it pushed for arranging loans to other financial institutions or sales to other institutions in addition to regular withdrawal management for normal loans. For non-performing loans, it pushed for a rapid and systematic method through the process resulting from demand for debt repayment → disposal of mortgage → probe of debtors' assets (separately from KDIC's investigation) → and the request for voluntary repayment through a cut in debts.

Figure 13.1 shows such an asset recovery system. Meanwhile, KDIC called for withdrawal of guaranty money for leasing and securities within one year through auction or sales of mortgage real estate. As for real estate, it conducted public sales or entrusted an outside institution with the public sale within one year.

In the middle stage of 1–2 years after bankruptcy, for general loans, it conducted an intensive probe of debtors' assets and requested debtors to pay back loans voluntarily by slashing debts. For special credit (companies placed under work-out, court receivership and composition), it pushed for a collective disposal by combining assets of various bankruptcy estates into one and issuing asset-backed securities (ABS). For real estate that failed to sell through public sales within one year after bankruptcy, it entrusted an outside institution with its public sale or sought collective disposal with special credit.

Even after passing through these procedures, assets that KDIC failed to dispose of will remain. Particularly among estates where a sufficient period has passed since the setup of a bankruptcy estate, such inefficiencies as the expense of keeping bankruptcy estates may exceed the withdrawal amount achieved thereafter. Accordingly, KDIC pushed for early settlement of bankruptcy procedures to maximize dividends to creditors and advance withdrawal of public funds. We look into this matter carefully later in this chapter.

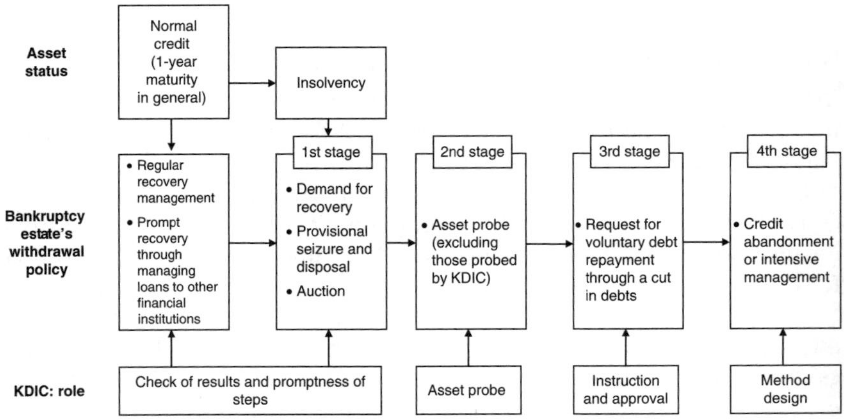

Source: KDIC (2002), p. 33.

Figure 13.1 KDIC's resolution system of bankruptcy estates

Maximization of recovery value of assets held by the bankruptcy estate

Besides the step-by-step method for withdrawing assets, KDIC pushed for various tools and means for efficient recovery of assets. One of the methods is its effort to maximize the recovery value of assets held by bankruptcy estates. First of all, to support activities to withdraw credit, it carried out a probe on the status of ailing debtor companies, assets of ailing debtors, flow of funds and legal proceedings.

Under the judgement that efficiency of sales and synergy effects fell, owing to the promotion of sales of holdings of assets by each bankruptcy estate and poor sales results due to a lack of PR activities, KDIC introduced a joint-sale method for some assets. For assets held by bankruptcy estates, it mapped out a disposal method by type. In the case of real estate, art products, securities and foreign currency loans, whose sale is more effective not through individual sale but through joint sale, it carried out joint public sales or auctions by type, enjoying good results.

In the case of real estate held by bankruptcy estates, KDIC staged active PR activities with a guide to sales of real estate on its homepage and exerted a great effort to activate sales through joint public sales. As a result, it sold off 170.3 billion won worth of real estate for 202 bankruptcy cases as of the end of August 2004, 353 billion won for 464 cases in 2003, 493.3 billion won for 566 cases in 2002, and 123.3 billion won for 258 cases in 2001.

Implementation of a system allowing a bankruptcy trustee to manage plural estates and a regional unit management system

By taking into consideration the characteristics of financial institutions, the scale of holding assets, and business capacity, KDIC allowed a bankruptcy trustee to manage plural estates, seeking flexibility of manpower operation and effectiveness. To help bankruptcy estates reduce personnel expenses and other unnecessary costs stemming from operation of an independent office, it also integrated offices of estates for effective operation.

Along with this, to manage all bankruptcy estates systematically, it implemented the *Regional Unit Management System*, which calls for division into regions centred on competent provincial courts and a management system led by a regional representative trustee. As of the end of 2004, 89 bankruptcy trustees were appointed to a total of 456 estates, thus a single trustee was in charge of an average of 5.2 estates. With this step, KDIC achieved effective management of bankruptcy estates and a reduction in expenses for office leases, building management and other such issues.

Enhancement of management effectiveness of bankruptcy trustees and assistants

For bankruptcy trustees, KDIC introduced a results appraisal system to manage their business results thoroughly. It also introduced an incentive system for their assistants, encouraging their activities in withdrawing credit. It operates a business investigation team of bankruptcy estates at all times and demands that bankruptcy trustees and assistants rectify errors or inconsistencies, if found. KDIC also holds regular workshops for re-education of bankruptcy trustees. To prevent possible financial accidents stemming from the long-term management of the same estate by a single trustee and to enhance business efficiency, KDIC carried out a *Regional Rotation Disposition System* and a *Cross Working System within Regions*.

It determined a suitable number of assistants per estate after analysing asset volume and composition, the number of lawsuits and types of bankruptcy estates. It also effectively controlled estate management manpower by implementing an additional cut in the number of assistants of bankruptcy estates after considering the quantity of reduced business. As a result, it saved expenses to bankruptcy estates and enhanced effectiveness of the estate management business.

Also, it arranged an information-sharing system between bankruptcy estates and published cases and its experiences with the bankrupt property management business in the form of a manual. It has made great efforts to raise the quality of the bankrupt property management business through accumulation of its business know-how.

Early settlement of bankruptcy procedures

KDIC has encouraged estates that have been delayed in the conversion of assets into money among those where a certain period has passed since bankruptcy, to conduct sales of remaining assets and to pay final dividends. This procedure is called the early settlement of bankruptcy procedures. It is designed to maximize the payment of dividends to creditors and withdraw injected public funds at an early date. KDIC selects the objects for early settlement according to the KDIC-set *Guideline on Selection of Estates for Settlement*. For selected estates, it arranges matters related to settlement in advance, appraising the assets held and getting due approval from a competent court. After this, it sells the remaining assets held by bankruptcy estates in a lump sum to KDIC's affiliate, the Resolution and Finance Corporation (RFC). If there are no lawsuits in progress or related assets, the estate concludes the legal bankruptcy procedures and makes the payment of final dividends.

However, a legal conclusion is impossible for estates placed under such lawsuits as a suit to fix credit in advance, a suit applying implementation of debt, and a suit applying damage compensation. For these estates, accordingly, it pushes for '*de facto* conclusion' (or 'quasi-conclusion'). This entails selling the remaining assets, excluding assets related to suits, in a lump and paying mid-term dividends to minimize expenses so the estate survives. The KDIC integrates estates that have come to *de facto* conclusion and lets a trustee of an integrated bankruptcy estate perform the remaining business. If financial resources for dividends are obtained as a result of a lawsuit, the estate implements a final dividend and concludes the bankruptcy procedures. In such an early settlement system, KDIC maintains consistency in the resolution system by requesting *its affiliate,* RFC, to sell off the remaining assets of the bankruptcy estate. It also makes it possible to withdraw public funds additionally through RFC.

The early settlement system was introduced in August 2001 for the first time. In the initial stage, KDIC selected 20 credit union estates first and pushed for their early settlement. That is because each had no problems with early settlement, as KDIC's credit ratio is 100 per cent and all suits were finalized. In case of estates in the midst of lawsuits, it transferred the suits to RFC without compensation, and pushed for conclusion in the form of post settlement. In principle, however, the conclusion of bankruptcy procedures under the bankruptcy law was impossible until the suits of bankruptcy estates in progress were finalized. There was also a problem regarding the proper qualifications of those concerned in the transfer method of a suit for damage compensation under the premise of post settlement after conclusion. Accordingly, for the estates in the midst of lawsuits, KDIC made an attempt at *de facto* conclusion, excluding suit-related assets from being objects for sale. The remaining assets, excluding assets related to suits, are sold in a lump, integrating estates and letting a trustee of an integrated bankruptcy estate to perform the remaining business. The *de facto* conclusion system was implemented in September 2002.

The early conclusion business of bankruptcy procedures is carried out according to a formalized system after preparing detailed instructions and step-by-step guidelines. First, the selection of the objects for early conclusion follows the KDIC-set *Guideline on Selection of Objects for Early Conclusion.* As a first step, it compares some indicators, including effectiveness of conversion into money, efficiency of expenses and stagnation in asset recovery of bankruptcy estates, and calculates rankings by estate. Then also taking into consideration KDIC's credit ratio, size of holding assets and status of lawsuits, it finally selects estates subject to early conclusion.

For the estates selected for early conclusion, they sell their holding assets to RFC and implement a dividend at an early date. To this end, KDIC prepared a *Guideline on Purchase of Assets from Conclusion Estates* after holding consultations with an accounting corporation. Based on the guideline, it appraises the asset value and sells assets to RFC in a lump. Under the asset purchase guideline, the empirical recovery rate is calculated based on the credit amount, and a proper price is decided after considering commissions necessary for credit withdrawal. The selling price of special credit among the assets subject to sale is finally decided by an accounting corporation's additional inspection to ensure fairness and objectivity.

For assets with no profit from conversion into money or no possibility of conversion into money of holding assets, KDIC requests the estate to abandon the assets according to the *Guideline on Asset Depreciation and*

Abandonment as a means of preventing unnecessary suits and seeking early settlement. Based on the guideline, it classifies assets for depreciation or abandonment after considering characteristics of bankruptcy estate's assets. It follows post-management procedures for the depreciated assets after passing through property inspection and depreciation screening. In the meantime, it keeps and manages documents of concluded estates according to the *Guideline on Remaining Documents of Concluded Estates*.

Estates that have paid out their final dividends and received a judgment for conclusion of bankruptcy from the court have no general business. On the other hand, *de facto* concluded estates have to carry out business related to lawsuits in progress. As the bankruptcy estate still exists legally, the estate has to deal with businesses related to settlement and final dividends. To carry out post management business of *de facto* concluded estates effectively, KDIC prepared the *Way for Post Management of Concluded Estates* and manages the estates. In particular, it designates trustees and assistants in charge of conclusion for each of the nation's 13 provincial courts in an attempt to manage concluded estates effectively.

As a result of propelling such an early conclusion, 264 out of the total of 457 bankruptcy estates were concluded as of the end of October 2004, covering 57.8 per cent of the concluded results. In particular, a number of bankruptcy estates of banks and merchant banks that faced difficulties in reaching conclusion owing to complex lawsuits and various asset compositions since 2003 finally came to conclusion. As time passed, the average asset volume of concluded estates increased compared with that in the initial stage of propelling conclusion, achieving an improvement in the quality of the results.

13.3 Concept of simple and discounted dividend rates

As mentioned above, KDIC has exerted its best effort to maximize the withdrawal rate by guiding the recovery of bankruptcy estates' assets at the highest price possible at an earlier date, and to save operation costs through early conclusion. KDIC has pushed ahead with maximizing net recovery of bankruptcy estates, in a nutshell defined as the amount after deducting operational expenses from asset withdrawal amounts. To analyse the economic performance of such efforts, we introduce the concept of net recovery more precisely by using a simple numerical formula.

First of all, assume that a bankruptcy takes place at time 0, and the bankrupt procedures conclude at time T. Also assume that asset recovery is made at each point of time $t = 0, 1, \ldots, T$, and the recovery amount and operational expenses are R_t and C_t, respectively. In this case, the net recovery at every point in time can be expressed as $(R_t - C_t)$. Assume that the asset value of the bankruptcy estate appraised at the bankrupt time 0 is A.

We define *recovery ratio* as the ratio of the recovery amount to asset appraisal. While the asset appraisal amount is the value appraised at the point of time 0, the net recovery amount is the amount appraised at every point in time. Hence, we have to discount the net recovery amount by the interest rate to compare these amounts. Under the simple assumption that the interest rate of the unit period is fixed at i over the whole period from 0 to T, the *discounted net recovery rate* (r) can be expressed as follows:

$$r = \sum_{t=0}^{T} \frac{(R_t - C_t)}{(1+i)^t} \times \frac{1}{A} \tag{1}$$

The right-hand side of equation (1) represents the sum of net recovery amounts discounted by the interest rate, and divides it by the asset appraisal amount. Given the asset appraisal amount A the goal of the bankruptcy trustee is to maximize the net recovery rate r. To attain this, the trustee is to make efforts for effective asset recovery and cost saving by carrying out bankruptcy procedures at a rapid pace.

If the interest rate changes at every period and it is expressed with $\{i_1, \ldots, i_T\}$, the discounted net recovery rate will be:

$$r = \sum_{t=0}^{T} \frac{(R_t - C_t)}{\prod_{s=0}^{t} (1+i_s)} \times \frac{1}{A} \tag{2}$$

where i_0 is defined as 0. Using the term dividend D_t, instead of the net recovery amount $(R_t - C_t)$, in the above formula, and indicate it as the discounted dividend rate d is as follows:

$$d = \sum_{t=0}^{T} \frac{D_t}{\prod_{s=0}^{t} (1+i_s)} \times \frac{1}{A} \tag{3}$$

Now consider the following situation. There are two candidates for a trustee in a bankruptcy estate with an asset appraisal amount of A; K (KDIC) and L (lawyer). Assume that the discounted dividend rate is d_K when K is a trustee, and d_L when L is a trustee. If d_K is bigger than d_L, we can say that trustee K performed more efficiently. The present value of the total discounted dividend $d_K A$ for K, is larger than that for L, $d_L A$. The discounted dividend rate defined above is the yardstick for appraising the bankrupt property management business comprehensively. Other things being equal, the higher the discounted dividend rate, the more efficient the procedure.

The increase in dividend (E) coming from the trustee K (instead of L) can be expressed as follows:

$$E = (d_K - d_L) \times A \tag{4}$$

Where there are n bankruptcy estates and not just one we express their asset appraisal amount as $\{A_1, \ldots, A_n\}$. Maintaining the assumption that there are two trustee groups, K and L, we compare the dividend results of the groups, under the realistic assumption that the discounted dividend rates are different for each bankruptcy estate. We express the discounted dividend rates of K and L groups as $\{d_{K1}, \ldots, d_{Kn}\}$ and $\{d_{L1}, \ldots, d_{Ln}\}$. In this situation, the increase in dividend (E) coming from the trustee group K (instead of L) can be expressed as:

$$E = (d_{K1} - d_{L1}) \times A_1 + \cdots + (d_{Kn} - d_{Ln}) \times A_n$$

Rearranging this:

$$\begin{aligned} E &= (d_{K1}A_1 + \cdots + d_{Kn}A_n) - (d_{L1}A_1 + \cdots + d_{Ln}A_n) \\ &= \left(d_{K1}\frac{A_1}{\sum A_j}A_1 + \cdots + d_{Kn}\frac{A_n}{\sum A_j} \right) \sum A_j - \left(d_{L1}\frac{A_1}{\sum A_j}A_1 + \cdots + d_{Ln}\frac{A_n}{\sum A_j} \right) \sum A_j \end{aligned}$$

The terms in parentheses on the right-hand side of the second equality are the weighted average of the discounted dividend rates of each of the K and L groups based on the asset appraisal amount of the corresponding bankruptcy estate. We call them the *weighted average of discounted dividend rates* and indicate them as $\bar{d}_K$ and $\bar{d}_L$, respectively. Hence:

$$E = (\bar{d}_K - \bar{d}_L) \sum A_j \tag{5}$$

13.4 Estimating the economic performance of efficient asset recovery and early conclusion

Data

Of the ailing financial institutions that took public funds, the number that received a decree of bankruptcy from the court was 457 (including liquidated institutions) as of the end of October 2004. By sector, there were five banks, nine insurance companies, six securities companies, 22 merchant banks, 76 mutual savings banks (old mutual credit unions) and 339 credit unions.

Table 13.2 shows the conclusion of bankruptcy estates by sector. Only Chungcheong Bank was concluded among the five liquidated banks in 1998, showing the lowest conclusion rate of 20 per cent. Mutual savings banks showed the highest conclusion rate at 68.4 per cent, followed by credit unions with 58.7 per cent. Of the total 457 bankruptcy estates, 61 estates were concluded legally, 203 estates were *de facto* concluded and 193 estates had not yet been concluded, showing an overall conclusion rate of 57.8 per cent.

Table 13.2 Number of bankruptcy estates by the status of conclusion (as of the end of Oct 2004)

Status	Sector						
	Banks	Insurance	Securities	Merchant banks	MSBs[a]	Credit unions	Total
Concluded							
Legally	0	1	1	0	0	59[b]	61
Actually	1	4	1	5	52	140	203
Not yet concluded	4	4	4	17	24	140	193
Total	5	9	6	22	76	339	457
Conclusion rate (%)	20.0	55.6	33.3	22.7	68.4	58.7	57.8

Notes: a. Mutual savings banks.
b. Included bankruptcy-abolished estate (Jeonbuk Daeil Credit Union).

In this part of the chapter, we place the focus of our analysis on credit unions, whose analysis is most credible as the number of bankruptcy estates is greater than in any other sectors. After this, we apply the same analysis method to merchant banks and mutual savings banks in order to analyse comprehensive economic achievements.[4]

First, we excluded 140 estates, which have not yet been concluded from the total of 339 credit unions, from the analysis.[5] After additionally excluding from the list a bankruptcy abolished corporation (Jeonbuk-Daeil Credit Union), a liquidated corporation (Isabel Credit Union), and six estates (Namdonggongdan, Nonsan, Mudeungilbo, Inwha, No. 2 Dongin, Chungil Credit Union) which did not report asset appraisal amounts or dividends, we analysed dividend results on 191 concluded estates. The data on dividends and asset appraisal amounts at the time of bankruptcy were based on the *Current Status of Bankruptcy Estates* reported by bankruptcy estates to KDIC every month and the *Current Status of Post Management of Concluded Estates* reported by concluded estates to KDIC every month.

Table 13.3 shows the dividend rate by time of each dividend for the 191 concluded credit unions.[6] In the table, the simple dividend rates are obtained by dividing the dividend appraisal amount by the asset appraisal amount at the time of bankruptcy. On the other hand, the discounted dividend rate converts the dividend amount into value at the time of bankruptcy (present value) and divides it by the asset appraisal amount. We calculated the average price of the overall estates by the time of each dividend. It is not the arithmetic mean but the weighted average based on asset appraisal amounts.[7]

The average total simple dividend rate shown in Table 13.3 is 90.66 per cent. Over half of the total dividends were made in the first dividend (46.29 per cent of asset appraisal) and three quarters (75.48 per cent) in the

Table 13.3 Average dividend rate of bankrupt credit unions by the time of dividend

Dividend rate	1st	2nd	3rd	4th	over 5th	Total
Simple	46.29	22.14	11.94	5.53	4.76	90.66
Discounted	43.70	19.94	10.22	4.72	3.98	82.56

first and second dividend rates combined (68.43 per cent of assets appraised). As the time progresses, the dividend falls sharply, so the total dividend rate for the 4th dividend and thereafter reached a level only slightly more than 10 per cent.

The discounted dividend rate shown in the second row of the table used the weighted average of time deposit interest rates (based on fresh dealings) compiled by the Bank of Korea shown in Table 13.4.

To convert dividends into value at the point of bankruptcy, following the method set out in the previous section, we should discount dividends by the relevant interest rate after considering the period between each dividend. For instance, assume that an estate went bankrupt on 1 August, 1998 and paid its first dividend on 31 July, 1999. In this case, the number of days referring to the year 1998 is 152 and the interest rate is 13.39 per cent, the discount rate during the period is 13.39×(152/365) = 5.58 per cent. Likewise, as the number of days referring to the year 1999 is 212 and the interest rate is 7.05 per cent, the discount rate during the period is 7.05×(212/365) = 4.09 per cent. Accordingly, if the first dividend paid on July 31, 1999 is D_1, converting it by the value as of 1 August, 1998 gives:

$$\frac{D_1}{(1+0.0558)(1+0.0409)} = 0.91D_1$$

Using this method, we discounted all dividends and divided the sum of them by the asset appraisal amount at the point of bankruptcy to calculate the discounted dividend rate.

Discounting thus has a major impact on the dividend rate shown in Table 13.3. The total dividend rate of the 191 estates is an average 82.56 per cent, clearly lower than the simple dividend rate. The dividend rate falls only slightly from 46.29 per cent to 43.70 per cent for the first dividend, and the

Table 13.4 Weighted average of time-deposit interest rates (annual %)

Year	1998	1999	2000	2001	2002	2003	2004
Interest rate	13.39	7.05	7.08	5.46	4.71	4.15	3.90

Source: Bank of Korea, *Monthly Bulletin*, relevant editions.

relative gap between the two dividend rates widens as the time for dividends progresses because the discounting is compounded.

All of the 191 credit unions subject to analysis paid dividends at least once (Table 13.5). The average period from the point of time of declaring bankruptcy to the point of the first dividend was 12.89 months. Nineteen estates were concluded after paying their first dividend so only 172 went on to pay a second dividend. The average period between the first and second dividends was 12.41 months, slightly shorter than the period needed for first dividend. Such a trend continued until the 5th dividend, but thereafter the period between dividends lengthened. The 191 estates paid dividends an average of 3.13 times. The period from the point of bankruptcy to the point of time to declaring conclusion was an average of 39.66 months (3.31 years). The period necessary for dividends varied widely according to the estate. For instance, the shortest period, until payment of the first dividend, was 2 months and the longest 67.46 months (5.62 years).

Dividend rates and the period needed for conclusion by group

If a KDIC trustee and a non-KDIC trustee manage bankruptcy estates with a similar status of assets, independently, during the whole period from the point of bankruptcy to conclusion, it would be simple to compare the two group's performances. However, even this is not a completely fair test because that would be the purely hypothetical case of managing the identical estate under the same conditions.

KDIC staff began to be appointed as trustees of bankruptcy estates in earnest after March 15, 2001 when the Constitutional Court of Korea ruled that the article concerning appointment of KDIC officials as bankruptcy

Table 13.5 Number of estates that paid dividends by the time of dividend

Time of dividend	1st	2nd	3rd	4th	5th	6th	7th	8th
Number of estates	191	172	124	66	32	17	5	1
Average period needed for dividends (months)	12.89	12.41	10.94	10.56	9.29	10.19	10.51	6.48

Table 13.6 Accumulated distribution of KDIC's participation in bankrupt credit unions (based on year-end figures)

Year	1998	1999	2000	2001	2002	2003
KDIC participation/ Total estates	0/27	0/99	23/142	164/165	166/167	191/191

trustees was constitutional. Table 13.6 shows the status of KDIC's participation in 191 bankrupt credit unions as a trustee by year on an accumulated basis. At the end of 1998, 27 out of the 191 estates were in bankruptcy. Of them, there was no case that KDIC staff was appointed as a trustee. Until the end of 1999, there were no KDIC-appointed trustees in a total of 99 bankruptcy estates. Around the end of 2000, however, KDIC participated in 23 out of the 142 estates as an independent or joint trustee, bringing the KDIC's participation rate to 16.2 per cent. From the beginning of 2001, KDIC staff had begun to be appointed as trustees in earnest. And, at the end of the same year, all but one out of the 165 estates had KDIC staff as their trustees.

There were 129 cases where a non-KDIC trustee carried out business at the point of bankruptcy but was replaced with a KDIC trustee in the middle of the process. Out of the 191 estates subject to analysis, there was not a single estate where a non-KDIC trustee managed the whole process from the point of bankruptcy to conclusion.[8] This fact makes it difficult to classify KDIC-managed estates and non-KDIC-managed estates. Namely, as KDIC managed bankruptcy estates from the point of bankruptcy to conclusion in many cases, it is easy to calculate the dividend results. However, it is difficult to compare those results with the dividend results of non-KDIC trustees as there were no dividend results for them. It means that the dividend results of non-KDIC trustees should be estimated in some sort of way in order to evaluate the economic performances of KDIC trustees.

To estimate the dividend results of non-KDIC trustees, we classify the 191 bankruptcy estates into four groups and look at each group's dividend results. The criterion of classification is the period from the point of bankruptcy to KDIC's participation. The first group is bankruptcy estates where KDIC was appointed as a trustee from the point of bankruptcy: 32.5 per cent of estates belong to the group. In each KDIC managed the entire process from the point of bankruptcy to conclusion. We call them 'KDIC-affiliated estates' from now on. In the other estates non-KDIC trustees (mainly lawyers) were in operation at the point of bankruptcy but were replaced with KDIC trustees later. As we cannot regard the group as a pure KDIC-affiliated estate, we call it 'quasi-KDIC-affiliated estates' from now on and classify them into three small groups according to the period for KDIC's participation in the estates after the point of bankruptcy. Namely, Group I consists of 12 estates in which KDIC trustees participated within one year after bankruptcy, Group II of 76 estates in which they participated between 1 to 2 years, and Group III of 41 estates in which they participated two years or more after bankruptcy.

From the simple and discounted dividend rates of the four groups shown in Figure 13.2 we can see a trend where the dividend rates are lower the later KDIC participated in the process. The difference the discounted dividend rates between KDIC-affiliated groups and quasi-KDIC group III was 21.17 per cent points. One noteworthy feature is that groups in which KDIC did not participate from the start see a bigger gap between the simple dividend

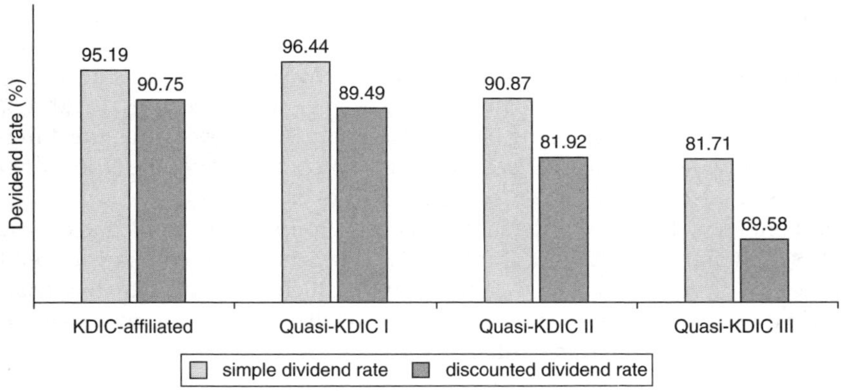

Figure 13.2 Average dividend rate of credit union bankruptcy estates by group

rate and the discounted dividend rate, implying that groups where KDIC participated later in the process were sluggish in asset recovery and required a longer period for conclusion.

As shown in Figure 13.3, it took 2.11 years for the KDIC-affiliated estates to come to conclusion from bankruptcy. On the other hand, it took a longer period for groups in which KDIC participated later in the process. In particular, in the case of quasi-KDIC group III in which KDIC could not participate for over 2 years after bankruptcy, the period needed for conclusion reached 4.63 years, more than twice that of KDIC-affiliated estates, while the period needed for conclusion for quasi-KDIC group I, in which KDIC participated within one year after bankruptcy, was delayed for about one year compared with that of KDIC-affiliated estates.

We can expect from these results that if KDIC had not participated in the bankruptcy procedures in the middle and non-KDIC trustees had managed independently until conclusion, the dividend rate would probably have been

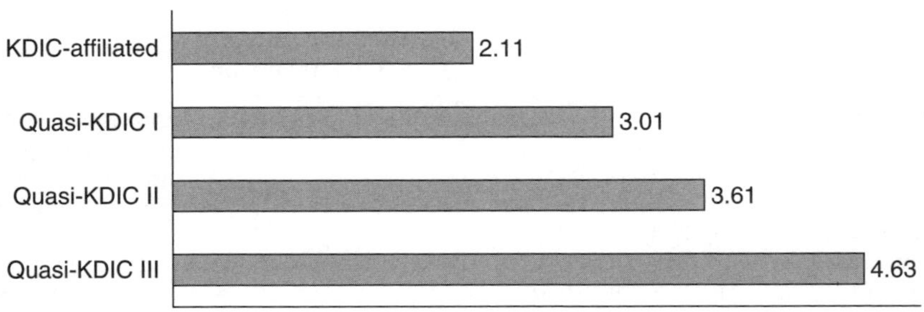

Figure 13.3 Period needed for conclusion of credit union bankruptcy estates by group (unit: number of years)

lower than even that of quasi-KDIC group III. However, for this expectation to hold, bankruptcy estates of each group would have to be in similar conditions in terms of asset volume, the degree of insolvency and business-cycle factors. As KDIC only participated in bankruptcy estates in earnest in 2001, if the environment surrounding bankruptcy estates differ over time, the difference of dividend results between each group could have come from other factors besides the trustees' effective asset recovery efforts.

There are substantial differences between groups in terms of book value as well as appraisal amount (Table 13.7). However, when comparing credit unions with other sectors, we cannot say that such differences are big, relatively speaking. Moreover, it is difficult to establish whether it is more favourable to recover assets from bankruptcy estates with fewer assets or those with larger assets.[9]

The degree of insolvency of assets also varies (see Table 13.7). The point of bankruptcy for KDIC-affiliated estates is the most recent – after March 2000. In general, as the financial institutions which went bankrupt right after the financial crisis suffered from a relatively high degree of insolvency and there were many estates that suffered from financial accidents, this may explain much of the big differences of asset insolvency between the groups. To take account of this we compare the dividend amounts divided not by book value but by asset appraisal amount, as the ratio of dividend to asset appraisal amount is an indicator that takes the degree of asset insolvency into consideration.

We can consider various factors affecting the results of asset recovery of bankruptcy estates besides the asset volume and the degree of insolvency, such as the ease of recovering assets and the financial policies and changes in business-cycle environment during the period in progress of the bankruptcy procedures. Our analysis does not take this into account.

Table 13.7 Average asset price of credit union estates

Group	Point of bankruptcy	Average asset price at point of bankruptcy (100m won)		Appraisal/book value average ratio(%)[a]
		Book value	Appraisal	
KDIC-affiliated	Mar 2000–Jun 2003	81.73	57.98	71.14
Quasi-KDIC I	Apr 1999–Dec 2000	67.43	41.46	62.46
Quasi-KDIC II	Jan 1999–Mar 2000	107.58	70.88	65.11
Quasi-KDIC III	Aug 1998–Apr 1999	120.31	55.22	49.52

Note: [a] The group average ratio of each appraisal/book value.

Estimation of economic performance of the KDIC trustee system

In this section we estimate the dividend rates of *non*-KDIC-affiliated estates, based on the dividend results of KDIC-affiliated estates and quasi-KDIC-affiliated group III. The quasi-KDIC group III is nearest to the non-KDIC-affiliated estates among quasi-KDIC-affiliated estates. Although we will look into it again later, in the case of quasi-KDIC group III, the first dividend was, in general, implemented by non-KDIC trustees while the second and subsequent dividends were carried out by KDIC trustees except in a few special cases.

It is clear from Figure 13.4 that a higher dividend rate was obtained from KDIC-affiliated estates, and this shows that the difference stems from the disparity of the first dividend rates, both simple and discounted. The total dividend rates of the second time and thereafter, are roughly the same for the two groups, whether estimated on the simple or discounted basis. These results indicate that KDIC-affiliated estates recovered assets promptly in the initial stage of bankruptcy procedures and effectively carried out their business. The slight improvement in the performance of KDIC affiliated estates when discounting is allowed for occurs because the period needed for dividends and conclusion for quasi-KDIC affiliated group III is much longer than that of KDIC-affiliated estates.

The period needed to attain the first dividend after bankruptcy, which was 7.42 months for KDIC-affiliated estates but 20.83 months for quasi-KDIC-affiliated group III (Figure 13.5), about three times as long. Mainly owing to these factors, the gap in the total discounted dividend rates between the KDIC-affiliated estates, which have a relatively high first dividend as a result

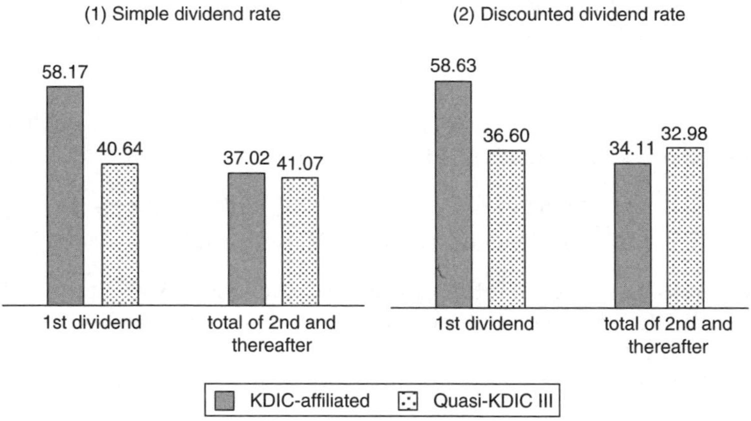

Figure 13.4 Average dividend rates of credit union bankruptcy estates by time of dividend

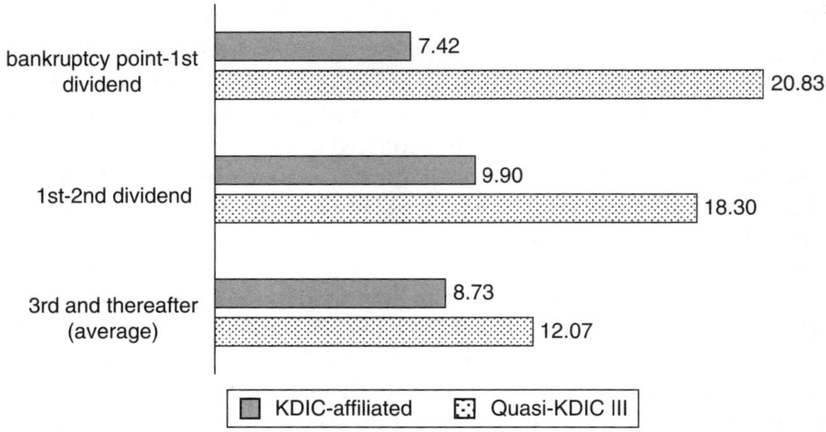

Figure 13.5 Average period needed for dividends of credit union bankruptcy estates (unit: number of months)

of carrying out asset recovery intensively and effectively in the initial stage of bankruptcy, and the quasi KDIC affiliated group III widened further.

In 35 out of the 41 estates belonging to the quasi-KDIC-affiliated group III, non-KDIC trustees implemented the first dividend. Whereas, KDIC trustees could not participate until the second dividend in only 6 out of the 41 estates. Accordingly, we treat the first dividend of quasi-KDIC-affiliated group III as being the result of non-KDIC trustees but adjust the dividend results of the second and subsequent dividends as follows:

Estimate of total dividend rate for non-KDIC-affiliated estates
= 1st dividend rate for quasi-KDIC group III
+ α × Total dividend rate of 2nd and thereafter for KDIC-affiliated estates

where α is an adjustment coefficient, based on the gap in the first dividend rates between KDIC and quasi-KDIC-affiliated group III:

$$\alpha = \frac{\text{1st dividend rate for quasi-KDIC-affiliated group III}}{\text{1st dividend rate for KDIC-affiliated group}}$$

This therefore assumes that the gap between the first dividend rates of KDIC and non-KDIC-affiliated estates will continue at the same rate for the second dividend and thereafter. Hence, the estimate of the discounted dividend rate of non-KDIC-affiliated estates by this method for credit union bankruptcy estates is:

$$36.60\% + \frac{36.60\%}{56.63\%} \times 34.11\% = 58.65\%$$

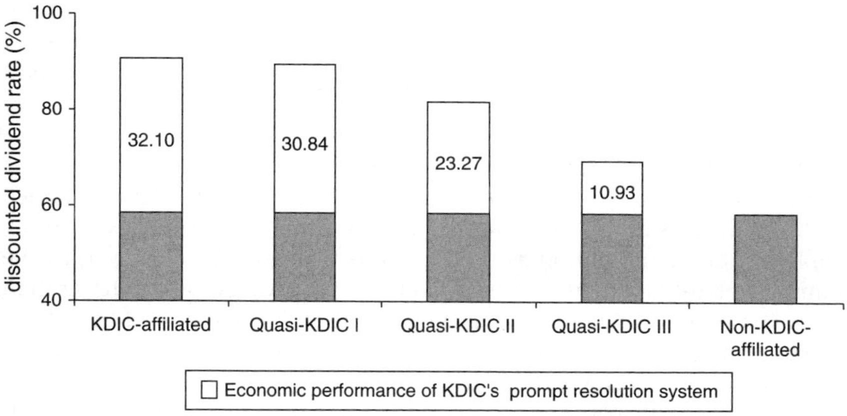

Figure 13.6 Results of the increase in discounted dividend rates by KDIC trustees of credit union bankruptcy estates by group

We can extrapolate this to provide an estimate of economic achievements made by KDIC trustees as shown in Figure 13.6. The gap in discounted dividend rates between KDIC-affiliated estates and non-KDIC-affiliated estates was 32.10 per cent points. Secondly, the later KDIC trustees participated the lower the estimated gain from their efforts.

These percentage differences are converted into monetary values in table 13.8. The table covers all 332 credit union bankruptcy estates, including estates that were concluded or have not been concluded yet. We calculated the economic performance under the assumption that the dividend rates of unsettled credit unions will be the same as those of concluded estates.

As shown in the table, the total amount of asset appraisals was 2.455 trillion won for the 197 KDIC-affiliated estates in which KDIC trustees participated from the point of bankruptcy. The increase in dividends due to the KDIC trustee system using equation (5), is 788.1 billion won. When

Table 13.8 Increase in dividends by KDIC trustees of credit union estates

Group	**No. of estates**	**Total asset appraisal (100m won)**	**Increase in discounted dividend rate (%p)**	**Increase in dividends (100m won)**
KDIC-affiliated	197	24,550	32.10	7,881
Quasi-KDIC I	16	1,242	30.84	383
Quasi-KDIC II	77	5,418	23.27	1,261
Quasi-KDIC III	42	2,327	10.93	254
Total				9,779

the results of quasi-KDIC-affiliated estates where KDIC trustees participated in the middle of bankruptcy procedures are included, the total increase in dividends attained by KDIC trustees in the credit union sector is 977.9 billion won under this estimation method.

Estimating economic performances in other sectors

In this section, we analyse the effects of the increase in dividends attained by KDIC trustees in the merchant bank and mutual savings bank sectors, by applying the same method as used for the credit unions. However, as the number of bankrupt merchant banks and mutual savings banks is fewer than that of bankrupt credit unions, we compare the dividend results of the overall bankruptcy estates in the sector, including estates that were concluded or have not been concluded yet.

In the merchant bank sector the number of bankruptcy estates is relatively few at 22. Six estates are KDIC-affiliated estates where KDIC trustees participated from the point of time of declaring bankruptcy; three estates belong to quasi-KDIC-affiliated group I in which KDIC trustees participated within 2 years after the sentence of bankruptcy; and 13 estates belong to quasi-KDIC-affiliated group II in which KDIC trustees participated 2 years or more after the sentence of bankruptcy.

Table 13.9 shows that as in the case of credit unions, groups in which KDIC trustees participated late posted a lower dividend rate. We estimate the dividend rates of non-KDIC-affiliated estates by comparison of KDIC-affiliated estates and quasi-KDIC-affiliated group II using the same method applied to the credit union sector. The result is:

$$50.69\% + \frac{50.69\%}{54.25\%} \times 34.52\% = 82.94\%$$

The reason the estimation was possible using the same method as applied to the credit union sector is that the first dividend of 13 estates belonging to the quasi-KDIC-affiliated group II of merchant banks was made by non-KDIC trustees but the participation of KDIC trustees has increased at a rapid pace since the second dividend. The calculated results of economic achievements attained by a KDIC trustee system in the merchant bank sector are an increase in dividends of 530.2 billion won as shown in Table 13.10.

Table 13.9 Average discounted dividend rates of merchant bank estates

Group	No. of estates	1st dividend	Total of 2nd and thereafter	Total
KDIC-affiliated	6	54.25	34.52	88.77
Quasi-KDIC I	3	39.79	45.98	85.77
Quasi-KDIC II	13	50.69	33.01	83.70

Table 13.10 Increase in dividends by KDIC trustees of merchant bank estates

Group	Total asset appraisal (100m won)	Increase in discounted dividend rate (%p)	Increase in dividends (100m won)
KDIC-affiliated	56,509	5.83	3,294
Quasi-KDIC I	42,897	2.83	1,214
Quasi-KDIC II	104,377	0.76	793
Total			5,302

Finally, we analyse the mutual savings bank sector. However, it is difficult to classify mutual savings banks into groups. Of the total 76 mutual savings banks bankruptcy estates, 43 (20 of them were concluded estates) belong to KDIC-affiliated estates but the remaining estates are those that KDIC trustees participated in within 2 years after declaring bankruptcy. In the case of these quasi-KDIC-affiliated estates, moreover, 70 per cent of the total is estates in which KDIC trustees participated before the first dividend, clearly different from credit unions and merchant banks. Accordingly, it is difficult to regard the results of the first dividend as the result of non-KDIC trustees. In the case of mutual savings banks, KDIC trustees in general participated in the initial stage of bankruptcy, so it is difficult to determine the objects for comparison of results with KDIC-affiliated estates. As for mutual savings banks, accordingly, we present the results of only KDIC-affiliated estates.

Table 13.11 shows the average discounted dividend rates of 43 mutual savings banks managed by KDIC from the point of declaring bankruptcy. We can see that the total discounted dividend rate for the mutual savings banks is 92.23 per cent, slightly higher than those of credit unions and merchant banks.

If we compare the dividend rates of KDIC-affiliated estates as a whole of the three sectors – credit unions, merchant banks and mutual savings banks, as shown in Figure 13.7, we can see that the similarity among the sectors is very high in terms of the absolute level of dividend rates and in the trend of dividends by time. One of the reasons seems that, in the case of KDIC-affiliated estates, trustees did not carry out bankruptcy procedures independently, but they guided asset recovery and early conclusion through

Table 13.11 Average discounted dividend rates of KDIC-affiliated MSBs

	No. of estates	1st dividend	Total of 2nd and thereafter	Total
KDIC-affiliated	43	56.93	35.30	92.23

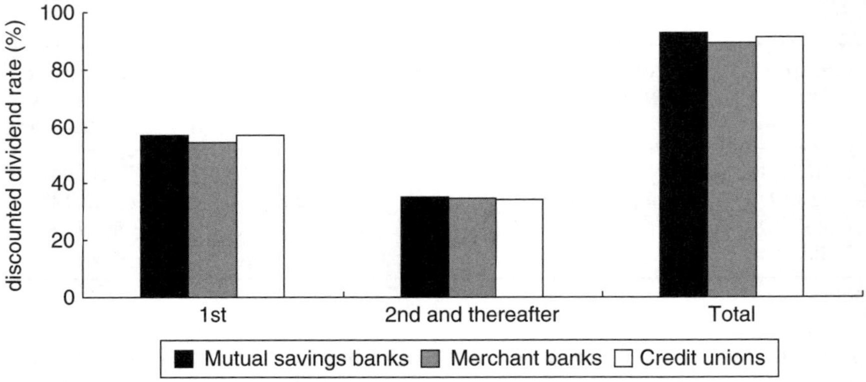

Figure 13.7 Discounted dividend rates of KDIC-affiliated estates by sector

a standardized system for the whole process, from the point of declaring bankruptcy to its conclusion.

13.5 Conclusion

Bankrupt financial institutions have many factors and characteristics that hamper efficient asset recovery. Since 2001, when KDIC began to participate in bankruptcy estates as a trustee in earnest, it has exerted its best effort to enhance the efficiency of bankruptcy procedures. It has reduced operational expenses of bankruptcy estates by creating an early conclusion system and enhanced the efficiency of asset recovery by mapping out various methods and tools.

In this chapter, we analysed the economic performances of credit unions stemming from enhancement of efficient bankruptcy procedures propelled by KDIC. The results showed that estates in which KDIC participated as a trustee from the initial stage of bankruptcy carried out bankruptcy procedures more effectively than estates in which KDIC participated as a trustee late, whether in terms of dividend rates or the period needed for conclusion. Converted into money, it is estimated at 977.9 billion won. Applying the same method to merchant banks the effect of the increase in dividends amounts to 530.2 billion won.

However, it is difficult to say that this analysis fully evaluated the economic performances of a system for early conclusion of bankruptcy estates propelled by KDIC. In particular, we failed to expand our analysis as there were no objects for comparison in the case of mutual savings banks. While comparing and analysing dividend results of KDIC and non-KDIC-affiliated estates, we assumed that factors other than asset volume and the degree of insolvency worked on the two groups identically. We can say that this was one limitation of our analysis as economic conditions improved considerably in the years following the financial crisis.

Systematic investigation into asset recovery and resolution costs of bankrupt financial institutions has an important implication, not only for enhancing effectiveness of bankruptcy procedures but also for deciding the deposit insurance premium rates and resolution methods. Accordingly, we can say that a follow-up study is needed.

Notes

1 The contents of this chapter were made based on the *Annual Report* and various internal reports published by KDIC and the *White Paper on Management of Public Funds* published by the Public Fund Management Committee of the Ministry of Finance and Economy. Detailed indications of quotations were omitted.

2 Article 20 of the *Public Funds Oversight Special Law* (special cases of bankruptcy procedure): in the case of dissolution or bankruptcy of financial institutions subject to deposit insurance (including those whose contract transfer was decided according to the *Act on the Structural Improvement of the Financial Industry*), the court appoints the KDIC or KDIC staff as bankruptcy trustees, despite Article 531 of the Commercial Law, Article 147 of the Bankruptcy Law, or other laws and regulations concerning the appointment of liquidator or bankruptcy trustees in case that effective withdrawal of public funds is needed. In the case that KDIC is a liquidator or a bankruptcy trustee according to Clause 1, the regulations of Clause 2 of Article 539 of the Commercial Law, and Article 157, 187, 188 of the Bankruptcy Law do not apply.

3 The contents of this chapter are based on various internal reports published by the KDIC and the *White Paper on Management of Public Funds* published by the Public Fund Management Committee of the Ministry of Finance and Economy. Detailed indications of quotations were omitted.

4 Banks along with insurance and securities companies with less than 10 bankruptcy estates were completely excluded from the analysis.

5 In the case of estates that have not yet been concluded, it is difficult to compare dividend rates as the dividend is in progress. Even in the case where a bankruptcy estate was concluded legally, if additional assets are found later, additional dividends should be made. Also, in the case of an actually concluded estate where the bankruptcy estate wins the suit, there are then funds for further dividends. Accordingly, in case of a concluded estate, the final dividend is not fixed, but in general additional dividend volume is much less than that of an estate that has not been concluded yet.

6 Bankruptcy estates report dividends to KDIC by dividing them into mid-term, final and additional dividends. In this chapter, however, we called them the first dividend, the second dividend, and so on, without such classification.

7 Weighted averages reflect the dividend rate for all the assets taken together as appraised at the start of the bankruptcy procedures.

8 Of the total 339 credit union bankruptcy estates, including those that have not been concluded yet, the number of estates where KDIC had not been appointed as a trustee is only one, Hanyoung Credit Union, which went bankrupt in September 1998 but it has not yet been concluded.

9 In the case of the USA, studies on bankrupt banks showed that the results were different according to the timing. According to the studies of McDill (2004) and Salmon *et al.* (2003) on bankrupt banks during the 1984–2002 period, banks with a bigger asset volume showed a higher recovery rate. In the case of studies of banks during the 1997–2002 period, however, banks with a bigger asset volume showed a lower recovery rate.

References

Bank of Korea, *Monthly Bulletin*, relevant issues.

Korea Deposit Insurance Corporation (KDIC) *Annual Report*, relevant issues.

Korea Deposit Insurance Corporation (KDIC) 2002 *In-Service Manual of the Bankrupt Property Management Business*.

McDill, K. (2004) 'Resolution Cost and the Business Cycle,' Working paper, FDIC.

Public Fund Management Committee, *White Paper on Management of Public Funds, Ministry of Finance and Economy*, relevant issues.

Salmon, R., Allston, L., McBride, J., Trimper, D., Nelson, E., Barr, D., Almond, B., Hudson, G., Kinser, D. and Robinson, V. (2003) 'Costs Associated with Bank Failures,' Working paper, FDIC.

The authors also had access to internal documents produced by the Korea Deposit Insurance Corporation which are not publicly available.

14

The Role of Deposit Insurance in Promoting Financial System Stability in Nigeria

Ganiyu A. Ogunleye

Prior to the establishment of the Nigeria Deposit Insurance Corporation (NDIC), there were two major formalized government-provided safety nets for the Nigerian banking industry. They were the lender of last resort facility provided by the Central Bank of Nigeria (through the provision of temporary liquidity support to solvent depository institutions) and bank supervision. The government provided an implicit blanket guarantee to depositors and, by extension, other stakeholders by bailing out troubled banks.

There was also no formal arrangement regarding how the implicit protection could be funded; in fact, it was largely provided through the government's budget. Thus, the scheme was a contingent liability of the Federal Government and was characterized by the usual uncertainties about the level and scope of coverage. Other problems included a slow response to a crisis due to a debate as to whether there was a need for a budgetary provision and government's sole burden in banking distress resolution.

In 1986, the implementation of a Structural Adjustment Programme (SAP) facilitated the deregulation and liberalization of the Nigerian economy. Prior to that time, especially in the late 1970s and early 1980s, the Nigerian economy, like many sub-Saharan African countries, had undergone a series of severe economic crises. This situation was reflected in an unprecedented deterioration of all economic indicators including falling output, high rates of inflation and unemployment, increasing budgetary deficits due to rapidly falling government revenue, huge balance of payments deficits occasioned by the collapse of oil prices and worsening terms of trade as well as escalating external debt service obligations (Afolabi and Mamman, 1994: and Afolabi, 1995). By 1986, international and domestic developments exerted strong pressures that compelled the government to adopt the SAP (Adeyemo and Iwayemi, 1995). It was designed to adjust the macro-economic policy framework, strengthen the institutions and provide appropriate signals to producers in the real sector. The basic policies included public expenditures stabilization, foreign exchange market deregulation, and selective import liberalization, a rationalization of public enterprizes as well as the liberalization and deregulation of the financial system, among others. The liberalization and deregulation of the financial sector, as a major pillar of SAP, was hinged on the belief that a successful implementation of the programme required the development of an efficient financial sector.

With liberalization and deregulation the number of banks increased from 48 in 1988 to 120 in 1990. This development triggered keen competition as well as an increase in the risks to which banks and consequently depositors were exposed. An explicit deposit insurance system (DIS) was introduced to protect the depositors, particularly the small ones, from the adverse consequences of the increased risks being taken by the banks. Without a doubt the phenomenal growth in the number of banks over-taxed the managerial capacity available in the banking system.

The foregoing necessitated the introduction of an explicit deposit insurance system (DIS) in 1988. NDIC commenced operations in March 1989 and provided a further layer of protection to depositors by strengthening the Central Bank of Nigeria's (CBN's) supervisory activities to help ensure a safe and sound banking system. The DIS, like most other explicit systems, adopted a number of best practices including specifying the maximum insured sum and it adopted a clearly defined *ex ante* funding arrangement, among others, (Garcia, 1998; Financial Stability Forum's Working Group on Deposit Insurance, 2001; and Sundararajan, 2002). Participation in the system was made compulsory for all licensed deposit-taking financial institutions. NDIC was also given responsibilities for monitoring the health of member institutions as well as the risk exposure of the Deposit Insurance Fund (DIF) and providing an orderly failure resolution mechanism. In effect, the DIS in Nigeria was designed as a risk minimizer.

The next section of this chapter takes an overview of the regulatory framework and information-sharing arrangement while the following section discusses the functions of the NDIC and the design features of the DIS. We then highlight the main contributions of the NDIC to financial system stability while the penultimate section highlights the main lessons that can be learnt from Nigeria's experience. The final section summarizes the chapter.

14.1 Regulatory framework in Nigeria

The critical areas of focus of regulation, which are required to ensure the establishment of a sound financial system and address any emerging problems in the system in any country, can be broadly grouped into three, namely: entry; risk evaluation and containment; and failure resolution. In essence, regulatory activities can span the potential 'life cycle' of a financial institution from its cradle to its grave.[1]

The main activity involved in the entry process is licensing. Regulators should have the ability to screen ownership and management so as to ensure that only individuals with requisite qualifications, professional competence, experience, financial capacity, and sound ethical standards are allowed to obtain a banking licence. In most emerging markets, this responsibility rests either with the central bank, a separate regulatory body, or the Ministry of Finance.

The CBN is at the apex as the regulatory authority for the banking industry as enshrined in the Banks and Other Financial Institutions Act (BOFIA) No.25, 1991. Under that Act, the CBN has the power to license banks and other deposit-taking financial institutions and to supervise licensed institutions. However, the CBN was required to obtain the approval of The President to de-license a banking institution. That requirement subjected revocation[2] of a banking licence or de-licensing to the approval of a political authority. Consequently, between 1988 and 1998, NDIC was confronted with delays in granting approvals for the revocation of the licences of terminally distressed banking institutions. In effect, a situation of 'free entry, no exit' prevailed over the period as illiquid and insolvent banks remained open. The President's requirement for approval for de-licensing was removed in 1998 through an amendment to BOFIA, thus giving the CBN full failure resolution powers. As well, up to 1998, the CBN had the power to appoint NDIC as the provisional liquidator of failed banks and such appointment was deemed to have been made by the Federal High Court (FHC) and that arrangement ensured an effective exit mechanism. Unfortunately, CBN lost that power when the BOFIA was amended in 1998 and NDIC was required to apply to the FHC to be appointed as liquidator. The new dispensation created opportunities for legal challenges and protracted litigations, which has resulted in undue delay of failure resolution.

Banking supervision is the joint responsibility of the CBN and NDIC but it is not a case of needless overlap and duplication. This is because the responsibility is carried out through on-site examination and off-site surveillance where, to avoid duplication of efforts and/or role-conflict, the two institutions engage in consultations. In particular, the two institutions meet at the beginning of every year to agree on a bank examination programme. This arrangement guarantees that a bank is examined once a year. At the end of each examination by any of the institutions, the examination report is sent to the other institution. Banks examined by an institution in one period are allocated to the other institution in the following year to minimize over-familiarity with employees of examined institutions as well as to promote peer review mechanism.

In the case of off-site surveillance, the two institutions use the same set of prudential bank returns for appraising the financial condition and performance of both the industry and individual institutions. In order to ensure credible results, the two institutions developed and use a Bank Rating System. It is currently being enhanced to electronic Financial Analysis and Surveillance System (e-FASS). Bank ratings generated individually by the two institutions are compared to harmonize the results of their off-site analysis.

The two institutions have also established joint committees on supervision both at the executive and technical levels and they meet on a regular basis. This arrangement enables the two institutions to review developments in the banking industry and proactively address any emerging supervisory challenges.

NDIC also shares responsibility for failure resolution with the CBN.[3] The two institutions have developed a Contingency Planning Framework for Banking Systemic Crisis, with thresholds for intervention indicating when and how each institution is to intervene. To avoid conflict of role in the provision of liquidity support, there is a framework for liquidity support. This framework clearly demarcates when the NDIC liquidity support is needed as against the lender-of-last-resort role of the CBN. When a banking licence is revoked by the CBN, the NDIC serves as Liquidator.

Given that the licensed banks are universal banks engaging in money, capital and insurance markets' activities under the supervisory purview of different regulatory authorities, the need for cooperation amongst the regulatory agencies is imperative. This is accomplished through the Financial Services Regulation Coordinating Committee (FSRCC) with the CBN Governor as Chairman. Other members of the committee include the Chief Executive Officers of the NDIC; the Securities and Exchange Commission, the main regulatory body for the capital market; the National Insurance Commission, regulatory agency for Insurance business; the Corporate Affairs Commission, (the registrar of companies); and a representative of the Federal Ministry of Finance. The specific objectives of the Committee are to:

1. co-ordinate the supervision of financial institutions especially conglomerates;
2. minimize arbitrage opportunities usually created by differing regulations and supervision standards among supervisory authorities in the economy;
3. deliberate on problems experienced by any member in its relationship with any financial institution;
4. eliminate any information gap encountered by any regulatory agency in its relationship with any group of financial institutions;
5. articulate the strategies for the promotion of safe, sound and efficient practices by financial intermediaries; and
6. deliberate on such other issues as may be specified from time to time.

A Memorandum of Understanding (MOU) was executed by all the members of the FSRCC to facilitate access to prudential information and it contains safeguards for confidentiality of information.

In recognition of the inherent fragility of the banking system, the CBN announced in 2004 a bank consolidation programme to promote mergers and acquisition. Under this, each bank is required to attain a minimum shareholders' fund of ₦25 billion (about US$180 million) by 31 December 2005. It is envisaged that with a stronger capital base, banks would be able to support economic development as well as compete effectively both domestically and off-shore. At the end of 2005, the bank consolidation programme resulted in a reduction of banks from 89 to 25 better capitalized banks.

The bank consolidation programme also resulted in the de-licensing of 14 banks that failed to meet the new capital requirement. Given that the DIS was not designed to address either a systemic crisis or bank reform-induced failures, the CBN had to extend a blanket guarantee to private depositors in the banking system during the second half of year 2005. Under that guarantee, private depositors were assured that their deposits in any bank that failed to meet the consolidation requirements would be refunded in full. The guarantee stemmed the prospects of either a flight to safety or deposit run on banks that were perceived to be weak. The resolution of the 14 failed banks through a Purchase and Assumption (P and A) option is currently being undertaken by the NDIC.

As part of the institutional support for the bank consolidation programme, the CBN and NDIC promoted the establishment of the Asset Management Corporation of Nigeria. It was designed as a vehicle for the resolution of non-performing assets of the banking system.

14.2 Main features of the DIS

The functions of NDIC are to:[4]

1. insure deposit liabilities of licensed banks and such other financial institutions so as to promote confidence in the Nigerian banking system;
2. give assistance in the interest of depositors, in case of imminent or actual financial difficulties of banks particularly where suspension of payments is threatened; and avoiding damage to public confidence in the banking system;
3. guarantee payments to depositors, in case of imminent or actual suspension of payments by member banks or financial institutions up to the maximum amount specified in the Act;
4. assist the monetary authorities in the formulation and implementation of banking policy so as to ensure sound banking practice and fair competition among banks in the country; and

5. pursue any other measures necessary to achieve the objects of the Corporation.

The main design features are:

Ownership

NDIC is wholly owned by the CBN and the Federal Ministry of Finance in the ratio of a 60:40 shareholding structure.

Governance

The governing body is the Board of Directors which is responsible for policy formulation and oversight. Members of the Board are appointed by The President and the Corporation is under the supervisory purview of the Ministry of Finance.

Participating institutions

Participation is compulsory for all licensed banks and other deposit-taking financial institutions. However, NDIC has since inception extended the deposit insurance coverage to licensed universal banks only. With the licensing of community banks (CBs) and primary mortgage institutions (PMIs) which commenced in 2003, NDIC is in the process of extending deposit insurance coverage to those institutions. In this regard the Corporation has established a full-fledged department to handle the insurance and supervision of other licensed deposit-taking financial institutions. NDIC has also proposed amendment to Section 8 of its Act to create separate insurance funds for each category of insured institutions.

Level of coverage

All deposits in member institutions are insured with the following exclusions:

1. Insider deposits, that is, deposits of staff including directors of the licensed bank or financial institution;
2. Counter-claims from a person who maintains both deposit and loan accounts, the former serving as a collateral for the loan; and
3. Such other deposits as may be specified from time to time by the Board.

NDIC guarantees the payment of the insured deposits up to a maximum of ₦50,000 in the event of failure of a member financial institution. The maximum coverage, which was the equivalent of US$10,860 in 1988, is currently worth US$382 as a result of depreciation of the national currency (the Naira) over the years. There is a proposal to raise the maximum insured claim from ₦50,000 per depositor per bank to ₦200,000 per depositor per bank and ₦100,000 per depositor per CB or PMI to the National Assembly to reflect developments in the industry and the economy. Coverage has to be limited to limit moral hazard. While an unduly large coverage could encourage excessive risk-taking, a too low coverage limit could undermine the credibility of the system.

Funding

There is a deposit insurance fund (DIF) that is generated from periodic premiums paid by member institutions. Premiums are assessed on a flat rate basis but there is a goal to shift to a differentiated premium assessment. The operations of the NDIC are, however, financed solely from the interest earned on investments of the DIF in government securities such as Treasury Bills (TBs). Unlike in some jurisdictions, funding is *ex ante* in order to ensure the credibility of the system.

14.3 Contributions to financial stability

The activities aimed at insulating the industry from destructive runs and instability are:

Provision of a deposit guarantee

NDIC guarantees repayments to depositors in the event of failure of a member. At the commencement of the system, the maximum insurance limit was set at ₦50,000 per depositor. That limit was based on the fact that depositors with balances up to that amount constituted over 85 per cent of total depositors at that time and since DISs are intended to protect small savers, that limit was considered adequate. At this time, an increase to ₦200,000 per depositor per bank is under consideration.

The Corporation had paid out about ₦3.29 billion to depositors, representing 63 per cent of total insured claims of ₦5.2 billion of 34 closed banks to the end of 2005. The owners of the remaining 37 per cent of the insured deposits are being encouraged to come forward through periodic media campaigns.[5] However, due to poor depositors' response, the claim-filing period had been extended with a view to sustaining confidence in the system. These efforts have, no doubt, gone a long way in engendering depositors' confidence in the nation's banking system thereby promoting the stability of the nation's financial system.

Despite the efforts to reach out through publications, seminars, workshops, press briefings and advertisement, the general public seems unaware of the benefits and limitations of the system. For instance, there had been pressure for full coverage as against the best practice of limited coverage.[6] Furthermore, it is still common to find stakeholders confusing deposit insurance with the conventional insurance business. All these factors depict an inadequate understanding of the workings of the system. For deposit insurance to be effective, it is important that the public be well and adequately informed of its benefits and limitations.

Ensuring prompt repayment is necessary for maintaining credibility and confidence in the DIS. However, the provisions of the NDIC Act make it difficult to reimburse insured deposits even when depositors have ceased to have access to their money. Unless a bank's licence has been revoked, it is practically impossible for the NDIC to pay insured deposits. As well, even where licences have been revoked, litigations by shareholders/directors have frustrated re payment of insured deposits.[7]

Promoting financial stability through effective banking supervision

Banks are supervised to protect depositors, ensure monetary stability and promote an effective and efficient payment system. Banking supervision provides the oversight required to preserve the integrity of, and promote public confidence, in the banking system. The Nigerian system is modelled after that of the Federal Deposit Insurance Corporation (FDIC) (NDIC, 1997). It was established as a risk minimiser,[8] hence supervision is included as one of its key functions. As noted earlier, however, NDIC's involvement can be regarded as a complement or reinforcement of the existing framework but with an emphasis on depositor protection. Thus, banking supervision can be regarded as an essential element of the DIS as it seeks to reduce the potential risk of failure and ensures that unsafe and unsound banking practices do not go undetected. It also provides the oversight required to preserve the integrity of, and promote public confidence in the banking system.

NDIC's involvement in on-site examination has significantly shortened the bank examination cycle such that despite the increase in the number of banks and their branches, banks are now examined annually as against once in two to three years prior to the establishment of the Corporation. However, the challenge of this important supervisory function (especially off-site surveillance), has been the perennial issue of inaccurate and unreliable prudential returns. Many of such returns fail to reflect the true state of affairs of the reporting institutions. For example, there were instances when banks were unable to meet matured obligations but still recorded high liquidity ratios. Inaccurate returns impair assessment of banks' financial condition and hinder identification of potential problems which require prompt corrective action.

In order to enhance its effectiveness, NDIC has been vigorously pursuing capacity building through focused training and through the acquisition of relevant skills for off-site surveillance. In that regard, more staff in the on-site and off-site supervision departments have been exposed to new techniques of banking supervision at both local and foreign regulatory institutions such as the USA Federal Reserve System, FDIC, Office of Comptroller of the

Currency (USA), Toronto Leadership Centre (Canada), Financial Stability Institute (Switzerland), and Financial Services Authority (UK). In addition, through the customized training on Audit Command Language (ACL) and Computer-Assisted Audit Technique (CAAT), the quality of IT Examination by the Corporation has improved considerably as acknowledged by the examined banks.

The main tool for off-site surveillance, the Bank Analysis System (BAS), is being enhanced to electronic Financial Analysis and Surveillance System (e-FASS). Upon completion of the project, NDIC will have access to banking information on an on-line, real-time basis and that will help to enhance access to more reliable data for bank analysis.

In conjunction with the CBN, NDIC is in the process of adopting and implementing the new Basel Capital Adequacy Measurement Framework known as Basel II Capital Accord. When it comes into effect in 2007, it will replace the existing 1988 Capital Accord or Basel I. Preparation for the implementation of the new capital accord also includes the development of a framework for risk-based supervision which has now become imperative in view of current developments in the financial services industry at both the domestic and international levels.

All the activities stated above are expected to further enhance the effectiveness of the supervisory activities of the Corporation in promoting safe and sound banking practices and hence contributing to the stability of the financial system. NDIC examiners have been carrying out their duties with the sole aim of ensuring a sound financial system and this has been demonstrated in their findings over the years.[9] NDIC maintains a policy of zero tolerance against unprofessional and unethical behaviour.

Examiners place an emphasis on risk management frameworks of banks. Focus is also on non-financial risks such as reputation and operational risks, which had not received adequate attention.

Distress resolution

One of the primary roles of NDIC is to ensure that failing institutions are resolved in a timely and efficient manner. This presupposes the existence of legal powers that support early intervention and prompt corrective action, the ability to close troubled banks promptly, and legal provisions for the prompt and orderly liquidation of assets and resolution of creditors' claims. NDIC is empowered to provide assistance to failing or distressed banks in the interest of depositors. Financial assistance can take the form of loans, guarantees for loan taken by the bank or acceptance of accommodation bills. Technical assistance may include the take over of management and control of the bank, changes in management or assisted merger with another viable institution.

Responsibility for distress resolution is shared with the CBN. A Contingency Planning Framework for Banking Systemic Crises introduced in 2002 facilitates prompt resolution of problem banks. The framework seeks to reduce the incidence of systemic distress by improving the supervisory processes, providing transparent and objective thresholds for regulatory intervention and promoting self-regulation among banks.

It is worth noting that NDIC was established when the banking system was already in distress. Indeed, there were seven technically insolvent state-owned banks in the system in 1988. It, therefore, had to grapple with the resolution of distressed banks at an early stage of its existence. Depending on the severity and peculiarity of the situation, NDIC and CBN have, over the years, successfully adopted the following measures, among others, to address bank distress:

- Accommodation facilities were granted to ten banks which had serious liquidity crises ₦2.3 billion (about US$500 million) in 1989 following the withdrawal of public-sector deposits from commercial and merchant banks and the transfer of same to CBN during that year. The disruption as a result of the policy-induced shock largely reflected the financial fragility of the system. The crisis occurred barely three months after NDIC commenced operations;
- Take-over of management and control of 28 distressed banks by CBN/NDIC to safeguard their assets. The most recent intervention was the removal of the respective Boards and Managements of three banks in 2005 and their replacement with new Boards and Managements to save the banks from reckless mismanagement and dissipation of depositors' funds;
- Acquisition, restructuring and sale of seven distressed banks to new investors; and
- Closure of 36 problem banks that failed to respond to various regulatory/supervisory initiatives. While the liquidation of Savannah Bank of Nigeria and Peak Merchant Bank were suspended due to court action, it is noteworthy that all the banks were closed with minimal disruption to the banking system. In this regard, the closure of 26 banks on 16 January 1998 was particularly significant. The closure of 14 banks on 16 January 2006 was also quite important.

The combined effect of these measures prevented deposit runs that would have created instability in the financial system.

Bank liquidation

Bank liquidation is always adopted if found to be the most effective as compared to other distress resolution measures.

The liquidation process involves the orderly closure of a failed institution with minimum disruption to the banking system, cost-effective realization of assets, and settlement of claims of uninsured depositors and creditors. Depositors are given priority over all other creditors in consonance with the primary objective of the deposit insurance system.

Achievements in this regard include:

1. Payment of liquidation dividend to depositors. In addition to the repayment of insured funds, depositors with credit balances in excess of the guaranteed limit were paid dividends based on the volume of proceeds of the closed banks' assets realized by the Corporation. At the end of 2005, the sum of ₦5.95 billion had been paid out to the depositors of 32 of the 34 banks in liquidation. This is more than half of the ₦10.75 billion declared as liquidation dividends. Out of the 32 banks, the Corporation had declared a 100 per cent dividend (that is, full recovery) for all uninsured depositors of ten banks while recovery is as high as 93 per cent in some other banks;
2. Payment of a liquidation dividend to general creditors. In keeping with the priority of claims under the Companies and Allied Matters Act (CAMA), liquidation dividends had also been paid to some general creditors of some of the banks. For example, the general creditors of five banks-in-liquidation, namely: Alpha Merchant Bank Plc, Amicable Bank Ltd, Nigeria Merchant Bank Ltd, Pan African Bank Ltd and Rims Merchant Bank Ltd had received the sum of ₦659.56 million out of ₦753.31 declared in their favour as at the end of October, 2005;
3. Payment of liquidation dividend to shareholders. After settling the claims of depositors and creditors, whatever funds that are left are appropriated to shareholders of failed banks in the form of dividends in keeping with the provisions of CAMA. Consequently, shareholders of liquidated Nigeria Merchant Bank Ltd (that is, United Bank for Africa Plc and Ministry of Finance Incorporated) were paid liquidation dividends totalling ₦620 million based on their ownership ratio of 40:60. Similarly, the sum of ₦293 million had been paid to former owners of Pan African Bank Ltd (Rivers and Bayelsa State Governments) as liquidation dividend. Payments of dividends have commenced to the shareholders of the defunct Alpha Merchant Bank Plc for whom ₦600 million had been declared;
4. Recovery of debts owed failed banks. In order to encourage debtors of failed banks to repay their debts, balances as at the date the banks were closed were frozen and accorded non-accrual status. All the interest accrued after liquidation were reversed while several requests for interest waivers were considered on their merit. Indeed, in 2000, post-liquidation interest amounting to ₦5.16 billion (about 14.6 per cent of the aggregate debt portfolio of failed banks) were written off which made aggregate debt portfolio of failed banks to fall from ₦35.37 billion to about ₦30.21 billion. The strategies adopted had assisted in the area of debt recovery. As

at the end of 2005, a total of ₦5.47 billion had been recovered from the debtors of the closed banks. The Corporation also facilitated the repayment of ₦3.10 billion debts owed by governments and their agencies to both healthy and distressed banks in 1997. That exercise improved the liquidity of many banks.

NDIC is still being faced with some constraints in its debt recovery efforts. Some of the constraints include business failures, unwillingness to honour obligations and large volumes of unsecured or fraudulently granted loans. Instead of seeking ways to settle their debts, some debtors had challenged the jurisdiction of the Federal High Courts to adjudicate in matters between them and the closed banks while the Court of Appeal gave a ruling in their favour. It is important to note that the NDIC had successfully challenged the ruling of the Court of Appeal at the Supreme Court which affirmed that the Federal High Court has jurisdiction over debt recovery matters. It is also important to stress that unless debts are expeditiously recovered, uninsured depositors and creditors cannot be paid most of their claims. This has serious consequences for public confidence in, and stability of, the banking system;

5. Disposal of fixed/tangible assets. NDIC has achieved appreciable success in this area but there are a few prime real estate properties yet to be sold. The inability to dispose of these properties is attributable to certain problems. The legal title of some assets is the subject of litigation while some of the assets are located in towns or communities where there is the low demand for such purpose-built properties. At the end of 2005, a total of ₦4.52 billion had been realized from the sale of fixed/tangible assets of the closed banks;
6. The implementation of The Failed Banks Act. NDIC, in its capacity as a liquidator, facilitated the enactment of the Failed Banks (Recovery of Debts and other Financial Malpractices in Banks) Act No. 18 of 1994, which was enacted to expedite recovery of debts owed to banks as well as subject perpetrators of financial malpractices in banks to a due process of the law. The Corporation facilitated the implementation of the Act in the following areas:

- collating information and supporting documents on bank frauds and financial malpractices;
- lodging criminal complaints to the police for investigation;
- providing necessary technical and logistic support for police investigation;
- maintaining liaison with prosecutors appointed by the Attorney-General of the Federation for the successful prosecution of criminal cases;

- appointing solicitors to file applications before the Tribunals to recover debts owed to failed banks; and
- coordinating and monitoring of criminal and civil cases.

Following the implementation of the Act, about ₦4.3 billion was recovered.

Liquidation challenges

As a liquidator NDIC is faced with a number of challenges. Prominent among them are:

1. Procedures for appointment as liquidator. A deposit insurer, while acting as a liquidator of closed banks is expected to be vested with special powers. The special powers are to expedite the liquidation process in order to maintain confidence and stability of the banking system as well as to ensure cost effectiveness of the liquidation process. Up to 1998, the CBN had the power to appoint NDIC as provisional liquidator of a failed bank and such an appointment was deemed as having been made by the Federal High Court. Unfortunately, the CBN lost that power in 1998. At the same time, NDIC was required to apply to the Federal High Court to be appointed as a liquidator. NDIC is also subject to the general companies winding-up rules,[10] which, among others, require that notice of winding-up petitions should be advertised before appointment. Predictably, the shareholders/directors of two banks, whose licences were revoked in 2002 and 2003, challenged NDIC's application for appointment as Liquidator. Regrettably, the cases were still pending in court as at the end of June 2006. The law suits challenging the revocation of the banks' licences were equally pending in court. The trend, if not checked, can threaten the stability of the banking system and erode confidence. The damage that is associated with protracted litigation is a very serious concern.
2. Lack of legal protection. The directors, officers and staff of the NDIC are not protected by law against civil liability suits that might be brought against them in connection with decisions or actions taken in good faith on behalf of the Corporation. This has a tendency to undercut the independence that the DIS should have as fear of personal liability could deter its staff from taking needed actions, (APEC Policy Dialogue on Deposit Insurance). However, proposals for such protection were included in amendments to its Act recently passed by the National Assembly.

14.4 Lessons learnt

The Nigerian experience offers some useful lessons for other countries wanting to start up a DIS and to those undergoing reform. These lessons include:

1. Licensing (chartering) of banking institutions should take cognisance of the available managerial capacity in the banking industry. The phenomenal growth in the number of deposit-taking institutions between 1988 and 1991 over-taxed the managerial ability of the banking system and contributed to the banking distress witnessed in the early 1990s;
2. Bank regulators should have the ability to screen access to ownership and management of banking institutions. A diagnostic study jointly confirmed that abusive ownership and mismanagement contributed significantly to the failure of banks in the 1990s;
3. Bank licensing authorities should have uninhibited power to de-license. While the CBN (before 1998) had the power to licence banks, it was required to obtain the approval of the President to de-license them. As a result of delays in granting such approvals, many illiquid and insolvent banks remained open thus posing contagion risk to other banks. The CBN was only granted the full powers to de-license in 1998;
4. Effective coordination and collaboration between the bank regulator/supervisor and the deposit insurer is imperative especially where they have joint responsibility as in the case of Nigeria. Both agencies undertake bank supervision, hence a collaborative framework was established in order to avoid duplication of efforts or role conflict;
5. The existence of multiple regulators (each with its distinct mandate) as in Nigeria where banking, insurance and securities businesses are under the purview of different regulators, require the establishment of a formalized framework for the coordination of supervisory activities. The framework should seek to minimize arbitrage opportunities for financial institutions and promote information sharing amongst the regulators;
6. Participation in the deposit insurance system should be mandatory in order to mitigate adverse selection which could manifest if only healthy financial institutions are covered by the system. The Nigerian DIS which provided coverage for all licensed banks irrespective of their state of health engendered public confidence and promoted financial stability;
7. The debate as to whether intervention should be 'rule based' or 'discretionary' was manifested in the Nigerian experience. Even though thresholds for regulatory intervention were covered by BOFIA, a strict application of 'rule based' intervention was not achieved. The supervisory authorities did exercise discretion as to the timing and mode of intervention in resolving troubled or insolvent institutions;
8. The loss of the CBN's power to appoint NDIC as the liquidator of failed banks opened the flood gate for litigation which had inhibited prompt liquidation of failed institutions. That development weakened the exit mechanism and denied depositors prompt payment of their guaranteed sums;

9. The dissolution of the Failed Banks Tribunals and transfer of debt recovery cases to the regular courts inhibited the Liquidator's ability to recover debts owed to failed banks. The consequences of this development have been delays in payments of uninsured deposits and other creditors and erosion of public confidence in the banking system; and
10. The lack of legal protection for the deposit insurer's staff and directors did not deter them from proactive intervention in troubled or insolvent institutions. Rather, delays experienced in taking corrective actions were caused by the agency problems of regulatory forbearance or non-approval of requests to de-license terminally distressed banks by the political authorities.

14.5 Concluding remarks

Nigeria proactively reacted to the imperatives of the wave of economic deregulation by establishing a deposit insurance system as another component of the financial safety net. NDIC has spent the last 17 years putting in place measures designed to protect the economy from the risk of deposit runs and thus contributing to the stability of the financial system. Apart from insuring the deposit liabilities of all licensed banks, the establishment of NDIC has generated the required stability and confidence through its activities. However, the system is still being faced with many challenges which include an inability to recover liquidated banks' loans through the courts, an unhelpful public perception of deposit insurance, a cumbersome judicial process, and weak corporate governance in banks which has manifested itself in insider abuse and mismanagement, and inadequate legal powers for the NDIC for failure resolution, among others. In spite of these challenges, the prospects for a better and stronger deposit insurance system are quite bright. The prospects are hinged on the following developments, amongst others: the amendment of the NDIC Act to increase deposit insurance coverage, to facilitate prompt corrective actions and to ensure an effective liquidation process; the bank consolidation programme of the CBN; the current efforts to enhance public awareness about its activities as well as the benefits of the system to the economy; and the commitment of the management and staff in running an efficient institution that is responsive to the needs of the stakeholders in a bid to promote stability and confidence in the nation's banking system.

Notes

1 It is not all financial institutions that fail. It is only the poorly managed ones or those that take excessive risks without the requisite capital that will go to their grave.

2 The conditions under which a bank's licence may be revoked by the CBN are when a bank: ceases to carry on the business for which the licence was issued for any

continuous period of 6 months or any period aggregating 12 months; goes into liquidation or is wound up or otherwise dissolved; fails to fulfill or comply with any condition subject to which the licence was granted; has insufficient assets to meet its liabilities; fails to comply with any obligation imposed upon it by or under any legislative framework; and fails to maintain specified level of capital funds unimpaired by losses. Prior to 1998, the CBN required The President's approval to close a bank. Since 1998, the CBN no longer requires such political approval before de-licensing a failed bank.

3 S.34 of BOFIA requires CBN to turnover significantly or critically under-capitalized banks to NDIC for distress resolution while NDIC is required to recommend the revocation of licences of terminally distressed banks to the CBN (S.36). NDIC's mandate as a liquidator is contingent on revocation of a banking licence by the CBN.
4 Section 5 of the NDIC Act stipulates the functions of the Corporation.
5 Statutorily, if a depositor fails to file claims within eighteen (18) months after the appointment of the Corporation as the Liquidator of the failed institution, such deposit shall fall within the uninsured category.
6 See for example, Garcia (1998) and Financial Stability Forum's Working Group on Deposit Insurance (2002) for the discussion of best practice in deposit insurance.
7 For example, the lawsuits instituted by the shareholders/directors of Savannah Bank whose licence was revoked in 2002 is still before the court as at June 2006.
8 The risk minimizer model was chosen in view of the prevalence of distress in the banking system at the time NDIC was established coupled with the rapid growth in the number of banks as a result of government policy of financial deregulation and liberalization under SAP. The Deposit Insurer was required to monitor its risk exposure on an on-going basis.
9 For instance, NDIC's Examiners' findings facilitated the removal of the Chief Executive Officers of two banks as well as the Chairman, Vice Chairman and Executive Director of another bank all in 2004 on accounts of unsafe and unsound banking practices.
10 For details of the winding-up rules in Nigeria, see the Companies Winding-up Rules made pursuant to the Companies and Allied Matters Act, 1990.

References

Adeyemo R. and Iwayemi, A. (1995) 'Nigeria's Macroeconomic Crisis 1970–1986: An Overview' in Iwayemi A. (ed.), *Macroeconomic Policy Issues in an Open Economy: A Case Study of Nigeria*, Ibadan, Nigeria: NCEMA Publications.

Afolabi J.A. (1995) 'Resource Boom and Macroeconomic Performance' in Iwayemi A. (ed.), *Macroeconomic Policy Issues in an Open Economy: A Case Study of Nigeria*, Ibadan, Nigeria: NCEMA Publications.

Afolabi J.A. and Mamman, H. (1994) 'The Dynamics of Savings in a Deregulated Economy: The Case of Nigeria', *NDIC Quarterly*, vol. 4, no.4.

Canada Deposit Insurance Corporation (2004) 'APEC Policy Dialogue on Deposit Insurance: Policy Conclusions Paper', June.

CBN/NDIC (1995) 'Joint Collaborative Study: Distress in the Nigerian Financial System'.

Federal Government of Nigeria (1988) Nigeria Deposit Insurance Corporation Act No.22.

Federal Government of Nigeria(1990) Companies and Allied Matters Act.

Federal Government of Nigeria (1991a) Central Bank of Nigeria Act No. 24.
Federal Government of Nigeria (1991b) Bank and Other Financial Institutions Act No.25.
Federal Government of Nigeria (1994) Failed Banks (Recovery of Debts and Other Financial Malpractices in Banks) Act No.18.
Financial Stability Forum Working Group on Deposit Insurance (2001) 'Guidance for Developing Effective Deposit Insurance Systems'.
Garcia, Gillian G. (1998) 'Comparative Analysis of Established Deposit Insurance Systems', paper presented at the FDIC's International Conference on Deposit Insurance, September.
Llanto, Gilberto M. (2005) 'Deposit Insurance: Role, Limitations and Challenges' Philippine Deposit Insurance Corporation (PDIC) Occasional Paper No. 1.
Sabourin J.P. (2004) 'The Deposit Insurer's Role in Maintaining Financial Stability', paper presented at the Chicago Federal Reserve Bank Conference on Systemic Financial Crises: Resolving Large Bank Insolvencies, 30 September.
SEDESA (2004) Symposium on Deposit Insurance, Argentina.
Sundararajan, V. (2001) 'The Role of Deposit Insurance', paper presented at the International Workshop on Deposit Insurance System Organized by People's Bank of China, Shanghai.
Umoh, P.N. (1997) 'Bank Deposit Insurance in Nigeria'. Nigerian Deposit Insurance Corporation, Abuja.
Umoh, P.N. (1999) 'A Decade of Deposit Insurance in Nigeria: Issues and Challenges' Nigerian Deposit Insurance Corporation, Abuja.
Umoh, P.N. (2003) 'The Role of Deposit Insurance in Financial Sector Stability', paper delivered at the Fifth CBN Seminar for Finance Correspondents and Business Editors, October 27–29, Owerri, Imo State, Nigeria.

Index

City University
Library Information Services
ss Learning Resource Centre

368.854
CAM

UFCLL

WITHDRAWN